THE VOICES
OF THE SILENT

THE VOICES
OF THE SILENT

Cornelia Gerstenmaier

Translated from the German by Susan Hecker

Hart Publishing Company, Inc.
New York City

CONTENTS

FOREWORD   13

ABBREVIATIONS   15

INTRODUCTION   17

PART I

THE LONG-AWAITED REFORM MOVEMENT 29
  The First Thaw   31
  De-Stalinization and the Second Thaw   39
  The Pasternak Affair   49
  The Search for New Values   55
  The Camp Literature   61
  The New Campaign   69
  The Growing Emancipation of the Intellectuals   75
  Cultural and Political Developments Following
      the Fall of Khrushchev   81

PART II

THE DEMOCRATIC MOVEMENT   89
  Initial Opposition   91
  Samizdat   101

Writers Under Pursuit 115

The "Cause Cèlebré": Siniavski and Daniel 123

The Struggle Intensifies 133

Journals of Social Criticism 143

The January Trial, 1968 151

A Flood of Rebellion 161

The Rulers' Revenge 167

Anti-Stalinist Spokesmen 173

The Role of Sakharov, The Atomic Physicist 181

Chronika 191

The Leningrad Trials 203

The Democrats' Program 211

Dissidents in the Army 221

Andrei Amalrik and The Discussion about
the Future of Russia 229

The Defenders of Czechoslovakia 241

General Grigorenko: Symbol of Opposition 259

The Solzhenitsyn Case 267

The Alienation between the Administration
and the Writers 283

Early Signs of Freedom 295

DOCUMENTS 309

NOTES 547

INDEX 573

THE VOICES
OF THE SILENT

. . . It is a question of honest self-evaluation, of thinking about ourselves as we are today, of leaving lies behind and looking for the truth. Then we will march onward, more quickly than the others because we are following them; because we can learn from their experiences, we can learn from all that has happened throughout the centuries preceding us. Europeans are making a curious mistake in their dealings with us; they insist upon relinquishing us to the East; by some sort of European instinct they relegate us to the Orient to be rid of us in the West. . . Let us discover our future for ourselves and not ask the others how we should go about it. . . The day will come when we will play an integral role in the intellectual life of Europe, just as we have already taken our place in European politics, but then more mightily with our spirit than we now do with our material strength. This will be the logical result of our long isolation: Monumental events always spring from deserts.

Petr Chaadaev

FOREWORD

The purpose of the following record and documentation is to provide evidence of the existence and extent of the intellectual opposition in the Soviet Union. In the writing of this report the author has tried to let herself be guided by the criteria of accuracy and objectivity; and in so doing has tried to observe the personal requests of several of the people, indeed friends, who appear in it. None of these individuals wish to be "glorified" in the minds of Western readers. They neither want nor need personal recognition, and they also have no desire to be the focal point of any political campaign. They simply want to prove that they exist, that they are not "criminal" or "insane" as Soviet propaganda declares them to be, and that they act, as they believe, in accordance with the dictates of their own consciences.

One hears over and over again that protests or reports about internal Soviet opposition that are not publishable there but only in the West, could have deleterious consequences for the participants. It has been repeatedly demonstrated, however, that in totalitarian systems, simply remaining silent could result in further terror and misfortune. For this reason Soviet civil-rights fighters, despite the very high personal risk they are taking in trying to make their protests heard, hope not only for a scrupulously accurate report in the "free world" but also for moral support in the Soviet's fight for human rights.

Many events described in this book will be introduced with the words, "It was reported" or "It has been learned." This does not in any way mean that the facts presented are based upon or represent unsubstantiated rumors. It does mean, however, that the events described in such terms have been widely ignored or unreported by the Soviet press and therefore there are no official sources of information available.

I would like to thank Mr. Michael Slavinski, who was always available and eager to supply information and suggestions. I am also grateful to Dr. Galina Berkenkopf and Mr. Peter Reddaway, who contributed much time and energy to the revision of the manuscript as well as moral support to its author.

CORNELIA I. GERSTENMAIER

Abbreviations for the names of journals and other periodicals which appear in the text and in the footnotes.

Chr = *Chronika Tekuscich Sobytij* (Moscow)

Gr = *Grani* (Frankfurt am Main)

Iz = *Izvestia* (Moscow)

KoPr = *Komsomolskaya Pravda* (Moscow)

LG = *Literaturnaya Gazeta* (Moscow)

NM = *Novy Mir* (Moscow)

NRS = *Novoe Russkoe Slovo* (New York)

NZZ = *Neue Zürcher Zeitung*

O-P = *Ost-Probleme* (Bonn)

P = *Posev* (Frankfurt am Main)

Pr = *Pravda* (Moscow)

INTRODUCTION

This book bears witness to the "other Russia." Its reality is documented by the contemporary intellectual class in the U.S.S.R. No one can estimate the number of political dissidents who now oppose in various ways the Soviet regime they inherited from Stalin and his successors. This opposition was not born of previous interests or of political resentment, but was conceived in the indestructible demand for self-determination and free individual expression. Indeed, it is the spiritual absolutism of this opposition that leads to political consequences. For the future of Russia and of the world, these two cases are equally meaningful.

This introduction attempts to outline the development of the so-called "cultural opposition," the development of that literary avant-garde that refused to criticize the policies and ideology of the Soviet regime in the wake of the "thaw," but did criticize its dogmatic cultural policies. From this avant-garde evolved the "democratic movement" with its currently wide-range intellectual and political opposition. For this reason it seems expedient to touch upon the very first manifestation of nonconformist thought, which can be essentially distinguished from the fundamental demands of today's "democratic movement" by style and content. As hopes for reform within the power structure faded away, along with concessions in cultural policies, the "cultural opposition" became political; and the boundaries less acute between "legal" opposition of the artists—that is, the opposition tolerated by the Party—and an incipient, bitterly opposed "democratic movement." Within the literary world, such evolution seems most clearly depicted in the Solzhenitsyn affair.

This book will not concern itself with religious opposition existent in Russia for many years. The documents of that movement would widely exceed its framework.[1] Moreover, the religious struggle has its own particular injustices to contend with, although one must admit that the religious and secular opposition groups are moving closer together. A most important example of this tendency can be seen in the religious philosopher Anatoli Levitin-Krasnov, who is equally zealous in his support of Church interests and the demands of the civil-rights movement. And there are also large numbers of Christians—or other religious adherents— among the spokesmen of the secular opposition.

This report will not consider in any detail the resistance movement of national minorities, such as the Ukrainians, the Jews, the Crimean Tartars, etc. The anti-Stalinism and the anti-Sovietism of these groups are based on historical roots quite different from those of the Russian civil-rights movement. But here again, similar, if not identical, arguments crop up increasingly in the opposition of the national minorities. This justifies the inclusion of a document produced by one of the Ukrainian writers (*see page 535*), as well as the "Memorandum of the Estonian Scholars" (*see page 486*) and the letter from the 139 Citizens of Kiev (*see page 404*), all of which bear witness to a supra-national humanism.

That opposition from the deported Crimean Tartars is closely bound to the efforts of many Russian intellectuals, provides reason enough for including the appeal on page 399. The active support that such pleas command from wide circles of the Russian intelligentsia offers further indication of a growing victory over remnants of Stalinist thought and despotism. An incipient, and at first weakly organized, political opposition is beginning to make itself heard in the various dissident groups that are linked to-gether under the so-called "democratic movement" or "civil-rights movement." Their ideological and political con-ceptions are still fairly hazy, and vary somewhat within each group. Their common goal lies in the establishment of a constitutional state, assuring the value of the individual and his fundamental rights as a human being.

Very few of the present-day Soviet dissidents consider themselves revolutionaries. They do not want a violent *coup d'état,* and their opposition is expressed within the framework of strict observation of existing laws. In this manner the civil-rights advocates hope to force the state organs into illegal actions. For they are the groups who, by persecuting political dissidents, violate the actual law of the Soviet Union—guaranteed at least on paper.

At present, it is not possible to determine how many people actively support or sympathize with this democratic movement. But the number has increased significantly since 1966—the year of the trial against Siniavski and Daniel—and particularly since 1968, attaining a size not thought possible forty years ago. In any event, organized protest has grown significantly in spite of, or perhaps even because of, increased pressures from above. Since the "trial of the Four" (involving Yuri Galanskov, Aleksandr Ginzburg, Aleksei Dobrovolski, and Vera Laskova in January of 1968), about five hundred petitions and letters of protest signed by more than two thousand Soviet citizens have managed to find their way to the West. (This figure does not include the numerous documents concerning religious opposition.) The official Soviet press did not publish a single letter or petition of the many addressed to it, nor did it even mention any of them; and none of the official authorities receiving such documents ever answered them.

It is noteworthy that representatives of this movement for a constitutional state are to be found in almost every level of society today. The so-called intelligentsia, however, forms the nucleus of the movement, for whom—in contrast with other social groups—it has succeeded in audibly expressing discontent and socio-political ideas. But what is really meant by the term "Russian intelligentsia"?

The old Russian intelligentsia was neither a social rank nor class; its members belonged to various social levels but failed to become identified with a single group. Though dominated at first by the nobility, the so-called *raznochintsi* grew in number—representatives of all ranks and nationalities. They were united by a common social-ethical principle finding expression in their strivings for reform and eventually in various revolutionary programs. The intelligentsia thus brought together utopians, anarchists, socialists, and other reformers. They were all supported by a fiery devotion, a sacrificial involvement that frequently exceeded the bounds of real discernment and understanding, but which, however, made up the uniqueness of the Russian intelligentsia at that time and assured it of a particular place in European intellectual history.

Through its most radical representatives this old intelligentsia gave rise to the October Revolution of 1917 and was subsequently almost completely annihilated by them. The newly grown Soviet intelligentsia seems to share little more than a name in common with these predecessors. The new intelligentsia is less concerned with political and intellectual attitudes than it is with social position, education, and contribution beyond the demands made by membership. In addition to the academically educated and the artists (the so-called "creative" intelligentsia), the huge army of technologists, as well as higher officials and functionaries, are today considered a part of this group. The old name actually signifies a totally new, or so-called "third," class. In its social position the intelligentsia has been more or less assimilated into the bourgeois society, much more solidly than its predecessor ever had. It is, of course, lacking in their spiritual determination. Up until a few years ago this was also true of the "creative" intelligentsia. Inasmuch as the latter devoted themselves almost exclusively to the areas of art and science, it turned away from the grip of the state and in so doing renounced from the start any possible cooperation with the state in matters concerning social and political life. Only since the end of the 1960's have its most determined representatives begun to raise their voices against the policies of the regime, against policies for which they do not want to share guilt by remaining silent.

Perhaps it is too early to answer the question whether this sector of the contemporary intelligentsia has finally overcome the disastrous utopianism, the intolerance bordering on despotism, and the blinding Messianism which almost completely annihilated it at one time. The most recent documents of the newly growing intelligentsia have a positive answer to offer. It may be that the horrible October inheritance cured the intellectual ranks of Russia of its ideas of anarchy and utopia. But how dearly did they have to pay for this realization!

During the last few years, uncensored literature in the Soviet Union has reached considerable proportions as a mirror of the ever-intensifying conflict between the Party and the intelligentsia. In order to understand the full significance of these inner altercations, one must look to the statements of the "underground" for assistance, even as the contemporaries of Gercen (Herzen), Kropotkin, or Solovev did.

One of the first literary documents to reach the West secretly from the u.s.s.r. was Boris Pasternak's *Doctor Zhivago*. This was followed by a large number of predominantly literary works at first, among them the satirical stories by Abram Terz (Siniavski) and Nikolai Arzhak (Daniel) or the novels of Aleksandr Solzhenitsyn. Particularly since the middle of the 1960's, outspoken political manifestations appeared, the most famous example of which was the memorandum by the atomic physicist Andrei Sakharov, which attracted great attention in the West.

The manuscripts managed to reach the West partly through the help of friends and with the consent of the authors, as for example in the cases of Pasternak, Siniavski, and Daniel. Sometimes they even reached the outside world without the knowledge of the author. This occurred with Solzhenitsyn, whose works appeared in the West after their publication in the Soviet Union had been denied by the Soviet Writers' Union.

Solzhenitsyn's forbidden books and the works of numerous other authors circulate underground in the Soviet Union in the form of typewritten and photocopied editions; that is, they appear in *Samizdat*. The conception of *Samizdat* (self-publisher) includes all publications which have appeared independently of the state publishing houses and therefore beyond the censor. Among others, the writer Georgi Vladimov stressed the extent and growing significance of *Samizdat:* "The unpublished works of Bulgakov, Cvetaeva, Mandelstam, Pilniak, Platonov and others, still living, authors, whose names I cannot mention for obvious reasons, travel from hand to hand and from reader to reader in the form of seven or eight typescripts . . ." Turning his attention to the authorities, he continued: "If they instigate mass house searches, if they confiscate all tape recorders, all manuscripts, if they arrest the authors and all those who have anything to do with the circulation of their works—there will still be one copy somewhere and it will be reproduced in even greater numbers than before." [2]

Since the nonconforming intellectuals are understandably concerned that the world should learn of the documents of this "other Russia"—documents of which the intellectual groups are much prouder than the hack work produced by the mediocre propagandists—they send their manuscripts into the free countries of the world by evading the censor, without whose stamp not even a bottle label may be printed.

A further, more important reason for such behavior is the effort on the part of the opposition to realize the widest possible circulation for their papers, information, and proclamations in their own country. For this purpose such papers must first reach the West, and especially must reach particular radio stations (the BBC, Radio Liberty, Deutsche Welle, Voice of America, Kol Israel, and others). From here they are rebroadcast into the Soviet Union (in Russian, of course) where a steadily growing number of listeners receive these Western broadcasts, which are, in reality, forbidden and have been increasingly interfered with during the last few years. By means of this detour, many Soviet citizens receive a clear picture of the events in Czechoslovakia, for example, and of the activities and goals of their opposition spokesmen.

The letters Pavel Litvinov and Larisa Daniel received from their fellow countrymen concerning their "Appeal to World Public Opinion" demonstrate the success of this practice (*see page 363*). And the furious tirades with which the Soviet press scolds not only the above-mentioned radio stations but also these people who provide those stations (and the foreign press) with information underscores the effectiveness of this practice. In an Open Letter to the Editor in Chief of the weekly journal *Literaturnaia Gazeta*, Aleksandr Chakovski, who had attacked in his paper the activities of these foreign broadcast stations and their Soviet correspondents in connection with the "Trial of the Four" (January, 1968), the imprisoned civil-rights fighter Lev Kvachevski wrote that those who wanted to learn the truth about the trial could refer to the objective information broadcast by foreign radio stations. In England, the United

States, and West Germany, these had become a "connecting link between the Soviet people and a portion of their intelligentsia," for millions of Soviet citizens heard their broadcasts.[3] Most recently, the writers Yuri Galanskov and Vladimir Bukovski have emphasized the importance attributed to these broadcasters in the battle for freedom and the future fate of Russia.

With exception the dissidents want the publications of *Samizdat* to be understood not as "underground literature," but rather as "uncensored" or "unofficial" writings. According to the Soviet Constitution (and in agreement with the Declaration of Human Rights), it is just as legitimate to compose and circulate written materials as it is to express complaints and protests or to participate in demonstrations.

There is no Soviet law forbidding one to send unofficial—that is, simply uncensored—literature into the West and of publishing it there. The Soviet functionaries are behaving in an illegal manner when they attempt to employ all the means at their disposal to hinder this type of literature from reaching the outside or from finding circulation within the u.s.s.r.

For the publication of *Samizdat* materials (in the past two years alone more than five hundred letters, petitions, essays, and books have reached the West), the Russian émigré publications *Posev, Grani, Novoe Russkoe Slovo, Russkaia Mysl'*, and others are extremely active. The Aleksandr Herzen Foundation has also taken an important place recently among these publications. The foundation is based in Amsterdam; its honorary directors include the leading critic of Slavonic literatures Karel van het Reve (University of Leyden); the historian Jan Bezemer (University of

Amsterdam); and the political scientist Peter Reddaway (University of London). The Aleksandr Herzen Foundation acts as publisher and trustee of those authors who are banned by, but still live in, the Soviet Union. The earnings of the works published by this foundation, as well as those *Samizdat* materials released through the Posev Publishing House, are deposited in special savings accounts under the names of these authors, in the hope that one day they themselves or someone authorized by them can withdraw their well-earned honoraria.

Even those authors who through the publication of their works in the outside world are much more imperiled than, let's say, Solzhenitsyn was because of the printing of his anti-Stalinist novels, send their manuscripts to the West completely aware of the risks they incur by so doing. (The simple circulation of "anti-Soviet" *Samizdat* materials in the u.s.s.r. is punishable by a three-year term in a work camp.) Only rarely today do such documents appear anonymously. In those cases where these materials might be published in the West under a pseudonym, it is much more a question of caution on the part of the publisher than fear on the part of the author.

One frequently hears the objection that documents published outside the Soviet Union have in some way been falsified. (In such cases, these alleged "falsifications" are usually attributed to Russian emigrants "caught up in illusions.") But every Western foreigner who has the opportunity to observe the workings of the anti-Stalinist intellectual and artistic circles—and most of the documents mentioned and reproduced in this book stem from these circles—will contradict such objections on the basis of his own personal experience. Up until now hardly any *Samizdat* author has ever denied a work published in the West under his name—something he could easily do in the event of some falsification and something, incidentally, that the KGB[4] often demands. And, finally, the authenticity of uncensored documents is directly or indirectly established by the Soviet press itself,[5] which repeatedly defames "apostate" writers and political enemies in trials against them.

The credibility of *Samizdat* literature, and the activities of the illegal opposition, is most impressively guaranteed by the fact that their spokesmen have been confined in concentration camps, prisons, and "insane asylums." Siniavski, Daniel, Galanskov, Ginzburg, Bukovski, and literally thousands of others were condemned to severe deprivation of freedom after only the barest hint of official legal proceedings. Pavel Litvinov, Larisa Daniel, and many others live in Siberian exile. Perhaps the greatest of Russia's living authors, Aleksandr Solzhenitsyn, was expelled from the Writers' Union and has since ceased to be officially recognized as a writer. After the publication of his memorandum in the West, the highly decorated atomic physicist Sakharov lost his most important posts. His indispensability in research was probably the only protection he had against more severe reprisals. Moreover, times have altered since Stalin to such an extent that the rulers no longer dare persecute or perhaps do away with Solzhenitsyn or Sakharov in consideration of their international reputation and in the light of the great admiration these exponents of free thinking enjoy in wide circles of the Soviet public.

PART I

The Long-Awaited Reform Movement

THE FIRST THAW

*Despite the fact that victory did not
bring the moral upsurge and freedom
one longed for, nevertheless the entire
postwar period had an expectancy of
freedom in the air, and this characterized the historical meaning of these
years.*

BORIS PASTERNAK

For millions of Soviet citizens, Stalin embodied the Communist promise of salvation. When he died on March 5,
1953, their political establishment faced the grave problem
of finding a successor—a task rendered even more difficult
in a totalitarian state. The masses responded to the news of
their dictator's death with expressions of relief as well as
genuine sorrow, but above all, with a sense of confusion.
"All of Russia is numb with grief . . . All of Russia is tor-
mented by just one question: Now what?" [1] In these words,
years later, the novelist A. Karanin described the mood of
those days when both press and radio warned incessantly
against "anxiety and panic." [2]

Stalin's heritage was a fairly well-established but insecure system of terror; it quaked without falling as pre-

31

tenders to the dictatorship fought among themselves. Nevertheless, the ruler's death and posthumous discredit marked the beginning of a spiritual emanicipation that led to occasional power shifts, if not revolts, among Moscow's tributaries, and still causes anxiety among Kremlin masters today.

For about a decade, during the fifties and early sixties, hostile political currents found expression, amost exclusively in literary works. This followed a Russian tradition— since the nineteenth century began—of employing the written word as the only weapon at hand in the war against existing grievances. Over and over again, it became possible to direct ideas against officially sanctioned propaganda by means of such writing, a method which at times has even functioned as spokesman for the opposition. Thus, Russian literature now represents not only the art of these people, but beyond that, the voice of their conscience.

The words of the poet Yevgeny Yevtushenko bear witness to the far-reaching significance of Russian literature for almost two centuries:

> *In Russia the word "author" is almost a synonym for "fighter."*

And he continues:

> *In no other land in the world does literature have as strong a tradition of political engagement. It is no accident that Russians considered their writers spiritual leaders, "de-*

fenders of the truth." Every tyrant in Russia
considered poets his worst enemies . . .[3]

And in Aleksandr Solzhenitsyn's great novel, *The First Circle*, the diplomat Volodin maintains:

The man of letters should indeed be a mentor
of the people . . . A great writer comes close
to representing an alternative government.
Therefore no government has ever loved the
great poets, just the minor ones.[4]

In hardly any other country did literature pursue so tortured a path as in Russia after the Bolsheviks came to power. The greatest symbolist poet, Aleksandr Blok, died of hunger in 1921, the same year that Nikolai Gumilev was executed. The lyric poet Sergei Yesenin committed suicide in 1925, as did Vladimir Mayakovski five years later. Both yearned for the Revolution and welcomed it; both were crushed by its reality. Some writers, Yevgeny Zamiatin for example, were fortunate enough to emigrate as early as the thirties. Mikhail Bulgakov, who tried in vain to escape, died disillusioned and impoverished in 1940; his great novels were not published in the Soviet Union during his lifetime. Sergei Tretiakov, the "Japanese spy," was executed. Mikhail Kolcov, Boris Pilniak, Isaac Babel, Osip Mandelstam and countless others perished in Stalin's camps. (In his letter to the Fourth Soviet Congress of Writers, Aleksandr Solzhenitsyn spoke of more than six thousand writers and poets who died in Stalin's prisons in those years.) Marina Cvetaeva, the returned emigrant, hanged herself in 1941. The circumstances surrounding Maxim Gorki's death are uncertain; rumor has it that OGPU (the secret police at that time) poisoned him. Mikhail Zoschenko, as well as the great poet Anna Akhmatova, was excluded from the Writers' Union; for years afterward, their works, along with those of many others, were censored.

The cultural self-mutilation of the Soviet system has continued to this day. It began in the post-Stalinist era with the defamation of Pasternak, and continued with the condemnation of Andrei Siniavski, Daniel and others, right up to the recent Solzhenitsyn case. It is precisely these outlawed contemporary writers, however, who enjoy the greatest popularity today, along with still unpublished authors of the twenties and thirties and writers of the nineteenth-century classics. The deferential regard with which the verses of Mandelstam or the prose of Pasternak is read and secretly duplicated betrays more than a simple fascination for the forbidden. (Gumilev's works sell for as much as one hundred rubles apiece in the black market.) The level of understanding that an author finds among his readers today determines just how closely his thoughts reflect the opinions of the public—at least those of several segments comprising this public.

In 1954 Ilia Ehrenburg, a man peculiarly sensitive to imminent political upheaval—the poet Mayakovski captured this quality when he once called him Paul Saulovic—published his short novel, *The Thaw*.[5] The political symbolism of its plot, and several of his ideas, considered truly liberal for that time, were finally lost in mazes of ideological compromise. Nevertheless, this story lent its name to an important historical period. It also marked the awakening of a unique, but long dormant, literary function, which now strove to break loose from the sterile, officially approved system of values—or at least, if that proved impossible, to guide it in a more human direction.

Although an overwhelming majority of the literati immediately applauded *The Thaw*, very few actually dared to support and defend it as openly as Vera Panova or Leonid Zorin did. Panova's novel, *The Seasons*,[6] and Zorin's drama, *The Guests*,[7] were greeted initially with the approval of critics who became progressively unsure of themselves as the course of political tensions developed. But after an appropriate order had been issued to those reviewers who acted as mouthpiece for the Party, a flood of invective broke over Vera Panova, and Zorin's already performed play was banished from the stage. Even Ehrenburg was not spared the critics' brimstone. Apart from *The Thaw*, his essay "Concerning the Work of a Writer"[8] was also considered an act of provocation, because in it Ehrenburg rejected the principle of a literature dictated "from above."

Even sharper and more discriminating was the criticism that Vladimir Pomerancev unleashed in his essay "Concerning the Integrity of Literature." Here Pomerancev strongly declared himself against popular optimism, that prevalent veneer (*lakirovka*) in Soviet writing, whose application reduced it to a dull and mendacious uniformity. While criticizing the official pressure brought to bear upon writers, the author equally censored the opportunism of those who all too willingly bowed to such compulsion. In this essay Pomerancev, assuming the role of a reader, defines his ideas and hopes to authors and clearly defends the goal of the new interpretation of literature:

. . . Don't deny any part of my individual-
ity, do not force anything upon me that is
incompatible with my being, but seek a syn-
thesis. In its center I stand—my work, my
thoughts, and all the elements of my sensi-
tivities—much of which I myself am unaware
of, but which you from your new heights
will more easily discover. The important
thing, however, is that you lift me to these
heights, so that I can better understand the
world.[9]

By merely stating these adamant demands Pomerancev
had already exceeded the permissible limits of speaking
out. He was accused of regressing toward "idealistic
aesthetics," of questioning the fundamentals of socialistic
reality, and many other similar offenses. Alexei Surkov, as
secretary of the Writers' Union, sullenly verified equally
"disturbing" views found, by chance, in essays by F. Abramov, M. Lifsic and M. Sceglov. The final answer to Pomerancev's article came slightly later with his expulsion
from the Writers' Union. Publication of that essay also
brought a strong reprimand to the newspaper *Novy Mir*
(New World), which has become, despite all outside pressures, the "legal" forum of the intellectual, especially the
literary, elite of the country. Accused of heresy by the
dogmatists early in his career, its courageous chief editor,
Aleksandr Tvardovski, was forced to yield his seat in August of 1954 to Konstantin Simonov, still very doctrinaire
at that time.

At the opening of the Second Congress of Writers in

December, 1954, the Party challenged all insubordinate writers. "Literature," announced Surkov, the main speaker, "is closely related to, and dependent upon, politics." [10] While Ehrenburg and Panova, among others, had to submit to the degrading ritual of criticism and self-criticism, another group of unorthodox writers was permitted to speak, among them the well-known Leningrad poet, Olga Berggloc; the somewhat older Veniamin Kaverin; Semion Kirsanov; and Valentin Oveckin, who later was committed to an insane asylum, thanks to his description of the misery rampant in the country. The speeches of these writers contained cautiously worded but nonetheless bitter charges against the emasculation of Soviet literature resulting from the stern directives of Andrei Zhdanov.[11]

Compared with the cultural-political organizations of the previous fifteen years, the Second Congress of Writers could meet in a relatively open atmosphere. During its sessions several authors who had been killed or persecuted under Stalin were restored to their former status. In the final resolution adopted, which included a pledge of allegiance to the Party, one sensed a renewed chill that ultimately brought the first "thaw" to a premature end. Its short span, however, underscored the fact that, throughout almost forty years of Bolshevik control, the literary avant-garde of Russia might indeed be physically suppressed, but even so, the Party never succeeded in unconditionally bringing under its yoke the newly emergent class of writers and poets.

DE-STALINIZATION AND
THE SECOND THAW

While the grotesque struggle over power proceeded "above," progress "below" stumbled toward its destiny. It grew, expanded, exploded like hot steam into the sky, and forced the authorities in some cases to yield, in others to resist. But to put an end to this process was out of the question. It pierced the surface everywhere, like grass between the cobblestones.

SVETLANA ALLILUYEVA

The sometimes violently enforced attempts to choke the cautiously inaugurated literary opposition did not last long. Khrushchev's famous secret speech of February, 1956, during the Twentieth Congress of the Communist party, branded Stalin an outright "enemy of the people," a mass murderer; and this shook the already precarious relationship between intellectual circles and the regime much more seriously than the chaos following Stalin's death. Ties between Party leadership and intellectual circles began to deteriorate from that moment. Among those continually sub-

39

jected to abuse was the writer and literary scholar, Andrei Siniavski. As a student, Siniavski became an active member of the Komsomol [1] (Organization of Communist Youth) and an unyielding advocate of the official doctrine. But his father's arrest in 1951, Stalin's death, and the events of 1956 finally resulted in Siniavski's total renunciation of Marxism.

The older generation, in particular, who had long equated the name of Stalin with the concepts of progress and socialism, now found themselves spiritually bankrupt because they were unable to separate Stalin himself from the ideals of the Revolution. The younger generation, on the other hand, now began to identify the image of the dead dictator with oppression, lies, and capricious despotism. Moreover, because of their silence, many people of both generations were haunted by a vague feeling of guilt for the crimes of the past decades. This strongly developed feeling of responsibility may be one of the most important reasons for the acute, increasingly violent protest of a hitherto small, but steadily growing group, against the encroachments of Party bureaucracy.

Certainly it would be unfair to Khrushchev to insinuate that he had launched this de-Stalinization process simply as a tactical maneuver, providing a cover for the elimination of political opponents. Most probably, the former Premier had also hoped to force the morally corrupt and politically isolated Party apparatus out of its deadlock and, no less important, to present the Party to foreign powers in the West as once again open to negotiations. With his overthrow eight years later, Khrushchev was to pay dearly for the miscalculation which led him to believe that he could excommunicate Stalin without at the same time discrediting the Party. In this respect his puritanical comrades in the Party were more realistic—they grasped very clearly the resultant danger for both Party and political system from any such attack on Stalin. Inevitably, a slur on the man was equally an attack on the Party's very structure, since Stalin had been its power source for almost thirty years. In her witty and informative second book,[2] Stalin's daughter, Svetlana Alliluyeva, described how Khrushchev fruitlessly struggled, through the Party system, to force rehabilitation of the victims of 1937-38. Subsequent development of Soviet domestic policy since 1964 shows that Khrushchev's loss of power was not simply the result of internal Party rivalries, or the failure of some of his more curious economic policies—especially in agriculture—but rather, signified the end of the dispute over the extent of de-Stalinization.

Though Khrushchev accused Stalin of being almost solely responsible for the crimes of the past regime of terror, he was equally determined to check every serious discussion concerning them. Thus he deliberately hamstrung any significant reforms of Stalinism, and from the beginning, forfeited any possibility of surmounting the past. In this manner the Premier hoped to control the extent of the de-Stalinization process and, more importantly, to guarantee the infallibility of the Party apparatus, which had suffered a tremendous loss of confidence during those years. But the reaction of the public, especially within literary circles, far exceeded any expected response. The intelligentsia had no intention of limiting a battle against the personality cult to those narrow guidelines set up by the Party. Instead, they did exactly what Khrushchev could have least wanted

and began investigating the roots of the personality cult
and its reign of terror. The novelist Karanin wrote:

> *Many had hoped that Russia would take up
> the battle against the personality cult, with-
> out seriously considering the factors which
> had brought it about. But that didn't hap-
> pen. Our perceptions have sharpened.*[3]

For many, the official renunciation of Stalin meant a
critical appraisal of their own ties to the system. Khrushchev's exposures instantly destroyed the myth of Party
infallibility, and all faith in it as the embodiment of absolute truth and justice. The intellectuals and artists were
not alone in realizing that the moment had come to demand
the surrender of dogmatism, however manifested, as well
as other allied reforms.

Meanwhile, a heretical avant-garde, whose most important representative in those years was unquestionably
Yevtushenko, gained a growing literary audience. The
young poet's publications related to the Twentieth Congress, permitted him to appear as spokesman for the
majority of Soviet youth. In "Zima Junction," his autobiographical poem published in 1956, Yevtushenko confronts
the reader with what has since become for millions of
young Soviet citizens a burning problem; the search for
truth.

> *What is my goal? asked the youth of twenty-
>   three,
> I should like to fight gallantly,*

> *But whatever leads me to the fight*
> *Must always accompany that flicker of truth*
> *Which shall remain an integral part of me.*[4]

The same problem appears even more emphatically a few years later in another poem:

> *. . . Let us truly be open,*
> *The free word be our shield.*
> *. . . What once was will not come again,*
> *We want to be new, new even in word.*[5]

Yevtushenko characterized Stalin's burial day as the turning point in the life of his generation. Like many of his contemporaries, he passionately condemned all those who established in the name of Communism a tyranny which then proceeded to compromise the teachings of Marx.

The fact that Yevtushenko's poem "Zima Junction" was published in the reactionary literary journal *Oktyabr (October)*, *Novy Mir's* counterpublication (in comparison to which it was so lightly regarded that most of its issues end up as wastepaper), indicates that a liberating current managed to exist, however temporarily, even in the most dogmatic of Party agencies.

In August of 1956, *Novy Mir* published the first installment of Vladimir Dudintsev's *Not by Bread Alone*,[6] a novel so well received in the West that it was shortly available in eighteen translations. Though lacking any special artistic worth, it became the literary sensation of the year. In this novel Dudintsev became the first to blame bureaucracy openly for the moral breakdown of the collective.

This deterioration, he felt, robbed the spiritually independent human being of every possibility to fight for his ideas on any level except at risk of his own life. By deliberately making one individual his "positive hero" and at the same time portraying Party members in a negative light, Dudintsev earned not only the wrath of puritan criticism, but also the sympathy of millions of readers and the praise of distinguished older writers, Konstantin Paustovski among them. Paustovski's defense of the novel took the form of a bitter charge against the "new middle class," the "beneficiaries and sycophants" who took it upon themselves to speak in the name of the people—those who had become accustomed to regarding the people as "dung," and whose "upbringing consisted of acting in accordance with one's lowest instincts," whose "weapons are treason, slander, and moral or physical murder . . . We see these people around us every day . . . They are a burden which weighs heavily on our land." [7]

Although the vilifications against him intensified toward the end of 1956 and the beginning of 1957, Dudintsev steadfastly refused to submit to self-criticism. In the following years this writer was able to publish very little. For a while he and his family lived under wretched conditions. His uncompromising posture and his candor in communicating with foreigners almost cost him his life. One day two trucks, whose drivers could never be "ascertained," rammed his automobile. As a result, the already-aging Dudintsev was hospitalized for a long time. He had scarcely been released when he was mysteriously shoved from a streetcar. Strangely enough, in this case too, the scoundrels were never found. The public has long expected a new novel from Dudintsev which reportedly concerns the tragic history of Vavilov.[8] This particular theme, however, is too controversial, even today, for Dudintsev to have the slightest chance of publication.

Other authors, including Daniel Granin, Semion Kirsanov and Aleksandr Yashin, succeeded the novel *Not by Bread Alone* with a whole series of stories, expressing their own grievances. To some extent, all these stories turned against institutionalized hypocrisy and, as in the case of Kirsanov, called upon the reader to "plan, think and seek." The year 1956 also saw a group of liberal writers in Moscow publish two anthologies under the title of *Literaturnaya Moskva (Literary Moscow)*.[9] Apart from short stories, verses of several "thaw" poets, and essays by critics such as Viktor Shklovski, these volumes contained poems by Anna Akhmatova, the last living representative of the "Silver Age." Although silenced for a long time, she had never really lost the love of her former public and quickly became an idol of Russian youth.

Finally, the playwright Aleksandr Kron attracted attention with an article deploring the wretched state of contemporary art. He began with a total repudiation of the personality cult, and rejected every type of "cult" as "scandalous" and "unpatriotic." "Even the cultish deification of the people . . . has its deficiencies; it degrades the individual person," [10] wrote Kron, who considerably exceeded the pardonable limits of criticism with this assault on the officially sanctioned chauvinism.

Attempts to liberate art and literature from their dogmatic chains continued, leaving the Party in a state of considerable unrest. The Hungarian uprising, effectively quelled by Soviet troops in the autumn of 1956, inevitably led to a reinforcement of Soviet domestic policy that was felt most noticeably in the cultural-political sector. From the beginning of 1957, one writers' conference after another was called, including the Plenum of the Writers of Moscow in March and the third Plenum of the Board of the Union of Soviet Writers in May. Nevertheless, the insubordinate writers, who had been asked to deliver self-accusations, amazed the assembly not only by their failure to repent, but also by their outright rejection of the criticism as unjustified. According to the official report of the March Plenum, the writer Veniamin Kaverin even threatened "his adversaries with a lawsuit." [11] At the same time, Yevtushenko, who had been dubbed the "complaining Komsomoler" by angry functionaries, fell into violent arguments with Komsomol authorities. These were finally settled with his expulsion from this young Communist group.

In a speech before the Central Committee, and in another one before writers, painters, sculptors and composers (May 13 and 19, 1957), Khrushchev strongly took the rebellious "culture creators" to task. That same year, in August, mouthpieces for the Party published excerpts from both speeches.[12] In them Khrushchev denounced the management of *Novy Mir* and *Literary Moscow* for having published "unpatriotic works." He defended the Party's claim to absolute authority, even in questions of art; and, following his custom, tried to force stubborn writers and artists back to the official Party line through threats or solicitude.

The press eventually reported that several had indeed admitted their errors. (Among those singled out for criticism, incidentally, was the once-loyal Konstantin Simonov, who as editor in chief of *Novy Mir* had fought almost as earnestly as his predecessor Tvardovski to give the newspaper a more liberal tone.) The depth and sincerity of these surrenders did not seem to satisfy the Party, however; no detailed information concerning them was ever released. Instead, the critics became outraged again when their adversaries entered into the now famous "conspiracy of silence." This type of retaliation—a boycott of Party assemblies and refusal to express any opinions—was a completely novel approach, against which the Party functionaries found themselves helpless. The writers, on the other hand, rejoiced in their discovery of this passive resistance as a means of exerting pressure. However weak it may have been, this ploy enabled them to escape complete political subjugation and, more importantly, helped introduce a new feeling of solidarity.

Until recently this "front of silence" represented the only form of protest in which writers, artists, and lately scientists, could safely take part. Seldom had this strategy been applied before in the same manner as in recent years when signs of a modification of neo-Stalinism became increasingly apparent. Even the present leadership recognizes its dependence upon the allegiance of intellectual groups, and tries to assure itself of their support, if not their loyalty. This situation has hardly changed since Khrushchev was in power, though his successors have indicated less willingness to compromise. Since the authorities are determined to maintain power in accordance with their reactionary, dogmatic guidelines, even risking greater loss of prestige at home and abroad, the lot of Soviet writers has again deteriorated, as witnessed by the recent Solzhenitsyn case. At the same time, these events emphasize the differences between the present neo-Stalinism and the Stalinism of the thirties and forties. This gap is most apparent in the fact that the present government no longer dares to rid itself of intellectual opposition by means of mass terror and execution.

Khrushchev's statements of August, 1957—better described as a decree—and the subsequent campaign against any liberalizing of literature put an ostensible end to the second "thaw." In the meantime, however, a great number of younger writers and other talented people joined forces with many scientists (particularly those of the natural sciences, but also including philosophers and historians) in a decision to support the moderate concessions they had won and, wherever possible, to expand them. As early as the 1950's, seeds were germinating for a new political opposition to the incumbent system, but nothing came of this. The writers and scientists comprised a very influential group that focused a clearly growing opposition upon the cultural policies of the Party, especially its suppression of research. Yet it was precisely in these areas that the regime demanded unconditional allegiance to those guidelines dictated by the Party. Artists, as well as researchers, found themselves faced by a growing contradiction between ideological dogma and personal commitments to truth. Such a clash could only lead them toward a more hostile confrontation with the Party.

THE PASTERNAK AFFAIR

They carried him, but not to bury him.
They carried him, to crown him.

ANDREI VOZNESENSKI

In April, 1954, the journal *Znamia (The Banner)* published ten poems from the appendix of *Doctor Zhivago* and announced the expected publication of the novel within coming months. Since he had obviously managed to 'break the enforced silence of years, Boris Pasternak's re-emergence aroused general excitement. The public, encouraged by reports that all arrangements had been concluded with a state publishing house, anxiously awaited the new novel's appearance. All hopes were dashed, however, in the autumn of 1956 when the Writers' Union refused publication of the work. (Two years later their letter finally appeared in the press.[1]) Meanwhile, however, a copy of the manuscript had reached the hands of Giangiacomo Feltrinelli, a publisher in Milan. Despite all efforts of the Soviet authorities to obstruct its publication, *Doctor Zhivago* appeared in 1957 in Italy and shortly thereafter in many other Western lands. A libelous campaign against Pasternak closely followed the book's publication—an attempt at calumny unparalleled even by the later treatment of Solzhenitsyn.

The Union of Soviet Writers criticized Pasternak's work on the grounds that "[he] denied the socialistic revolution." Obviously, the religious elements expressed in *Doctor Zhivago* and its unmistakable renunciation of Marxism, combined with the description of suffering endured by the Russian intelligentsia after 1917, hit Party representatives in a very sensitive spot.

The campaign against Pasternak reached its climax on the twenty-third of October, 1958, when the poet was awarded the Nobel Prize for Literature. Pasternak accepted this honor with a telegram to Stockholm: ". . . eternally grateful, moved, proud, joyful, humbled." A few days later the author felt he was being pressured by Party dignitaries to recant his acceptance of the distinguished award. On October 28 Pasternak was expelled from the Writers' Union. In pamphlets circulated by the press he was denounced, among other things, as a "traitor," a "malevolent philistine," a "decadent formalist." V. Semichastni, then Chief Secretary of the Komsomol, exceeded the level of general hysteria with his vulgar invectives comparing Pasternak to a sow except "that swine never dirty the place where they eat."[2] At the same time, Semichastni demanded that the author be forced to emigrate. As a result, Pasternak was compelled to address a letter to Khrushchev in which he begged the Premier to save him from emigration.

> *Leaving my motherland would be equal to death for me, and that is why I ask that you do not take such extreme measures in this case.*[3]

The situation died down during the following months. Not one of the "liberal" writers yet dared to speak openly in his defense, as happened nearly ten years later in the case of Solzhenitsyn. Even in Moscow, their protest exhausted itself with a boycott of the official writers' assemblies.

When Pasternak died on May 31, 1960, the intellectual elite of Russia mourned for the death of one of their greatest poets, and many young writers lamented the loss of an important teacher as well as an artistic exemplar. His funeral in the writers' colony of Peredelkino resembled a demonstration, with hundreds of people present to pay their last respects to the poet. Among them were students, workers and well-known artists. His sons, and the writers Siniavski and Daniel, carried the coffin out of his home, accompanied by the pianist Sviatoslav Richter. At the conclusion of the funeral oration, delivered by the professor of philosophy V. Asmus, the mourners surrounded Pasternak's grave and recited some of his verses as a final tribute.

What Pasternak feared during his lifetime actually occurred after his death. Olga Ivinskaya, his old friend and co-worker (who served as model for Lara in *Doctor Zhivago*) was arrested in August, 1960, humiliated by public defamation, and sentenced to eight years in a labor camp. She had been charged with "currency offenses," having accepted Pasternak's foreign fees as authorized by him. Her daughter Irina was also indicted and received a five-year term. Irina's release came after one year, and Olga Ivinskaya's sentence was reduced by half. This amnesty may have come about because everyone knew that the charges against Pasternak's friend were unjustified; also, perhaps, the men who had succeeded Khrushchev to power believed such an act of clemency would favorably influence nonconforming intellectuals.[4]

A volume of Pasternak's poetry appears in 1961, thanks primarily to the ubiquitous literary critic Andrei Siniavski. This, too, sold out almost immediately, as did a later volume of verse (with an introduction by·Siniavski) in 1965. Again, a rumor circulated in the early 1960's—a period promising some relaxation of domestic policy—that *Doctor Zhivago* was close to being released for publication. Even Ilia Ehrenburg spoke in favor of this. Nevertheless, the discrepancy between the novel's intellectual position and the ever anxiously guarded taboos of the power system afforded little support for such conjectures.

Pasternak regarded *Doctor Zhivago* as his "most decisive and significant work . . . the only one of which I am not ashamed and which I wholeheartedly support."[5] In another passage, he further described the autobiographical experiences in this work. He once told a visitor:

We have learned we are guests of existence, travelers between two stations. We must find our security in ourselves. During the short time we are permitted to live, we need to define for ourselves our relationship to the world in which we live, and our place in the universe. That means, as I see it, a renunciation of the materialistic concept of nineenth-century life. It means a rebirth of the spiritual values of one's inner life, of

religion. I do not mean religion as dogma,
as the church without life . . .[6]

Soviet readers are still waiting in vain for the release of all the works of Pasternak and Solzhenitsyn, the greatest Russian writers of this century. The faith with which they have waited for such publication was unforgettably expressed in the words of a worker who cried out above Pasternak's open grave:

Farewell, honored Boris Leonidovich. We don't know all the works you have written. But the day will come when we will read them all. This we swear to you in this hour . . .[7]

THE SEARCH FOR
NEW VALUES

*I don't want the wind to determine the
  direction of my life—
I want to master the questions, that is
  our duty.
Greatness calls and beckons and forces
  us to think,
We will devote ourselves to it and prove
  ourselves equal.*
                    YEVGENI YEVTUSHENKO

The risk of Russia's slipping back to conditions that existed
before 1953 and 1954 was completely wiped out by the
Twentieth Congress. Even Khrushchev's dogmatic campaign
of 1957 couldn't change that; although he defined the limits of de-Stalinization even more narrowly than ever before,
writers and artists no longer allowed themselves to be mis-
led. Besides, Khrushchev was shrewd enough to grant writers modest concessions. He did this primarily to provide a
certain ventilation for the pent-up emotions of the opposition, but secondly, for reasons of political expediency. A
definite measure of de-Stalinization simply had to appear
in cultural policies.

Naturally the Party did not spare its bitter criticism

of insubordinate writers, and even Yevtushenko was eventually forced to submit to self-criticism, though he had so long remained outwardly loyal to the Party line. Because of this capitulation he lost the sympathy, and shook the confidence, of many readers. Indeed, he has been reproached again and again for his willingness to compromise with the regime under pressure.

But while the pressure exerted from above noticeably lessened, along the fear of reprisals, the number of literary works unsympathetic to the Party increased. Actually, one may regard any totally apolitical literature as deviating from the Party line. And it is precisely this overall lack of political implication that characterized the literature of 1958 through 1960.

The growing anticipation of a possible clear-cut separation between art and official propaganda was the underlying cause of the writers' apolitical posture. Younger writers shared this attitude, for they were generally bored by the political hues of literature and the constant editorial intrusions of the Party. Questions involving happiness, the purpose of life—good and bad—glutted the literary output of those years. The prevalent mood was defined by doubt concerning official goals and standards, the longing for new values, and the desire to escape from the constraint of the collective and "equality." All these ideas lay far removed from the insincere, utilitarian pathos of the Party.

Apart from Yevtushenko, there are a number of writers whose actions have been the subject of suspicious Party surveillance since the end of the 1950's but who still command high respect from millions of readers. These include Andrei Voznesenski, Viktor Nekrasov, Yuri Kazakov, Vladimir Tendriakov, Yuri Naghibin, Vasili Aksyonov, Rimma Kazakova, Valentin Katayev, Bulat Okudzhava, Aleksandr Galic, Boris Slutski, and Bella Akhmadulina, naming but a few. Along with many others, they have contributed to the return of the humanistic tradition in Russian literature, a tradition which has been stunted during the course of the last twenty years. In so doing, they also have given fresh expression to the best characteristics of their people: compassion, incorruptibility and integrity.

One of the literary sensations of 1961 was a public recital by Yevtushenko on the so-called Day of Poetry (October 8). Beneath the impressive Mayakovski monument, a popular spot for poetry readings, a mob interrupted the official recital in progress, in order to push Yevtushenko onto the rostrum. The crowd spontaneously recited in unison his recently published poem, "Babi Yar." [1] The critical reaction to this occurrence bristled with indignation, particularly since a group of several anti-Semitic functionaries considered the poem an intolerable provocation. The critics reproached Yevtushenko with a lack of "internationalism" and labeled his politics adolescent. He was accused of presenting a one-sided description of the sufferings of the Jews while ignoring the sufferings experienced by Russians, Ukrainians and other national groups during the German occupation. Moreover, he had allegedly neglected to identify the Fascist criminals. The management of the journal that published the poem—*Literaturnaya Gazeta (The Literary Gazette)*—was subject to disciplinary action. Its chief editor, Valeri Kosolapov, lost his position.

Russian intellectuals were moved by Yevtushenko's "Babi Yar" to adhere even more strongly to their own frequently pro-Jewish attitudes. Though hardly intending to grant the Jews a privileged position, they did oppose discrimination against any minority and saw, in anti-Semitic remarks especially, another symptom of inhumanity and cultural backwardness.

According to Soviet newspaper announcements, unofficial poetry reading was held in June of the same year in Tambov. There the poet Viacheslav Gogin, and several others after him, read some of their own poems followed by works of Blok, Yesenin and other controversial writers. As a result of this recital, Gogin was accused of "illegal formation of a group" and "propagation of inferior poetry." He lost his membership in the Komsomol.

By somehow avoiding the censor, almost a decade after these incidents, one of the major works of post-revolutionary Russian literature appeared in the West. Nadezhda Mandelstam, the widow of the poet Osip Mandelstam, published her memoirs. In the midst of a tale of suffering, confusion and unrealized hopes, she managed to shift attention to the early signs of a still distant but brighter future:

> . . . the values we thought had been abolished forever are being restored . . . This has come as a surprise, both to those who never gave up these values and to those who tried to bury them once and for all. Somehow or other, they lived on underground, taking refuge in all those hushed homes with their dimmed lights. Now they are on the move and gathering force. . . . The keepers

*of the flame hid in darkened corners, but
the flame did not go out. It is there for all
to see.*[2]

THE CAMP LITERATURE

*Memory is man's most precious
     possession.
Without it, there is neither conscience
     nor honor, and no spiritual
     creativity . . .
Remembrance of the past is the only
     reliable key to the present.*
                              LIDIA CHUKOVSKAYA

The Twenty-second Congress of the Communist Party, held
from October 17 through 31, 1961, rivaled the Twentieth
Congress as a landmark in the history of the u.s.s.r. During this congress, the new program of the Communist party
of the Soviet Union was adopted and the Stalin "problem"
further debated. The new Party program devoted considerable attention to the theme of "art and literature," and
the numerous speeches concerning it bore witness to the
extensive discussions of Party dogmatists caused by unman-
ageable writers and artists. The final effect of their provocations, however, was soon overshadowed by Khrushchev's
new and even sharper condemnation of Stalin, which resulted in the removal of the dictator's body from its mauso-
leum to new interment outside the Kremlin walls.

The reaction to this second wave of de-Stalinization resembled the first in the sense that it found earliest and most obvious expression in literature. As far back as the previous Third Writers' Congress in May, 1959, Tvardovski demanded from his colleagues the courage to risk writing what their consciences dictated. (Khrushchev highly respected this poet, a fact most probably responsible for his reinstatement as editor of *Novy Mir* in 1958.) It was in this spirit that Tvardovski published, barely a year later, his now-famous poem, "From Distant Reaches." Surprisingly enough, it also appeared in *Pravda.* The poem criticized Stalin's faults and crimes. Its final verses emphasized not only his generation's responsibility for these crimes, but more importantly, the involvement of writers because of their unpardonable silence and delusion.

And still everything remains the same
Just as it was, because nothing passes away.
All that has been written down by the pen
Still withstands the attacks aimed against it.

There is no way to avoid the truth.
It is something you cannot escape.
For, better than anything else, truth knows
That silence is often nothing more than a lie.

Perhaps not for all, but definitely for a poet
Silence can afford neither fame nor glory.
What will happen tomorrow, when a strict judge

Calls you to account for your deeds and your
    silence?

Now, my little friend, where was your voice?
You wanted a peaceful life, no problems.
You are lying, for those awful times, those
    terrible years
Were long since a thing of the past.

No! You have only stolen the time,
Already accustomed to apathy.
But you never neglected to collect
Your wages punctually from your muse.

I will go immediately to the judge;
Perhaps I've been waiting for him.
It may be that I was never able
To say the one word which said all.

What I did say came from the depths of my
    soul.
I shall not delay in preparing myself.
I was there, and when I am not
I am responsible for all of it.[1]

The controversy between Soviet youth and their parents became one of the ever-recurring themes of the times.
The younger generation reproached their fathers for silence
in the face of tyranny, and blamed their apathy for the misfortune and death of millions of fellow citizens. Those of

their elders who had been victimized were chided for being unprepared and thus not defending themselves. Complained the young Jarik to his uncle in *The White Flag*, a play by K. Ikramov and V. Tendriakov.

> *They dragged you off to Magadan . . . and you forgave them.*
>
> *With guns they forced you to clear the forests—and you pardoned them. They lined you up against the wall, and you died shouting the slogan: Long live Stalin! You've forgiven, you've compromised . . . You're not dead yet, you're still alive and as long as you live so does submission. The detestable, unscrupulous submission!* [2]

Short stories and novels concerning the day-to-day existence of the approximately twelve million political prisoners who filled Stalin's prisons over the decades, flooded the pages of literary journals, including *October*. Another sign of the steadily growing liberation even managed to carve out for itself a separate category in Russian folklore. The bitter songs of labor camps and their prisoners quickly spread throughout the country. Mikhailo Mikhailov, sentenced to an extended prison term in Yugoslavia for his political views, described in his report, "Moscow Summer, 1964," how the students at Moscow University enthusiastically sang the new prison songs in small spontaneous groups on the landings and in the halls of their school.[3]

We have admitted the mistakes of others
And have set out in search of our destiny.
In those days we had more confidence in you,
   Great Stalin,
Than we ever did in ourselves.

Your uniform boasted many decorations,
Your hair has grown grey with care.
Back then you were rescued six different times
While I haven't managed to succeed yet.

Just yesterday we buried two Marxists.
And their graves were not draped with flags.
One of them was a right wing radical,
While the other proved himself something quite
   different . . .

Dying, he offered you all his possessions—
His tobacco pouch and his loyal oath.
He begged you to return order to our state
And whispered, "Stalin, he's our captain." [4]

Thus one song celebrates an unfortunate victim's blind faith in the man who, directly or indirectly, was responsible for his suffering.

Unquestionably, the most important work of his genre was Aleksandr Solzhenitsyn's novella *One Day in the Life of Ivan Denisovich*.[5] A physicist and mathematician, born in 1918, Solzhenitsyn graduated with honors but was forced to interrupt his studies in literature to serve on the front in

1941. In East Prussia in 1945, the distinguished artillery officer was arrested, stripped of his rank, and condemned to eight years in a forced-labor camp. Upon his release, Solzhenitsyn was further sentenced to "eternal" exile in Kazachstan. His punishment had been prompted by letters sent from the front to a friend back home that contained derogatory remarks about Stalin. On March 5, 1953, the day Stalin died, the critically ill Solzhenitsyn was released from prison only to go into exile. He later described the disease and his subsequent convalescence in his novel *Cancer Ward*. Rehabilitated in 1956, Solzhenitsyn returned to Rjazan in western Russia where he was employed as a mathematics instructor.

In 1962 he offered his description of a normal day in the life of a Soviet concentration-camp inmate to Tvardovski, chief editor of *Novy Mir*, for publication. Tvardovski received the book enthusiastically, and Khrushchev, eager for an authentic first-hand revelation of Stalin's atrocities— especially considering the resistance he met from the Party —not only approved publication but even went so far as to defend it emphatically in the Party Presidium against the opposition of several members. After Tvardovski presented the manuscript to Khrushchev, Solzhenitsyn is supposed to have telephoned Moscow frequently to learn what he could about his own fate and that of Tvardovski—a grim reminder of the tremendous risks taken by these men to publish the truth.

As expected, the appearance of *Ivan Denisovich* in *Novy Mir*, caused a sensation. That particular issue exhausted within a few hours, and 100,000 copies were sold in less than half a day. This set a record, even for *Novy Mir*, whose issues are usually gone within two or three days. (Even the alleged "loyalists" actually snatched the journal from newsboys' hands.) *One Day in the Life of Ivan Denisovich* established Solzhenitsyn's lasting reputation as one of the most respected, if not most popular, writers in the Soviet Union. No less than four dissertations concerning his work were submitted to the philological faculty of Moscow University in 1963 alone.

In his first literary endeavor, Solzhenitsyn focused on one of the most dismal chapters in Soviet history, and at the same time immortalized in the figure of Ivan Denisovich, a Soviet Platon Karatayev,[6] the best qualities of the Russian people. For the most part critics greeted the narrative favorably, at times even enthusiastically. Gregori Baklanov, who courageously supported Solzhenitsyn even in the earliest campaigns against him, wrote:

> *It has become clear that since the appearance of Solzhenitsyn's book we will never again be able to write as we have done till now.*[7]

THE NEW CAMPAIGN

*The inability to find the truth and then
to say it, is a deficiency that can never
be camouflaged by our ability to talk
about lies.*

BORIS PASTERNAK

Despite the fact that the principles of "socialist realism"
and the dogma of "Party-mindedness" endured much the
same as ever, 1962 was generally known as a golden year
for Soviet art and literature. Recent modifications in domestic policy, and a more cautious approach to cultural matters,
made possible an expansion of the official norms under
which the artists and writers, now become much more self-
confident, could function.

However, since every relaxation of state pressure in cultural, especially literary, affairs resulted in a weakening of
official control, as well as a diminution of totalitarian
strength, it hardly came as a surprise when the party leadership launched a new attack against the heretics in art
and literature. Leonid Ilyichev, Secretary of the Central
Committee and Chairman of the Ideological Commission,
spoke toward the end of the year before successive joint
sessions of representatives of the Party and the regime (De-

cember 17) and representatives of art and literature (December 26). On both occasions Ilyichev sought again to reinforce the Party's claim to infallibility in cultural matters.[1] An exhibition of plastic arts in Moscow acted as springboard for both of Ilyichev's speeches, as well as a resultant month-long dispute between the Party and the artistic intelligentsia. While visiting the exhibition, Khrushchev expressed his displeasure at abstract artistic creations as alien to the people. Referring to several paintings, he said that one could hardly determine whether they had been daubed at "by the hand of a man or the tail of a donkey." (It may be pertinent to note that later, during his long days of retirement, Khrushchev allegedly amused himself by trying his own hand at this very pursuit.)

Ilyichev hastened to heap "sharp but justified criticism" on the artists and their "pathological endeavors." Among others, such criticism was aimed at the well-known logician, Aleksandr Yesenin-Volpin, author of *Vesennij List* (*A Leaf of Spring*). The poems and meditations contained in this book, secretly smuggled to the West and published in New York, Ilyichev characterized as "misanthropic," the "nonsense of a rogue," a "poisonous toadstool rotten to the core."[2]

Interestingly enough, this chief theoretician also mentioned several letters that various groups of scientists and artists had addressed to Khrushchev and the Central Committee of the CPSU regarding plastic arts. These letters contained an urgent plea to "put a stop to regressive trends toward earlier methods which run contrary to the whole spirit of our times."[3] With the single exception of this quotation, Ilyichev never made these letters public. He branded them as a "call for peaceful coexistence within the realm of inimical ideologies," and his response to such provocation was summarized in the statement:

> *We have complete freedom to fight for Communism. We do not have any freedom to fight against Communism, and there can never be any such freedom.*[4]

March 7 and 8, 1963, witnessed an encounter between Party leaders and the "creators of literature and art." Joining the undaunted Ilyichev as main speaker was the Party chief himself, Nikita S. Khrushchev. Ilyichev started things off by praising those who had "felt the loving care of the Party in their hearts" and consequently acknowledged their "errors." The writers Andrei Voznesenski and Yevgeny Yevtushenko, and the heavily censored sculptor Ernst Neizvestny, belonged to this group. As for the others, however, Ilyichev censured the continuing opposition of many writers and artists, who not only "stubbornly cling to erroneous notions," but worse, try to "persuade others of their convictions." The situation looked equally dismal for those writers who simply remained silent:

> *"Silence in itself means something, it too betrays a point of view."* [5]

Khrushchev's speech by comparison seemed rather mild. As usual, he digressed frequently and took pains to single out those "culture creators" whom he favored, since he was concerned for the most part with chauvinists most truly devoted to "socialist realism." Viktor Nekrasov bore the brunt of his criticism, as did Ehrenburg's memoirs *Men-Years-Life*,[6] a book that had caused considerable uneasiness among the dogmatic cultural functionaries. The Poem "Babi Yar" also earned an official reprimand for Yevtushenko. In spite of this, however, the poet continued to enjoy Khrushchev's somewhat divided favor. Several months earlier, upon instructions from the Party chief, he published in *Pravda* his long poem entitled "The Heirs of Stalin." This poem warned of a Stalinist revival and was aimed at all those who secretly hoped for one. Khrushchev's reason for supporting this poem had earlier brought about the publication of Solzhenitsyn's *Ivan Denisovich*. He saw it as an effective weapon in the battle against his old pro-Stalinist opposition within the Party.

Following a few other assemblies and meetings with the young writers, the Party was able, laboriously, to establish once more in the public mind an impression of ideological unanimity. Several writers who had provoked the wrath of the authorities were sent on month-long bus expeditions (officially known as "creative trips") to remote provinces. Vasili Aksenov, for example, was dispatched to a construction site in Siberia; Andrei Voznesenski was required to spend a portion of his time in various northern factories. Thrown back upon the grass-roots of reality, as it seemed, they were encouraged to take advantage of such "retreat" for reevaluating their convictions. Thus they would return home penitent and burning with a desire to sing the Party's praises. Indeed, several of them actually did fulfill their obligations upon their return, according to plan, and issued self-criticisms. But these "confessions" perished of their own superficial nature; the repentant phase did not last. Contrariwise, these recent attempts of the Party to muzzle them only intensified the feeling among writers and artists of the absolute necessity for independence. Eventually this enabled them to place the demands of conscience above Party dictates.

THE GROWING
EMANCIPATION OF
THE INTELLECTUALS

*For thousands of years mankind has
been accumulating precious experiences,
but we tend now and then to underesti-
mate them. It would be wrong to believe
that real life began only after the October Revolution and is to be found
only in socialist countries.*

ALGIMANTIS BALTAKIS

In the cultural-political campaign of 1963, the artistic intelligentsia recognized very clearly that nothing more significant than an abandonment of the criminal abuses of the
personality cult lay hidden behind the first and second de-
Stalinizations, and that this departure alone offered little encouragement for the long-awaited freedom of the press.
Any real undoing of the past was thus impossible. Guarantees blotting out the chances of a return to the terror of the
thirties and forties were equally shaky. The breach between
an appropriate degree of de-Stalinization, as regarded by
the power system, and what seemed necessary to the young

intellectuals, who had not personally experienced all its horrors, grew wider than ever.

This increasingly intense search for truth by young people soon became one of the most pressing themes of the liberal group in literature, and this equated their efforts to overcome the past. "There is no truth—if there really is a truth at all—which our literature wouldn't make use of, whether dangerous or meaningless, just as there are no lies which could in any way be useful to it." With such words Aleksandr Tvardovski raised an urgent appeal for the "whole truth" in an essay which appeared in *Novy Mir* in 1965. Clearly he was demanding historical candor, as well as veracity, in the reporting of everyday events.[1]

As a result of the Party's claim to infallibility in cultural questions, working writers saw themselves exposed to relations far more strained than those of the scientists—at least the natural scientists, who, because of their indispensability in the technical development of research, were allowed greater concessions than those employed in any other discipline or business. (This was proved, for example, in the case of Sakharov, who dared give free expression to his opinions.)

The First All-Union Congress for philosophical questions in the natural sciences, held in October of 1958, legitimized the theory of relativity and quantum mechanics. During the Second All-Union Congress, in April of 1965, discussions were held concerning logic, pathology, cybernetics and scientific methodology. Since 1964, biology and genetics have been pursued once more beneath the shadows of Vavilov's rehabilitation and the victory over Lysenko's law of heredity. In 1962, the name of the Kharkovian professor E.

Liberman became inextricably linked to the beginning of economic reforms as yet incomplete.

The stagnation of philosophical research in the USSR is second only to that imposed upon the historical fields, mainly because philosophers, as interpreters of the "classics" (Marx, Engels and Lenin), are not only subjected to every vacillation in the ideological-political realm, but are also confined in means of expression by definite and unalterable postulates of ideology. But even in this area, which includes the history of philosophy, natural philosophy and ethics, a frequently heated debate has developed since the end of the fifties; and also—no less importantly—in the disagreement over alienation, philosophical anthropology, and philosophy of ethics.

The growing need within philosophic circles for joining the cultural tradition and development of Europe, as well as the desire to overcome an unnatural isolation fostered by five decades of Bolshevik rule, found a means of expression in literature. Another demand, especially from young intellectuals, to study and evaluate the spiritual heritage of pre-Bolshevik Russia grew as steadily as the desire to orient themselves toward Europe. It must be noted, however, that in all this they did not simply equate Europe with the "West" of that time, its living standards and thought processes.

Since Lenin, and more precisely since Stalin, the Soviet power structure has almost completely withheld the history of nineteenth- and early twentieth-century Russian ideas from its intelligentsia. It has succeeded in doing this either by silencing this history or by garbling it beyond recognition. The single exception to this rule is classical Russian literature, which is widely, though not exhaustively, published in great quantity today. The contribution of pre-Revolutionary literature should not be minimized, for it has provided the nation with a natural defense against cultural self-mutilation. Russian classics offer many people a moral standard which has occasionally stood in flagrant opposition to the goals and doctrines of the "new class"; such literature remains today an important corrective within a world that has been steered off course. It also accounts for the inner identification of the Russian reader with his writers.

In his *Soviet Men*, Klaus Mehnert relates an anecdote that powerfully illustrates the essence of this bond. Shortly before the Twentieth Party Congress, it was reported in Soviet newspapers that on February 9, 1956 (the seventy-fifth anniversary of Dostoevski's death), a subscription offer for a ten-volume edition of his works would be made available. The issuance of a thirteen-volume edition in the late 1920's, and the appearance of several books in 1931, were the last publications of Dostoevski's works in the Soviet Union. His name had disappeared from the annals of literary history unless related to a negative appraisal. In 1955, several of his works were finally allowed publication. Early in 1956, when Mehnert attempted to subscribe to the publicized edition through one of Moscow's larger bookstores, he was informed that the supply had been sold out three days earlier—indeed, before noon, on the first day of the subscription offer. Many people had stood in line overnight in icy zero weather, relieving one another in shifts, just to be sure they got their names on the list. The same story was repeated in other cities of the USSR. The extensive 300,000-copy edition had been sold out within a few hours.

Mehnert, who gradually came to believe that the attempt of the Bolsheviks to ban Dostoevski from the conscience of the people was simply a "test case," added these words: "The new spiritual upper class was unwilling . . . to have its version of the history of the people's ideas dictated exclusively by the Party and announced in official Party writings or edicts. Their curiosity, and their need to form their own impression of Dostoevski's works, was so overwhelming that the followers of Stalin had no choice but to capitulate finally on this point." [2]

In Communist Russia today, the relationship to great writers of the past is probably more essential than ever before. The best contemporary writers identify themselves with the classics, as for example, the highly respected and beloved Bulat Okudzhava, who wrote:

> *I wish that love could occupy the place it deserves in human life, that human society would not evolve into a barracks, that every human personality had the opportunity of a single individual development . . . that all relics of the personality cult would disappear . . . and democratic procedures become the general habit . . . For that reason, the great Russian literature of the nineteenth century, which preaches man and his freedom, is especially dear to me.* [3]

CULTURAL
AND POLITICAL
DEVELOPMENTS
FOLLOWING THE
FALL OF KHRUSHCHEV

Despite all obstacles, error always falls back before the assault of truth; at worst, it is a question of time or of the number of victims, as the history of mankind shows, starting with the victims of the Inquisition and even earlier.

PETR KAPICA

The overthrow of Khrushchev on the sixteenth of October, 1964, caused no particular uneasiness among the intelligentsia and certainly evoked none of its sympathy. Apart from the deterioration of relations between the now powerless Party chief and the artists and writers, his dilettantism in many fields and the public displays of his temper, especially abroad, were strongly disapproved. Moreover, intellectual circles were least likely to pardon his failure to push the de-Stalinization process toward more meaningful accomplishments. Even less willing were they to forgive the fact that he had compromised himself during his earlier co-operation with Stalin.

In their efforts to firmly establish their authority, Khrushchev's successors tried to assure themselves of the loyalty of noncomforming intellectuals by granting them greater concessions. Thus a new "thaw" developed, which allowed liberal forces to gain some ground for the future. In preparing the way for this milder climate, the new administration remained deliberately neutral at first. For example, a few days after Khrushchev's removal, an article by Dudintsev appeared which took exception to the catastrophic official principles in biology, particularly those concerning laws of heredity, and turned against Lysenko, whom Khrushchev had so avidly supported.[1] A whole series of similar articles followed. Very shortly, during one of the meetings of the Academy of Sciences in January, 1965, the pseudo-scientific stars of Stalin's and Khrushchev's eras were officially denounced and excommunicated from the society. That same month Ilyichev, Chairman of the Ideological Commission for the Central Committee of the CPSU, was compelled to abdicate his position in favor of the less doctrinaire Peter Demichev. Finally, several bards of "socialist realism," including Vsevolod Kochetov, L. Sobolev and G. Markov, also lost their posts in the Moscow writers' organization, at least temporarily, because of increasing pressure from the liberals.

In October, 1964, three representatives of the literary avant-garde—Yevgeny Yevtushenko, Rumma Kazakova and Bella Akhmadova—were permitted to hold a poetry recital before an audience of almost 2,000; it was the first time

since the campaign of 1963 that such well-known nonconformist poets could appear before so large a gathering.
Also very unusual was the fact that the Party press followed
this recital with a vigorous defense of the liberal-minded
intellectuals; indeed, the editor in chief of *Pravda* (at that
time), A. M. Rumjancev, contributed two articles about
"The Party and the Intellectuals," which emphasized the
right of intellectuals and artists to free, individual creativity, without which there could be no art at all. He said:

> *Genuine creativity is possible only in an at-*
> *mosphere of searching, of experimentation,*
> *of the free expression, and mutual clashes,*
> *of opinion. A salutary development of art de-*
> *mands the presence of different schools and*
> *directions . . .*[2]

A few months later Rumjancev was transferred from
his influential newspaper post to the sciences, a position
considered far less risky from the official point of view.
(He has since become Vice President of the Academy of
Sciences.)

As the progressive movement of the intelligentsia grew
stronger in its more frequent demands for complete abolition of all traces of Stalinism still present in culture, politics, justice and the economy, the new leaders again felt
compelled to tighten the reins. Even Khrushchev knew
he could not make allowances for the demands of youth,
because the power system had never really discarded, much
less overcome, the precepts of Stalinism. His successors,
far less confident with Brezhnev at the helm, feared the

loss of control, and with it the loss of all power in the face of ever-growing reform movements. They did not necessarily want to revert to terrorist methods, but at the moment that seemed the only way to guarantee free exercise of their own power.

Even so, one cannot honestly speak of a regression to Stalinism, or for that matter, even a return to Neo-Stalinism. Rather, the present Party bureaucracy seems to be setting itself into a course reminiscent of the policies employed during the period from 1953 to 1956. Such a course depends upon condemnation of the personality cult while maintaining Party control of the secret police. (The infamous Ministry of Internal Affairs, the MVD, once decentralized by Khrushchev, had regained its former power as a result of the new centralization in 1968.) The present administration is also concerned with efforts to restrain open terrorist tactics and to insure a minimum of inalienable civil rights. And finally, since the fall of Khrushchev, the Presidium of the Supreme Soviet has been given greater control over the Party Secretariat, a move that supposedly will prevent the possible emergence of a new one-man dictatorship.

Official criticism of Stalin, his terrorist methods, and his political and military mistakes has dwindled noticeably. The rehabilitation of victims of that era suffered a setback in following years despite the fact that works of once-censored writers, such as Andrei Platonov or Mikhail Bulgakov, were now permitted to appear. Military leaders were at least partially successful in reinstating Stalin as Commander in Chief of the Second World War. Soviet history, and in particular Party history, appeared now and again in new and revised versions. The attempt to re-ideologize, closely associated with the "hard" approach of the new domestic policy, caused the Party ever since 1966 to undertake authentic "sociological field trips" in order to win back the youth who had become indifferent toward, if not rebellious against, the official Party catechism. They instituted a campaign to remind scientists more frequently than ever of the principle of "Party-mindedness." These attempts of the ideologists to persuade the natural scientists, by nature generally skeptical of any utopia, were greeted with the same lack of success as their attempt to win back the youth who, in direct reaction against previous half-truths, had become totally immune to ideology.

During the Twenty-third Party Congress (the twenty-ninth of March through the eighth of April, 1966), to which the machine "bosses" gave their approval, the Party leadership could not refrain from speculative reflections. By this time Stalin, whose name was never even mentioned, had traversed the road from demigod, past posthumously accused criminal, toward his final degradation as a non-person. In order to ease the growing fear in many places that partial rehabilitation of the former dictator was definitely afoot, a group of well-known artists and scientists entreated Brezhnev, in a letter delivered the evening before the Party Congress, not to retard the de-Stalinization process.

Although the import of the speeches delivered at the Congress differed in many ways from those at the previous assembly, they again acknowledged allegiance to the tenets of the Twentieth Party Congress and once again denounced the personality cult. And, not surprisingly, they again raked the nonconforming writers over the coals. The top level of leadership assigned this task to second-echelon functionaries, including Egorychev, then Party Secretary of Moscow. The editorial management of the journal *Junost,* second only to *Novy Mir* as ranking mouthpiece for the literary avant-garde, subjected itself to self-criticism. A candidate for the Central Committee of the CPSU, Tvardovski had just lost his membership in that group; his position as editor in chief of *Novy Mir* hung by a slender thread. But to the satisfaction of his many friends, and the annoyance of the doctrinaire camp, he continued to resist every attack aimed against the publication just four years earlier of Solzhenitsyn's *One Day in the Life of Ivan Denisovich.* As the Party saw it, this short novel preached "pessimism, skepticism and decadence," and supposedly "distorted reality."

Mikhail Sholokhov played a particularly ugly role in the Party Congress. Sholokhov, a cold, unfeeling man and a writer of questionable talent, had slandered the writers Daniel and Siniavski a few weeks after their harsh condemnation. He considered their punishment too lenient. Siniavski and Daniel had been arrested in September, 1965, and sentenced the following February to seven and five years, respectively, at hard labor in the work camps. They weren't the first during the past years to be apprehended and put away because of illegal publications at home or material smuggled abroad for publication. But it was the judgment against these two outstanding representatives of the Russian intelligentsia that brought about today's steadily growing opposition to such arbitrary practices of the regime. Never before had the spiritual victory over the

Stalinist terror made itself so evident as in the open protest occasioned by this trial, a protest proving that an awareness of one's rights and an audacious attitude had taken the place of terrified silence and crippling resignation.

PART II

The Democratic Movement

INITIAL OPPOSITION

We are a caste.
We are separate.
We are heralds.

A. SUG-SUCHT

An unofficial, or illegal newspaper literature, duplicated by students of various Soviet high schools has been available alongside nonconformist, but officially published, literature ever since 1953, and even more readily so after 1956. Early references to such uncensored student papers were found in the Soviet press. Thus toward the end of 1955 the *Komsomolskaya Pravda* mentioned the *Figovy List¹* (*Fig Leaf*), which was secretly circulating around the University of Vilna. Shortly thereafter the same source reported on several newspapers printed in the high schools in the vicinity of Leningrad: *Goluboy Buton²* (*The Blue Bud*), *Svezie Golosa³* (*Fresh Voices*), and *Eres⁴* (*Heresy*). None of these journals were seen in the West.

Angry commentaries in the Party press seemed primarily concerned with literary works being reproduced to ridicule "socialist realism" *ad absurdum.* The milder climate following the Twentieth Party Congress, however, fostered widespread currents of opposition, first apparent among the academic youth. Among other things, earnest (yet unsuccessful) attempts were undertaken by these groups to reform the Komsomol along more democratic lines.

One of the doctors responsible for accelerated growth of internal hostility was the suppression of the Hungarian uprising in 1956. The internal Soviet reaction to Hungarian events was naturally a great deal weaker than what followed the occupation of Czechoslovakia in August, 1968. The average man in the Soviet Union knew relatively little about the Hungarian drive for independence. Even news of Polish disturbances at that time flowed more sparingly than it did twelve years later from Czechoslovakia. Nevertheless, the ever more insistent cry for greater freedom and spiritual revival in Poland and Hungary became universally more audible in Russian intellectual and artistic circles. The news of the Hungarian tragedy destroyed many of the hopes emanating from the Twentieth Party Congress and spread fear and dismay among the intelligentsia, despite the fact that there were always a few, even among the students, who candidly supported suppression of Hungary.

While there is little reference to direct protest actions by Moscow students, various sources reported how a substantial number of Leningrad students brandished the slogan "Hands Off Hungary!" and marched before the Winter Palace (now the Hermitage) during the Hungarian revolt. According to one conference report of the Leningrad Komsomol organization, 4,300 students were expelled from Leningrad high schools during 1956 and 1957 alone[5]—an unmistakable response to the spirit of rebellion spreading throughout the schools. On the other hand, unofficial assemblies had met in Moscow, as well as in Leningrad, to discuss Hungarian events in a perspective rather different from that of the Party. Copies of authentic commentaries, including several from English transmitters of the BBC, were allegedly displayed on the bulletin boards of various high schools and institutes of higher learning.

In 1957 many political prisoners, predominantly students from Moscow, Leningrad and Kiev, were sent to labor camps because of intrigues inimical to the state. Among them was the student writer Aleksei Dobrovolski, at that time about twenty years old, who was sentenced to three years for circulating uncensored reports of the Hungarian uprising.[6]

In their unequivocal renunciation of Marxism, Dobrovolski and the long-since disillusioned Siniavski (both now converted to Christianity) do not stand alone. The fact that many people shared their convictions was proved in *Feniks (Phoenix)*, an illegal anthology appearing in 1961. The majority of dissident intellectuals and artists of the 1950's (and even thereafter) did not fight the Communist system, but rather, a privileged caste, which had taken advantage of this system to pursue its own personal power. The political views of the rebels can be described as "neo-Leninist" inasmuch as they acknowledged the basic precepts of Leninism and the goals of the October Revolution. At the same time, however, they reproached the Stalinists, along with the present Party bureaucracy, for having betrayed these goals. Specifically, they decried their liquidation of revolutionary leaders, the setting up of a one-man dictatorship, the establishment of a system of suppression rather than promised freedom, and finally, their having become embroiled and imprisoned in a bureaucratic institution working against the people. Especially during the middle and late 1950's, a considerable number of predominantly "neo-Marxist" groups appeared openly at various universities. Sooner or later they were discovered, and their members often faced harsh imprisonments, as happened with the "Krasnopvcev-Rendel Group," whose leaders (bearing those names) were sentenced to ten years in a labor camp.

During a public meeting of the Komsomol at Moscow University, which was attended by students of the Physics Faculty, the assembly demanded a white book concerning all the victims of the Stalinist purges. The moral foundations of official Party policy were also questioned at this meeting, whose subject was "Nihilism in Politics." Several students criticized the Party leaders' cowardly and ineffective handling of the personality-cult problem during the Khrushchev era. The faculty member who chaired the meeting as Komsomol secretary seems to have successfully opposed a proposal to end the discussion,[7] made by the secretary of the Party committee.

At that time (the late fifties and early sixties), one could find numerous references in the Soviet press to individual acts of political opposition; today, such occurrences frequently remain unreported. Thus the official newspaper *Izvestia* reported a group of Moscow students being held responsible for "anti-Soviet speeches" and allegedly distributing anti-Establishment handbills.[8] Another news note was concerned with an engineer who had written and distributed letters directed against the "socialist order." [9] Anti-Soviet leaflets and flyers, great quantities of which were tossed into the mailboxes of private houses, seemed a popular means of communicating underground propaganda. Newspapers continually reported the discovery of mimeograph machines and other devices used for duplicating and distributing anti-Soviet literature, and these, too, were available everywhere, sometimes in the humble huts of peasants and farmers.[10] Incidentally, even the printing facilities of the state became involved, with the full cooperation of print-shop directors as well as workers.[11] Moreover, most of these political crimes were not so named, but were frequently disguised, especially in more recent years, under the general heading of "criminal offenses."

Illegal amateur radio transmitters (known as *Samefir*, self-perpetuators) sometimes plugged into official programs and thus stole considerable audiences for their own propaganda. The organs of the Soviet press reported angrily on the "subversive" broadcasts of these "radio rowdies" whose activities seemed particularly zealous in many regions, but chiefly in Kazakhstan around Tula. In Belaya Cer'kov alone, two hundred illegal transmitters were confiscated.[12] Although the majority of these ham operators probably have been discovered, they were able to pursue their methods for years and some continue today. A great number turned out to be students and workers, many of them less than twenty.

At first, the broadcasts were mostly nonpolitical (they had names like "Twist," "Boxer," "Carnival," etc.), and limited themselves to the broadcasting of officially proscribed modern music and unofficial cultural broadsides. Eventually, this means of communication came to be used for the transmission of otherwise unavailable news items and critical commentaries. Just how serious the Party considered these attempts to break through the state monopoly on information was demonstrated by the numerous sharply worded journalistic notes that branded such operators as "radio pirates," "criminals," and "gangsters of the air waves." [13] As a further means of stifling this propaganda, an ordinance was provided in 1963 (still in effect) that would define "increased liability for the illegal manufacture and use of radio transmitters." So far as can be known, punishment for violations of this ukase have ranged from a fine of fifty rubles to a four-year sentence in prison or work camp.[14]

Besides these underground actions, the years between 1959 and 1963 saw an increase in isolated open strikes by workers and prolonged protest demonstrations by the general populace. One orderly demonstration took place in Temir-Tau in Kazakhstan, where approximately three thousand young workers of both sexes struck against their miserable housing accommodations—they were living in tent colonies without sanitation facilities. During the course of the uprising, these workers disarmed the military who had been summoned for Temir-Tau's defense and occupied it. According to unofficial reports, the military troops were sympathetic to the workers' demands and refused to obey the command to fire. Special detachments of security police were finally successful in putting down the demonstration by barricading the city on all sides. It was also reported that one breakthrough attempt claimed the lives of ninety demonstrators and hundreds more were left wounded.[15]

In many places, the slightest excuse sufficed to release pent-up anger and frustration growing out of years of hollow Party promises. Inadequate arrangements for distribution of supplies, coupled with a lessening of fear after the

Twentieth Party Congress, provoked strikes and demonstrations in many parts of the Soviet Union during 1961 and 1962. Isolated disturbances occurred in the following years. By March, 1963, the situation was bad enough allegedly to trigger a work stoppage at Elektrosila, the electric power station in Leningrad. One month later the dock workers in Odessa refused to load cargo destined for Cuba. Similar outbreaks occurred in the northern ports of Archangel and Murmansk. Several Moscow factories waged demonstrations against stepped-up production which brought with it no increase in already insufficient pay. Strikes were called at the Gubkin Institute of Moscow in response to Soviet hydrogen-bomb tests. Demonstrations brought about by food shortages and encroachments of the local military broke out in Odessa, Gorki, Volgograd (formerly Stalingrad), Krivoi Rog, Krasnodar, Tashkent, Vladimir, Omsk and other cities. Vladimir, a city located northeast of Moscow and famous for its cultural-historical monuments, remained barred to all tourism during the summer months of 1961.[16]

Growing tensions accompanied the price increases for butter, milk and meat, which went into effect June 1, 1962. One strike followed another in the industrial centers, especially in Donec-Becken within the Donbas region. In June of 1962, an uprising occurred in Novocherkassk.

There a large part of the population joined in a massive demonstration that was brutally suppressed. Almost helpless in cases like this, the military was forced to call up reinforcements. But even these additional troops allegedly refused to fire into the crowd after the commanding officer shot himself in front of their eyes. Accompanied by tank units, the MVD troops (consisting for the most part of non-Russian nationalities) finally put an end to the mass demonstrations. According to unofficial reports, several hundred people were killed.[17] The insurgents in the Donbas region reportedly considered the suppression of the demonstration in Novocherkassk unsuccessful mainly because they rebelled there without the consent of the strike organization offices in Rostov (on the Don), Lugansk, Taganrog and other cities. This would confirm rumors and reports concerning a headquarters for organized opposition in Donbas, but also explain that a planned co-ordinated demonstration didn't develop because of tumult breaking out over the price increases before final preparations could be made. (The agitation was supposedly instigated for the most part by students and intellectuals, abetted by a few Ukrainian nationalists.)

Even though these protests were doomed from the start, the fact that they took place at all under the conditions of a totalitarian state should not be underestimated. Though they were brutally suppressed, they did succeed in forcing the regime to do all in its power to make sure that the level of public provisioning did not sink below a definite minimum. Those in power were so unsure of themselves that they did not dare, as in the Stalin era, to meet every emerging opposition with a greater degree of brutality and exploitation.

The circumstances described here clearly reveal the stubborn and unbroken determination of almost every level of the population to fight against injustice and bondage, even when the odds were overwhelmingly against them. If the socialist revolution,[18] already taken place in Russia, failed to show it, these protest actions should have disproved the myth of the "dull, fatalistic Russian," the myth of a people so long-suffering that apparently nothing could push them out of their lethargy. The virtues of patience, humility and contemplation were undoubtedly responsible for the tenacity that made it possible for millions of Russians, especially during the last fifty years, to endure wars, occupations—one need only think of the almost three-year siege of Leningrad—and the unimaginable tortures of concentration camps. It would be frivolous in this case to equate unpretentiousness with a lack of civilization, and the ability to suffer pain with indifferent passivity. The history of Russian uprisings is almost as old as the history of Russia itself. It extends from the Russia of the czars to the anti-Bolshevik demonstration of Kronstadt in 1921, from the numerous peasant uprisings of the 1920's (including those protests against the forced collectivization which were paid for with millions of human lives) to the workers' revolts in the face of Soviet totalitarianism of the 1960's. Obviously, these protests could not really threaten the power system which had firmly established itself in the 1930's and had secured its position by extensive terrorism. However, since the regime has managed to satisfy neither the workers nor the farmers, and is losing the support of the intelligentsia—at least, of the intellectual elite—in increasing numbers, there is hardly anything today's rulers fear more than an alliance of workers and intellectuals pitted against them. Such an alliance among the Czechoslovakian intellectuals, artists, and workers led directly to the downfall of Novotny and the Stalinist clique in 1967-1968 and paved the way for the "Prague spring."

There is little indication in the Soviet Union today of a similar active solidarity between intellectuals, on the one hand, and workers and farmers on the other. Yet the disturbances of Novocherkassk, in which workers and students participated equally, and the gradually increasing role of workers in demonstrations in Moscow, Leningrad, and other cities, seem to hint more frequently that such a development could come about in the USSR.

SAMIZDAT

No, it's not against us
  you should aim your pistols!
But for the most significant times
  the epoch created writers,
  and these created soldiers.

N. NOR

Sintaksis

Samizdat literature (a term translated as "self-publishing house") refers to those clandestine typescript works that cannot be published because of Soviet censorship. The first to reach the West were three issues of *Sintaksis (Syntax)*.[1] This journal, apparently aimed at a large readership, appeared in 1959, and again in 1960, in Moscow and Leningrad, in editions ranging from 120 to 300 copies. (It is generally assumed that only five issues of the journal have been published.) Among the many contributors to *Sintaksis* were several students expelled from Leningrad schools in 1956, and some who considered themselves independent writers: Bella Akhmadulina, Uri Pankratov, Bulat Okudhzava, and Boris Slutski.

The verses of these generally very young poets reveal a strong affinity for the poetry of the "Silver Age." They are uncritical of society and contain no political undertones whatsoever. Instead, they express a striving toward new forms, toward things foreign to their everyday life, and finally, toward individuality. These works proclaim a new and different life style, and in so doing, have provided sufficient reason for the Party press to brand them "pessimistic" and "nihilistic." [2]

Under pressure from the state police, *Sintaksis* was forced to suspend publication in 1960. It's editor in chief, Aleksandr Ginzburg (born in 1936), was accused of violating Paragraph 70 of the Penal Code of the RSFSR[3](Russian Soviet Federated Socialist Republic). Since all concerned knew that this accusation could not be justified, Ginzburg was sentenced in accordance with Paragraph 196/1 (falsification of records—he had completed a test for a fellow student) to two years in a labor camp. After serving his term Ginzburg worked, among other places, in the State Museum of Literature, and enrolled in evening courses in journalism and history. The press attacked him again in 1963, this time accusing him of trying to make contact with foreigners, and reproached him for allegedly having defended "abstractionism." A few months later he was again harassed for "circulating anti-Soviet literature." Secret-police pressure finally caused him to publish in the newspaper *Vechernyaya Moskva* a confession dictated by the KGB (People Commissariat of State Security). Among other things, this statement admitted his reading the émigré publications *Posev* and *Grani*.[4] In a letter to Premier Kosygin, Ginzburg later absolved himself from all responsibility for this confession.

The first issue of the journal *Boomerang* appeared in conjunction with *Sintaksis* in Moscow during 1960. Its contents were never made known in the West. Shortly thereafter its editor in chief, Vladimir Osipov, along with the writer Eduard Kuznecov, was sentenced to seven years in a work camp, presumably in accord with Paragraph 70 of the Penal Code. However, both men are said to have been put on trial mainly because of their participation in the monthly *Feniks*.

Feniks I

Outspoken and even revolutionary in its opposition, the almanac *Feniks (Phoenix)* was first published in 1961.[5] This anthology, primarily devoted to the publication of poems, consists of 140 typewritten pages. No one knows the present circulation of *Feniks;* it is considerably less than that of *Sintaksis,* however.

Unlike those of *Sintaksis,* the poems published in *Feniks* are mostly political. Though several of its poets identify themselves as active supporters of the October Revolution, as "legitimate great-grandsons of 1917" and as the "nucleus of the truth which is being mangled" (Sug-Sucht), others are surprising in the intensity of their anti-Communistic activities. A few students expelled from Moscow schools (several of them openly suspended right after the appearance of *Fenix*) are among the twenty-three contributing authors, most of whom were born between 1940 and 1944.

Their verses, showing forth varied, and at times extremely high, poetic standards, impress readers with their many-sided symbolism and their uncompromising demand for freedom. One popular subject is the tragic Hungarian uprising of 1956 (*see the poem by A. Petrov, page 316*).

These young poets vacillate between hope and doubt, between nihilistic resignation and passionate protest. Gloominess dominates most of their poems, an apocalyptic foreboding of imminent catastrophes which is sometimes reminiscent of the poetry of 1917 written on the eve of the Revolution.

A. Vladimirov expressed it in one of his gripping poems:

> *Listen!—Do you hear it?*
> *Is somebody calling you?*
> *I can hear its echoes creeping*
> *Over valleys and furrows.*
>
> *Now the rumbling is nearer.*
> *Evil is approaching. Evil!*
> *The resounding deed is travelling*
> *Over land and sea.*[6]

And N. Gorbanevskaya warns:

> *My friend, disaster is pursuing you.*
> *The color of the ocean's wave is deceitful.*
> *It hides the ubiquitous, surrounding nets.*[7]

If some poems herald the coming of death and a terrifying end of the world, hope for a spiritual rebirth and longing for new and higher values find expression in others. Not in vain is this poetic collection named after the legendary phoenix, symbol of immortality and resurrection. Goals and wishes may have merged into one another, but the call for freedom and the demand for truth remain clear. The motto appearing on the masthead of *Feniks* is significant:

> *Write only the truth so the word can live;*
> *So that thoughts, hidden under veils*
> *But as tense as the pen*
> *Can defeat her enemies.*[8]

"What justice," asks the writer M. Mercalob, "is given me in poetry and truth? Because of them I have been tortured with lies and poison."[9] The hopeless resignation of the author A. Onezskaya

("Just lies. Just the lies of exhaustion . . .

Everything is wonderful in my native country, built on top of bones . . ."[10]) stands in opposition to the defiantly provocative determination of N. Nor:

> *When you come to take me away*
> *And to lock me up in an iron cage,*
> *With head held high I will leave this life*
> *With no regrets about my deed.*[11]

> *Enough, that's sufficient!*
> *Comrades of the Soviets!*
> *A. Shukin said to the writers—*
> *Remember 1917!*
> *How could you have forgotten?*
> *Our poets of today personify*
> *The Russia of the 'sixties.*[12]

And V. Nilsky issues an undisguised call for revolt:

> *Rise up!*
> *Now!*
> *In this blue night!*[13]

The greatest force and most outstanding talent, however, is found in J. Galanskov's "Human Manifesto" (*see page 311*). Here the discarded values are clearly replaced by new ones. Little wonder that the ignominious articles aimed at two *Feniks* contributors by the official press bore particular animosity against Galanskov, reproaching him for having sought to "corrupt the morals of minors." [14]

Official commentaries have revealed the true names of several writers whose works appeared under pseudonyms. Among these is the biology student Vladimir Bukovski. According to *Komsomolskaya Pravda,* the readers of such young poets must expose themselves to the works of "poetic toadstools," "parasites," "bums who rummage around in rubbish heaps," and similar dregs of humanity. With deepest abhorrence, the journalist Elkin once reported the repeated appearances of poets under the Mayakovski monument where they allegedly tried to speak publicly about "progress," "equality," and "justice." [15]

The response of the servile Party hacks to such efforts is significant:

> *We know all about these pygmies!*
> *Let them beat us into rings of steel.*
> *We are not a beacon-lit monument;*

Yet the citizens protect your affairs
And mount guard over them! [16]

Sfinksy

On its last page, *Feniks* has drawn attention to the
monthly *Koktejl'* (*Cocktail*), which appeared under similar circumstances. In conjunction with *Cocktail,* three numbers of *Sirena* appeared in Moscow, along with *Vremena
Goda* (*The Seasons*). In February of 1953, *Fonar* (*The
Lantern*) was published, and in October of 1964, *Masterskaya* (*Workshop*) appeared. *Bom* came out in March,
1964, and in August of the following year *Seja (Neck)*. In
1963, Leningrad saw the first edition of *Antologiya Sovjet-
skoy Patologii* (*Anthology of Soviet Pathology*), and was
followed in 1964 by another *Anthology.* Unfortunately, none
of these uncensored publications ever reached the West.

Only the journal *Sfinksy (The Sphinx),* a few months
after its debut, managed to be published outside the
USSR.[17] This new collection of unofficial poetry differs
from its predecessors in printing works of the very young
alongside those of an older generation of writers, the most
famous being Valery Tarsis, who has functioned as the journal's editor.

At least two names familiar to readers of *Feniks* were
found among the contributors to *Sfinksy:* V. Kovshin and J.
Stefanov. Pessimism, and the lack of any viable alternative,
characterizes most of the works appearing in *Feniks,* but
many poems in the Sphinx group exhibit composure and
clear resolve. Even here, however, the poets boldly come forward as spokesmen against oppression. While it is possible to

find a glimmer of approval of the October Revolution in the works of several Sphinx poets, the majority reject even the historical origins of Communism in their land. Under the title, "Song of the Old Party People," Yevgeny Golovin writes:

> *Everything is just as before—no face,*
> *   no sound of complaint.*
> *Like Nero's living torches,*
> *The red flags continue to burn,*
> *Forged to the chains of October.*

Bitterly mocking the sacred emblems of the Bolshevik rulers, the poet continues:

> *Our confident words*
> *Merrily show their teeth to the scarlet slogans*
> *. . .*
>
> *There, where like freshly spilled blood,*
> *The mausoleum clutches the plaster.*[18]

Much of the Sphinx poetry glorifies Russia, not with the official, seemingly chauvinistic pathos of Soviet reverence for home and hero, but rather with a love for "Holy Russia" reminiscent of Dostoevski and other Slavophiles.

"Russia (Rossija)—July, 1965" stands on the title page of *Sfinksy* and identifies its publisher as ARI (Avangard Russkogo Isskustva—Avantgarde of Russian Art). The term

Rossija disappeared from the official vernacular almost half a century ago, and many of the old names for Russian cities have been replaced by new ones. It is therefore rather unusual that one of the Sphinx poets should place the old term "moskva-Petrograd" beneath his contribution. Petrograd is the Russofied name of the czarist capital and residence, and was used early in the first World War to replace the old Germanic form, St. Petersburg. Later it was changed yet again by the Bolsheviks to Leningrad. (As a matter of fact, it is not unusual to hear young people today substitute the old name, St. Petersburg, for the new. Whether anything more than a distinct awareness of tradition and history lies hidden behind this cannot be known.

Along with an attempt to resurrect old *Rossija,* the religious revival is a characteristic feature of *Sphinx* writing. Many of the poems which are brighter and more hopeful than their counterparts in *Feniks* owe their energy to this phenomenon. Granted that much bitterness is expressed in Sphinx poetry, as for example in the works of Artiomi Mikhailov (*see page 316*) or in the poem by Aleksandr Galich, "Silence is Golden":

> *We know that silence is more useful*
> *For silence is gold.*
> *It's so easy to amass a fortune;*
> *It's so easy to join the authorities;*
> *It's so easy to become an executioner.*
> *Just keep still, still, still.*[19]

Yet there seems to be a call to action buried in the conviction expressed in the journal's editorial introduction:

> *We are not able to say how long the condi-*
> *tions will last under which Russian art must*
> *presently develop. We simply dare to assert*
> *that these conditions will not continue for-*
> *ever. It's a question of the logic of historical*
> *evolution. People cannot exist without art.*
> *The state cannot exist without the people. If*
> *the functionaries of the state do not possess*
> *the capacity and talent sufficient to under-*
> *stand this, then, as statesmen, they are all*
> *deplorable.*[20]

SMOG

Most of the representatives of underground literature, particularly the younger ones, were united in the early 1960's as members of an independent organization called SMOG. The initials stand for *smelost'*, *mysl'*, *obraz* and *glubina* (courage, thought, form and depth). A second, ironic version of the group's name was "youngest society of geniuses" (*samoe molodoe obscestvo geniev*). Like most other dissident groups, the SMOG movement seemed to be concentrated in Moscow and Leningrad, but was also active in other areas of the Soviet Union. Thus, in 1965, there were newsletters available from at least the *Jugo* (southern) SMOG, one from the Ural SMOG and one from the Odessa group.

The members of SMOG, including not only writers and poets but also musicians, painters and sculptors, see their task as the protection of Russia's cultural heritage and the revival and fostering of pre-Revolutionary traditions in Russian art. Their models are Dostoevski, Pasternak, Marina Cvetaeva and others. Even Tarsis, who still lived in the Soviet Union at that time, was listed on their manifesto next to the great painter of icons, Andrei Rublev, and Aleksandr Radischev, the first important writer to be critical of Soviet society. One of the SMOG appeals reaching the West early in 1966 carried a request for the publication of Russian works in Western newspapers. The proclamation declares:

> *We are few, yet very many—thrust upon fruitful ground, like sprouts of what will come. Today we have to fight against everything from the Cekisten to the bourgeoisie, from ineptitude to ignorance—everything is against us.*

Nevertheless, the SMOGers depend upon the support of the people. "Our people are for us, with us!" The proclamation ends with a plea for aid from the free world.

> *Help us, do not allow our budding activity to be trampled by clumsy boots. Remember that we are here and that there is such a thing as SMOG in Russia.[21]*

The activities of SMOG reached their climax in 1965, extending not only into a wide field of uncensored literary publications, but also into social and political movements. On April 14, 1965, the anniversary of the death of Mayakovski, the SMOG group organized a meeting described as "literary-political" by its initiators. Approximately one thousand people attended. The report of a participant, a Moscow University student, appeared in the West (*see page 324*).

In all probability, a manifesto of the SMOG organization was read at this convocation. At least an angry columnist in the *Komsomolskaya Pravda* quoted a few sentences from such a document, allegedly read aloud "somewhere, publicly, near a monument" (most probably the Mayakovski monument). Among other things it stated that:

> *Contemporary art is in a cul-de-sac and can find no way out. It is permeated with the fumes of foreign literature and art to the point of being transformed into the art of imitation. National art is dead. It is our duty to restore it to life once again.*[22]

Official sources later revealed at least five additional "illegal" poetry recitals during July, August, and September, during which "anti-Soviet" verses were supposedly quoted. The poet Vladimir Batsev ended one of his poems with the words: "And the Mayakovski Plaza has become for us the Senate Plaza," [23] referring to the Senate Plaza in Petersburg. There, on the fourteenth of December, 1825, the Decembrist uprising was broken up by artillery fire.

Whatever effect the literary activity of SMOG may have had, the journal *Sfinksy* must be listed among its accomplishments. In addition to *Sfinksy*, SMOG secretly published *Avangard* (I and II), the anthology *Smog,* the newsletter *Cu!* (*Listen!*), and a great number of poems, short stories, and essays by various authors. Some of these reached the West, including the journal *Cu!*, which appeared in Moscow shortly before *Sfinksy*. The poems in *Cu!* are somewhat esoteric, but all are rich in allegory. Many relate to a confrontation between the author and the power system. In Yuri Kublanovski's "Fragment from the poem 'Harlekin' ",[24] the poet (Pierrot) commits suicide. These completely political verses, often disguised as enigmatical satire, are skeptical, sad, even fatalistic, as shown by the very young Julia Visnevskaya's poem dedicated to the logician Yesenin-Volpin. Despite disillusion over the retreating thaw, a sign of hope remained for the *Cu!* writers. Their goal, to introduce changes while liberating oneself from lies, fear and sepsis, remained intact. And, finally, there was Kublanovski's poet, Pierrot. On the very spot of the gloomy, snowy street where he killed himself with the words, "Father, forgive," snow melted and grass grew.

WRITERS
UNDER PURSUIT

The past has not been forgotten . . .
It's finished, but it still lives on.
You teach us how to write
And what to write about.

For every word we write
We are threatened anew by prison.
And, not unlike the practices of the past,
They have descended upon Brodsky.

VADIM DELONE

Mikhail Narica's novel, *The Unsung Song,* the short stories of Valery Tarsis, the poems and philosophical meditations of Aleksandr Yesenin-Volpin, and the poems of Josef Brodski have all been published in the West; in their native land they have as little chance of legal publication as Pasternak's *Doctor Zhivago,* Solzhenitsyn's great novels, or the prose of Siniavski and Daniel.

Mikhail Narica

Mikhail Narica, a sculptor from Leningrad who was born in 1906, spent the years between 1935 and 1940 in a

concentration camp as a victim of the "purges." In 1949 he
was arrested again, and sentenced to one-year imprisonment
and permanent exile in Karaganda. When rehabilitated, he
returned to Leningrad in 1957. Having completed his strongly autobiographical novel, *The Unsung Song,* in which he
described the ideals of a once-loyal Communist now shattered by reality, he managed to smuggle it out in 1960. The
book appeared immediately in the West under the pseudonym of M. Narymov in the journal *Grani*.[1]

After vainly seeking permission to emigrate with his
family, Narica sent a carbon copy of his book to Khrushchev,[2] together with a letter informing the Party chief that
the novel had been sent abroad simply because there was no
chance for its publication in the Soviet Union. Although the
book contains no sharp political overtones, and there is no
law that forbids sending manuscripts abroad, Narica was declared insane and confined to a psychiatric ward. For three
years he remained imprisoned in this notorious Leningrad
clinic. His second request for permission to emigrate in
1966 remained unanswered. The response came as a surprise raid on his home, organized by neighbors who belonged to the Party. During the course of this action he was
seriously wounded.

Like innumerable other dissidents in the Soviet Union,
Narica lived on beneath the Damoclean sword of another
forced confinement in the mental institution. Aleksandr Solzhenitsyn compared this, perhaps the most terrifying of all
imprisonments, to the gas chambers of the Nazis; the historian Andrei Amalrik saw in it a blatant confession that the
state did not know how else to treat its opponents than to
declare them insane, "a sure sign of the regime's complete

capitulation in the face of its opponents." [3]

Valeri Tarsis

Unlike Narica, the writer Valeri Tarsis (born in 1906) had the good fortune to emigrate to the West. Tarsis came from a family that had joined the Revolution as far back as 1905. His father died during the 1920's in a concentration camp. By the thirties Tarsis was already busy as a writer. He spent the war years on the front as a newspaper correspondent with the rank of captain. As his relationship with the ruling powers became increasingly strained, his manuscripts were no longer approved for publication. Having been a Party member for decades, Tarsis broke off his connection in 1960. Shortly thereafter he began to send manuscripts to England where they appeared at first under the pseudonym of Ivan Valery. As a result of noncompliance with official directives and refusal to return his manuscripts, Tarsis was confined to one of Moscow's insane asylums in 1962. After his release the following year, he recorded his impressions of the place in the short story entitled *Ward 7*.[4] In it, Tarsis described the atmosphere of a mental institution that housed only a few disturbed inmates, the majority of these very young "patients" being freedom-loving political dissidents. Such punishment offered the power system a convenient solution. It eliminated the travesty of a trial, usually needed to place political opponents behind bars, and in this way one could send them up for an undetermined length of time. Behind the ambiguous phrase "medical care" the authorities could use whatever measures they pleased to torture prisoners not only physically but mentally as well.

Petr Grigorenko, a political protestor writing from his own experience, states:

> The "patient" in a so-called "special psychiatric clinic" does not even possess the rights of a prisoner in a concentration camp. He has absolutely no human rights. They can do to him whatever they want, and nobody interferes. Nobody will defend him, and none of his pain will ever reach the outside world. His only hope is a decent doctor.[5]

In his short story, Tarsis drastically settled his accounts with the Communist system, whose attempt to realize its own goals he considered a political and spiritual atavism. Through one of his patient-characters, he says:

> I have come to the conclusion that Marxism and the Soviet order represent a regression of mankind . . . The official philosophy—Marxism—is in reality inferior pragmatism and dogmatic scholasticism . . .[6]

It was presumably the trial of Siniavski and Daniel in February, 1966, that saved Tarsis from another arrest. The Soviet authorities, undoubtedly eager to divert attention from the trial, deported the rebellious writer to England shortly before it took place and simultaneously divested him of his citizenship.

Josef Brodski

One of the most disturbing events to occur since Stalin's death and following the threats against Pasternak was the judgment against the Leningrad writer Josef Brodski (born in 1940). Brodski, an unusually talented poet, illegally published his verses in various periodicals, including *Sintaksis,* and was well known for his translations from romance languages. An article by a former official of the secret police appeared in *Vecerny Leningrad* on November 29, 1963, which maligned Brodski as an "idle loafer" and disparaged his poetry. The article attracted the attention of the *KGB,* which subsequently arrested the poet and sentenced him to five years of forced labor in exile for "parasitism." This punishment was enforced despite the fact that several prominent writers—Anna Akhmatova, Kornei Ohukovski and Samuil Marshak among them—spoke in his defense.

The charge was based solely on the allegation that the poet had been employed as a writer "without permission." The judge's question was significant, for he demanded to know who had "admitted Brodski to the ranks of writers." Brodski answered with another question: Who then had admitted the judge to the ranks of mankind? [7]

Because of poor health the poet was allowed to return to Leningrad in November, 1965, before completing his sentence, but not before being compelled to spend a portion of his term on a *sovchov* (state farm) in the northern regions around Archangel. Since his "amnesty" followed directly on the heels of the arrest of Siniavski and Daniel, there was a strong belief in intellectual and artistic circles that the authorities thought Brodski to be the man behind the pseudo-

nym of Abram Tertz and had therefore pronounced the outrageous sentence. In reality, Tertz was Andrei Siniavski.
Actually Brodski's poems, although not directly political,
were so far removed both in content and form from official
standards that his persecution probably rested on these
grounds alone.

Aleksandr Yesenin-Volpin

Yesenin-Volpin, the former university lecturer in mathematical logic, was born in 1924, a year before his father, the
well-known lyric poet, Sergei Yesenin, committed suicide.
Yesenin-Volpin studied under the famous Moscow mathematician Sofia Janovskaya who died in 1966. Because of two
anti-Stalin poems Volpin was confined to a "nerve clinic." A
year later the scientist was exiled to Karaganda, where he
finally received pardon after Stalin's death. From 1954 to
1959, he directed a seminar in mathematical logic at Moscow University. His scientific reputation soon spread beyond
the borders of the Soviet Union, and the high esteem accorded him by colleagues and students alike remains un-
impaired today. Politically, he was always a thorn in the
flesh of the ideological grail keepers; and in 1959, they denied
him permission to take part in an international conference
held in Poland; his contribution to the assembly had to be
read by one of his colleagues.

His collection of anti-Communist poems, along with his
Free Philosophical Treatise, was published in New York in
1961, and earned for the scientist not only another period
in an insane asylum but also the loss of his chair at the
university. In his *Treatise*, Volpin pursued the Marxist con-

ception of freedom *ad absurdum* and represented dialectical materialism as a false doctrine.[8] In 1961, he was once again released, only to be confined to still another institution in 1962-63. Volpin is the author of numerous scientific essays, which have been published in Soviet periodicals despite his various "retreats" in "psychiatric clinics." Many of his works concerned chiefly with legal questions circulate in *Samizdat*.

On December 5, 1965 (Constitution Day), during a demonstration he helped organize at Pushkin Plaza in Moscow, Volpin carried a placard bearing the slogan: RESPECT THE CONSTITUTION! He was quickly taken into custody pending investigation but was released a few days later. Ever since the trial against Siniavski and Daniel, Volpin has actively participated in all protest demonstrations against the persecution of political dissenters. His protest against the "Trial of the Four" (January, 1968) provided reason enough for the secret security police to take the internationally renowned mathematician, philosopher and poet into custody once more. On Saint Valentine's Day in 1968, Yesenin-Volpin disappeared for the fifth time behind the walls of a psychiatric clinic, this time in Ward 5, whose "therapeutic practices" consisted of starvation diets, party newspapers as the only reading material offered, and the confinement of political prisoners with the criminally insane.

A letter of protest from ninety-nine mathematicians, whose number included seven Academy members (*see page 169*) helped bring about Volpin's release three months later on May 12, 1968. Fifteen scientists later retracted their signatures in a public declaration directed to the United States on the grounds that the letter was passed on to

Western newspapers and radio stations without their knowledge or permission. It was reported, however, that they released this statement on condition that Yesenin-Volpin be released immediately from prison and reinstated in his old post as scientific assistant in VINITI[9]—All-Union Institute for Scientific and Technical Information. Following his release the allegedly "mentally disturbed" mathematician was indeed allowed to resume his work in this institute.

THE "CAUSE CÉLÈBRÈ": SINIAVSKI AND DANIEL

I maintain that the works of Tertz and Arzhak are dictated by the love of these writers for their native land and people, by the pain of the suffering these people have experienced, by the efforts never to see this suffering repeated, and from their own personal experience of today's abuses. It is the literature of a brightly burning flame of mutual responsibility and the greatest sincerity; it is a truly patriotic literature.

—EXCERPT FROM A LETTER BY THE
MATHEMATICIAN JU. I. LEVIN TO THE
EDITOR OF *Izvestia*

Early in September, 1965, the public was finally able to identify the writers who for years had hidden behind the pseudonyms of Abram Tertz and Nikolai Arzhak. On his way to a lecture on September 8th, the literary scholar Andrei Siniavski (Tertz) was arrested. Three days later, upon his return from Novosibirsk, secret police officials took the translator Uri Daniel into custody at Moscow Airport.

Siniavski and Daniel were both born in 1925, both came from intellectual backgrounds (Daniel's father was a well-known Jewish writer), both were eighteen when they found themselves on the front. After the war Daniel found employment as a teacher. Later he was able to support himself by making translations from several languages. His sharp, politically accented short stories, published abroad, are satirical but less farcical and fantastic than the works of his literarily more talented friend Siniavski. Neither Daniel nor Siniavski ever had the slightest hope of their works being published in the Soviet Union. So they sent them abroad from the very beginning.[1] Siniavski's essay on "Socialist Realism" (*see page 147*) was written as early as 1956 and was first published in Paris in 1959.

After completing his philosophical studies, Siniavski studied the history of literature at Moscow University. His former teacher, the lecturer Viktor Duvakin, later appeared at the Siniavski trial as a witness for the defense, and before the court, testified to Siniavski's distinguished qualities, personal as well as professional.

> *At first I sat in on his lectures, but soon realized that it was no longer necessary to do so. I saw in him a lecturer who was more qualified than I. I was reminded of the duck that turned into a swan. He was the ugly duckling turned into a swan.*[2]

Siniavski later worked at the Gorki Institute for World Literature where he came to know Svetlana Alliluyeva. The latter describes her friendship with the writer in her book,

Just One Year. Until his arrest Siniavski was a highly respected critic, and was admitted to the Writers' Union in
1960. Renowned literary journals, such as *Novy Mir* and
Voprosy Literatury, published his essays. One of his last
works to be published in the Soviet Union, an evaluation
of the poetry and personality of Pasternak, was written as
an introduction to a volume of poetry he edited in 1965.[3]
(The book was subsequently taken out of circulation and
replaced by another with an introduction by Kornei
Chukovski.)

The pseudo-public court proceedings (to which foreign correspondents had as little access as did the friends
of the defendants) took place from the tenth to the fourteenth of February, 1966, before the Moscow District Court.
The significance attached to the case was emphasized by
the fact that Lev Smirnov, the Chief Justice, was authorized
to hear it.

The request by the prominent writer Konstantin
Paustovski to speak in defense of the accused was denied,
and other testimony on the defendants' behalf by the literary scholar V. Ivanov and the writer Lev Kopolev could
not be recorded in the minutes. Instead, two fairly obscure
members of the Writers' Union, Zoya Kedrina and Arkadi
Vasilev, assumed the role of public plaintiffs. As a result
of such actions, their names became symbols of despicable
deceit among nonconformist intellectuals.

The proceedings caused a sensation; for the first time
in about four decades, accused men declared themselves
not guilty. Instead, they demanded respect for the freedom of creativity and the freedom of conscience . . .
Siniavski and Daniel have broken the repugnant "tradition

of 'repentance and confession.' " [4] *(See page 335.)* Their dignified appearance and stubborn refusal to accept the burden of guilt laid upon them marked a turning point in the history of Soviet justice. To this day their example encourages numerous political dissidents to assume the same tenacious position in court. Although Siniavski and Daniel challenged every point of the charges against them and tried to disprove them, they were sentenced, in accordance with the ignominious Paragraph 70 of the Penal Code, to seven and five years, respectively, at hard labor in a work camp. They were denied the right of appeal. The sentence had not even been handed down when the radio commentator B. Belicky declared in an English-language broadcast on January 3, 1966, that "without wishing to anticipate the sentence," he felt sure that these men had been called to account for slimy works published abroad. These words are misleading because even according to Soviet law the sending of manuscripts abroad is not illegal. Daniel and Siniavski were brought to trial simply because of their literary activity. The court was completely indifferent to the literary value of the authors' works. Their short stories were considered anti-Soviet in nature, and they were condemned on these grounds alone.

Reports of the arrest of the two writers did not reach the Soviet public until January 12, 1966. But artists and intellectuals were well informed of the proceedings. In a letter to Kosygin, Aleksandr Ginzburg protested the arrest of the two men. *(See page 328.)* The wives of Siniavski and Daniel defended their husbands in equally resolute letters to the Party leadership and the state attorney. "Just how much fool's freedom does this state have?" asked

Siniavski's wife, and further indicated that even she was threatened with arrest by the security police.[5] Daniel's wife protested against the methods of the examining magistrate who recommended she not try to find an advocate for her husband since he would only interfere with the course of the trial and could in no way influence the decision.[6]

Handbills calling for participants in a demonstration planned for the fifth of December (Constitution Day) were distributed early in December, 1965, probably through the initiative of SMOG, around Moscow University and various other institutions. The proclamation demanded that legal proceedings against Siniavski and Daniel be made public.[7] Approximately two hundred people, mostly students, took part in the rally beneath the Pushkin monument. At that time a convocation of people (in whose midst scrolls were unrolled) presented a strange sight in the USSR, not to mention Moscow. On the fringes of the crowd, passers-by stood dumfounded, unable to comprehend what it was all about. The thought of a demonstration never occurred to anyone; most people believed it to be the outdoor filming of some movie.[8] In accordance with the guidelines of its announcement, the demonstration proceeded in an orderly and disciplined manner. Nevertheless, the participants were violently dispersed by members of the secret police force. "A mean act of revenge," [9] as later reported in a flyer, "was perpetrated" against the students of MGU. This paved the way for the expulsion of several students from the university. According to Ginzburg's white book, three of those persons responsible for the announcement were arrested on December 2 and confined to a madhouse. Those arrested included the SMOG contributor Leonid Gubanov, Vladimir

Bukovski, and Julia Visnevskaya, then only 16 years old, who was arrested while attending classes.

The first two malicious articles by D. Eremin[10] and Z. Kedrina,[11] published in the papers *Izvestia* and *Literaturnaya Gazeta*, formed the prelude to a hysterical campaign against Siniavski and Daniel. Both articles, however, provoked a flood of letters addressed to the editors of the papers in question. The writers of these letters, courageous literary scholars for the most part, spoke up in defense of the vilified writers.

The minutes of the trial were secretly recorded on tape and thus managed to reach the public. In his *White Book* Aleksandr Ginzburg summarized the proceedings of the trial, as well as all available witnesses for and against the accused. The book gave a simple but moving impression of the dignified posture of the two men, an equally perceptive description of their wives' sense of duty, and the courageous acknowledgments of friends, colleagues, and many members of the intelligentsia. Ginzburg sent this document to the Supreme Soviet and to the KGB with the request that sentence be immediately revised. Shortly thereafter he was arrested.

It was disclosed in the *White Book* that art historian, I. Golomstok, had refused to give testimony that would add to the burdens of Siniavski and other parties concerned—a decision probably as novel and unexpected to the Soviet courts as was the declaration made by Duvakin in their defense, and the sympathetic testimony in favor of the defendants given by many witnesses before the court. Golomstok's refusal to testify netted him six months of forced labor at his place of work. (This meant a 20 percent reduction in salary, a severe hardship, considering the already shamefully low salaries of most academic employees.) Several witnesses were expelled from the Party because of "clumsy attempts to protect the accused." The literary scholar Duvakin lost his lectureship at the university, but even this caused an unlooked-for reaction. In telegrams to the Twenty-Second Party Congress, held in March and April of 1966, more than one hundred scientists and writers demanded Duvakin's reinstatement.[12] This sharp public protest actually succeeded. Although the authorities kept Duvakin far removed from any activity as lecturer, for the time being, they did accept him for research within the MGU. Today, once again, Duvakin has a chair on the Philological Faculty of Moscow University.

Also included in the *White Book* are the letter of journalist Lidia Chukovskaya to Mikhail Sholokhov (*see page 344)* and a "Letter to an old Friend." (Ginzburg refused to identify the author of this letter before the court; it is possible that he really didn't know who wrote it.) The epistle addressed to the Supreme Soviet by sixty-two well-known Soviet writers requesting the release of Siniavski and Daniel against their security (*see page 356*) lacked an important legal prerequisite, as Ginzburg pointed out in his report, since according to law only those people could be released on bail who had "acknowledged their guilt and sincerely repented of it."

After their sentencing, Siniavski and Daniel were brought to Dubrovlag/Mordwinien. There the friends were separated and assigned to different camp areas. While little is known of the fate of Siniavski, considerable news concerning Daniel has reached the outside world. In July,

1967, there appeared in the West a letter addressed to Soviet leadership and the Party Presidium from Larisa Daniel, wife of the accused. In it she complained of the inhuman treatment to which Yuli Daniel was being subjected in the concentration camp. She also reported about the poor state of her husband's health and declared that necessary medication had not only been denied him but even taken away from him. Declared Larisa Daniel:

> In 1967, the fiftieth year of Soviet power, prisoners are still being handled according to methods which the Soviet Codex of the 1920's described as torture.[13]

With the approach of the fiftieth anniversary of the October Revolution, many men in the Soviet Union and abroad hoped for an amnesty for Siniavski and Daniel. Meanwhile only criminals were pardoned, while the prisons and labor camps still overflowed with political prisoners. Even today, according to the statements of Soviet political prisoners, these camps extend in a gigantic, intricate spider web throughout Russia. Within them,

> in spite of all international agreements and even those ratified by the Soviet leadership themselves, forced labor and inhuman exploitation are the rule; . . . people are systematically starved . . . they are humbled and their honor trod upon by the feet of others. An uninterrupted stream of men whose numbers reach into the millions flow through these

*camps, men who are eventually returned to
society crippled in mind and body.*[14]

Anatoli Marchenko, a political prisoner who wrote a
report about Dubrovlag which was published in the West,
described his meeting with Daniel.[15] Suspicious at first
because of a general distrust of writers—many had sketched
a rose-colored, unrealistic picture of Soviet life—Daniel's fellow prisoners soon tried to ease his work load. He fast became the central figure of his prison unit, with all the others
grouped about him. For this reason he was transferred
eventually to another area.

In the summer of 1969, along with five other political
prisoners, Daniel sent a petition to the Supreme Soviet requesting improvements in prison living conditions. Several
months earlier he had participated in a hunger strike of two
hundred political prisoners to emphasize their demands for
better treatment. In July, 1969, Daniel was transferred from
Dubrovlag to the infamous prison at Vladimir on the
grounds, according to the words of a fellow prisoner, that
he had remained, even in prison, "a singer of freedom
and truth."

In a plea for help addressed to the English novelist
Graham Greene, Daniel's eighteen-year-old son expressed his
great concern over the future fate of his father.[16] The youth
considered it highly possible that his father, for one reason
or another, might not be released in September, 1970, as he
was supposed to be, but might perhaps receive a new sentence. According to his son, Daniel would hardly survive
another prolonged term in prison or in a labor camp. Despite all fears to the contrary, however, Daniel was released

on September 12, 1970.

News of the early release of Andrei Siniavski was announced in early June, 1971. His freedom—fifteen months short of his sentence—was mentioned repeatedly in connection with the imminent Fifth Congress of Soviet Writers. Rumors from several sources maintained that Siniavski, whose health is poor, was prematurely "pardoned" because of good behavior. The writer had continually declined offers from camp authorities to request a pardon for him. Because of his unselfishness, his strength of character and his personal integrity, Siniavski is said to have enjoyed not only the affection of his fellow prisoners but also the respect of the camp administration.

It was not sheer chance that the Western press reported so extensively the release of these two writers—men who had been relatively unknown until their condemnation. The names of Daniel and Siniavski may stand as a most important landmark in the history of the Russian "democratic movement," a turning point in the modern history of their country.

THE STRUGGLE
INTENSIFIES

*We are demanding from you vigilance
and opposition. We are challenging you
to look honestly into your conscience,
and not to strangle the natural expressions of your conscience in the noose of
calculations, inevitably imperfect. We
are asking you to look into the depths
of your own souls. Should you discover
there a miserable wretch who has already lost his head, but who still trem-
bles with every single hair on that lost
head, then we are asking you not to
deceive yourselves.*

—EXCERPT FROM A PROCLAMATION OF
THE GROUP "OPPOSITION" (PUBLISHED IN
MOSCOW IN DECEMBER, 1965)

The unusually harsh sentence in the Siniavski/Daniel case,
obviously intended as a cautionary deterrent to this sort of
boldness, boomeranged. Not one single influential writer—
with the exception of "blood and earth" Mikhail Sholokhov
—aligned himself with the Party. Several hundred artists,

writers, scientists and students protested openly and vig-
orously against this regression toward Stalinism. One result
of the trial was the rapprochement of forces that considered
themselves "liberal," but had hitherto remained loyal to the
regime, and those that had always been compelled to act
illegally. According to Galanskov, "The proceedings against
Siniavski and Daniel have accelerated the polarization of
the forces: At one pole you find some given standards and
at the other pole you find the antitheses of these
standards."

Most people held the concerted action of their rulers
responsible for bringing about a revival of the terrorism
they all believed had long since been eliminated, and this
deceit inspired the anti-Stalinist forces to instigate the so-
called "democratic" or "civil rights movement" which today
represents probably the greatest potential threat to the ruling regime. The literary critic Anatoli Jakobson reminisces:

> *Since the sentencing of Siniavski and Daniel
> in the year 1966, not one single act of des-
> potism and force on the part of the adminis-
> tration has gone without public protest.*

In the letter mentioned here, sent to the Premier on
the eve of the Twenty-Third Congress of the Communist
Party, scientists and artists anxiously warned against a revival of Stalinism. A few weeks earlier, on March 5, 1966—
the anniversary of Stalin's death—a number of intellectuals
demonstrated against the partial rehabilitation of the dictator. Authorities tried to softpedal the announcement, and in

the meantime arrested several of the instigators of the February 24th demonstration. The majority of those arrested were released a short time later, among them the former Major General Petr Grigorenko, the teacher Ilia Gabai, and the student Vera Laskova. Alexei Dobrovolski, a former political prisoner, was confined for two months in a psychiatric clinic. The talented SMOG poet Vladimir Batsev, born in 1947, was brought to trial; in April 1966, like Brodski two years earlier, he received sentence as a "parasite" to five years exile under forced-labor conditions. Batsev, whose father supposedly held an influential position with *Glavlit*,[1] published poems in *Sfinksy, Cu!,* and other journals. The grounds for his verdict were revealed in the announcement of April 25th:[2] as far back as 1956 Batsev had been expelled from school because of "political invectives against the Soviet power." He had subsequently kept busy as a worker, and later as a free-lance contributor to *Moskovsky Komsomolec,* but was fired after several months because he supposedly read "tendentious" poems at a public poetry recital. Again, as in the Brodski case, the court accused the young Batsev of being engaged in questionable literary undertakings without being a member of the Writers' Union.

The supplement to Paragraph 190 in the Penal Code of the RSFSR evoked general indignation when announced on September 16, 1966. Sections one and three intensified the penal legislation that large portions of the public already considered illegal.[3] The first section of the paragraph was obviously intended to guard against future cases resembling those of Siniavski and Daniel. Twenty-one members of the creative intelligentsia protested against this new paragraph in a petition to the Supreme Soviet. (*See page 385.*)

The leaflet of the "December 5th Movement" (*see page 477*) also referred to the unconstitutional law. This flyer was circulated late in 1966 shortly before a Constitution Day rally. No more detailed information is available about the December 5th Movement except that it was apparently connected in some way with members of the "democratic movement." But their handbill indicated a demand for radical reforms in the current judicial system of the USSR.

The demonstration on Constitution Day has become a tradition ever since its first appearance in 1965. From that time on, it has taken the form of a silent assembly in Moscow's Pushkin Plaza. The protest of December 5, 1966, in which several well-known Soviet writers took part, proceeded without incident; but the KGB bore down on a group of about thirty such demonstrators one month after the rally, on January 22, 1967. They were protesting with banners against the arrests of Galanskov, Dobrovolski, Vera Laskova and Pavel Radzievski, all apprehended between the seventeenth and nineteenth of January because of their collaboration on a new edition of *Feniks*. (Radzievski was later released.) Fewer participants than expected found their way to the demonstration, however, for on that same afternoon a public exhibit of modern art was scheduled to open. Unfortunately the exhibit had to be closed down after several hours because too many of its pictures were abstract in nature. During the course of the demonstration, cries such as "Down with the dictatorship!" and "Freedom for Dobrovolski!" became louder and more frequent, until the police, with security forces, intervened and arrested several of the demonstrators on the spot. Among those arrested were a worker, Viktor Chaustov, and a writer, Yevgeny

Kuschev. A few days later, on the twenty-fifth and twenty-sixth of January, Vladimir Bukovski, Ilia Gabai, and the poet Vadim Delone were also arrested.

The physicist Pavel Litvinov drew up a white book containing details and a secretly recorded copy of the minutes of the proceedings against Chaustov, Gabai, Kuschev, Delone, and Bukovski.[5] Among other things it disclosed the fact that several students of Moscow University had organized a signature drive as a protest against the arrest of demonstrators in February, 1967. Those in whose possession the KGB found this document were forced to leave the university.

The trial against Chaustov and Gabai was held on February 16, 1967. Ilia Gabai, born in 1925, was released for lack of evidence, but did not receive her freedom until April. Viktor Chaustov, born in 1938, and up until the time of his arrest employed as a worker in a rug factory, declared himself not guilty as charged before the court. He tried, as did Bukovski a little later, to exonerate friends accused with him by assuming complete responsibility for having organized the demonstration. Questioned as to his political and moral views, Chaustov confessed his preference for the English parliamentary system, a system which he felt was the most desirable form of government. At the same time he acknowledged his respect for the philosopher Kant and his rejection of the Marxist-Leninist ideology. Chaustov was sentenced in accordance with Paragraph 190/3 and Paragraph 206/2 (rowdiness) to five years of hard labor in a state camp. The violation against Paragraph 191/1 (opposition to the supreme power) was modified in the appeal, reducing the sentence to three years.

If one studies the records of later trials against Bukovski,

Delone, and Kuschev, a definite helplessness on the part of
the prosecution becomes more and more evident. The
charges are predominantly based on infringements of Paragraph 190/3 (disturbing the peace), according to which
demonstrations and convocations are effectively forbidden.
In total awareness of their civil rights, however (granted
these rights only exist on paper), the accused could appeal
to Article 125 of the Constitution, which grants the citizen,
along with freedom of speech and freedom of the press, freedom of assembly and a full right to demonstrate. Significantly, the prosecution right from the beginning steered a course
between calumny of the accused and an attempt to divert
attention from the trial. Thus the observation that the accused does not work appears again and again in the indictment against Bukovski, Delone, and Kuschev. Yet Kuschev's
mother proved that her son did work at the Lenin Library
and had made various translations from the Spanish of some
works of García Lorca for *Junost.* At the same time, the
minutes of these trials revealed that in every case the defendants had taken their duties much more seriously than
had, for instance, the writers Siniavski and Daniel.

From the thirtieth of August to the first of September,
Vladimir Bukovski, Vadim Delone, and Yevgeny Kuschev
stood before the court. Bukovski, born in 1942, is the son of
the critic and essayist, K. Bukovski. Vladimir Bukovski had
obviously worked on *Feniks* (1961) and on the anthology
SMOG. According to Soviet sources, Bukovski wrote a
treatise (1961?) in which he attempted to prove that the
Komsomol de facto did not exist.[5] In 1961, his last year
at school, Bukovski ran into difficulties with the authorities
as a result of his editing the illegal journal *Muchenik*

(Martyr). He was expelled from school and denied permission to pursue his studies elsewhere. Despite this prohibition he registered in the Agronomy Faculty of Moscow University.

A year later the authorities caught up with him, and Bukovski was once again expelled. In 1963 he was taken into custody for "circulation of anti-Soviet literature." (A copy of Milovan Djilas's *New Class* was found in his possession.)

Diagnosed as "feeble-minded," the young writer was confined to the infamous Leningrad psychiatric prison where the prisoners were subjected to the most inhuman "special treatment." During the SMOG demonstration on April 14, 1965, his friends and former colleagues demanded not only his release but also the release of other political prisoners (*see page 324*). Shortly thereafter, Bukovski was set free. He immediately participated in organizing the demonstration held on the fifth of December, 1965, and was resentenced to confinement in the psychiatric clinic, where he remained until the fall of 1966.

After taking part in the rally of January 22, 1967, Bukovski was again arrested and detailed in the clinic for the duration of the investigation. His three imprisonments as an alleged "madman" in insane asylums seem particularly grotesque when one considers the fact that during his trial, on September 1, 1967, he was declared mentally and emotionally sound. Bukovski assumed total responsibility before the court for the organization of the demonstrations, once more in an effort to exonerate his co-defendants. However, he declared himself not guilty as charged. His impressive summation ended with the assurance:

I do not regret having organized these dem-
onstrations at all . . . When I am free again,
I will organize demonstrations again.

In accordance with Paragraph 190/3 of the Code Bukovski was sentenced to three years in a work camp. Following his release in January, 1970, Bukovski devoted himself with, if possible, even greater determination and fearlessness than before to the battle for human rights in the USSR. Toward the end of March, 1971, he was arrested for the fourth time and charged with violating Paragraph 70 of the Penal Code. Out of a total of nine months of investigation, he had to spend three of them in the Serbsky Institute, a psychiatric institution connected with the courts, before he was even brought to trial on January 5, 1972, where he was sentenced to seven years' deprivation of freedom (two years imprisonment and five years at hard labor) followed by a five year term of exile. In his concluding statement the accused explained once again that he would not give up his convictions but would continue to fight for "law and justice." Shortly thereafter Andrei Sakharov addressed a letter to Party Secretary Brezhnev and Prosecutor General Rudenko demanding the release of the illegally convicted Bukovski. At the same time, an appeal for help signed by fifty-two of Bukovski's friends reached the Secretary General of the United Nations. These appeals expressed not only the indignation over a new exhibition of illegality on the part of the regime, but also concern for Vladimir Bukovski's health, for he had suffered a heart attack during his previous prison term and therefore might not be able to endure the physical hardships which now faced him.

The two co-defendants, Kuschev and Delone, also arraigned in 1967, who in the course of the trial had expressed their political views no less clearly and courageously than Bukovski, made a partial confession of guilt. Vadim Delone, born in 1947, had had connections with the SMOG group. On these grounds he was expelled from the Philological Faculty of the Moscow Pedagogical Institute and banned from the Komsomol. A year after his trial, on August 25, 1968, Delone participated in a rally on Red Square and was subsequently sentenced to three years' imprisonment.

In 1964, Yevgeny Kuschev, then seventeen, took part in the founding of the independent Ryleev Club and was co-editor of the uncensored journals *Russkoe Slovo* and *Tetradi Socialisticeskoy Demokratii*. Several of his poems appeared in *Feniks* in 1966. Kuschev also actively supported Siniavski and Daniel, and later, along with Delone, spoke up for Ginzburg and Galanskov. Questioned during the trial about his religious feelings, Kuschev proudly and eloquently declared himself a "believer" who had been baptized a few years before. He described his political position as "Christian Democrat," and he claimed the Decembrists as his historical models. (*See his poem, page 320.*)

Kuschev and Delone were both sentenced to one year on probation. At the conclusion of the hearing, they were released and greeted by a great number of friends and like-minded enthusiasts who had gathered outside the courthouse. Like the trial against Daniel and Siniavski, admittance to the proceedings had been denied the public with the exception of those who were subpoenaed.

The former general Grigorenko defended the accused

in a letter dated December, 1967, addressed to the Supreme Soviet of the USSR and to the public prosecutor general, using this opportunity to reproach the court with having abused the law.[6] Pavel Litvinov, grandson of the former Foreign Minister Maxim Litvinov, undertook to gather the official records of the hearing into a white book as Ginzburg had done in the case of Siniavski and Daniel. When this reached the ears of the KGB, Litvinov was ordered to a conference, during the course of which one of the state security officers warned him against an "illegal" publication (that is, delivery of the white book abroad). Litvinov courageously countered the officials by appealing to Soviet legislation, but was urgently advised nevertheless to destroy all such writings in his possession. Following this conference, Litvinov wrote down the discussion verbatim from memory. He sent this text to Soviet, as well as Western, Communist papers, but it was never published. The text first appeared in December, 1967, in an edition of *Il Giorno*.[7] Later, Western radio stations broadcast it into the Soviet Union. As a result of these activities in defense of the rights of Bukovski and his friends, Pavel Litvinov was relieved of his duties as assistant for physics at the Moscow Institute for Chemical Technology on January 3, 1968. The formal grounds for dismissal were reported as "violation of the work discipline."

By 1967, the Soviet's fiftieth anniversary of its founding, a year which began with so much pomp, the Soviet power structure seemed anything but a self-confident, internally secure governmental system. Rather, her judicial practices in particular, dictated by fear and hate, inevitably conjures up the image of a kangaroo court executed in secret.

JOURNALS OF
SOCIAL CRITICISM

*There is no freedom of the press in
Russia, but who would maintain that
there is also no freedom of thought!*

ALEKSANDR YESENIN-VOLPIN

Tetradi

In 1965, issues seven and eight of the *Tetradi Socialisticeskoy
Demokratii (Notebook of Social Democracy)* appeared in
Moscow. These two were the only ones ever to reach the
West. Yevgeny Yevtushenko's "Letter to Yesenin" appeared
in it, along with (among other things) a historical study
entitled "Who killed Trotsky?", poems by Brodski, and the
treatise "In the Hour of Dawn" by the Christian journalist
and writer Anatoli Levitin-Krasnov. (*See page 537.*) This
treatise is devoted to the question of morality in society and
sets forth the author's conscientious attempt to propose
means of establishing spiritual values in a secular world.

Further details are not known concerning the ultimate
fate of *Tetradi*. The eighth issue announced that any further
appearance of the journal after January of 1966 could not be

assured, and even stated that the journal might never be printed again because of certain unforeseeable circumstances. It is highly unlikely that this journal has been published since the end of 1965, most probably because of confiscation by the authorities.

Russkoe Slovo

The literary journal *Russkoe Slovo* (*Russian Word*), whose very first edition appeared in the West,[1] was edited by the founders of the Ryleev Club, Yevgeny Kuschev and Vladimir Voskresenski. The Ryleev Club was established on June 6, 1964. Its members had intended it as a literary, socially critical organization, and as such, a successor to the Society of the Russian Word (*Obschestvo Russkogo Slova*), a circle of literary Decembrists led by the poet Kondrati Ryleev.[2]

In the first issue's foreword, the editors briefly outlined the history of the journal's famous predecessor and namesake, which had been founded in 1859 in Petersburg by Count Kuleshov-Bezborodko, and later became the legal mouthpiece of the *narodniki*[3] and the *raznocinci* until its prohibition in 1866. The editors hoped to insure a continuity by alluding to the fact that their newly founded journal had once again taken up the work of the former *Russkoe Slovo* "after a century of interruption." (*See page 522.*)

Although the new management of *Russkoe Slovo* counted on the strong appeal made by the name of the former periodical of the *narodniki*, their present political and moral posture seemed to favor the Decembrists.[4] This is particularly true in the case of Yevgeny Kuschev, whose poetic cycle "The Decembrists" is dedicated to the five executed leaders of that movement. In their fate he sees his own prescribed; to complete their unfinished work seems to him an absolute necessity:

> *We are exterminated like a pestilence . . .*
> *But it is certainly too early to repent. Maybe*
> *we should try things one more time.*[5]

There has always been a preference for the *narodniki,* even today, among the post-Revolutionary Soviet intelligentsia. And although the Decembrists have always commanded the attention and respect of later generations (the Bolsheviks even made use of them when it was in their interest to do so), doubtless their spiritual tradition has never attracted so unspoken a following in the Soviet Union as members of the Ryleev Club clearly display today. This is all the more significant because it indicates a trend toward abandoning the anarchical-utopian dreams to which the Russian intelligentsia, including many of their Soviet descendants, were sacrificed. Even beyond the respect all revolutionary and progressive idealists felt for the worth of the individual, the principle of civil service and civil obedience, not civil disobedience, received the highest priority, and such influence on the majority of the intelligentsia of the nineteenth century helped pave the way for the coming doom.

It was reported in one of the articles published in *Russkoe Slovo* that the work of the Ryleev Club proceeded with the slogan "culture, truth, honor." The famous poem "The Citizen" by Grazdanin serves as the Ryleev motto and appears on every issue of its journal.

Feniks II

Early in 1967, the Paris bureau of *Grani* received a copy of the second edition of *Feniks*,[6] which was published late in 1966. The volume of 376 typewritten pages contained letters, poems (particularly by the SMOG poets), short stories, and documents.

This periodical, actually an anthology, appeared under the editorship of Yuri Galanskov, born in 1939, who was expelled from the university because of his collaboration on the first *Feniks* and had been confined for a period of several months in an insane asylum. Galanskov, one of the most capable men in the dissident movement, came from a working-class family and before his expulsion had studied philosophy and history. In 1965, before the American Embassy, he picketed a solitary four hours against American intervention in the Dominican Republic. For awhile he worked as secretary in a technical school, as an electrician, and finally, like Ginzburg, in the State Museum of Literature.

Besides the editorial introduction, two articles from Galanskov appeared in *Feniks*. One, advocating the necessity for world-wide total disarmament, supplemented his argument with a series of suggestions.[7] (Galanskov described himself as a "social pacifist.") The other was an open letter to Mikhail Sholokhov, who had won a Nobel Prize the previous year. Following the actions of the journalist Lidia Cukovskaya, Galanskov opposed Sholokhov in support of the writers Siniavski and Daniel. Galanskov, who termed Sholokhov a member "of a military state, where only one's toes in one's boots could move freely," observed:

> *The Russian intelligentsia . . . will never*
> *forgive Western culture for its distinguishing*
> *Sholokhov, a man who . . . busily takes*
> *part in an activity fatal to Russia and to the*
> *freedom of art in Russia.*

This high honor conferred upon a man considered so mediocre both personally and literarily evoked both dismay and indignation from Russian intellectuals. Galanskov's open letter is one of the most significant documents of the underground; in it the young poet paints an impressive picture of a Russian underground writer as a man continually pursued who nevertheless maintains his integrity as citizen and gentleman. In this letter Galanskov characterizes illegal writings as the only "authentic" literature in Russia today. Similar sentiments appear in the thoughts of Osip Mandelstam, the poet who died in Stalin's camps in 1939 and whose essay "The Fourth Prose" (until that time unpublished) appeared in *Feniks*. In this piece Mandelstam confesses that he "divides all works of world literature as authorized or written without permission. The former is trash, the latter the secretly inspired air." [8]

Two of the articles appearing in *Feniks* were already familiar to Western readers. One was Siniavski's treatise on "Socialist Realism"; the other, the stenographic records of the Pasternak affair in the Writers' Union in 1958. [9] A second essay by Siniavski, "In Defense of Pyramids," [10] is based on Yevtushenko's poem "Bratsk Station," published in 1965, and takes critical exception to it. The work is a brilliant example of literary criticism. Its publication (the article was originally written for *Novy Mir*) was, for obvious reasons, denied by the "legal" press.

The theological treatise by the young writer Alexei Dobrovolski, born in 1938, on "The Correlation between Religion and Understanding" [11] offers another high point in the collection of *Feniks* articles. Dobrovolski was sentenced for the first time in 1957 for "anti-Soviet propaganda" and received three years in a concentration camp. (He had circulated authentic reports on the Hungarian uprising.) He was prematurely released in 1961, but during his imprisonment converted to Christianity. It is said that Dobrovolski considers himself a student of the religious philosopher Nikolai Berdjaev. In 1964 Dobrovolski was arrested again and detained for six months in a Leningrad psychiatric prison. As an organizer of the March, 1966 demonstration, he again suffered imprisonment for several months (this time as a "preventive" measure) in a mental institution. Before his arrest in January of 1967 he had worked as a printer and finally, along with Galanskov and Ginzburg, in the Literature Museum.

Many of the pages of *Feniks* were devoted to the battle against Stalinism, as for instance the open letter of the journalist Ernst Genri addressed to Ilya Ehrenburg, and the transcript of a speech delivered in December of 1965 by the philosopher and Oriental scholar, Grigory Pomerantz, at the Moscow Institute for Philosophy. *(See page 430.)* And, lastly, the journal published the stenographic records of a discussion that took place in 1966 with the participation of many old Bolsheviks at the IML[12] (Institute for Marxism/Leninism within the Central Committee of the CPSU). The theme of this conference was the printing of the third volume of the *History of the Communist Party of the Soviet Union.*[13] A situation similar to the debate, well-known even abroad, concerning the book by the historian Aleksandr Nekrich, occurred when a furious dispute erupted between pro- and anti-Stalinists.

An essay entitled "The Russian Road of Progress toward Socialism and Its Results,"[14] falsely attributed (for the most part in the West) to the well-known economic theoretician and formerly active politician Yevgeny Varga, was compared to Milovan Djilas's *New Class.* Investigations have proved that Varga could not possibly have written it. Nevertheless, the article, presumably written in 1962 by an anonymous, progressive Soviet Marxist, remains a significant document.

In his editorial foreword, Galanskov referred to the recently amended Paragraph 190 of the Penal Code.

> *The state authority attempted another criminal step in order to strengthen the regime of "restraint and oppression." Now all that remains is to wait for this "restraint" and this "oppression" . . . The publication of this journal alone provides sufficient grounds for the application of some anti-democratic law or a similar ordinance. . .*
>
> *You could win the battle, but it won't make any difference, because you will lose the war. The war for democracy in Russia. The war, which has already begun and in which justice will inevitably prevail . . . .*[15]

THE JANUARY TRIAL, 1968

This trial is a stain on the honor of our state and on the conscience of every one of us.

PAVEL LITVINOV AND LARISA DANIEL
(IN THEIR PROCLAMATION TO THE
PEOPLES OF THE WORLD.)

Yuri Galanskov and his co-workers did not have to wait for long for their "oppression." A few months, if not weeks, after the appearance of *Feniks*, between the seventeenth and the nineteenth of January, 1968, Galanskov, Dobrovolski, and Vera Laskova were taken into custody. During the five-hour search of his house which preceded Galanskov's arrest, the police found and confiscated, among other things, the draft of a new edition of the journal drawn up by a group of young people. On the twenty-third of the month, Aleksandr Ginzburg was arrested for publishing his *White Book* concerning the Siniavski/Daniel case.

Despite repeated protests of more than a hundred scientists, and other renowned intellectuals, against the unlawful extending of their detention during the supposed investigation, the trial originally scheduled for the eleventh of December, 1967, finally took place before the Municipal Court of Moscow on January 8, 1968. Well-known scholars and artists drew up two petitions demanding an open trial,[1] but once again the courtroom was filled with members of the KGB and the auxiliary police (*durzininki*: plain-clothes men); the defendants' closest relatives were granted admission only under the most unusual circumstances and after great effort. Admission was equally denied to a representative of Amnesty International who had traveled to Moscow for the express purpose of attending the trial.

As a sign of protest against their exclusion from the courtroom, approximately sixty friends and colleagues of the accused staged a one-hour "silent" demonstration in front of the courthouse. The Western press was unanimous in its description of the constant number of people who, during the four days of the trial, congregated in the corridors or outside the courthouse and, even more significantly, openly argued with party-line Komsomolers and secret-police officers.[2] These debates were primarily concerned with the guilt or innocence of the accused and the question of whether—and just how much—criticism of the state was allowed. Members of the security forces persistently attempted to hinder an exchange of information and opinions between the friends of the accused and the representatives of foreign-news organizations. They photographed the foreign correspondents and particularly the intellectuals who had shown up.

These attempts at intimidation, however, bore very little fruit; the trial's opponents, among them Larisa Daniel, Pavel Litvinov, Petr Grigorenko, Yesenin-Volpin, and the historian Petr Jakir, continued to seek open contact with Western journalists. Grigorenko was apprehended while handing over a copy of a petition to representatives of the foreign press, but reappeared later on. Shortly thereafter, Ginzburg's mother and Galanskov's wife invited foreign-press representatives to a private press conference. Soviet authorities had no compunctions about harassing the correspondents who attended, and threatened them by telephone with possible loss of accreditation.

Pavel Litvinov managed to complete literally on the eve of his own arrest, a *White Book* of approximately 200,000 words, which contained a record of the trial. Eventually, it found its way to the West and is now available in an unabridged version. *(See note on page 363.)* According to report, the reading of the indictment alone dragged on for more than three hours. The main defendant was Yuri Galanskov, charged with violating not only Paragraph 70 (anti-Soviet propaganda), but also Paragraph 88/1 (currency offenses). All four of the accused were charged with having made contact with the Russian émigré organization, NTS.[3] Armed with this indictment, the authorities apparently sought to denounce the defendants as tools of inimical foreign bodies and to present their case as a type of espionage trial, rather than a hearing against political dissidents.

The co-defendant Dobrovolski strengthened already heavy charges against Ginzburg and, above all, Galanskov, not only by making a confession of guilt and repentance, but also by "confessing" to having been enlisted by Galanskov and Ginzburg to cooperate with the NTS. Except for Brocks-Sokolov, who played an unpleasant role in the trial,[4] Dobrovolski was apparently the only witness the prosecution could use successfully to give support to their accusations. Something had obviously happened during his one-year confinement preceding the trial that explained the testimony—completely contradicting his earlier statements— that an extremely unsteady and somewhat eccentric Dobrovolski was forced to give. The growing suspicion that he was a secret agent of the police seems highly unjustified since Dobrovolski had repeatedly sat out months and years in camps and mental institutions because of his political and religious convictions, and had been sentenced once again to a term in a concentration camp for his connection with *Feniks*. Recently released from prison and working in Moscow, Dobrovolski discredited himself in the eyes of his former friends and colleagues, probably for life, by his behavior before the court. Rumor has it that he is completely isolated, although Galanskov, who bore the brunt of Dobrovolski's confessions, spoke up for him again and again in his letters from the camp.

The other three defendants denied any connection with the NTS. All three stood completely and absolutely by their story of having composed (edited for printing), gathered, and circulated the writings of which they were charged. Vera Laskova was only accused of having transcribed the *Feniks* manuscripts. At the same time, however, they defended their constitutional right to do what they did, even as Siniavski and Daniel before them. Ginzburg uttered the sentence that has since made this case famous:

> *A patriot should be ready to die for his native land, but not to lie for it.*

Toward the end of his summation, he said:

> *I consider myself innocent. I have done what
> I have done because I was convinced that
> it was right. My counsel has pleaded for a
> fair judgment in my case. I know that you
> will find me guilty, because no one who is
> accused of violating Article 70 is ever
> found innocent. I will go peacefully to the
> camp and sit out my time. You can stick me
> in prison, send me to a camp, but I am sure
> that not one single honorable man will judge
> me guilty. I ask the court for just one thing
> —make my sentence no shorter than that of
> Galanskov.*[5]

Vera Laskova also pleaded not guilty, but was nevertheless sentenced to one-year imprisonment. She was set
free, however, having already spent this year in detention
during the investigation. In accordance with Paragraph 70,
Ginzburg was sentenced to five years at hard labor in a
work camp. Convicted by the same paragraph, and Paragraph 88/1 as well, Galanskov received seven years in a
state work camp. Each defendant was given the maximum
sentence imposed by the public prosecutor. Later a general
request for appeal was denied.

In their *Call to the World*, Larisa Daniel and Pavel
Litvinov described the treatment allotted the witnesses for
the defense who were forcefully cleared from the courtroom, partly as a result of the abuse which the subpoenaed
"public" hurled at them. *(See page 363.)* In a letter ad-

dressed to the highest Party and court positions, 13 witnesses protested their unconstitutional treatment.[6] The proceedings, whose characteristics reminded Pavel Litvinov and Larisa Daniel of a witchcraft trial, betrayed even more obviously the state's lack of confidence in its own power. Like all previous hearings, this one was a parody of justice and law, a farce, in which the concept of revenge overwhelmed the administration of justice.

As for Ginzburg, Boris Zolotuchin—the defense counsel —made a new and unusual plea for the release of his client. He called upon the prosecutor general who had earlier observed that "opinions" alone, even if they should be anti-Soviet in nature, are not punishable, and maintained that Ginzburg had behaved as a citizen who was gravely concerned "if an innocent man is led away." [7] These courageous arguments earned for Zolotuchin his expulsion from the Party. Several months later he lost his membership in the bar and as a result was compelled to give up his profession.

The Soviet press reported the trial only after the sentence was handed down and then overstressed its virulent accusations and false reports about the condemned group. According to Komsomolskaya Pravda and Izvestia, those who stood before the court were not freedom-loving men of letters, but rather, parasitic loafers who had joined foreign "espionage organizations," such as the NTS, out of greed and personal need for recognition.[8] The editor in chief of Literaturnaya Gazeta, A. Chakovski, used his paper as a sounding board for the suggestion that the four defendants be deported on grounds that "agitators of this sort" should not be supported by public means.[9] Anatoli

Marchenko wrote an open letter to Chavoski[10] in the same tone, describing the living conditions in the camps and the extent of the needed forced labor there. *(See page 389.)*

Ginzburg, Galanskov, and Dobrovolski, whose heads already had been shaved during their investigation and were shockingly emaciated, according to reports, were brought to the camp complex at Dubrovlag. Also, reliable sources said that the condition of Galanskov, who suffered from stomach ulcers during his detention, had become critical since denial of proper medications and treatment. Petitions from his fellow prisoners and friends to save his life remained unanswered.[11] Though in grave condition and in need of an operation, he was forced, when possible, to continue his hard labor. This case, as well as many others, proves that no significant changes have occurred since Stalin's time except that immediate liquidation of political dissidents has been replaced by lingering, tortured deaths.

In a note composed at Dubrovlag during February of 1970, Galanskov looked toward Western Communists for exertion of their influence on the Soviet power system to bring about several fundamental reforms. Among these reforms he recommended complete amnesty to those persecuted because of political or religious convictions. Galanskov credited the West with great power; he emphasized its responsibility for the future development of the Soviet Union. At the same time, he criticized those Western intellectuals who had passively observed the crimes Stalin committed in earlier years. *(See page 345.)*

Together with Daniel and other political prisoners, Galanskov repeatedly participated in hunger strikes; as a sign of solidarity with Ginzburg—according to reports in the uncensored journal *Chronika Tekuschchich Sobyty* (Chronicle of Current Events)—he took part in a hunger strike lasting several weeks during May and June of 1969 in an attempt to obtain official permission for Ginzburg to marry his fiancée, Irina Zolkovskaya. Despite Ginzburg's model behavior in the camp and regardless of innumerable petitions, the authorities did not permit the marriage until August, 1969. In the meantime, Irina Zolkovskaya was relieved of her duties as lecturer in Russian at Moscow University.

In August, 1970, the alarming news was made public that, along with Daniel and others, Ginzburg had been transferred to the prison at Vladimin. There he possessed still fewer rights and was more isolated from the eyes of the public than he ever had been in the camps at Mordvinia. Ginzburg's transfer was the result of a trial held on August 18 in Javas, in which Ginzburg was called to account because of his participation in hunger strikes and because of his allegedly "bad influence" on the other prisoners. The intensified conditions of his imprisonment probably stemmed, in part, from the fact that Ginzburg had discussed with his fellow inmates a tape recording made in the camp and smuggled out to the West. In this recording, sent to many Western countries along with secretly filmed interviews with other Soviet dissidents (Bukovski, Yakir, and Amalrik), Ginzburg described the total helplessness of the political prisoners.

> In this concentration camp . . . there is a single doctor for all the prisoners; thousands are robbed of their freedom, and the life

of each one of them is in danger . . . We are surrounded by camps and prisons and the death of those who were close to us, but nevertheless we still hope to hold out.

According to Ginzburg's words, it is not the so-called. . .

determined position of the Soviet Union, nor the good will of the governments of other great powers, that will save the dissidents. Rather, it will be "the anger, the protest, and the solidarity of all respectable men in the world, all of those to whom human dignity, democracy, and peace are dear."

Ginzburg continued:

"In their decisive "no" to the Soviet barbarism, I see the true guarantee of respect for human rights, here and in the whole world.[12]

A FLOOD OF REBELLION

One might proceed from the assumption that truth is essential simply for its own sake and not for any other reason; that the integrity of the individual does not allow him to put up with evil, even when it is beyond his control to prevent it.

ANATOLI YAKOBSON

The proceedings and sentences in the case against Ginzburg and Galanskov inaugurated the so-called Year of Human Rights in the Soviet Union, and the resultant indignation was deeper and more overt than that following the trial against Siniavski and Daniel.

The most prominent spokesmen for the rapidly growing protest actions were Pavel Litvinov and Larisa Daniel (née Bograz). On January 11, 1968, they composed and circulated a public proclamation demanding the release of Ginzburg and Galanskov, as well as a "public review of the shameful trial and punishment of the guilty." *(See page 363.)* Litvinov and Larisa Daniel forwarded this proclamation to the foreign press, and through it the Soviet public was provided with an accurate description of the proceedings in the Moscow municipal court. Western radio stations transmitted it behind the Iron Curtain, thus informing millions of Soviet citizens of the sordid details. In turn, they made their response known in numerous letters and telegrams eventually reaching Litvinov after the broadcast. (*See page 363.*) According to reports by Western correspondents, fifteen letters of protest bearing the signatures of seven hundred persons[1] found their way to the mailboxes of foreign correspondents. Sharply critical letters from almost every region of the Soviet Union were sent to the Supreme Soviet, to the Supreme Court, and to other authorities and leading Party functionaries. Almost every protester condemning such despotic practices referred in his letter to the proclamation of Litvinov and Larisa Daniel as one of the reasons for his indignation.

One petition addressed to the Supreme Soviet was signed by 224 people, a record number for a single protest letter. "As long as this despotism continues, no one can feel secure," declared the authors of the letter, mostly scholars and technicians, but also including workers and housewives.[2] One hundred and twenty-one scientists condemned the judgment against Ginzburg and stated that it was impossible to consider this trial as anything but "an attempt to revive once again the methods employed in the trials of 1937."[3] Another letter of protest was signed by eighty well-known scholars, plus workers, students, and civil employees, who asked:

> *Isn't it incredible, that men who performed their acts in the open . . . are judged secretly? A lawful court would not have any-*

thing to fear from openness, indeed would welcome it.[4]

Most of the petitions (including those of the Novosibirsk scientists (*see page 372*) repeated the demand made by Litvinov and Larisa Daniel for appropriate punitive actions against all who acted illegally in connection with the trial.

In a letter addressed to the members of the Central Committee and the Supreme Soviet, the former Major General Grigorenko wrote:

Apart from the moral-ethical, political, and legal aspects of the case, as one familiar with military proceedings, I should like to point out that it is difficult even to estimate the great number of allies which our land has lost [because of this trial] . . . Not even our most dangerous enemies could have done us more harm.[5]

In a letter addressed to the Politburo and the Presidium of the Supreme Soviet, the brothers Boris and Yuri Vachtin— both members of the Academy of Sciences, demanded a review of every known political trial during the past two years.

We cannot tolerate the recent illegality, for, if we did so, our lives and our work would lose all meaning and would be reduced to

nothing more than a mere biological func-
tion . . . We demand light, truth, and an in-
formed public! Our right to make this de-
mand is guaranteed by the Constitution, by
our declaration of the rights of a man both as
a citizen and as a private individual, and
finally, by the desire to see our native land
great and pure—in big as well as little things.[6]

In a lengthy document sent to the editorial management
of *Komsomolskaya Pravda,* the engineer and mathematician
Leonid Pliusch explained why he gave more credence to
publications appearing in *Samizdat* than to the announcements made in the official press. (*See page 468.*)

This remark caused him to lose his job. The student
Victor Voronin wrote an open letter to the editor of *Izvestia*
in which he denounced the scandalous article defaming the
accused.[7]

As a citizen of the country which more than
any other embraced freedom and justice, I
protest your newspaper's publication of the
article by T. Aleksandrov and V. Konstan-
tinov. As a citizen of the RSFSR,[8] *in whose*
name this disgraceful conviction has been
carried out, I protest this sentence and the
judicial farce that took place in Moscow. I de-
mand an immediate, open, and impartial in-
vestigation of the case, to take place publicly
and in the presence of correspondents from
the foreign press. I demand a public review

*of all trials held against political dissidents
behind closed doors, and the punishment of
those who have violated the administration
of justice. I demand the reinstatement of
truth and justice.*[9]

In an attempt to draw wider attention to the injustice
rampant in their land, 12 spokesmen for the intellectual
opposition sent a letter to the delegates of the Advisory Assembly, representing governments beyond Soviet influence
in East European countries, held in Budapest in February
and March of 1968. (*See page 426*.) In a proclamation addressed to representatives of science, art, and culture, Ilia
Gabai and Yuli Kim, both teachers, as well as Petr Jakir,
historian, used this trial as a basis to point out once again
the danger and increasing signs of a revival of Stalinism.
They warned the "heirs of the humane tradition of the Russian intelligentsia" not to promote a new despotism, "a new
1937," [10] through further silence.

Unlike public reactions to the trial of Siniavski and
Daniel, which demands were limited for the most part to the
question of intellectual freedom and artistic creativity, and
which protests were concentrated within the intellectual
circles of Moscow and Leningrad, the wave of indignation
over the conviction of Galanskov and Ginzburg rose from
many parts of the Soviet Union and represented many different vocations. The extent of their demands increased in
direct proportion to the number of protesters. By now the
opposition had crystallized in a matter of demanding greater
legal security and increased civil rights. The defiant tone of
all this differed considerably from the cautiously worded

ambiguous hints and allegoric parables which the writers, particularly, had employed in their earlier criticisms of widespread injustice.

If the Siniavski-Daniel trial had brought about a rapprochement between the moderate and the more radical groups, how much more these new events succeeded in driving the originally loyal forces toward closer and closer association with the uncomprising opposition. This solidarity of political and artistic protest lent a different character to the initially unpolitical "cultural opposition" and helped make it a dissident front that could not be dismissed.

THE RULERS' REVENGE

> *We, the participants in the democratic
> movement, will be arrested . . . But
> there is no turning back. If we weren't
> the dissidents, others would be . . .
> They will strike us down and kill us.
> But it won't make any difference, be-
> cause men will continue to think in-
> dependently.*
>
> —PETR YAKIR

In constant fear of losing some of its control and for many
years unwilling to enter into peaceful negotiations, the
power system continued, indeed escalated, the war against
the intellectuals. Several of the spokesmen protesting the
January trial were arrested, including the mathematician
Yesenin-Volpin and the poet Natalia Gorbanevskaya. They
were apprehended in their homes on the fourteenth and
fifteen of February, 1968, and were confined in mental institutions without a proper hearing. Natalia Gorbanevskaya,
a talented poet whose reputation had been established in
the first *Feniks*, described her experiences during her two-
month enforced stay in an insane asylum in a short piece
that appeared in *Samizdat*[1] under the ironic title "Free
Medical Treatment."

Pavel Litvinov was spared any drastic persecution—probably because of his famous grandfather. All the same, he did lose his job. Along with Petr Jakir, Larisa Daniel, and Petr Grigorenko, Litvinov also was subjected to so-called "prophylactic" interviews in the main offices of the KGB. While Jakir's wife lost her job shortly thereafter for having signed several petitions, the secret police told the son of the famous commander: "You are not the spiritual heir of your father! We are his spiritual successors." [2] About a year later it was revealed that Jakir, too, was prevented from continuing his work as a scientific consultant in the Historical Institute of the Academy of Sciences. Since then he has become a librarian.

In a letter addressed to the Party Secretary, M. Suslov, the *kolkhoz* (collective farm) chairman, Ivan Yakhimovich, not only complained bitterly about the illegal trial, but also expressed grievances that he felt existed in many areas of Soviet life; as a result, he lost his job and was expelled from the Party. At approximately the same time, his wife, a teacher, was given notice. The instructors Kim and Gabai, who with Petr Jakir had composed the proclamation to leading figures in science and art, also lost their posts, as did Petr Grigorenko.

The police launched open inquiries against all those who had signed the numerous petitions. While many of the signers got off with a reprimand, others lost their jobs or, if they happened to be members, were expelled from the Party or the Komsomol. As a rule, expulsion from the Party not only accompanied the loss of one's job, but also made it more difficult for that particular person to find another position. Very often, therefore, such expulsion was a successful means of jeopardizing the very existence of those people the Party considered incorrigible.

In its issue of June 30, 1968, the uncensored *Chronicle of Current Events (Chronika)* published under the heading "Illegal Political Reprisals" a list of ninety-one people who during the first months of 1968 had lost their jobs or membership in the Party, or had been subjected to some other act of repression. Among those listed for loss of job or Party membership were many renowned scientists, writers, and editors, including the mathematician, I. Gelfand, winner of both the Lenin and State Prizes; the well-known Moscow professor of philosophy P. Gaydenko; and the philosopher A. Ogurcov. The last two named had written several noteworthy articles which appeared in the philosophical journal *Voprosy Filosofii*. A leading secretary of the Komsomol also was listed as having been excommunicated from the Party. The authorities were driven to rigorous action in Akademgorodok, the "City of Scholars" not far from Novosibirsk. Here the Department for Mathematical Linguistics was abruptly disbanded after several of its professors signed their names to the *Letter of the 99*. *(See page 121.)*

The historian Andrei Amalrik, who was banned from all legal publications and by now had resorted to the underground press, wrote a brilliant and thoughtful analysis of the possible future of the Soviet empire. In it he maintained that the "most human, probably if not least enticing, goal that the Soviet regime had set up for itself in the course of the past 50 years was based on the assumption that everything should remain as it was."

Continued Amalrik:

*The regime does not want the system to be
shaken by any dangerous and unusual reforms; it does not act, but simply defends itself. . . .*[3]

In the year of the "Prague spring" and with the increasing discontent in their own land, the Soviet rulers saw themselves pushed into a position more defensive than they had
known in 20 years.

With the help of a corrupt and controllable press, simply
the organ for the transmission of Party propaganda, the administration sought to get the rebellious intelligentsia se-
curely in its grip. Printing apparatus of all sorts is one
resource against such daring opponents, while ominous
decisions of the Central Committee, press campaigns, and
a huge army of agitators sent to mingle with the people are
others. "Vigilance against the internal and external enemy,
against spies and other dissidents" was a rallying cry that
had found little acceptance among the public since the
death of Stalin. Writers' and artists' organizations were
"purified," students were expelled, teachers and professors
fired. Not only those writers denounced as "mercenaries of
imperialism" disappeared behind the walls of concentration
camps and prisons, but also all who openly or covertly supported them were, and continue to be, summarily damned
as traitors seeking personal recognition.

Conformist writers such as Sholokhov, who have
noisily taken over the positions once held by those well-
known writers who have been muzzled so long, openly condemn the "rebels."

> *As long as these subjects [the insubordinate*
> *intellectuals] spread their stench and call*
> *upon foreign armies for help, please make*
> *sure, our dear dictatorship, that you do not*
> *grow weaker and die out!* [4]

These words of holy indignation are drawn from a loathsome poem by the unknown Sergei Smirnov, who not long ago received the State Prize of the RSFSR for such eloquence.

ANTI-STALINIST
SPOKESMEN

We have learned from bitter experience what freedom, democracy, and human rights mean. We have paid for this knowledge with our blood, with years of insanity and degradation.

EXCERPT FROM A LETTER ADDRESSED TO
PAVEL LITVINOV

Guidelines for de-Stalinization were defined in the Twentieth and Twenty-Second Party Congresses; the process itself soon became a focal point for a gradually increasing opposition within the Soviet Union. The very moment it actually began to ignore the directives of the congresses—although never admitting this in so many words—the administration fostered an opposition among the intellectuals which would have been unimaginable before. Not a branch of cultural or scientific life exists in Russia today whose most determined representatives do not openly rebel against a revival of Stalinist terror, even if it takes the form of a rebellion against so seemingly trivial a thing as the partial rehabilitation of Stalin himself.

The first example of this new approach was the proclamation addressed to Brezhnev on the eve of the Twenty-Third Party Congress in 1966 signed by well-known artists and scholars.[1] These included the physicists Andrei Sakharov, Petr Kapica, and Igor Tamm, the film producer Mikhail Romm, the prima ballerina Maya Pliseckaya, the writers Valentin Kataev and Kornei Chukovski, and others. "The Stalin era shall not repeat itself. It all depends upon us." [2]

So read the text of a leaflet that Olga Iofe (then fourteen years old) distributed through the mail, with nine of her schoolmates. None of the pupils were arrested at that time. It was three years later that Olga Iofe, by this time a student of economics, was arrested and accused of having violated Paragraph 70 of the Penal Code. Shortly before the anniversary of Stalin's ninetieth birthday she and several of her friends had printed up handbills warning against a new revival of Stalinism. One of the students involved informed the authorities of the plan and, as a result, the flyers were confiscated before being distributed. On August 20, 1968, the Moscow Municipal Court arranged for Olga Iofe's admission into a "psychiatric clinic." Though two of her friends—Viacheslav Bachmin and Irina Kaplun—confined to similar institutions, were released a few months later, she remains imprisoned.

A book by the historian Aleksandr Nekrich, entitled *1941-22. Ijunja (June 22, 1941)*, was published by Nauka and aroused considerable response. In his treatise, Nekrich attempted to explain Stalin's disastrous and incredible errors both before and at the beginning of the war—errors that cost the Red Army such fearful losses. But this publication caused Nekrich to enter the public arena at a time when such critical appraisal of Stalin had long since ceased to be opportune. He further harmed his position by questioning the "historic legalities" of the Soviet victory, thus inadvertently confessing himself guilty of heresy.

In February of 1966, a discussion concerning this contested work took place behind closed doors at the Institute for Marxism-Leninism (IML), under whose aegis the book was originally published. During this discussion, a particularly heated dispute arose between the anti-Stalinists on the one hand and the old-line Stalin supporters on the other. The minutes of the meeting, in which 130 historians, military people, and Party functionaries took part, were secretly smuggled to the West and published there.[3] Nekrich's book was confiscated shortly after its appearance in the U.S.S.R. and its author accused of having referred to "bourgeois history falsifiers" and having betrayed the "principles of Marxist-Leninist historiography."[4] In July of 1967, Nekrich was expelled from the Party. The "Nekrich Affair" not only provided the occasion for Petr Grigorenko, the civil rights fighter and former major general, to write a brilliant defense of Nekrich (never published in the Soviet Union[5]) but also for many other anti-Stalinists to scrutinize the current extent of de-Stalinization. The critic and German scholar, Lev Kopelev, who was a decorated officer of the second World War, like Solzhenitsyn, unexpectedly found himself in a concentration camp, to be rehabilitated only after Stalin's death. (As one of Solzhenitsyn's fellow inmates, he appears in the novel *The First Circle* as Lev Rubins.) Upon Nekrich's expulsion from the Party, Kopelev wrote that a vindication of Stalin today would be the same thing as a defamation of socialism.[6] This letter cost him his second dismissal from the Party and the loss of his post at the Historical Institute.

Another "Letter to a Comrade" circulated in Moscow and appeared anonymously in the West:

> *Surely you have already noticed for yourself how the political dregs, who crept back into their caves after 1953, are again turning up everywhere. The followers of the Twentieth through the Twenty-Third Party Congresses are publicly accused in ever-increasing numbers of revisionism and a lack of patriotism; the frightened publishers and editors go through every manuscript with a fine-toothed comb, examine every word for its ideological import, and look for inconsistencies in Gauss's theory . . . It seems to me that, given the present circumstances, we do not have the right to stand on the sidelines. Of course, those who do keep silent are rewarded with successful careers. Still, our more than thirty-year membership in the Party has shown both you and me the sad results brought about by political fatalism, the naïve hope that, despite everything, all will go straight in the end, that history proceeds in the right direction . . . .[7]*

These words clearly describe the atmosphere of thought presently being fostered by those "above," which seems once again to have gained some control in the lower levels of political life. At the same time, however, this letter demonstrates the sensitive reaction the government could expect from opponents of any return to this sort of thought pattern.

Lidia Chukovskaya established her reputation through her "Open Letter to Mikhail Sholokhov." Her father was the famous novelist Kornei Chukovski, who died in 1969, and she herself is a journalist with a book about Aleksandr Gercen (Herzen), as well as a novel about the terror of the 1930's, to her credit.[8] (The latter has not yet been published in the Soviet Union.) Shortly before the fifteenth anniversary of Stalin's death, Lidia Chukovskaya wrote a letter to the editor of *Izvestia,* in which she not only revived the question of mutual responsibility of all those who were guilty under Stalin, but also indirectly attacked the pillars of the present-day system for failing to bring these known criminals to account (something they admittedly could not do without jeopardizing their own positions) and even managing, where possible, to praise them. (*See page 344.*)

The historian Roi Medvedev, brother of the famous geneticist Zores Medvedev and author of a three-volume work on the origins and development of Stalin, wrote a landmark essay in which he critically examined the attempts to rehabilitate Stalin. Like Nekrich, Grigorenko, and many others, Medvedev questioned Stalin's role as Commander in Chief. According to this historian, at the very beginning of the war, Stalin had failed as ruler of his people. During one of the most critical moments of Soviet history he "in fact deserted his post as head of state."[9] Medvedev sent his manuscript to the Party organ *Kommunist* for publication; as was expected, however, it had no more chance of being printed than his thousand-page monograph on Stalin. Both treatises were circulated in *Samizdat.* In 1969 it was announced that Medvedev had lost his membership in the Party, an event undoubtedly connected with his anti-Stalinist publications.

The *Kommunist* also refused to print Petr Jakir's "Open Letter" to the editor, a document that was published in the West. During his seventeen years as an inmate in a Stalinist camp, Jakir became one of the most important leaders of the civil rights movement, and continued this role following his release. In his letter he denounced the neo-Stalinistic tendencies evident in recent historical accounts, especially those concerning Stalin himself. The *Kommunist* itself had abetted this trend with its publication of a series of essays that partially rehabilitated the despot.

Asked Jakir:

> *On what grounds do the authors of the articles I mentioned above restore to good standing the most heinous criminal our land, in all its recent history, has ever had?* [10]

There is an obvious answer to this question so often posed by an uncomprehending younger generation. Since the determined opponents of Stalin not only equate Stalinism with the degradation of the "personality cult," but also with the violation of basic human rights, they attack—consciously or unconsciously—the very foundation of Marxist-Leninism, something more than a "temporary Stalinist deterioration" and, indeed, the basis of the present Soviet system.

When the Communist World Conference met in Moscow on June 5, 1969, eleven civil-rights fighters, including

Petr Jakir, Ilia Gabai, and Leonid Pliusch, tried to persuade the delegates to forestall any revival of Stalinism. Besides the trials against leading writers and the suppression of political dissidents, the proclamation mentioned the occupation of Czechoslovakia as an ominous symptom of a Stalinist revival and concluded with the usual plea:

> We beg you to do all that your conscience and understanding dictate, everything in your power, to prevent the unholy shadow of Stalin from darkening our future.[11]

On December 21, 1969, the centennial of Stalin's birth, approximately thirty people gathered around the Kremlin wall at the spot where the dictator was buried, with the intention of demonstrating against any possible pro-Stalinist actions. However, no pro-Stalinist announcements were made and no demonstration took place. One of those present, however—the literature critic Anatoli Jakobson—was arrested and fined for "rowdiness."

A comparatively restrained intervention by the police and the very cautious official article[12] in *Pravda,* not meant to praise Stalin, added support to the general assumption that the neo-Stalinist posture of the power system sprang less from intention than from a defensive strategy forced by its helplessness.

THE ROLE OF SAKHAROV,
THE ATOMIC PHYSICIST

The calling to arms of scholars and writers, whatever form it might take, always precedes every campaign of en- lightenment, every progressive thrust of education. They ought not be faint- hearted in their anger, since they have always been destined to stand in the front lines and take upon themselves all the dangers and all the wounds.

—A. S. PUSHKIN

In July, 1968, as Soviet troop maneuvers in Czechoslovakia heralded the coming doom, a 10,000-word manifesto of the famous Soviet atomic physicist Andrei Sakharov was pub- lished in the West. This memorandum, entitled *Progress, Peaceful Co-Existence and Intellectual Freedom*,[1] started a wave of unusual speculation. While some considered it a mere fabrication by foreign powers, others greeted it as ostensible proof that at least the leadership of the Soviet Union had found its way to "human socialism," to the "con- vergence theory," and to other similarly encouraging deci- sions. A third group viewed the document, especially after the occupation of Czechoslovakia, as something the Soviet leadership itself had dreamed up to bolster its own position or else a total falsehood propagated by that leadership—a shrewd but vain political attempt by the Party to shift public attention from the rebellion raging in Prague.

None of these hypotheses proved valid; as a matter of fact, they were all overturned by subsequent events. Nevertheless, despite many of its illusionary passages, the document is significant as the individual expression of a leading scientist in the Communist world; as such, it should not be underestimated. Sakharov speaks not only for himself, but for a large segment of the progressive intelligentsia, particularly, as set forth in the beginning of the work, for the scientific-technological elements within this group. Thus the physicist represents a group of people, who hitherto had shared absolutely no political power but whose influence on society had steadily increased nevertheless.

Sakharov is known in the West as the "Father of the Soviet Hydrogen Bomb." Although unusually young at the time—he was born in 1921—Sakharov had played a central role in the development of Soviet nuclear research. He was considered, with good reason, an ingenious *Wunderkind*. He has won the Lenin, Stalin, and State prizes, in addition to having been chosen on three separate occasions as "Hero of Socialist Work." In 1953, at the unusually early age of thirty-two, he became a member of the Academy of Sciences. With his more mature colleagues, Nobel Prize winner Igor Tamm, Petr Kapica, and others, Sakharov signed several petitions, among them the one dated March, 1966. He is not a member of the Communist Party. In fact, his treatise declared himself in total opposition to it, considering himself a Communist with "revisionist" viewpoints, as one who supported the Czechoslovakian variety of socialism. (Incidentally, many other members of his circle endorsed the Czechoslovakian reforms.)

Sakharov began writing his paper in April, 1968, and finished it the following June. The manifesto is not concerned solely with conditions within the USSR; apart from recommendations for the guarantee of intellectual freedom and propositions concerning world health, possible avoidance of a threatening nuclear war and the ravages of famine was carefully outlined. The author appealed to the leadership of his country, "to all citizens and to all peoples of good will throughout the world," and challenged them to a discussion of the urgent problems he had presented.

It appears that Sakharov had entertained some hope of legal release and circulation for his book within the Soviet Union, the only plausible reason why he took such pains, for example, to consider the Party leadership in the question of the economic capacity of the U.S.S.R. For instance, when he advocated the "convergence theory," that is, the possible mutual rapprochement of the two political systems —a theory widely supported in the West but completely disregarded by official Soviet spokesmen—the reader finds it difficult to assume that Sakharov considered the Soviet economic system really capable of convergence in its present state. Even the expanded economic reforms that Sakharov recommended would not make the Soviet economy a viable competitor with the West.

Sakharov made no secret of the fact that he saw a continuation of Stalinism in the present Soviet system, if in a more moderate form. The terror of the Stalin era, which the scientist equated with the horrors of the Hitler regime, had indeed ended, but guarantees of its total elimination had never been given. Sakharov cited the lack of press and speech freedom, the trials of writers, the incomplete de-Stalinization, the racial problem, and other things as proof of an intact Stalinism. He contested the Party's claim to total leadership, especially in view of its current composition. It was made up of beneficiaries of the Stalinist "pseudo-socialism" of members of a privileged caste, of a "bureaucratic elite" that accounted for 5 percent of the total population at that time, and which, according to Sakharov, enjoyed as much special treatment as "the corresponding groups in the United States of America." At the other end of the scale, moreover, he maintained that conditions were better for the average American than they were for the average Soviet citizen, about 40 percent of whom lived "under very stringent economic conditions" as opposed to only 25 percent of a similarly impoverished American population. Through this statement alone, the physicist assailed a fundamental principle of Soviet propaganda, the very doctrine of Leninism, his remark combined the observation that a class society did in fact exist under Communism with the equally daring observation that the dogma of "fading capitalism" was no longer completely tenable.

The suggestions and propositions Sakharov put forth for the final victory over Stalinism may be summarized as follows:

> (a) An intensification of the strategy of peaceful co-existence.

(b) A weakening of the dogmatic and bureaucratic chains which were hindering the economy.

(c) The complete unmasking of Stalin; release
of the archives of the NKVD (Peoples' Commissariat for Internal Affairs); curtailment of
the influence of the neo-Stalinists.

(d) Amnesty for political prisoners; reviews of
the trials against writers; prison reform.

(e) Repeal of all unconstitutional laws; positive
guarantees of human rights.

(f) Freedom of the press and freedom of information.

To insure that all this progressed along democratic
lines, Sakharov advocated a multiple-party system, even
though he did not see such a system as a "panacea against
all exigencies."

While the first five points hardly exceeded what spokesmen for the progressive intelligentsia had been repeating
for so long and had openly demanded, the appeal for an
abolition of censorship and the institution of a multiple-
party system showed more than a little daring. Certainly
this demand, too, was not new, but it was always whispered
and had never appeared in a publication such as Sakharov's. He was soon to learn that his hope for legal publication was unfounded. The 10,000-word manifesto became, in
the Soviet Union, just another piece of "underground" con-
traband. The authorities decided to take action against

Sakharov, after some length of time, but considering his reputation and his indispensability in the field of research, he was spared severe persecution. Nevertheless, in March of 1969 it was made known in the West that the physicist had been stripped of almost all his assignments. Recently, he has been employed in the scientific center of Cherno-golvka, nearly 50 miles from Moscow, although relieved of all consultative functions and forbidden to enter any teaching activities. At the present time, the KGB thwarts every attempt by Westerners to meet Sakharov.

Sakharov's memorandum aroused considerably more attention than other documents written by the noncomformist intelligentsia, especially in the non-Anglo-Saxon nations of the West, although discussion over its contents was never permitted to exceed very narrowly defined limits. The response which Sakharov's thoughts found in his own land was unquestionably much greater than anywhere else.[2] Although the matter was officially hushed up, Sakharov drew a sympathetic chord in unofficial circles. Igor Tamm and Petr Kapica publicly praised him. Kapica, who ranks among the models for Moscow students is in the very rare position of being able to express such candid support. As a former student of the English atomic physicist Ernest Rutherford, and as the present chairman of the mathematics and physics department of the Academy of Sciences in the U.S.S.R., Kapica himself had urged of the growing isolation of the Soviet ideologies during a philosophical conference in February of 1969, and had those present, in their exploration of Socialism, to consider not only the non-Marxists but also the revisionists. In addition, he felt that the scientific-technical development of the U.S.S.R. seemed to lag behind that of the u.s.a.[3]

The most remarkable contribution in support of Sakharov's document, which also made its way to the West, was a memorandum written by a group of intellectuals who enthusiastically applauded the manifesto but expanded upon several of the theses and suggestions presented by Sakharov. The scientists wrote:

> *Twelve years have passed since the Twentieth Party Congress, and we still wait and still ask our government for liberating reforms; we are even willing to wait a while longer and repeat our requests again. In the end, however, we will demand and act! Then they won't be sending tank divisions to Prague and Bratislava, but will have to station them in Moscow and Leningrad!*

A letter dated March 19, 1970, directed to the top echelon of the Soviet system, expressed the views of a "considerable number of the Soviet intelligentsia and the avantgarde of the working classes." (*See page 493*.) Written by Andrei Sakharov, the physicist Valeri Turchin, and the historian Roi Medvedev, it contained a program for reform that came exceedingly close to the democratizing program suggested by seventy-five Czechoslovakian scientists in July of 1968.[4] The essence of their program corresponded to Sakharov's points, while supplementing them with more precise suggestions. (For example, the authors recommended that voting privileges be made more democratic, that educational and judicial systems be reformed, that a unified passport system be adopted for all nationalities in the U.S.S.R., that general-information censorship be abolished, etc.)

These three prominent scientists emphasized the urgency of an immediate move toward a more social life in the Soviet Union. The introduction of such a process was absolutely necessary, if only to lessen the breach between Party and state apparatus on the one hand and the intelligentsia on the other.

> Under the conditions of a modern industrial society, a society in which the role of the intellectual becomes increasingly important, a breach of this type can be described in no other term than suicidal.

The authors of the letter analyzed the deficiencies of the present Soviet system, and particularly those in the field of economics. If a general and comprehensive reform program were not instituted, the U.S.S.R. would inevitably decline to the status of a "second-rate provincial power."

They wrote:

> There is no other way out of these difficulties . . . except to follow a more democratic course, which would be carried out by the CPSU according to a carefully worked out plan. A sudden switch to the right—that is, a victory for those tendencies directed toward a stronger administration, a "tightening of the

*screw"—cannot solve the problem; it would
only make matters worse by driving them to
extremism and would lead our country toward a tragic dead end. An attitude of passive waiting, on the other hand, would have
the same results eventually. One single possibility remains open to us today, to pursue the
right path and to institute urgently needed
reforms. In a few years it could be too late.*

Sakharov's commitment to the "democratic movement"
reached a new climax with his formation of a Soviet Commission for Human Rights, whose establishment was announced on November 15 in Moscow. In this venture he was
joined by two physicists, Valeri Chalidze and Andrei Tverdochlebov. Chalidze, a long-time contributor to *Samizdat*,
had been well-known especially for his right-wing political
writings; according to reports in *Chronika*, Tverdochlebov
had published at least one essay in *Samizdat* supporting
Sakharov's document. The principles of the commission were
defined in a cautiously worded *Five Point Manifesto*.[5] In it
the founders explained the commission's nonpolitical character, a fact they further emphasized by stating that participants would not belong to any party, other public organization, nor would they belong to any dissident political
organizations. The manifesto also announced that the commission, while bounded by legal limits, would examine the
status of those civil rights guaranteed by Soviet law and,
wherever necessary, offer constructive criticism. Guidelines
would be provided by the United Nations' Declaration of
Human Rights.

These politically neutral goals alone would create a problem for Soviet rulers legally seeking to form such an organization so long as it was properly registered. At first, the authorities said nothing concerning the establishment of the commission. Later, however, the Party press called for greater vigilance against the infiltration of bourgeois ideology. The scientists of the Lebedev Institute of Physics were repeatedly harassed in this connection because of their "uncritical" political posture.[6] Naturally no names were mentioned, but it was easy to see that the attack was aimed at Sakharov, one of the institute's leading figures at that time.

Even before the establishment of the Commission on Human Rights, Sakharov had actively supported political prisoners, including the geneticist Zores Medvedev, the student Olga Iofe, and the mathematician Revol't Pimenov. Toward the end of 1970, he protested in the name of the commission against drastic sentences being handed down to eleven Soviet citizens—almost all of them Jews—during the so-called "Leningrad Trial."

The actions of Sakharov and his colleagues clearly revealed the growing role of natural scientists—a rather apolitical group—in the battle for a constitutional state order. The fact that they are less limited in their professional fields than are liberal-arts scholars, artists, and writers in theirs makes the setting aside of ideological boundaries less of an existential necessity for scientists. True, Soviet rulers have dealt less repressively with leading natural scientists than others. On the other hand, proceedings against Zores Medvedev[7] and Revol't Pimenov[8] have shown that the regime does not stand in awe of famous scientists nor does it hesitate to take Draconian measures against them.[9]

CHRONIKA

Each man has the right to free expression of his opinions; this right includes the freedom to adhere to these opinions unmolested and to seek, receive, and circulate information and ideas by all means of communication regardless of boundaries.

ARTICLE 19 OF THE DECLARATION OF
HUMAN RIGHTS

It is said that Sakharov began work on his document in April, 1968, immediately after Soviet Party leadership publicized the notorious decision of the Central Committee to order an "offensive against the bourgeois ideology." [1] The intelligentsia responded at once with Sakharov's memorandum and the already mentioned *Chronika Tekuschich Sobytij (Chronicle of Current Events),* whose first number appeared on April 30, 1968, and which has continued to appear bimonthly ever since. The journal's first appearance coincided with the Year of Human Rights, and having survived that auspicious-sounding year, it has managed to continue publication to this day. Article 19 of the Declaration of Human Rights, quoted above, is reproduced on the masthead of every issue, usually comprising thirty to fifty pages.

This journal is primarily concerned with the reporting of protest demonstrations and provides a survey of illegal reprisals against political dissidents, as well as those perpetrated against members of national minorities, such as Jews, Crimean Tartars and Ukrainians, and against various religious denominations (mainly Russian Orthodox and Unitarian). In this respect *Chronika* assumed to a certain degree the function of a free press. On the final pages of its fifth edition, the journal described the difficult circumstances under which its editorial board sought to fulfill this assignment:

> *Although* Chronika *is not an illegal publication, working conditions are hampered by a peculiar conception of legality and the freedom of information by certain Soviet organs —disseminating news. Therefore, unlike other journals,* Chronika *cannot print its post-office address on the last page of each edition. Nevertheless, everyone who is interested and concerned that the Soviet public be informed about current events taking place in Russia can learn with little difficulty all pertinent information about the journal. Let the person from whom you received this paper know of your interest; he will pass on the information to the person from whom he received his copy, and the process will be repeated. It would be unwise, however, to pursue the whole chain yourself, for in that way you*

*would place yourself in the dangerous posi-
tion of possibly becoming an informer.*[2]

Those people who managed to get copies of the journal
either copied or photographed the individual issues and
passed them on to others. (The use of photocopying machinery or mimeograph equipment was avoided since the
secret police regarded such facilities as subversive and closely controlled their use.) A few of the several hundred
reporters who contributed to *Chronika* apparently were
members themselves of the higher circles of functionaries.
Neither the KGB nor the editorial board of *Chronika* itself
knows exactly how many anonymous informers this extraordinary publication really has. Despite this fact, *Chronika*
remains a model for accurate news reporting. In an early
issue it was reported that *Chronika* endeavors to maintain
a maximum level of reliability in those news stories it
prints. Occasionally, absolute certainty about one thing or
another is lacking; *Chronika* prefaces its report with the
caveat that the story may be only rumor. At the same time,
the journal warns its readers to be cautious and precise
when passing on information they read in it.[3] Considering the speed and high degree of accuracy with which
Chronika reports the news, including last-minute items,
some circles are convinced that it has access to computers,
or even Telex photographs, for transmission and circulation
of its published reports. This tends to support the conclusion that scholars, scientists, and technical people in important posts contribute actively to the production and research of the journal, because they are the only ones with
access to such equipment.[4]

Chronika, which can be described as an organ of the "democratic movement," is probably the most constructive element that the Russian underground has ever produced. The value of its contribution can perhaps be most significantly compared to the activities of the illegal Czechoslovakian radio stations following the occupation of that country on August 21, 1968. The working conditions of the Soviet dissidents are, if possible, even more difficult in Russia than those experienced by the Czechoslovakian amateur broadcasters. The phenomenon of *Chronika* is even more astounding, when one considers the fact that it is now in its fourth year of publication. Another indication of its strength lies in the similarity of various newsletters based upon the format of *Chronika.* In January, 1970, the first edition of *Vestnik Ukrainy (The Ukrainian Messenger)* appeared, and three months later Russian Zionists still living in the u.s.s.r. published their journal *Ischod (Exodus).*[5]

Chronika is an excellent example of the altered nature of *Samizdat,* which—particularly since 1968—has shifted its emphasis from the predominantly literary journals of its early years to publications of a political nature. "In this way," wrote the editor of *Chronika,* "*Samizdat* not only fulfills the function of book publisher but that of newspaper publisher as well.[6]

Besides petitions, essays, and books by Soviet authors, the works of foreign writers occasionally appear in *Samizdat.* The most recent and most important *Samizdat* materials are now published by *Chronika* in a special rubric. Foreign works, secretly translated into Russian—and particularly those of Russian writers and philosophers which were printed in the West and forbidden in the u.s.s.r.—are referred to as *tamizdat*, the prefix *tam* meaning "there" or "in that place."

The newspaper's style is characterized by a moderate form of reporting, along with an astounding lack of personal opinion and personal value judgments. The report concerning the Fetisov Group was one of the rare exceptions, although even in this instance the editorial board of *Chronika* rejected every expression of emotional polemic as being superficial and trifling.

The position of the Fetisov Group (named after its leader, the national economist A. Fetisov) follows a totalitarian and chauvinistic attitude that is, according to *Chronika*, anti-Semitic and intellectually untenable. The principal heroes of this misguided group are Stalin and Hitler. Fetisov himself voluntarily renounced his Party membership in 1968 as a protest against the efforts to rehabilitate Stalin, which he felt were unsatisfactory and insufficient. In 1969, Fetisov was confined to a mental institution with three like-minded comrades, all of them architects. Contributors to *Chronika* understandably rejected the fascistic ideas of the group but used it as a theoretical example to strengthen their own conviction that no one should be deprived of freedom because of his personal beliefs. The journal condemned as "immoral" the imprisonment in mental institutions of those who held different ideological convictions. Were they to do otherwise, the editors maintained, it would mean "equating ourselves with Fetisov, according to whose views Siniavski and Daniel should have been executed." [7]

Chronika portrayed a totally different group in its reports about the so-called Organization of Independent

Youth. This group, whose main concern is to conform strictly to the law, had applied for registration with the municipal government of Vladimir in December of 1968. But two type-written handbills distributed by the group disclosed that the leader of the organization, the worker and "learned" philologian Vladimir Borisov, had been imprisoned in a psychiatric clinic following a hearing with the KGB in May, 1969. Released two months later, Borisov was arrested shortly thereafter again and confined to an insane asylum. In July, 1970, it was learned that he had committed suicide in that institution.

According to its charter, the Organization of Independent Youth is a "self-sufficient and independent organization of young people which . . . determines and carries out its activities independently but within the boundaries of Soviet law." Its main objective is to foster "the development of socialist democracy and social progress with every means available" in their land. The demands of the group consist of "really free and democratic elections, genuine freedoms of opinion, press, and assembly, as well as the right of demonstration and assembly." In addition, the group demands "absolutely no persecution because of personal convictions, the publication of all works written by Soviet writers, abolition of the illegal and unconstitutional censorship, and a determined offensive against criminality." [8] These young people base their requests and their activity on the guarantees of Paragraph 126 of the Soviet Constitution (the right of assembly).

Additional reports in *Chronika* prove that this attempt to organize outside the jurisdiction of the Party and the Komsomol is no isolated case.[9] According to the journal, early in 1970 the members of three different political groups were brought to trial in Gorki, Rjazan, and Saratov. Accused of "anti-Soviet organization and propaganda," the leading parties concerned—almost all of them were students—were sentenced to rather severe punishments in concentration camps, ranging up to seven years. Whether any connection existed between the various groups was not determined in the reports of the trials. However, the groups from Rjazan and Saratov did show a distinct similarity in the choice of their names. The first called itself the Revised Marxist Party, and the second group identified itself as the Party of the True Communists. These circumstances show quite clearly that the activity of the opposition is no longer predominantly limited to the large cities (such as Moscow and Leningrad), but has penetrated into the provinces.

Chronika also reported extensively on the trial and conviction of the Moscow mathematician Ilia Burmistrovich, who was sentenced on May 21, 1969, to three years in a concentration camp for having "circulated anti-Soviet literature." When Burmistrovich had been arrested in May, 1968, the primary evidence against him was his possession of single works by Siniavski and Daniel.

The case of the former major, Genrich Altunjan from Charkov, is similar. Altunjan, who had been employed until 1968 as professor in the War Academy, was expelled from the Party in July of 1968 and discharged from the army after secret security police found in his possession a copy of Sakharov's treatise, Solzhenitsyn's *Cancer Ward,* and several copies of *Chronika.* Despite reprisals already instituted against him, Altunjan had come out in active support on the side of the civil-rights fighters and was confined on

June 11, 1969. Ten citizens of Charkov protested against his arrest in a petition addressed to the public prosecutor general of the u.s.s.r. on July 31, 1969. On November 26, Altunjan was sentenced to three years in a work camp. In its eleventh issue, *Chronika* reported the case of the writer and translator, Juriy Malchev. Like Altunjan, Malchev was a member of the so-called Initiative Group for the Protection of Civil Rights in the u.s.s.r. Since 1964 Malchev had repeatedly requested permission from the Supreme Soviet to travel outside the Soviet Union. In a letter addressed to U Thant and dated February 5, 1968, Malchev explained his reasons for wanting to emigrate and asked the United Nations for help. In so doing, Malchev referred to Articles 13 and 15 of the Declaration of Human Rights, which state that every person has the right to travel or live where he wishes, and the right to change his citizenship. In his letter to the Secretary-General of the United Nations, Malchev wrote: "I want to leave this land because I am prohibited from practicing my vocation as a writer. I reject the official Soviet ideology; I do not believe in Communism—it seems to me to be an imaginary abstraction. In a land in which Communist Party-mindedness in the arts is considered to be an irrevocable principle, I am condemned to spiritual annihilation. Without the possibility of expressing my own convictions, all that is left to me is the purely animalistic existence of a slave, an existence which is unworthy of man." [10]

Following this letter to U Thant, Malchev was brought before a military hearing and subjected to dire threats. Thereupon the writer complained to both the military and the Supreme Soviet. He even wrote a letter to the Human

Rights Commission of the United Nations describing the incident. In his letter he requested the commissioners to inform the public of what had happened to him, since the "relationship between the Soviet power structure and political dissidents" was particularly clear in this case. Reports of an intervention, or even an answer from the United Nations to Malchev's pleas for assistance, were never made known. In October of 1969, Malchev was interrogated concerning his intellectual convictions at the instigation of the secret-police authorities and was detained for a considerable length of time in a psychiatric clinic in Moscow.

The economics scholar Viktor Krasin was arrested on December 20, 1969, and, under the pretext of alleged "parasitism" received sentence of five years in Siberian exile. In less than four days Krasin was transported to the region of Krasnoyarsk. The sole justification for his banishment was the fact that he was unemployed. As a result of his activity within the Initiative Group, Krasin had lost his position and was unable to find a similar post elsewhere. A former inmate of Stalin's camps, the professor suffers from a heart condition and cannot endure heavy physical exertion. Respect for his personal integrity and his conduct as a so-called "ideologue"—that is, one of the spiritual leaders of the "Initiative Group for the Protection of Civil Rights"—has earned Krasin an enviable reputation within the "democratic movement."[11]

Also in its eleventh issue, Chronika published a list of those cases in which persons were condemned to concentration camps, prisons, and insane asylums, or were still serving time pending their trial. The list was valid only for the year 1969. It included sixty-two persons, all of whom

were convicted for violation of Paragraph 70 or 190/1 of
the State Penal Code, and covered the cities of Moscow,
Leningrad, Kiev, Tashkent, Charkov, Riga, Simferopol, Vladimir, Gorki, Tallinn (formerly Revel), Roshal, Perm, Dne-
propetrovsk, Kirov, and Rostov.

The history of the artist Yuri Ivanov reads like a
macabre drama. Born in 1927, Ivanov was the grandson of
a Czarist minister and the son of the artist Yevgeny Sivers
(who was executed in 1938 and then posthumously rehabilitated). He was arrested for the first time in 1947 and sentenced, along with two other students, to ten years in a
work camp, without the benefit of legal proceedings. The
reason: The three students had cut lectures on Marxist
Leninism. Thanks to the intervention of influential relatives,
Ivanov won release the following year and was permitted
to complete his studies at the Academy of the Arts. When
arrested again in 1955—this time for the "circulation of
anti-Soviet literature"—he received a term of forced labor
in Kuibyshev. Because he refused to "repent," he was not
released like so many others as a result of the "demasking"
of Stalin. Instead, he was wounded during a vain attempt
to escape, and another ten years were added to his sentence. He organized a strike committee in the infamous
Dubrovlag camp in 1956, resulting in a further ten-year
sentence. The entire previous year had been spent in solitary
confinement in Vladimir. In 1963, another ten years were
ordered for "circulating anti-Soviet propaganda within the
concentration camp."[12] In 1959, an art exhibition in London
managed to display some of the sketches Ivanov made
while in camp. These pictures from the camp, many of them
actual portraits of fellow inmates, including Aleksandr Ginz-

burg and Yuri Galanskov, found their way farther west in 1970.[13]

Significant in the disclosure of an insidious anti-Semitism poorly disguised as anti-Zionism, which condoned the scandalous discrimination of Jews in the u.s.s.r., were the extensive reports in *Chronika* concerning the case of the young radio technician Boris Kochubievski. Kochubievski was arrested in Kiev on December 7, 1968, following his public demonstration against the one-sided condemnation of Israel as the apparent "aggressor" in the Six Day War. Kochubievski, together with his non-Jewish wife, also had made application for permission to emigrate to Israel. Kochubievski's wife was subsequently accused of "Zionism" and expelled from the Komsomol. After a second mutual application for emigration, Kochubievski was arrested and sentenced on May 16, 1969, to three years imprisonment in a concentration camp, according to Paragraph 187/1 of the Ukrainian Penal Code. (This coincides with Paragraph 190/1 of the uk rsfsr.)[14] Testimonies of responsible leaders of the secret police, reprinted in *Chronika* reports, betrayed an anti-Semitism that would seem excessive even for the Middle Ages. Similar prejudices were expressed in the handling of the eighteen-year-old Aleksandr Daniel, son of the convicted writer and the exiled Larisa Daniel. Aleksandr Daniel had passed the entrance examination for the Physics Faculty of the University Tartu (formerly Dorpat) with honors. Nevertheless, he was not accepted. He then enrolled in a Moscow institute and was suspended a few months later—"according to his wishes" was the wording of the official records. The rector of the institute is supposed to have expressed his discontent at the large number of Jewish students in his faculty with the following words:

> *I am naturally no anti-Semite, but one must*
> *be an internationalist.*[15]

Such ominous expressions of the spiritual atavism among officials stood in flagrant opposition to the deeply rooted humanism of innumerable representatives of the Russian intelligentsia, whose distinct sense of justice was confirmed time and again by many of the *Chronika* contributors.

THE LENINGRAD TRIALS

We need freedom in order to be able
to fulfill our duty to Russia and to life.
—YURI GALANSKOV

The "Kolokol" Group

Early in 1966 the Western press reported the discovery of a
secret organization in Leningrad during November of 1965.
Nine of its leading members, among them the engineer
Valeri Ronkin, were brought to trial early in 1966[1] and sentenced to concentration-camp terms of two to seven years.

This organization is said to have had about 250 adherents calling themselves the Union of the Kommune Members, a name referring to the "proletariat democracy" of the
1871 Parisian Commune. Group leadership rested in the
hands of chemistry students of the University of Leningrad.
This illegal group—which apparently had branches in two
other Russian cities, Novosibirsk and Omsk—considered itself a "Marxistic circle" of "liberal" members. Their activity,
apparently based on Marxistic and, to all intents and purposes, early Leninistic precepts, was directed against the
form of communism then practiced by the Soviet authori-

ties. The group's main demand was freedom of speech and thought. It was reported that this considerably large union possessed its own printing facilities, and was thus able to publish the journal known as *Kolokol (The Bell)*.

If nothing more, the very name of this underground newspaper reminds one of the famous journal that the socialist Aleksandr Gercen (Herzen) published in the middle of the previous century while exiled in London. With this publication the Leningrad group obviously intended to continue the tradition established by those previous moderate socialists, whose newsletter had exercised great influence on the Russian intelligentsia of its time.

Number 24 of the Leningrad *Kolokol,* which is said to have attained a circulation of a thousand copies, managed to reach the West. *Posev*, an emigrant newspaper, published its four articles. Among other things, these articles were concerned with an essay obviously directed against Suslov, a member of the Politburo, and his questionable role in the racial policies of Stalin's regime.[2] In another article the author spoke of the dangers of a new Stalinism, and emphatically warned against its revival.[3] In still another essay, advocating the multiple-party system for the Soviet Union (*see page 480*), the author dutifully examined the pros and cons of such a form of government. His conclusions are especially interesting in view of the fact that many Soviet citizens reject a multiple-party system, largely because they believe that the rulers would neglect the true interest of the country in their battle to obtain for themselves the support of the voters.

The author of the essay (Volgin is apparently a pseudonym) decides, however, that in a state without an opposing party the power system is not subjected to any control and for that reason nothing stands in the way of despotism. As a result of the one-party system, the Soviet Union has managed to transform itself into one huge concentration camp.

The Christian Socialist Union

"Down with the Communist Party of the Soviet Union!" This and similar slogans are said to have appeared on bulletin boards in the philosophy, jurisprudence, and other facilities of the Leningrad University toward the end of 1966.

According to uncensored reports in *Chronika,* the trial against four members of an allegedly conspiratorial movement took place in November, 1967, in Leningrad. The movement identified itself as the All-Russian Christian-Socialist Union for the Liberation of the People. This organization, founded in 1964, was discovered in March of 1967. Considering the large number of state informers and secret-police officers active at that time, this group managed to exercise its underground activities for a surprising length of time. There are reports, however, that the KGB was already on the trail of the group one year after it was founded, but refrained from taking any action at that time, lacking the evidence which would have enabled them to ascertain and arrest the greatest number of members.

The exact size of this organization is unknown, but in February and March of 1967 approximately sixty persons were arrested, not only in Leningrad, but also in the Siberian cities of Irkutsk and Tomsk, and in Petrozavodsk, a city situated north of Leningrad. According to the report of a Swede who has recenty been released from Dubrovlag, a total of three hundred members of the group were supposedly arrested.[4] *Chronika* published a short synopsis of the group's program:

> *The establishment of a democratic order: The head of state will be elected by the entire population, and be responsible to the parliament. The controlling body, the Sobor (church assembly)—that is, the representatives of religion—possesses the right to veto the head of state and the parliament. The land belongs to the state, and will be leased to private individuals or to a collective (exploitation is prohibited); salaried work will be permitted only upon the foundation of equality. The greater part of industrial activities belongs to the workers' collectives; the most important branches of the economy, such as transportation, electricity, etc., shall be nationalized. The fundamental principle of the economy is personalism.[5]*

The obviously militant anti-Communistic program of the group (the full text of which is not yet available in the West) gives the impression that a liberation from the Communist regime is only possible through an armed confrontation.

> *For a complete victory, the people needs its underground army, which will overthrow the*

dictatorship and annihilate the Black Shirts
of the oligarchy.[6]

According to its announcements, the Christian-Socialist Union (abbreviated in Russian to VSCHON) regards Bolshevism as a "tragic stage in the national development" of its land; its precepts condemn it as amoral, anti-human, and anti-national.

The author of a *Samizdat* article, which was written in 1969 and has in the meantime reached the West (the essay was first published anonymously), offers critical arguments against the methods and goals of the Christian-Socialist Union. He rejects the militantly anti-Communist position of the group and compares it to a "belligerent religious order." According to him, the VSCHON considered voluntarism[7] a standard for political action. Moreover, the organization opposed Bolshevism as being above all a hypothetical force, and at the same time ignored the national-political power factor in Soviet Communism. To be fair, the author also praised some of the positive characteristics in the outline of the union's goals, including for instance its economic and cultural-political program, its concepts of private possessions, the humanization of justice, the normalization of cultural relations with foreign countries, and the reinstatement of Christian institutions.

The charter of the movement demonstrates its highly secret nature, based on a triple compartmental system:

Everyone knows the oldest and second oldest
members in his group. Moreover, he recruits

new members, forming another group of three, of which he is now the oldest. The head of the organization does not know the individual members; if necessary, they can appeal to him in writing or through the oldest member of any group.[8]

According to reports in *Chronika,* the organization was mainly concerned with obtaining new members and circulating forbidden literature. Among works to be circulated were *The New Class* by Djilas, works of the philosophers Berdiayev and Soloviev, *The History of Bolshevik Russia* by the German historian Georg von Rauch, etc. The works of Nikolai Berdiayev, the anti-Communist philosopher who died in exile, appear to have played a particularly important role in this underground body. One group, which stood in close relationship to the Christian-Socialist Union, called itself the Berdiayev Circle.

Most of the leading members of the organization were intellectuals. State accusations against them mentioned either conspiracy or high treason. In November, 1967, as a result of the proceedings, the Oriental scholar and translator Igor Ogurcov was sentenced to fifteen years at forced labor in a work camp. His colleague Mikhail Sado received thirteen years; Yevgeny Vagin, the literary scholar, ten years; and the lawyer Averochkin eight years. At the time of their conviction, the four accused were between twenty-eight and thirty years old.

The trial against seven other members of the illegal movement took place on the fourteenth of March and continued to the fifth of April, 1968. As with the December trial, these hearings took place behind closed doors. This time the accused were all between twenty and thirty-three years of age, and prominent among them was the Oriental scholar Vyacheslav Platonov. With the exception of a locksmith and a mechanic, all these men again were intellectuals; most of them were graduates of Leningrad University (LGU). Up until their arrests, one of them—Nikolai Ivanov—had been a lecturer at LGU; another, Leonid Borodin, was the director of a school. The sentences meted out to these men ranged from one to seven years.

The convicted men were brought to the camp complex at Dubrovlag. Ogurcov was later transferred to the prison at Vladimir. His physical condition was reported to have been so bad that for awhile he was not expected to survive. In an open letter written from the camp and addressed to Boris Polevoi, editor of *Junost,* the writer Aleksandr Petrev-Agatov wrote about his companions in suffering and the members of the Christian-Socialist Union: ". . . All that they wanted, and still want, is to· see their native country free from tyranny. In that, and in that alone, lies their guilt. It is not an accident that one of the prison songs runs as follows:

> *Yesterday while still students and soldiers,*
> *We were used to thinking and daring.*
> *Russia, our mother, rewarded us*
> *By dressing us in prison stripes.*[9]

As with the Kolokol Group, the proceedings against the Christian-Socialist Union were concerned with an outspoken underground organization which, unlike the movement for civil rights, was not involved with public activities since its program did not coincide with the letter of the Soviet Constitution. This might also apply to the underground groups mentioned in connection with Andrei Amalrik, the Krasnopevcev-Rendel group (whose members were sentenced in 1956), the Osipov-Kusnecov group (convicted in 1961), and the Dergunov group (discovered in 1967).

The diverse, often naïve, and frequently undeveloped theories which many of these groups proposed should not be judged primarily by their political relevance. The unmistakable value of the groups lies much more in their attempts, under conceivably adverse circumstances, to find alternative solutions for the problems facing them—solutions which, at that time, stood outside political and ideological systems but would eventually affect these systems in every area, especially in questions concerning morality and ethics.

THE DEMOCRATS'
PROGRAM

Socialism will develop through all phases to its most extreme consequences, and finally to insanity. Then, however, a stentorian cry for retribution will echo from the breast of the revolutionary minority and the fatal wrestling will begin all over again. But this time socialism will be in the place currently occupied by the conservatives, and will be defeated by the future revolution, although we do not know yet what form this revolution will take.

—ALEKSANDR GERCEN (HERZEN)

These words of the Russian freedom fighter and socialist stand at the head of the Program of the Democratic Movement in the Soviet Union.[1] Drawn up by the "democrats of Russia, the Ukraine, and the Baltics," this proposal is the first meaningful attempt to formulate in one general statement the goals of obviously different groups of Soviet dissidents, and to provide a vision of the possible political future of the country. The most remarkable thing about this plan is the fact of its being put together by individuals of different age and vocational backgrounds, and also by representatives of various moral, ethical, and political convictions. At the same time, representatives of various internal Soviet nationalities had a voice in determining and evaluating the title. In addition to the Russians themselves, these included mostly Ukrainians and Baltic peoples. Despite a few illusionary passages—those, for example, dealing with the potential effectiveness of the United Nations—the significance of this program cannot be disputed. Next to the letter of Sakharov, Turchin, and Medvedev (which can be loosely described as a program of the "reformed Communists"), the above-mentioned document is perhaps the most important political phenomenon that has yet appeared from the "democratic movement."

This program's similarity to the so-called memorandum of the Estonian scientific intelligentsia (*see page 486*) and also to the letter of Alekseev, allegedly the same as the one from fleet officer Gavrilov (*see page 440*), seems to support the conjecture that the authors of these two documents stand in close contact with those responsible for the overall plan. If this is so, it could mean that several of the supporters of this new draft of the Constitution are to be found within the ranks of the military.

Unlike Sakharov, Turchin, and Medvedev, the authors of the "democratic" program do not proceed from the CPSU's leadership, but rather work out their principles according to the guidelines of a parliamentarian democracy. (Of course, it is completely plausible that tactical factors forced Sakharov, Turchin, and Medvedev to go only halfway in their democratizing proposition. These considerations have had a lot to do with the possible acceptance of their suggestions by the ruling administration.)

The authors of the 14,000-word program acknowledge the Declaration of Human Rights as the foundation for the social concept they envision, and simultaneously maintain that the Constitution of the Union of Soviet Socialist Republics is an undemocratic imitation of a real constitution. Not even equality among the classes has been accomplished in the Soviet Union under Communism; the nation's development ironically enough appears to be dictated by the conditions characteristic of a democracy, but in fact has not been carried out according to the expected procedures of a "class struggle."

The program proposes the establishment of a new state, to be called The Union of Democratic Republics. Free elections, separation of power, establishment of a constitutional court system, and the abolition of the secret police are all demanded.

As for economic questions, heavy industry is to remain nationalized, light industry to fall to cooperative producers' associations, and small businesses to be turned over to private ownership. These three types of ownership are to have equal standing with one another. For the stabilization of the currency, a ceiling on the price of gold is recommended.

Racially the program provides for the realization of sovereign rights by means of a plebiscite under the supervision of the United Nations. Cultural and economic autonomy would be guaranteed to those groups who wished to remain within the political organization. Territorial conflicts are to be settled by an arbitration commission provided by the

United Nations. In addition, all non-Russian groups are to be reimbursed for losses of any kind resulting from governmental demands of earlier and, most particularly the current, regimes. The proposition states:

> *The progressive Russian intelligentsia understands and clearly realizes that without freedom for the various racial groups, there can be no freedom for the individual and no genuine democratizing of society.*[2]

In the area of foreign political affairs, the authors of the program suggest a reconciliation with capitalistic countries, particularly with the United States, hoping in this way to bring about a growing mutual rapprochement. At the same time, they look for a gradual reconciliation with China, which at the moment represents the most threatening of all external dangers to the Soviet Union. The "democrats" lay the greatest blame for this development on "irresponsible Soviet leadership and its social-imperialistic doctrine" (their own words). The supporters of the program seek a complete disarmament under United Nations control to be achieved within an appropriate length of time, not only in the U.S.S.R. but also in the United States and Western Europe. A United Nations commission should undertake a revision of the postwar boundaries in Eastern and Middle Europe; Germany should become one democratic political entity. The principle of noninterference in the internal affairs of the various socialist countries should be upheld; by means of free elections the people of these countries must decide for themselves whatever questions may arise concerning their political and economic systems. The Soviet troops must be recalled, and unequal treaties must be revised.

Soviet citizens themselves should not be subjected to any limitations in their travel, and a free exchange of information must be allowed. Complete freedom and noninterference from the state is demanded in art, culture, science, and research. Finally, the program concludes with a short six-point summation:

(1) In the political arena: individual freedom and a democratic state which guarantees the observation of the thirty principles of the Declaration of Human Rights.

(2) In the economic arena: social security (a system of public assistance) and an economic system that guarantees equal rights and access to whatever means of production are necessary in various undertakings that are either state, group, or privately owned.

(3) Complete self-determination and free decisions in plebiscites (in racial questions).

(4) In the cultural arena: freedom of creativity and noninterference by the state in the intellectual workings of society.

(5) In matters concerning foreign policy: reconciliation with the capitalistic countries and political self-determination for the socialist states.

(6) In matters concerning domestic policy: racial
and class peace, legal equality for all classes,
and a multiple-party system.[3]

Following this six-point summation, the authors have
appended an appeal to the citizens of the Soviet Union:

*We, the participants in the democratic move-
ment, young and old, representatives of various social levels, vocations, and nationalities
as well as different personal convictions, ma-
terialists and idealists, atheists and believers,
socialists, Communists and nationalists, con-
sumed by the desire for justice, for a humane
constitutional order, for freedom and the
sanctity of the individual, for a complete
democracy—we have used this document to
express our views, expectations, and hopes,
and have pointed out in it the paths to an
evolution in the reform of the Soviet society.*

*We would once again remind every citi-
zen of this country that fourteen million completely innocent people have died simply
because of the passivity displayed by every
social level of our society, and as a result of
the lack of democracy in our land. We would
remind them that this danger is still very real
today, despite a definite moderation on the
part of the regime. The forces of repression
are powerful—once again political trials are*

taking place, once again the concentration camps are being filled with honest and respectable men, once again healthy men are being confined in mental institutions. We would remind them that no single citizen of the Soviet Union—beginning with the simple workers right on up to the most respectable and highly honored personalities—is safe from despotism and coercion. Therefore we want to unite ourselves into one organized democratic order! Let each one of us render this smallest of services—to rebel everywhere and at all times against lawlessness, despotism, and exploitation!

We are appealing to the intelligentsia, to the creative and technical intelligentsia, to those holding governmental positions! Create new spiritual values and carry them to the people! Take a courageous stand behind your "I," behind your convictions!

Workers and farmers! Fight for your political rights and for a higher standard of living! Make use of the means of economic expression open to you—the strike! Our prosperity depends upon ourselves. Don't be mute slaves. Don't believe the demagogues who promise you and your descendants mountains of gold.

Youth! You are the future of the land! Courageously support democracy! The final fate of our society depends upon you.

Soldiers! Be alert in the fulfillment of your high duties to protect our native country. Don't aim your weapons against your fellow citizens, against your brothers and sisters. Be worthy citizens of our country so that society will not find you and your children deficient in those qualities. Be honorable, do not defile yourselves with the slaughter of a peaceful and unarmed people.

Members of the secret police! Your job is to fight against spies, but not against democratic forces. Don't forget that many of your colleagues, who eagerly fought against an alleged "counterrevolution" and against the "enemies of the people," have themselves been killed by their own swords. Consider the fate of your many predecessors!

We, the democrats of this country, declare that we are determined to fight without hesitation for the proclaimed values, to pay no deference to the difficulties and the sacrifices, to fight for the freedom and the prosperity of the people. We, the democrats of this country, call to all honest, thoughtful, and courageous citizens of all ages and sexes, of every class, nationality, and religion, to participate in the peaceful and nonviolent struggle for the high ideals of democracy. We, the democrats of this country, pass on our holy struggle for a free democratic society as a heritage to our glorious, uncompromising youth and to the coming generations, in the event we have to suffer a temporary defeat. Democrats of the Soviet Union! Unite, fight, win!

THE DEMOCRATS OF RUSSIA, THE UKRAINE,
AND THE BALTICS, U.S.S.R., 1969.[4]

DISSIDENTS
IN THE ARMY

*The immeasurably heroic deeds per-
formed during the war, and the taste
of victory over the enemy mean nothing—in the judgment of the spirit and
of the century—when compared to the
courage of the individual citizen of
the state.*

KONDRATI RYLEEV

Oleg Penkovski, a successful officer of the secret police, was
the first man of his rank to become a spy for the West because of his political convictions. Condemned to death in
May of 1963, Colonel Penkovski presumably faced the firing
squad in Moscow and was executed. His secret reports appeared in several translations in Western lands.[1]

Although the Soviet public was able to learn nothing
more specific about the case concerning Penkovski, they
played a greater part in the totally different fate of Major
General Petr Grigorenko, one of the most active and most
daring critics of the outdated Soviet dogmatism.[2] Even
Genrich Altunjan, the civil-rights fighter imprisoned in a
concentration camp in 1969 because of political opposition,

remained an instructor in the Academy of War at Charkov with the rank of major until his discharge from the army in 1968.

The army, and above all the officers' corps, has not yet recovered from the wounds which the Revolution, the civil and world wars, and, finally, Stalin's purges have inflicted upon it. In the current distribution of power, Soviet military organizations have been deprived of practically every influential role they might have played earlier in political events. Neither this fact nor the memory of the mass murders of their commanding officers have favorably affected the relationship between the Party leadership and the armed forces. And yet these very armed forces maintain the façade of an obedient rank of functionaries that continues even today to applaud Stalin, the man who not only decimated their ranks during the purges but who also at the beginning of the second World War had also senselessly sacrificed and continually degraded them.

Nevertheless, today there are unmistakable movements afoot in the army, not only those that are dogmatically Stalinist, but some that even appear to be thinking along the lines of a free and constitutional state. There are obvious groups in the army closely connected with the civil-rights movement or whose end goals at least betray a certain similarity to their civilian counterparts'.

A more spectacular incident than that concerning Penkovski occurred on January 23, 1969, when shots were fired into a column of vehicles belonging to the Party leadership. With the exception of a single chauffeur, no one was seriously injured. In an announcement by TASS two days later it was reported that the perpetrator (who had been arrested in the meantime) was an "agitator." More than a year later it was reported in the Soviet press that the assailant, a twenty-two-year-old lieutenant from Leningrad named Ilin, had been confined in a "special" psychiatric clinic as "mentally disturbed." [3] Any further particulars concerning this incident were kept strictly confidential by officials apparently taking great pains to hasten the incident into oblivion. Ever since the shot Fanny (Dora) Kaplan fired at Lenin in 1918, and the assault in 1934 that claimed the life of the Leningrad Party Secretary S. Kirov, no similar incident had been recorded in the Soviet Union.

Anatole Shub, a *Washington Post* correspondent who was deported from the U.S.S.R. in May of 1969, reported admittedly contradictory rumors being circulated on one side within the circles of the leadership and on the other by the offices of the secret security police. According to the KGB version of the story, Ilin had been under contract with a "counter-revolutionary group of conspirators," and some of his supporters were even high-ranking army officers. Obviously, representatives of the secret police saw in this incident an opportunity finally to initiate arrests on a grand scale. According to unofficial rumors, however, the Department of the Interior felt that the case concerning the lieutenant from Leningrad involved an "individual paranoid," a Soviet Oswald type. Ilin supposedly traveled from his Leningrad garrison to Moscow where he was said to have borrowed a police uniform from a relative, took up his position near the Borovicki Gate of the Kremlin, and from this vantage point fired the shots at the head of the Soviet leadership. (Ilin could not have known that arrangement of the automobiles was switched at the last minute, causing his bullets to be aimed unwittingly at a car carrying astronauts.)

Members of the "democratic" intelligentsia, according to Shub, compared the Leningrad lieutenant with officers of the Decembrists, as well as with *narodnik* terrorists. A rumor stemmed from this group that Ilin, when questioned by Andropov, chief of the secret police, as to his motives, made the statement that he wanted "to wake Russia up." [4] This may very well be a total fabrication, but it does express the currently reigning attitude among nonconforming intellectuals. The supposition, repeatedly mentioned in the West, that this case was analogous to the Kirov affair because the Leningrad lieutenant had been used by the administration as a cover for their own attempts at a new purge, seems unlikely.

Perhaps Ilin's unsuccessful attempt was the deed of a single individual who had acted out of the conviction that he was rendering his country a necessary service. Most of the progressive intelligentsia of Russia rejected this sort of militancy—not only because they felt that the risk was far out of proportion to the possible benefit of such an act, but also because they considered this approach as detrimental to their cause, if not totally immoral. They realized very clearly that the terrorist actions of the *narodnaja volja* (a group calling themselves "the will of the people") [5] and other extremist groups of the nineteenth and early twentieth centuries had only strengthened the reactionary forces of the state and caused the country further misfortunes. Disgusted by the brutality and despotism of the Party and the regime, the dissidents also had no desire to put themselves on the same level as that of their rulers. As Pavel Litvinov once expressed it when speaking about himself, the majority of the intellectuals had banished their former feelings and now were "against every form of coercion, whether it originated from positions above or below." [6]

According to several rumors circulating in Leningrad shortly after the abortive assassination attempt in Moscow, an underground organization had been discovered whose goal was armed rebellion against the regime and whose members mainly consisted of military officers. These rumors thickened as Leningrad was barred for the entire month of March, 1969, to foreigners then living in Moscow. (Unlike tourists, such aliens were not controlled by guides and leaders.)

In its eighth, ninth, tenth, and eleventh issues, *Chronika* reported the arrest of thirty-one civilians and members of the atomic submarine fleet in May, 1969. Approximately one quarter of those who had been apprehended are said to have been Estonians, and the majority apparently were supporters of the "democratic movement." Reports further stated that the officers had established a "League in the Struggle for Political Rights." (In other references reports speak of an "Alliance of the Soldiers for Political Freedom.")

Late in October of 1969 the Western press reported that in June of that year (actually in May) members of the Soviet submarine fleet had been arrested for "nonconformism." [7] *Chronika* mentioned three officers whose names were well known: Paramonov, Kosyrev, and Gavrilov. Gavrilov was identified as the author of the "Letter to the Citizens of the Soviet Union," Gennadi Alekseev (*see page 440*). The policy commissioner of the submarine fleet was also said to be among those arrested.

According to these reports, the officers had signed a

letter condemning the invasion of Czechoslovakia. Alekseev's letter also criticized the surprise attack on Czechoslovakia and took exception to Sakharov's memorandum. He praised the treatise but considered Sakharov's reform suggestions ineffectual because they were too mild and too superficial. Many clues pointed to the supposition that the arrest of the officers had resulted somehow from their mutual cooperation in composing the Program of the Democratic Movement or circulating it, and that these officers had perhaps participated in the evolution of this program. According to *Chronika*, the KGB held hearings of several hundred persons in connection with the arrest of the fleet officers and had instigated approximately thirty house searchings, particularly in Leningrad, Moscow, Tallinn, Riga, Baku, Perm, and Chabarovsk. If these investigations indicate anything, it would seem that such underground activity has permeated the entire width and breadth of the Soviet Union.

On September 2, 1970, United Press International (UPI) reported that Gavrilov had been sentenced to six years in a work camp and Kosyrev to two years imprisonment. Paramonov was confined to an insane asylum under forced "treatment." Sergei Soldatov, an engineer allegedly closely associated with the group, was also held in a "psychiatric clinic." In its eleventh issue, *Chronika* published the minutes of the five hearings held by the KGB in Soldatov's case. (It is assumed that these minutes reached the hands of the opposing intellectuals by means of a leak within the ranks of the secret police.) Soldatov's answers to the sometimes completely absurd questions of the secret-police officials revealed fearlessness and strength of character, as well as a high degree of intelligence. To the accusation that he imperiled the reputation of the Soviet Union with his loud arfd obvious protests against the arrest of political dissidents, Soldatov replied that it was not a question of national reputation but of the principle of the thing.

> *It is a question of the freedom of speech and creativity. Besides, one fearless defender of freedom is worth more than one million cowards.*[8]

Incidentally, during the police raid and search of his home, correspondence between Soldatov and the writer Vladimir Pomerancev was discovered, the same Pomerancev whose essay "Concerning the Integrity in Literature" had aroused so much attention in 1954.

It was reported that a few years before the events of June, 1969, nine officers of the atomic submarine fleet stationed in Leningrad were arrested for the "propagation of illegal literature" and then condemned to severe prison terms, ranging all the way up to fifteen years. This indicates that many of the illegal organizations discovered during the past years had their headquarters in Leningrad, formerly known as St. Petersburg, which had been known as the "Cradle of the Revolution" and the center of intellectual discontent ever since the Decembrist uprising in 1825.

ANDREI AMALRIK AND THE DISCUSSION ABOUT THE FUTURE OF RUSSIA

The time has finally come in which the basic ignorance of Russia has become a threat to our security. We must now recognize the fundamental causes which have forced this gargantuan regime to overstep its boundaries and painfully oppress the rest of the world.

PETR CHAADAEV

Andrei Amalrik is one of the most original, clever, and incorruptible figures, both intellectually and morally, of the intellectual opposition in Russia today. He was born in 1938 to a family boasting many well-known historians, and was expelled from Moscow University in 1961 because, in his dissertation about "The Normans and the Russians of Kiev," he supported a position contradicting the official interpretation of this historical event. Thereafter the talented young historian, whose scholarly career was now reduced to ashes, tried his hand at various vocations, first as a construction worker, then map maker, journalist, mailman, etc.

In his spare time he wrote short theater pieces, none of which were ever produced but nevertheless were indirectly responsible (along with his contacts with Western journalists) for his arrest in 1965 and his subsequent exile to Siberia for two years. He was prematurely pardoned in 1966, however, and later described his exile experiences in a book entitled *Involuntary Trip to Siberia*.[1]

Amalrik was arrested again on May 20, 1970, and accused of having violated Paragraph 190 of the Penal Code. A group of Soviet dissidents protested against his arrest, as well as some well-known French historians and a group of Dutch writers.

Sverdlovsk, one of the cities barred to tourists, lies about a thousand miles from Moscow, and it was here on November 12, 1970, that Amalrik received sentence to three years imprisonment in a work camp under severe conditions. (The physicist Leo Ubozhko had been accused of circulating *Samizdat* materials, including a piece written by Amalrik, and was condemned with him to the same camp.) The sentence exceeded the one demanded by the public prosecutor. In Amalrik's case, according to his accusers during the trial, the court was confronted, not with a historian, but rather with a "dimwitted slanderer." The most incriminating evidence against him turned out to be his essay, "Will the Soviet Union Survive the Year 1984?" Amalrik referred to the Soviet Constitution and declared the trial illegal. In his concluding statement that lasted an hour, Amalrik maintained that the general persecution and "witch-hunts" of the regime, as well as his own trial, aroused in him neither respect nor fear. "Everything that is taking place right now can only be described as the cowardice of the regime, which sees some danger in the circulation of any thoughts or ideas that are foreign to its bureaucratic elite . . . I believe that I am a better patriot than they, who blare out their love for their native country but really mean their love of their own privileges . . . It seems to me that the main task of my country today lies in casting off the burden of its heavy past. To do so, nothing is more important and more necessary than free critical discussion, not self-glorification." [3]

Amalrik's behavior before the court and the conviction of this particularly imperiled man, despite his poor health, provide sufficient proof against the irresponsible accusation, chiefly made by several Western journalists, that Amalrik's works were not conceived as a result of genuine political opposition, but actually were written with the knowledge and support of the KGB.[4] Less than five months later, suffering from tubercular meningitis, Amalrik was admitted to a hospital. From there, he was transferred in June of 1971 to the infamous "death" camp at Kolyma.

In his critical evaluation of his people and of the Russian intellectual tradition, Amalrik resembles more than anyone else the famous nineteenth-century Russian thinker, Petr Chaadaev.[5] Many Russian emigrants, and even some people who remained in Russia, accused Amalrik of a lack of patriotism, even of being a Russophobe. In his turn, the author of the essay about "1984" maintained that a good patriot was not he who sought to hide the mistakes and weaknesses of his country, but he who "exposes these wounds, in order to heal them."

Wrote Amalrik:

I love my land in which I was born and raised, and I can't think about her extraordinary fate without shedding tears. Separation from this country would be a great burden for me, but I confess with bitterness that I am not happy with this land. If it were possible for me to choose before my birth, I would have preferred to be born in a small country, a land such as Biafra or Israel, that fights for its freedom with weapons in its hands.[6]

Although he never participated in any of the political demonstrations (he had, however, along with his wife Gjusel, demonstrated in 1968 in front of the British Embassy against their weapon loans to Nigeria, and as a result had lost his job) and had refrained from entering his signature on any of the many protest documents of the civil-rights movement, Amalrik remains one of the most courageous and uncorrupted representatives of this movement.

Toward the end of 1969 he wrote an open letter to the writer Anatoli Kuznecov, who had by now fled to England. In it he congratulated the writer on his opportunity to live and work from then on in a free country. At the same time he defended the value of "inner" freedom as against that of "outer" or external freedom; this inner freedom was such that "under it the authorities could do many things to a man, but it made it impossible for them to rob this individual of his personal moral values."[7] Incidentally, this letter is less directed to Kuznecov personally than to the Soviet intelligentsia in general, who, according to Amalrik, allowed themselves all too willingly to be frightened by the practices of the secret police, instead of opposing them with a large measure of fearlessness, self-confidence, and moral conviction. The regime continued to exist—if not completely, at least mainly—on the taxes it gleaned from this fear, the bulk of which had been accumulating since Stalin's era. No repression, however, could be effective without people who were willing to submit themselves to it.

The first part of Amalrik's study, "Will the Soviet Union Survive the Year 1984?" is unquestionably one of the most profound analyses of Soviet society ever written, at least in this particular field. There were three main reasons which moved the author to write this book and he enumerates them elsewhere. The main reason concerned the alarming impression that his country was about to be thrown directly into catastrophe. The second had to do with the author's desire to refute a mistaken belief circulating in the West that the Soviet Union was progressively liberalizing. According to Amalrik, rather than becoming more liberal, it was in fact becoming more and more senile. As an example, Amalrik pointed to the immense extent and popularity of the *Samizdat* literature. These *Samizdat* writings owed their strength not to the fact that the ruling authorities forbade them, but that in the end the authorities were powerless to prevent their appearance.

A further reason for Amalrik's writing his book was simply that, like every author, he wanted to put his thoughts into words, especially since he had not succeeded in getting his opinions published in the official Soviet press.[8]

The author proceeded to characterize the "democratic movement" which appeared, he maintained, as the successor to the post-Stalinist "cultural opposition." Within the general demand for greater security under the law, Amalrik saw an essential prerequisite for the emergence of such a movement. In the analysis that followed, he divided contemporary Soviet society into four main groups: (1) supporters of the many-sided "democratic movement," (2) the "class of specialists," (3) civil servants, (4) the officers and the people. As he stated at the beginning of his work, Amalrik did not believe in a "liberalization" of the Soviet system; those incipient reforms just beginning to emerge tended toward nothing more than the illusion of reform. Amalrik pointed out the internal decline of power within the regime as the situation which the "democratic movement" had to confront. He hoped that in time the movement would construct a strong and inclusive program and would find numerous adherents.

To be sure, the author did not consider the strength of the so-called "middle class" (within which he included writers, scholars, and technicians)—always the first thing to be considered when talking about support for the "democratic movement"—as sufficient to allow the movement to "engage at some time in a real fight with the regime." Amalrik considered the movement's support throughout the masses of the people in a rather negative light, although he did admit that no one really knew "which approaches were effective among the masses." According to him, the discontent of the population was obvious all over the land and in the event of a standstill, or perhaps even a regression in the growth of prosperity, would lead to a commotion unthinkable in earlier days, even to acts of violence. The author realized, however, that the greatest obstacle facing the movement was the lack of a tradition of freedom in Russia.

He felt that the word "freedom" for the majority of the people was synonymous with the word "disorder," providing the possibility for committing acts that were dangerous and inimical to society. This lack of tradition and poor education were responsible for the lack of understanding on the part of the lower levels of the population when it came to upholding the worth of the individual. As a result of an untiring propaganda program that continually sought to polarize the "personal" against the "social," even the slightest emphasis on the latter was enough to keep the "interest for the personal" synonymous with "all that was ugly and egoistic." [9]

Amalrik states that any change is unacceptable to the Soviet power system since this would mean a loss of its own power. Therefore, the author investigates the possibilities that a change or alteration in the foreign political situation might create. In this connection he not only considers the possibility of war between the Union of Soviet Socialist Republics and China, but also maintains that an armed confrontation is inevitable in light of the progress of current developments. Armed with a very convincing argument, Amalrik proceeds in his assumption that such a war would hardly mean an atomic struggle between the two powers, but rather that the Chinese would eventually succeed in their attempt to force their superior techniques on the Soviet Union. This part of Amalrik's study is necessarily speculative and hypothetical; and least convincing (if not totally improbable) is the final part of the book. (The author completely ignores the possibility of at least a temporary Soviet-Chinese understanding after the death of Mao.) At this point in his treatise, Amalrik considers the possibility that a power shift in the West might benefit the Soviet Union. (By West he means the current East European satellite states.) Finally he prophesies the end of the Soviet empire, a situation brought about by its own voluntary isolation, as well as by the economic collapse such a war would cause, and finally, by the general distaste of the population for war. Since the actual confrontation would take place far from the important centers of the country, however, the population would never rise up in revolt as it did against the invasion of Hitler's Germany.

Amalrik saw the eventual possibility of a Soviet commonwealth as a salutary development and the disintegration of the present Soviet Union into a multiplicity of small individual states as an inauspicious development. Some of these would fall to China under certain circumstances, he believed. In any event, the author also considered the possibility that nothing he had predicted and explored would occur.

The Russian historian's statements are admittedly interesting, in many respects debatable and in many others even begging for contradiction. Naturally, they must be viewed as only hypothetical. The question remains about the kind of initial reception his fellow countrymen gave Amalrik's thoughts (always supposing they had some access to the work in the first place), and what this reception might be now. The brilliantly written study not only provided stimulating material for discussion, but actually seemed to approximate closely to suppositions of more than a few members of the intelligentsia. To be sure, two critical replies appearing in *Samizdat* described Amalrik as unrealistic and pessimistic.[10] On the other hand, in a letter published in *Chronika,*

the historian Petr Jakir greeted Amalrik's essay as an example of correct and clever thought. Although he expressed a
fundamental agreement with the theses Amalrik put forth,
Jakir nevertheless showed himself to be more optimistic
with respect to the future of the "democratic movement."
He admitted that at the moment this movement was not
especially popular with the people because few knew about
it and it was forced to operate under extraordinarily difficult conditions. Nevertheless, the ideas thus spawned had
begun to circulate throughout the country. "And that," continued Jakir, "is the beginning of an irreversible process of
self-liberation." [11]

The authors of another article that appeared in *Samizdat*
under the title "Time Doesn't Wait" were more skeptical.
These men, the Leningrad engineer N. Alekseev and the
teacher S. Zorin (these names are undoubtedly pseudonyms), warn of the dangers of a war in which the present
power system would unquestionably lead the country, as
long as those wielding that power maintained their present
course in domestic, foreign, and economic policy. The leadership was isolated from the population and insufficiently,
if not falsely, informed about the real state of the nation.
(This situation arose, beginning with the lowest level of
bureaucratic administration, because each individual, in the
interests of his own career, made his reports to the next
person in command not always according to facts, but more
often according to the current official version of those facts.)
A false evaluation of the general status, the ominous economic policy, and the underestimation of external enemies
were leading the land to the brink of catastrophe. At the
same time, according to Zorin and Alekseev, the threat of

external enemies would be incessantly played up for all it was worth, in an attempt to avoid internal problems. The Soviet Union, they felt, found itself at a turning point in history. Her leaders were faced with the choice of either initiating genuine reforms, which would mean "to slacken the deathlike grip with which they controlled the economy," or else to risk everything, including the possibility of a world-wide atomic confrontation. Zorin and Alekseev appealed primarily to the scholars and scientists to resist any military buildups. They emphasized the urgency of fundamental reforms which would guarantee the development of a political democracy—that is, above all, freedom of speech and freedom of the press and a multiple-party system. The one-party system, they felt, was synonymous with fascism.

Even if the adherents of the "democratic movement" saw the most natural and most acceptable solution to the present totalitarianism in an "evolution of the power system," they seemed at the time to have very little chance of accomplishing it. The experiences of the past years, the standstill, the regression of the reforms Khrushchev attempted to effect, and finally, the Soviet invasion of Czechoslovakia, afforded little encouragement for hopes of a Soviet Dubchek. Also, it was more difficult for the reform forces in the u.s.s.r. to oppose a dogmatic and despotic leadership than it was for the liberals in Czechoslovakia, Poland, or some other satellite state. In those countries the Stalinists were synonymous with Soviet "colonial" power, and it is easier to fight against foreign chains than against one's own. For the moment, at least, the opposition of the progressive intelligentsia does not bring sufficient pressure to bear on those in power. The latter are more willing to sacrifice the best of their intellectual minds—and if not to sacrifice, at least to silence them—than to institute the necessary reforms, for they see a threat to their omnipotence in the changes that would inevitably occur under such reforms. Asks the writer Aleksandr Petrov-Agatov, a prisoner in the camps at Mordwinia:

> *Is it possible that in the 20th century normal people put other normal people behind bars, simply because the latter think and write differently than they do, or because they believe in God? . . . The Communist Party is wandering in the footsteps of the medieval inquisition. Tvardovski was persecuted, Pasternak was killed,[13] Solzhenitsyn crucified. Daniel is in handcuffs, Siniavski shovels sawdust . . . And what about the troops in Czechoslovakia? What about the blood bath in Hungary? And what was the reason for the incitement of the Arabs against Israel and thus bringing the whole world to the brink of an atomic catastrophe?*

Petrov-Agatov further observed that every great empire eventually faces extinction.

> *Carthage was reduced to ashes. Ruins are all that is left of the Roman Empire. Byzantium has long since disappeared from the map. Genghis Khan, Napoleon, Hitler—all have dis-*

> *appeared . . . and the empire of Soviet Com-*
> *munism will not meet its end any differently.*[14]

Insecurity and deception characterize the Soviet leadership. They do not practice their authority for the good of the people, but for the express purpose of strengthening their own power. The question remains whether a system which to all appearances no longer believes in its own ideological and economic discretion, but nevertheless continues to express its belief in them—whether an empire which came into being through violence, and which continues to operate by means of this violence, is capable of inner renewal and in accord with the "convergence theory" could peacefully approach the West.

THE DEFENDERS
OF CZECHOSLOVAKIA

*For me there was never any question
of whether or not I would go to Red
Square. It was my duty as a Soviet
citizen to raise my voice against the
recent deeds of our government, deeds
which I could never condone.*

—PAVEL LITVINOV BEFORE THE MUNICI-
PAL COURT OF MOSCOW, OCTOBER 11, 1968

Before the Invasion

Thanks to the broadcasts of Western radio stations, which
could still be received with relatively slight interference in
the U.S.S.R. until August of 1968, the Soviet population was
very well informed about the developments of the "Prague
spring." Also, by means of these radio broadcasts, the news
continued to come through even after Czechoslovakian newspapers had disappeared from Soviet kiosks.

As stated above, Sakharov positively appraised the
Czechoslovakian version of reformed Communism in his
memorandum. In doing so, the famous physicist not only ex-

pressed his own feelings but also those of wide areas—if not the majority—of the intelligentsia. Even among the student population, the fascination of "socialism with a human face" made a deep impression. According to reports in *Chronika*, handbills were circulated around the University of Gorki in April, 1968, which urged the people "to follow the example of the Czechoslovakians." In November of the same year many students were expelled from the university for having circulated the 2,000-word manifesto of the Czechoslovakian writer Ludvik Vaculik.

The Prague reformers had long since become the targets of ominous Soviet persecution campaigns, and as the possibility of a military invasion gained increasing support in Moscow, five Soviet Communists of the Czechoslovakian Embassy in Moscow released a letter in July of 1968 expressing their sympathy and admiration for the progressive Czechoslovakians. (The letter was signed by Petr Grigorenko, Ivan Jachimovich, S. Pisarev, V. Pavlinchuk, and Aleksei Kosterin, a writer who has since died but who voluntarily resigned from the Party three months after the invasion of Czechoslovakia as a sign of protest against it.) *(See page 410.)* A short time later, on July 30, 1968, the young physicist Pavlinchuk from Obninsk died after he had lost his post and been expelled from the Party because of circulating *Samizdat* publications. (Pavlinchuk had been Secretary for his local Party office.) In their letter, addressed to "the Communists in Czechoslovakia and to all Czechoslovakians," these men criticized the "one-sided and unobjective" Soviet news reports about the occurrences in Czechoslovakia, as well as the threats official Soviet sources made against the Czech liberals.

On the first and second of August, 1968, five Leningrad intellectuals were arrested shortly after they had completed a letter of protest against the Soviet policy regarding Czechoslovakia and had even apparently succeeded in collecting a few signatures. Those arrested, all between thirty and thirty-three years of age, included the engineers E. Shashenkov and A. Studenkov, the chemical technician L. Kvachevski, and the lawyers Nikolai Danilov and Yuri Gendler. In the possession of some of these men, the security police found literature similar to that belonging to members of the Christian-Socialist Union.

Without benefit of legal proceedings, two of those arrested—N. Danilov and E. Shashenkov—were herded into psychiatric prisons as early as October, 1968. Ironically, Danilov had been an examining magistrate for the secret police organization during the fifties but had given up this position in favor of employment as a legal adviser, a job he had held ever since. Eventually he was dismissed, however, after he had sent a letter of complaint to Rudenko, the public prosecutor general, in March or April of 1968, together with Gendler, Kvachevaki, and Viktor Fainberg. A sojourn in a lunatic asylum was nothing new for Shashenkov: a letter he wrote to Stalin in 1950 while still a student was responsible for the first forced treatment he received in a mental institution. In 1963/64 he disappeared once again behind the walls of these "hospitals."

Kvachevski and Gendler were sentenced to four and three years, respectively, at hard labor in a state camp. Their co-defendant Studenkov, who declared himself guilty and had given testimony before the court which added to the burdens of the others, received the minimum punishment of one year and served his time in a Leningrad prison.

On July 22, 1968, Anatoli Marchenko, then thirty years old, sent an open letter to the editor of the Czechoslovakian newspapers *Rudé Právo, Práce,* and *Literárny Listi.* In it he sharply criticized the deceitful actions that the Soviet regime and other countries bound by the Warsaw Pact had perpetrated against the Czechoslovakians. At the same time he mentioned the danger of an invasion made ever more possible by the fear of these states for possible loss of their power and authority. "I am ashamed of my country," wrote Marchenko, "which all of a sudden has assumed the scandalous role of gendarme for all Europe." [1]

A few days after he posted his letter, Marchenko was arrested in Moscow under the pretense that he had supposedly violated the pass laws in some trivial respect. (As a former political prisoner who did not live in Moscow, he had been denied permission to reside in that city.) Marchenko was a worker, the son of simple parents (both his father and mother were illiterate), and had spent six years in prison camps following an abortive attempt in 1960 to flee to Iran. In a chilling report entitled *My Testimony,* [2] Marchenko described the sufferings he endured during his imprisonment. Other political prisoners have commented on this book, saying that the description is accurate to the smallest detail and is characteristic of the regimentation prevalent in concentration camps of Russia today. In the introduction to his book Marchenko wrote: "The purpose of this document is to state the truth about the present camps and prisons and to explain it to those who wish to hear it. I am convinced that my knowledge of the camps, and of life in them, is my single effective weapon in the struggle against evil and law-

lessness which is rampant today. . . ." [3] Marchenko was
well aware that publication of his book would mean another
imprisonment for him. Nevertheless, the only fear he had
was that he and his friends would not succeed in circulating
his report.

On August 21, 1968, the day the Soviets invaded Czechoslovakia, Anatoli Marchenko was sentenced for a second
time to one year at hard labor in a state camp. Because of
his book (which had appeared meanwhile in the West), the
now critically ill civil-rights fighter was sentenced on August
22, 1969, during a secret trial, to two additional years of
imprisonment.

A total of eight civil-rights fighters protested against
the arrest of Marchenko in August of 1968 with a petition to
the office of the public prosecutor and a proclamation to
the citizens of the u.s.s.r.[4] During the night of August 7,
Irina Belgorodskaya, an engineer, was arrested under the
pretense of having circulated letters in support of Marchenko. Before the court she declared herself not guilty as accused—that is, not guilty of propagating anti-Soviet propaganda—but nevertheless was sentenced on February 19,
1969, to one year in a work camp in accordance with Paragraph 190/1 of the Penal Code. As Petr Grigorenko, another leading figure in the civil-rights movement, observed
in his short sketch about the trial of Belgorodskaya, this was
the first time that a Soviet citizen was sentenced simply because he or she had spoken up in defense of another.[5] Up
until then the authorities had restrained themselves to less
severe reprisals in such cases.

At the time of Belgorodskaya's trial, approximately 150
people, consisting mainly of her friends and like-minded

colleagues, gathered in front of the courthouse. According to eyewitness reports, they applauded the accused and tossed flowers up to her, which were immediately trampled upon by the quickly assembling security police. Despite all fears to the contrary, legal proceedings were not taken against those who signed the petition, although in letters to the authorities they assumed total responsibility for the *Letter to the Citizens* while at the same time sharply protesting against the illegal nature of the trial.

After the Occupation

> *During the night of August 20, 1968, Russian panzer divisions invaded Czechoslovakia . . . On that day many people in Russia wept. This invasion, they said, heralded the turn toward fascism . . . I realized that I could no longer remain there, that every day, every month, and every year would only introduce even more horror and even more cowardice in my life.*[6]

These are the words of the well-known Soviet writer Anatoli Kuznecov following his successful flight to the West in July of 1969. Indeed, the occupation of Czechoslovakia seems to have thrown not only the intelligentsia but the whole Soviet population into such a condition of simultaneous depression and stimulation that the Party officials, at least those in the academic and scientific institutions, were generally forced to cancel those assemblies that were supposed to applaud the invasion. In almost every instance where duty demanded such convocations, there were reports that several of those present stood up and spoke out against the invasion.

> *Even if 95 percent of the unarmed population of the Soviet Union were to rise up in revolt, the remaining five percent, representing the powerful apparatus of suppression, would hold them down with armed force.*[7]

However, this sad truth, which Kuznecov wrote in another section of his report, also had validity—at least at that time.

In light of this fact, those who raised their voices loudly and fearlessly against the expansionary policies of their rulers, despite the growing dangers which might result from such actions, deserve much more admiration than was accorded to them. (These policies, when compared with those of the Czars, are even more explorative than the hypocritical phrases of Communistic history books indicate.)

Yevgeny Yevtushenko sent a telegram to Brezhnev and Kosygin venting his bitterness and horror over the Soviet action, and expressed his fears that the end results of this deed could not be overlooked. Complained the poet:

> *I don't know how I'm supposed to sleep any more, I don't know how I'm even going to go on living. All I know is that I have a moral duty to tell you the feelings that now overwhelm me.*[8]

Chronika reported numerous cases (17 stemmed from

Leningrad alone) in which Soviet citizens were either arrested, convicted, or pressured in some other fashion because of their protests against the invasion of Czechoslovakia. During the night of August 21, 1968, a twenty-year-old Leningrad youth was caught in the act of writing BREZHNEV, GET OUT OF CZECHOSLOVAKIA! on the various statues adorning that city's bridges. The young man (whose name was Boguslavski) was immediately condemned to five years hard labor in a concentration camp.

That same night, an Estonian student wrote CZECHO-SLOVAKIANS, WE ARE YOUR BROTHERS! on the walls of a movie house in Tartu. The student was so badly beaten while being arrested that he had to be hospitalized for serious internal injuries.

The police sought vainly those people responsible for writing the innumerable slogans which appeared on the walls of several office buildings in Akademgorodok during the night of August 25th. One of their slogans read: BAR-BARIANS, GET OUT OF CZECHOSLOVAKIA! A few days after the invasion, Vladimir Karasev, a physics student in Moscow, took up his position in the hall of the main building of Moscow University, set up a sign, and began to collect signatures protesting the invasion. Within a few minutes, indeed before he could collect five signatures, he was forcefully dragged off by suddenly ubiquitous security guards. Karasev's demonstration netted him a three-month confinement in a "psychiatric clinic." Following his release—in the meantime he had, of course, been expelled from school—he found a job as a stoker in a Moscow factory.

Valerija Novodvorskaya, a nineteen-year-old student, was arrested on December 5, 1969, as she passed out handbills during an opera intermission in the Moscow Kongress-palast. These handbills, written in the form of a poem, protested the occupation of Czechoslovakia and demanded observance of human rights in the Soviet Union. Once again, a talented student—one who had graduated with the highest marks in her class—was brought before the court in April of 1970 and declared feeble-minded, not responsible for her actions, and referred to an insane asylum.

The tragic fate of Ilia Rips from Riga, one of the shining lights of the university mathematics department, aroused particular sympathy. Rips was a recipient of the Lenin scholarship and had completed the requirements for his degree at the unusually young age of twenty. His professors considered his thesis good enough to use as the basis for his doctoral dissertation. On April 10, 1969, Rips was offered a position in the Physics Institute at the Latvian Academy of Sciences; this fact alone promised a glowing career. Three days later the young scientist carried a plac-ard with the slogan FREEDOM FOR CZECHOSLOVAKIA! during a demonstration at the Freedom Plaza in Riga and as a sign of the sincerity of his protest he set himself ablaze.[9] Some sailors who happened to be passing by rushed to his aid, and the brilliant student was admitted to a hospital under KGB guards.

Rips was later accused of having violated Paragraph 65 of the Latvian Penal Code—this corresponds to Paragraph 70 of the UK RSFSR—but was referred to a "special" psy-chiatric institution. His fellow students, who had offered to donate their skin for the necessary grafts, were said to have been censored by the university for having made such an offer. And according to recent reports in *Chronika,* Professor Plotkin, Rips' academic adviser, has been released from Riga University. Several of Rips' scientific articles, together with a biography of the talented mathematician, have appeared in *Samizdat*. Latest reports say that Rips is now busily engaged on scientific projects for the Latvian Academy of Sciences, although still confined to a mental institution. Apparently the Soviet authorities are none too keen on wasting extraordinary talent, even when such talent is officially declared irresponsible and feeble-minded.

Although he had been praised previously by the press for his outstanding contributions as chairman of a collective farm, the civil-rights fighter Ivan Yakhimovich was arrested on March 25, 1969, after he repeatedly called for the return of the Soviet troops from Czechoslovakia and supported the model of socialism that Prague had worked out. The day before he was arrested Yakhimovich delivered a moving speech to people he respected and admired. On April 18, 1970, the court declared him mentally ill and sentenced him to one year in a madhouse. *(See page 414.)*

These examples of protests and protesters against the occupation of Czechoslovakia could be continued for pages. They show quite clearly how much determination and how much personal sacrifice the members of the younger generation, particularly in the Soviet Union, were willing to expend in demonstrating their indignation over the power politics of the regime. Unlike methods employed against protesters in the West, these actions against official policy almost always mean a loss of freedom for the Soviet citizen, but in any event, always result in the permanent loss of a possible academic or scientific career and the complete renunciation of peaceful, private existence.

Demonstration of August 25, 1968

> *If while in London, Gercen (Herzen) single-handedly preserved the honor of the Russian people when he spoke up for the freedom of Poland one hundred years ago . . . then it goes without saying that seven demonstrators have preserved the honor of the Soviet people. The significance of the demonstration of August 25th should in no way be underestimated.*

This conclusion, drawn by the Soviet literary critic Anatoli Jakobson, is probably the most pertinent yet made about Soviet citizens who publicly protested on August 25, 1968, against the suppression of Czechoslovakia.

These seven demonstrators included the physicist Pavel Litvinov, the philologian Larisa Daniel, the linguist Konstantin Babicki, the art historian Viktor Fainberg, the worker Vladimir Dremlyuga, the writer Natalia Gorbanevskaya, and the poet Vadim Delone. There were actually eight demonstrators, but during a later interrogation by the KGB, Tatiana Baeva explained to the total satisfaction of the authorities that her presence in Red Square at that particular time was only accidental. She was subsequently released.

While the Czechoslovakian leadership faced their Soviet conquerors in the Kremlin—presumably Dubchek was still a prisoner at that time—a small group of people whom Jakobson called the "heroes of the 25th of August" proceeded toward the former execution site on Red Square. Their placards demanded FREEDOM FOR DUBCHEK! Some posters were written in Russian, others in the Czech language, but all proclaimed LONG LIVE A FREE AND INDEPENDENT CZECHO-SLOVAKIA! DOWN WITH THE OCCUPATIONAL FORCES! HANDS OFF CZECHOSLOVAKIA! FOR YOUR FREEDOM AND OURS!

In her book entitled *Noon*[10]—the demonstration took place at midday—Natalia Gorbanevskaya gives a detailed and impressive report of the protest action. This report, which could almost be called a white paper, describes many of the now-famous protest demonstrations against the occupation of Czechoslovakia, as well as the Czechoslovakian and official Soviet attitudes toward the invasion. Also included in her book were the minutes of the proceedings against five of the demonstrators. Her letter dated August 28th, sent to various Western newspapers, presents the very first short report about the events which took place on Red Square. *(See page 375.)*

Several of the demonstrators were brutally beaten up by secret-police agents who rushed to the scene. About a quarter of an hour passed before a squad of KGB officials arrived to carry the protesters off in their paddy wagons. At the same time, passers-by who had expressed their sympathy for the small group were taken. In a short interrogation the mental condition of the demonstrators was examined. Natalia Gorbanevskaya was released after many hours of questioning, presumably because she had brought along a three-month-old infant.

Since his front teeth had been knocked out on Red Square, Viktor Fainberg did not appear in court with the other defendants. He was tried in Leningrad on December 2, 1968, and confined to that city's psychiatric prison. The proceedings against Pavel Litvinov, Larisa Daniel, Konstantin

Babicki, Vladimir Dremlyuga, and Vadim Delone were held from the ninth through the eleventh of October, 1968. The prosecution based its case on Paragraphs 190/1 and 190/3 of the State Penal Code.

As in the earlier trials, friends of the accused, as well as foreign news correspondents, were barred from the court-room, although in a petition addressed to Brezhnev, Kosygin, and Podgorny[11] fifty-six people demanded a public trial. In another declaration, seven civil-rights fighters, including Petr Grigorenko and Petr Jakir, emphatically spoke up for the rights of the accused.

> *"Once again . . . men are being condemned not because of their behavior but because of their convictions! The conscience of the Russian people is being manipulated! . . . Comrade Judge," they wrote in conclusion, "if the interests of our people and our homeland mean anything to you, will you put an end to this artificial and dishonorably fabricated affair as soon as possible." [12]*

On the first day of the proceedings, protesters against the trial circulated this declaration in front of the court-house where once again about 150 people had gathered. General Grigorenko collected signatures. A considerable group of reserve militiamen arrived and attempted to obstruct the signature drive, but all they managed to do was come to blows with the civil-rights advocates.

The determined and fearless declarations delivered before the court by the accused have appeared in the world press; particularly impressive were the conclusions of the twenty-eight-year-old Pavel Litvinov *(see page 378)* and Larisa Daniel. Larisa Bograz-Daniel, born in 1929, spoke in her own defense and concluded with the statement:

> *I know the law. But I also know the practice*
> *of the courts, and therefore in my conclusion*
> *I will make no plea to this court today.*[13]

Questioned as to the grounds which moved her to participate in this demonstration, Larisa Daniel answered her judges:

> *I love life, and I value freedom. I fully real-*
> *ized that I would be risking my freedom, and*
> *it was something I didn't want to lose. But I*
> *was faced with the choice of acting or remain-*
> *ing silent. Had I remained silent, it would*
> *have meant giving support to an action that*
> *I cannot condone. It would have amounted*
> *to the same thing as lying. I do not consider*
> *my course the only right one. But for me it*
> *was the only possible one.*[14]

Vladimir Dremlyuga, born in 1940, had previously been punished for alleged "speculation." As he declared:

> *Ever since I was seventeen years old, I have*
> *actively participated in protests against those*
> *policies of the Party and the regime with*
> *which I could not agree . . . All my life I*

have wanted to be a citizen of the state—that is, a man who proudly and peacefully upholds his convictions. For ten minutes there [on Red Square] I was such a citizen of the state.[15]

Konstantin Babicki, then 39, asked his judges:

What kind of value systems do you want to impose upon the masses? Do you want to encourage respect and tolerance for the opinions of others, on condition that they are expressed in accordance with the law, or do you want to encourage hate and attempts on the part of the people to suppress and destroy every person who thinks differently? [16]

The youngest member of the accused group was the poet and former student, Vadim Delone (only 21), who, scarcely a year earlier had stood with Bukovski and Kuschev before the court. In his conclusion, Delone said:

Unlike the others accused, I knew what imprisonment means. I have served more than seven months in prison. In spite of that, I went to the demonstration.

(For this very reason the other participants had tried to persuade Delone not to take part in the rally. But he remained—smiling, as Tatiana Baeva, another participant, reported.) Delone continued:

*I was well aware that for five minutes of free-
dom on Red Square I would have to pay with
years of personal freedom.*[17]

While Vladimir Dremlyuga and Vadim Delone were
each sentenced to three years in a work camp (Delone received two years and six months in addition to the four
months he had spent in detention in September, 1967,
pending investigation), the court exiled the remaining three
defendants, a punishment seldom handed down until that
time. Pavel Litvinov was sentenced to five years, Larisa
Daniel to four, and Konstantin Babicki to three. Ninety-
five persons protested the drastic verdicts in a petition directed to the Supreme Soviet.[18] Several people who signed
that petition were subjected later to severe harassment.
Many were expelled from the Party, and others lost their
positions either as workers or students.

The official Soviet press restricted itself to several non-
committal opinions in which the convicted demonstrators,
as so often happens in such cases, were personally slandered.
According to the press releases, they had allegedly "surrendered themselves to drink" and were supposedly "aso-
cial loafers." (This last was one of the favorite accusations
used to arrest political dissidents and at the same time to
arouse public opinion against them.) In addition, the press
said that they apparently had acted out of the single desire
"to draw upon themselves the attention of the West." All
this, it continued, while the court itself had done all in its
power to let "humanity and compassion" reign in the
proceedings.[19]

In handing down the verdict of exile, the court was

following an old Czarist tradition. Details of the conditions under which the three exiled demonstrators are forced to live, however, clearly underscore the differences between Czarist and Bolshevik Russia. For instance, while Lenin's sojourn in exile in Sushensko—which was paid for by the state—more accurately resembled a forced convalescent retreat (Lenin wrote, fished, hunted, and according to reports from his wife, "abounded in strength and good health"),[20] Larisa Daniel had to fight for her very survival.

According to the report by Gorbanevskaya and other friends, the physically weak woman was at first forced to lug rafters more than nine feet in length in weather hardly ten degrees above zero; so doing, she rapidly lost weight. The attempts on the part of her friends to get her some translation work were unsuccessful, since none of the state publishing houses wanted to have anything to do with a political prisoner. Only after Larisa Daniel received a medical certificate—the doctor made it clearly understood that she would not survive if she continued to pursue such strenuous tasks—was she reassigned to lighter employment. At the present time, she works as an exile in a locksmith shop in the vicinity of Irkutsk.

On December 25, 1970, Konstantin Babicki was prematurely allowed to return to Moscow from the Komi Republic. Pavel Litvinov is employed as an electrician in the vicinity of Chita more than 7,000 miles from Moscow. Despite the fact that this area suffers from a dearth of instructors, the physicist is not allowed to hold classes. After his transfer to this area, Litvinov's wife was granted permission by the authorities to follow her husband into exile. In this respect she closely resembles the wives of the Decembrists, who in their time shared Siberian exile with their husbands.

Vladimir Dremlyuga was confined to a camp in Yakutia. Delone, who suffered greatly from hunger but even more so from isolation in the midst of criminals, was imprisoned in a camp near Tyumen. Despite rumors of an early release, he was given his freedom only in June of 1971.

Toward the end of her book *Noon*, Natalia Gorbanevskaya answered the often-asked question about the sense and purpose of the August 25 demonstration. "Was it worth it, to go to prison for the Czechoslovakians?" With their decision to go to Red Square, both she and her colleagues believed they were following not only the voice of their consciences, but at the same time trying "to atone for a small part of the historical guilt of their own people." Gorbanevskaya concludes:

> *I believe that our purpose lies in that very attempt, and therefore the goal of the demonstration has been accomplished.*[21]

The circulation of her book was probably the decisive factor moving the authorities to arrest Natalia Gorbanevskaya on December 24, 1969. On July 7, 1970, she was tried in absentia. The court, having taken counsel with "psychiatric assessors," found the writer to be mentally disturbed and therefore felt obliged to relegate her to an appropriate mental institution for an indeterminate length of time.[22]

GENERAL GRIGORENKO:
SYMBOL OF OPPOSITION

The plague kills indiscriminantly, but
the current regime plucks its victims
from the flower of the nation.
SERGEI KRAVCHINSKI (STEPNJAK)

Much has been written in the West about the former Major
General Petr Grigorenko, particularly after excerpts from
his diaries were published in Western newspapers.[1] These
dated his imprisonment and confinement to mental institutions.

Grigorenko was born in 1906 and until 1961 had occupied a chair for military cybernetics at the Frunze Academy in Moscow. In 1961 he criticized the policies of Khrushchev during a Party conference and as a result lost his
position at the military academy. As further punishment,
he was transferred to the Far East. His arrest occurred on
February 1, 1964, because of "Anti-Soviet activities" and
several months later he was confined for fifteen months in
the psychiatric prisons of Moscow and Leningrad. At the
same time he was expelled from the Party, stripped of his
rank, and deprived of all claims to his pension, after having

served a total of thirty-four years in the army. During this time he had been severely wounded in the war and had often been singled out and highly praised for his contributions.

Following his release from the institutions, Grigorenko sent letters to Brezhnev and Kosygin asking for rehabilitation and a resumption of his duties in the army,[2] but all in vain. Grigorenko described the details of his case in a later letter addressed to the voters of Moscow, encouraging them to cast their votes against Kosygin.[3]

In 1966, he participated in the demonstration against the convictions of Siniavski and Daniel and against the re-Stalinization attempts. During the trial against Galanskov, Ginzburg, Dobrovolski, and Vera Laskova, Grigorenko came forward as one of the spokesmen for the accused and as a result lost his position as foreman in a state construction company. The former major general wrote innumerable petitions and letters of protest to judges and Party leaders in favor of political defendants and political prisoners. Right up to his last arrest his name never failed to appear on any motion or resolution concerning the human rights movement. He defended Nekrich in a daring and, for that particular military historian, very informative study. He drew up a protest against the franchise, which at that time was only a paper right in the Soviet Union (see page 397), and delivered that stirring funeral oration at the grave of the writer Aleksei Kosterin in which he demanded an "uncompromising fight" against the Soviet totalitarianism then hiding behind the mask of the so-called "socialist democracy." Despite all attempts on the part of the secret-police agents to prevent his saying anything more, Grigorenko called out to the approximately three hundred mourners: "There will be freedom and there will be democracy!" [4]

Together with Ivan Yakhimovich, the fearless general spoke out in support of the reforms being carried out in Prague and later for the retreat of the Soviet troops out of Czechoslovakia. (See page 380.) He actively championed the interests of the deported Crimean Tartars for many years. In one protest statement concerning this problem, Grigorenko passionately appealed to Rudenko, the prosecutor general, against what he called the "illegal and unpatriotic" institution of the KGB:

> This parasitic organization, which eats up an immeasurable amount of the national income and in return takes from the people their best sons and inflicts upon them an incurable injury, must disappear from our society forever, and the sooner the better! [5]

Petr Grigorenko traveled to Tashkent on May 2, 1969, to speak in defense of ten Crimean Tartars during their trial. After his arrival it was learned that the general had fallen into a trap. An agent of the KGB, disguised as a Crimean Tartar, made a telephone call to Grigorenko in which he begged the general to appear at the trial, and despite the fact that the KGB threatened him with arrest should he go, Grigorenko proceeded to the Uzbekian capital. As it turned out, the trial, which had originally been scheduled for this particular time, had been postponed to a later date, but there was no way Grigorenko could have known this. Two hours before his scheduled return to Moscow, on the seventh of May, Grigorenko was arrested. Members of the security police conducted simultaneous house searchings in his Moscow residence and in the homes of six of his friends.

After the arrest of Grigorenko, who was in a sense the leader of the movement, one heard the name "Initiative Group for the Protection of Human Rights in the Union of Soviet Socialist Republics" for the first time within the "democratic movement." At the time of its founding (in May of 1969) the group included fifteen individuals, and of these original fifteen only nine are today still free. There are, however, at least forty to sixty additional people who in fact belong to the Initiative Group, for their signatures appear regularly on all its released statements. The first of these proclamations was addressed to the United Nations. In it the human (civil) rights fighters referred to the continued disregard of human rights on the part of the Soviet regime.

> *"We, the signatories of this letter," reads the introduction, "deeply disturbed by the unending stream of political persecutions in the Soviet Union, which we see as a return to the Stalin era when our entire country was in the grip of terror, appeal to the United Nations Commission on Human Rights to come to the defense of human rights that are being trampled upon in our country. We appeal to the United Nations because our protests and complaints, addressed for a number of years to the highest state and judicial*

*authorities in the Soviet Union, have elicited
no response of any kind. The hope that our
voices might be heard, that the authorities
would put an end to the lawless acts to which
we have repeatedly called their attention—
this hope has proved to be vain."* [6]

In a roll call directed to the citizens of the u.s.s.r., 55
civil-rights fighters spoke up for the release of Grigorenko.
Reports came in from several areas of the Soviet Union
describing protest actions against the arrest of the former
general. Larisa Daniel and Pavel Litvinov expressed their
indignation from their respective places of exile. In March
of 1970, 249 students of the Leningrad Pedagogical Institute
informed the general's wife, Zinaida Grigorenko, of their
sympathy concerning the fate of her husband and their indignation over the practices of the kgb.[7] Information about
Grigorenko had reached them by means of handbills and
fliers which the Norwegian, Swedish, and Danish smog
organizations printed up and distributed through Swedish
tourists.[8]

On June 6, 1969, five Crimean Tartars demonstrated for
their rights on Mayakovski Plaza in Moscow—that is, for
permission to return to their homeland. In addition, they
carried placards demanding the release of General Grigorenko. Irina Jakir, daughter of the historian Petr Jakir, also
participated in this demonstration. A few months later it
was reported that Irina Jakir had been expelled from the
Institute of Historical Archives where she had been study-
ing.

Not long after Grigorenko's arrest, reports were circulated about the arrest of the instructor Ilia Gabai, who had also been apprehended in connection with the Crimean trial in Tashkent on May 19, 1969, under the pretense of "anti-Sovietism." Gabai had been one of the leading figures in the civil-rights actions of previous years. On January 19, 1970, he was sentenced, along with the Crimean Tartar Mustafa Dzemilev, to three years in a work camp, in accordance with Paragraph 190/1.

At first Petr Grigorenko suffered more than five months of insulated KGB imprisonment. In October of 1969 he was subjected to psychiatric examination in the Serbski Institute of Moscow. In February of 1970 the authorities once again declared him mentally ill, and he was confined to the psychiatric prison in Tashkent. Since then the general, who had been kept completely isolated from the outside world for over a year, has been transferred to one of the infamous "mental institutions" under KGB supervision. He is now being held in Chernjackovsk (formerly known as Insterburg) in East Prussia.

Excerpts from the prison diaries Grigorenko managed to keep have appeared in the West, together with a statement by his wife. (Since then the general has been deprived of paper and pencil.) Zinaida Grigorenko, who indirectly passed her husband's writings on to the International Committee for the Protection of Human Rights, used the opportunity to appeal to "all democratic organizations that defend human rights and to all free citizens of the world" to rescue her husband.[9]

Shortly after the publication of Grigorenko's diary, the text of the letter[10] addressed to the Medical Academy of Sciences was printed in the West in which the old Communist

S. Pisarev called upon his personal experience with prison psychiatrists to give a very controlled description of the treatment one can expect to receive in such an institution. Pisarev exposed the practices of the Serbski Institute, whose corrupt staff is maintained for only one reason: to formulate incorrect psychiatric diagnoses arbitrarily and deliberately. According to Pisarev, hundreds of mentally competent and completely healthy men—for the most part politically "uncomfortable" scholars and artists, but even including Party functionaries and army officers—have fallen victim to this most scandalous despotic policy during the past two decades.

In these so-called "psychiatric clinics" physical and psychic tortures are part of the daily routine: The normal "politicals" are intentionally confined in close quarters with the criminally insane (who, incidentally, are kept in the KGB institution for camouflage purposes; they do not receive any treatment, but are available and can be trotted out whenever necessary) often for periods of eight years or longer. The dispensing of psychedelic drugs, which evoke indescribable tortures and have disastrous effects on the body, is another well-known means of breaking the morale of "unruly patients."

Grigorenko's entries provide a shocking document about the methods of physical and mental destruction with which the post-Stalinist Soviet regime is trying to silence political dissidents. The yet unbroken major general reports on his executioners' capriciousness and tortures, all of which are aimed at one thing—his ultimate death. (The public prosecutor Naumova frankly admitted to Grigorenko that they were just waiting for him to die.) In the meantime his family is continually subjected to persecutions growing out of the popular but illegal principle of liability of kinship.

An interesting passage appears in the discussion Grigorenko had (and later wrote down) with the psychiatric commission in the Serbski Institute. In it the general advocates a different version of oppositionary tactics:

> Our earlier approach was typically Bolshevistic: the creation of a strong illegal conspiratorial organization and the circulation of illegal pamphlets. Today, however, there is no organization, no pamphlets; but rather, open, undisguised attacks on the well-known tyranny, falsehood, and hyprocisy—attacks against every distortion of the truth. Earlier the goal was to do away with the reigning regime and to return to Lenin's starting point. Today, on the other hand, the goal is to solve the obvious grievances of society, to fight for the strict observation of the existing laws and for the realization of the rights guaranteed by the Constitution. Earlier they cried out for revolution. Today the battle to make life in our society more democratic is carried out in the open and within the letter of the law.[11]

THE SOLZHENITSYN CASE

No one can obstruct the path to the truth.
I am prepared to die for this path.

ALEKSANDR SOLZHENITSYN

Following his rather late literary debut with *Ivan Denisovich*, which became an overnight best seller, Solzhenitsyn had difficulty in publishing even a few of his short stories in *Novy Mir*. None of his works, with the exception of *Ivan Denisovich*, have appeared in book form in the Soviet Union. Instead—at least until now—they could only hope to appear in rough proof form. Following the fall of Khrushchev, *Ivan Denisovich* was actually forbidden. The 700-page manuscript of his novel *The First Circle*[2] (*The First Circle of Hell*) was written between 1955 and 1964 and later confiscated by the KGB even before Solzhenitsyn had had a chance to make the final revisions. This was also one of the reasons for the author's protests against publication of his works outside the Soviet Union—a plea he made after his novel, and later *Cancer Ward*, reached the West without his assistance.

Solzhenitsyn's *First Circle*, as the Slavic scholar Felix Philip Ingold so aptly expressed it—

> *(belongs) with the greatest works of the So-*
> *viet, indeed of all Russian literature. Sol-*
> *zhenitsyn had at his disposal the encyclope-*
> *dic knowledge and the superior intelligence*
> *of Lev Tolstoi, the explosive power of expres-*
> *sion characteristic of Dostoevski, a command*
> *of the language reminiscent of Leskov, the*
> *satiric qualities of Saltykov-Schedrin, and the*
> *gentle, underlying humor of Chekhov.*

Like his *Ivan Denisovich* and his *Cancer Ward*, Solzhenitsyn's *First Circle*, according to Ingold, is—

> *an autobiographical work without the I, a true*
> *story which is not related by him who lived*
> *it, but rather by witnesses (prejudiced and*
> *unprejudiced), by judges and those who were*
> *judged, by hangmen and their victims . . .*
> *Solzhenitsyn's contribution as chronicler of*
> *Stalinism stands alone, far above anything*
> *that the recent Soviet literature has produced,*
> *unless one were willing to accept the com-*
> *parison between it and a lyrical work—that*
> *is, Anna Akhmatova's* Requiem.[3]

Like *The First Circle, Cancer Ward*[4]—written approximately between 1963 and 1967—is heavily dependent upon
the great Russian classics of the nineteenth century. After
recognizing that the confiscated *First Circle* had no chance
for publication, Solzhenitsyn busied himself with *Cancer
Ward*, the novel he considered his "most important and most

personal" work. Following its appraisal by the prose section
of the Writers' Union, *Cancer Ward* was recommended for
publication.

Veniamin Kaverin asked:

> *"What is the underlying idea of the still in-*
> *complete* Cancer Ward? *"To confront people*
> *of different vocations, different levels of edu-*
> *cation, different moral positions, with death.*
> *That is an immense task—a greater one, in*
> *any event, than that in* The Death of Ivan
> Illich *(by L. N. Tolstoi). I honestly hope that*
> *the author will prove equal to this task. He*
> *gives us a clever psychological cross section,*
> *and the characters eventually see into each*
> *other's inner depths. That has to move us. We*
> *are all standing on the brink of death."* [5]

"It is clear to everyone that *Cancer Ward* must see the
light of publication," the writer Karjakin felt at the time,
and the poet Bella Akhmadulina, turning toward Solzhenitsyn, shouted to the assembly:

> *A magnificent man! We will pray to God in*
> *Heaven that He grant Aleksandr Solzhenit-*
> *syn good health!* [6]

A few months after this meeting, Solzhenitsyn wrote
his impressive open letter to the participants of the Fourth
Congress of Soviet Writers, in which he exposed the threatening situation of Soviet literature and attacked the institu-

tion of censorship. *(See page 454.)* The author had hundreds of copies of this letter made and sent one to each participant at the Congress. During the Congress, which was in fact boycotted by a majority of the well-known writers (even Ehrenburg, now an old man, excused himself), only the dogmatists were allowed to speak. Solzhenitsyn's letter was officially unrecognized, but unofficially it was hailed as the sensation of the Congress; more than one hundred writers praised the letter and demanded that it be discussed in the open. Eighty prominent writers, among them Yevtushenko, Tvardovski, Paustovski, and others, directed a similar letter to the Writers' Union. Following Solzhenitsyn's example, the critic and writer Georgi Vladimov also sent a letter to the Congress advocating the elimination of the censor. He passionately defended Solzhenitsyn as—

> the writer which my Russia needs most of all; the writer who will bring her glory in the face of the world and who can give us answers to all the painful questions about the tragedy we have lived through.

At the turn of the century, nine-tenths of the delegates here will have been forgotten as writers, but Solzhenitsyn's name will live on.[7] In a document addressed to Demichev, the Party secretary, the aged poet Pavel Antokolski supported Solzhenitsyn's demands and defended the author as a "rare talent," referring to him as—

> the rising hope of our realistic literature, the heir of the great humanistic tradition of Gogol, Lev Tolstoi, and Maxim Gorki.[8]

On September 22, 1967, under the chairmanship of Konstantin Fedin, the Secretariat of the Writers' Union once again considered the Solzhenitsyn case. Mikhail Sholokhov, a man who had already compromised himself by his behavior regarding the Siniavski-Daniel case, really outdid himself this time in his attempts to strengthen his reputation as an informer. In a written but unpublished opinion, Sholokhov described Solzhenitsyn as "crazy," one who would best be confined either in prison or in a mental institution. The writer Kozhevnikov reproached Solzhenitsyn with his statement:

> *We have lost a great deal of time reading this gray manuscript of yours that you don't even dare offer to a publishing house. For its pure naturalism* Cancer Ward *evokes disgust from its readers . . . .*[9]

While Tvardovski, the once-so-doctrinaire Konstantin Simonov, and a few others spoke up in favor of the novel's publication, Saripov, one of its members at the time, demanded Solzhenitsyn's dismissal from the Writers' Union. The dogmatists serving as leaders for this group demanded that Solzhenitsyn revise his *Cancer Ward* ideologically and that he renounce what he had said in his letter to the Congress of Writers. For his part Solzhenitsyn demanded the publication of his letter and refused to take back anything he had said in it.

Against the accusation that his novel was "antihumanistic," the author replied:

> *I absolutely fail to understand why you
> have accused* Cancer Ward *of being "anti-
> humanistic." The exact opposite is the case:
> It is the victory of life over death, the victory
> of the future over the past* . . . .[10]

Turning to the role of the writers, Solzhenitsyn continued:

> *The task of the writer certainly does not
> consist in defending or criticizing this or
> that means of distribution of a social prod-
> duct . . . The tasks of a writer concern
> more general and more lasting problems.
> They concern the mysteries of the human
> heart and the human conscience, the con-
> flict between life and death, the victory
> over mental and emotional pain, and all
> those laws of a widely scattered humanity,
> formulated in the unthinkable depths of
> thousands of years, which will only be raised
> up when the sun sinks.*[11]

In an interview Solzhenitsyn had once remarked:

> *The tasks of a writer ought not to be con-
> sidered solely from the standpoint of the
> duty which he has to perform in the public
> interest, but must also be considered from
> the standpoint of his important duty with
> respect to each individual person . . . To-*

*day, when technology rules over life, when
material prosperity is the most important
thing, and when the influence of religion has
grown increasingly weaker throughout the
world, a particular responsibility is laid upon
the writer. He must fill up many empty
vacuums.*

Questioned as to the writer's role in society, Solzhenitsyn replied:

*Society has to evaluate him objectively—
that's all. I don't see any serious mistake in
the fact that society treats its writers unjustly. In this way they are constantly being
tested. Writers shouldn't be pampered too
much . . . they have to learn to deal with
injustice. That is the risk of their vocation.
The fate of a writer will always be a hard
one.*[12]

Although Tvardovski had in the meantime expressed
his readiness to publish Solzhenitsyn's *Cancer Ward* in *Novy
Mir*, he was not granted the necessary permission from the
Writers' Union to carry out his proposal. In a letter dated
November 12, 1967, and addressed to the Secretariat of the
Union, Solzhenitsyn demanded the "immediate publication" of his novel. In other correspondence addressed to the
union the writer inquired about what measures the Secretariat had taken against the illegal ban of his books in
public libraries and what efforts had been undertaken to

return to him the manuscript of *The First Circle* and his pilfered records, both of which had been confiscated by the KGB. He also asked whether the union intended to protect him against the continual calumnies which had been hurled at him for the past three years. (Among other things, it was rumored that Solzhenitsyn was schizophrenic and that he had committed high treason during the war. In addition, Solzhenitsyn demanded that the union lose no time in persuading the Soviet regime to draw up some sort of agreement with the International Convention for the Protection of Copyrights, so that the copyright of Soviet authors might finally be recognized and observed outside the Soviet Union.[13]

After the announcement appeared in *Novy Mir* heralding the publication of *Cancer Ward,* and the text of the first part had even been set, the novel was called back in December of 1967. The following January the writers Aleksandr Tvardovski and Veniamin Kaverin sent letters to Konstantin Fedin in which they courageously and determinedly spoke up in favor of the publication of Solzhenitsyn's books. Both writers warned of a recurrence of the Pasternak affair, an episode in which Fedin had played a lamentable role. In his letter Kaverin also showed how fluid are the distinctions between "legal" and "illegal" literature. "You will hardly find a single writer who does not have a polished and thoroughly planned manuscript lying somewhere in his desk drawer that for inexplicable and incomprehensible reasons has been deemed unacceptable for healthy human consumption . . . Do you really fail to realize that powerful historical experiences demand their own personification and that you are allying yourself with those people who are trying to hinder this inevitable process in order to increase their own prosperity?" [14] A short time later the writer Georgi Svirski delivered an angry speech against censorship in a meeting before the Moscow section of the Writers' Union (*see page 462*) and was promptly expelled from the Party.

A considerable length of time passed before Solzhenitsyn and his supporters received an official answer. When it came, it took the form of a press release. On June 26, 1968, the publishing organ of the Writers' Union, *Literaturnaia Gazeta,* loosed a total attack against the writer. He was accused of having placed his talent in the service of foreign enemies. The article contained ominous insinuations and was rich in unctuous advice. For the most part, the article was a forecast of accusations made against Solzhenitsyn about a year later, which served as reasons for his expulsion from the Writers' Union. In a letter addressed to A. Chakovski, editor in chief of *Literaturnaia Gazeta,* the writer Lidia Chukovskaya protested the charges made in the article.[15] The famous physicist Valeri Turchin did not hide his indignation either. Turchin, a few of whose freelance articles appeared from time to time in *Literaturnaia Gazeta,* assured the editor that in retrospect he was ashamed of these contributions. He wrote to Chakovski:

> *I declare that as long as you are still the editor in chief of* Literaturnaia Gazeta, *I shall reject every offer, whatever form it might take, and that I refuse to subscribe to or buy this newspaper. I believe that this is the single possible reaction for everyone who*

> *shares my point of view in respect to the ar-*
> *ticle about Solzhenitsyn.*[16]

In light of the growing campaign against Solzhenitsyn, his friends began to fear for his safety. According to Western news reports, his friends formed a group of bodyguards for the writer and accompanied him whenever he left his house, probably to prevent any assassination attempts such as those perpetrated against Dudinchev.[17] As Solzhenitsyn celebrated his fiftieth birthday, on December 11, 1968, the Writers' Union neglected to pass on to him even one of the birthday greetings that were received from the outside world.

In late autumn of 1969 the campaign against Solzhenitsyn reached its climax with his expulsion from the Writers' Union. He was reproached with having displayed an "antisocial" attitude; in addition, he allegedly neglected to "oppose" the West sufficiently and was even said to have aided the enemy. Five members of the writers' group from Rjazan, Solzhenitsyn's place of residence, found themselves under pressure from the local Party officials concerning the expulsion; two were forced to excuse themselves because of illness in order not to participate in the distasteful ritual. Once again Solzhenitsyn defended his position as determinedly as ever. He replied to his expulsion with a letter in which he prophesied to the conformist members of the union that the "hour is approaching when each one of you will try to erase his name from this resolution." (*See page 473.*)

After Solzhenitsyn's expulsion was confirmed in Moscow, various groups of writers, among them poets like

Bulat Okudzhava and Gregori Baklanov, protested against this act of the Writers' Union. As a symbol of their protest several writers are said to have threatened to resign from the union. However, Solzhenitsyn encouraged them not to do so, for it would mean completely abandoning the field to the dogmatists. It is believed that Tatiana Litvinova, an aunt of Pavel Litvinov, demanded the convocation of an extraordinary Writers' Congress. Yevgeny Yevtushenko sent a wire demanding an appeal of the expulsion proceedings. Lidia Chukovskaya also sent a telegram and described the expulsion as a "national disgrace for Russia." In addition to various letters of protest written by well-known people, including the biologist Medvedev, two other letters circulated in *Samizdat,* bearing thirty-nine and fourteen signatures, respectively. Both of these looked upon the expulsion as a further manifestation of a reviving Stalinism.

As happened once before during the Pasternak affair, the Writers' Union released a statement on November 25, 1969, maintaining that no one would hinder Solzhenitsyn from "going wherever he might be welcome." He could go "where his anti-Soviet works and letters would be received with enthusiasm." [18] This statement was as much hypocritical propaganda ploy as the one concerning Pasternak, for everyone knew that Solzhenitsyn would no sooner leave Russia than Pasternak would have in his time, however tempting this invitation might have been.

With his expulsion from the Writers' Union Solzhenitsyn also lost his claim to the old-age pension which was guaranteed to members. The designation of "Soviet writer" had been officially denied him. For reasons of ill health many years earlier Solzhenitsyn had been forced to give

up his position as a mathematics instructor. At first, therefore, it was feared that the writer could be ordered off to
some factory or even be exiled as a "parasite." Contrary to
earlier reports from Western sources and according to the
most recent announcements, the condition of the writer's
health has not deteriorated. For a long time he lived on
the outskirts of Moscow as a guest of the famous cellist
and music professor Mstislav Rostropovich.

In July of 1970 the writer once again came forward
with an opinion in which he strongly protested the imprisonment of the geneticist Zores Medvedev in a mental
institution. (See page 395.) In his complaint Solzhenitsyn
denounced the Soviet habit of confining political dissidents
in insane asylums. Such an act was "spiritual murder." He
considered this a "modification of the gas chamber" and,
if possible, even more horrible, because here free-thinking,
healthy men were being slowly tortured to death. These
crimes would be as much remembered and as little forgotten as the gas chambers of the Nazis.

On October 8, 1970, Solzhenitsyn was awarded the
Nobel Prize for Literature. The writer accepted the honor
and declared at the same time that he intended to come to
Stockholm to receive the award. The decision of the Nobel
Committee was greeted with satisfaction and enthusiasm
by Soviet intellectual circles. In a letter passed on to a
foreign correspondent in Moscow, thirty-seven of Solzhenitsyn's fellow countrymen congratulated the Swedish
academy on its decision.

At first Soviet officials kept their silence. Soon, however, the Writers' Union and the Party presses began to issue
reprimands to the Nobel Committee, which, in the course

of the next few weeks, intensified to ultimately massive abuse. The conferring of the prize on Solzhenitsyn represented a provocation, a clumsy piece of imperialism, which in the distribution of Solzhenitsyn's "anti-Soviet" works endeavored only to serve its own "bloody policy." The Swedish academy was denounced as a depository of reactionary elements. When four years earlier Mikhail Sholokhov received the Nobel Prize from the hands of those very same "reactionaries," the jubilation of the Party accompanied him. But now a campaign was released against Solzhenitsyn that, although it never reached the heights of the earlier persecutions of Pasternak, nevertheless played an important role in the writer's decision not to travel to Stockholm. In an open letter to the Swedish Academy of the Arts, Solzhenitsyn thanked them for the honor they had granted him, an honor which he shared with all of his "predecessors in Russian literature, who as a result of the difficult conditions in the last decades did not live long enough to receive such a prize." [19] But the animosity expressed in the official press undoubtedly contributed to Solzhenitsyn's fears that his enemies could use his trip to Stockholm as an opportunity to bar his return to Russia. For the authorities this would probably have been, in fact, a very welcome inducement to relieve themselves of an uncomfortable opponent by depriving him of his citizenship (which they actually did in the case of Tarsis). In this way the intellectual opposition in Russia would be deprived of one of its most important and influential leaders.

It was left to *Pravda*, the Party mouthpiece, to provide the most threatening attack against Solzhenitsyn, and it did so on December 17, 1970. In naming Solzhenitsyn, now branded an "enemy of the people," in the same breath with the leading political prisoners Vladimir Bukovski and the recently convicted Andrei Amalrik, the article deepened the fears one heard all over that Solzhenitsyn too could be brought to court and tried for alleged "defamation of the Soviet Union."

The hate-filled accusations on the part of the official mass media stood in direct confrontation with the significant expressions of others, especially the fearless acknowledgment of the cello virtuoso Rostropovich. In an open letter dated October 31, 1970, and addressed to the editorial boards of the leading Soviet newspapers, the musician passionately defended Solzhenitsyn and attacked the cultural policies then being employed by incompetent functionaries. *Samizdat* saw to the publication of the letter, which was naturally ignored by the official press and which would inevitably reap very severe reprisals for Rostropovich, the winner of both the Lenin and the Stalin prizes. The right of independent thought must be accorded to everyone, Rostropovich wrote, as well as the right to express his experiences, his opinions, and his reflections, rather than to express only those opinions which he is prompted to say. Continued the musician:

> *I know that there will no doubt be a so-called "opinion" released about me because of this letter. I am not afraid of that, but rather, I say what I think. I know many of Solzhenitsyn's works. I value them and feel that the suffering he has experienced has won him the right to write the truth as he sees it. I see*

> *no reason to change my opinion of him sim-*
> *ply because a campaign against him is now*
> *being launched."* [20]

Aleksandr Solzhenitsyn, whose novels[21] have been read by a great part of the Soviet intelligentsia thanks to *Samiz-dat* publications (on the black market today, for example, his *Cancer Ward* sells for seventy rubles), is considered by many of his readers as the "pride of Russian literature," as a "new Dostoevski," and honored as "the conscience of the nation." In their letter to the Party leadership the scientists Sakharov, Turchin, and Medvedev describe him as the "most important and most popular (!) Soviet writer." The esteem in which Solzhenitsyn is held in the minds of the progressive intelligentsia today is best expressed in one of the popular jokes now circulating in the Soviet Union. Early in the next century Russian pupils will be asked about Brezhnev. "Brezhnev," so the answer will go, "wasn't he a politician in Solzhenitsyn's time?"

THE ALIENATION BETWEEN
THE ADMINISTRATION
AND THE WRITERS

My voice has long been silenced.
What does it matter?
People memorize and write out
All that I say—stolen, secretly.
Such a notebook is a greater honor
Than any published book could be.
                    —MAXIMILIAN VOLOSHIN

The proceedings against Siniavski and Daniel, and to a
greater extent the sentences handed down to Galanskov and
Ginzburg, proved to be the spur that drove the persistent
"cultural opposition" to take a political stand and also
aroused forces, which had hitherto remained loyal to the regime, against the power structure. Today formerly successful writers stand, if not in open opposition, then at least in
silent protest, assuming a sort of prolonged strike against the
ever more reactionary policies of the Party leadership.

In 1967 alone, as those in power prepared for a glorious
celebration of the fiftieth anniversary of Soviet rule, the
nervous leadership was delivered a series of severe blows.

Svetlana Alliluyeva, Stalin's daughter, sought political asylum in the United States. Employing a rare first hand knowledge of the internal affairs of her country, she exposed the Soviet power lords and renounced the version of Communism they were trying to establish.

"During the past few years," declared the famous emigrant to the press, "the Russians have begun to think and to discuss. We no longer automatically believe everything we are told . . . And religion, too, has played a large part in my decision to leave. . . ." [1]

Andrei Voznesenski, a poet who up until then had indeed been an *enfant terrible*, but one who had nevertheless remained loyal to the Party, wrote an indignant letter to *Pravda* (which, not surprisingly, neglected to print it, but other Western newspapers did publish it) in which he protested certain practices of the Writers' Union. "The leadership of the union apparently does not consider writers as human beings. One runs across their standard of behavior—lies, evasions, insults—as common practice all over the place . . . One is surrounded by nothing more than lies, lies, lies, impudence, and more lies. I am ashamed to find myself in the same union with such people. . . ." [2] As Yevtushenko did before him, Voznesenski fell out of favor with this letter. Since then both have been permitted to publish very little of their works. One of Voznesenski's poems, entitled "It's Impossible to Write Any More," appeared in *Novy Mir* in 1969:

I am in the midst of a crisis.
My soul has grown dumb and speechless.
"No day should pass without a few verses,"
My friend tortures me with his advice.
But I—I have neither days
Nor verses.

Thus my accuser
From among the critics
Will remark in his essay
That, out of anger and resentment,
I alone experience crisis.
In this, of all systems, the
Most devoid of crises . . .[3]

The symbolism in Yuri Levitanski's poem, *New Year on the Danube,* which was published in *Novy Mir* shortly after the poem by Voznesenski, is rather obvious:

An ice-cold wind howls over our streams.
Snow covers Russia. But what is hidden un-
der the snow?
Who is it, what does this blanket of snow
conceal, what is beneath it?
Who's there—sighing and laughing, and
weeping bitter tears?[4]

Solzhenitsyn's letter of May, 1967, addressed to the Fourth Congress of Soviet Writers is a high point in the history of Soviet literature, and it has found positive support with a majority of the reputable men of letters. *(See page 454.)* A few weeks later F. Burlacki and L. Karpinski, two editors of *Pravda,* published an essay aimed against censorship in theatrical life,[5] and as a result were removed from that newspaper's editorial staff. The editor in chief of *Komsomolskaya Pravda,* who in turn published the essay in his paper, also found himself without a job.

The ever more vociferous and ever more frequent criticism on the part of officials against the avant-garde *Novy Mir* was symptomatic of the increasing alienation of the Party from the intelligentsia. While many of the existent journals, and particularly those of a literary bent, sounded the views of the Party more than ever before in politically indistinguishable editorials, to the eternal tedium of their readers, *Novy Mir* had attempted to remain uncompromisingly loyal to its motto of honesty and sincerity. Many readers who had access to the paper (because of the censors' activities it appeared weeks, and sometimes even months, after its original issue date) had gradually got into the habit of checking the masthead of the paper before they read any further, to see if Tvardovski's name was still included in the roster. Tvardovski, now sixty, had been a one-time Stalin apologist and then for almost twenty years an outspoken defender of the greatest possible freedoms a legal organ of the press in Soviet totalitarianism could ever achieve.

In February of 1970, he was forced to step down after endless disputes. Unlike 1954, however, they did not dare remove him from his position. For years on end, the courageous writer had opposed the assaults of the dogmatists; only after four letter-loyal "controllers" were assigned to the

editorial staff of the newspaper was the now infirm and
ailing Tvardovski persuaded to leave. His latest poem, *The
Right to Think*,[6] had previously appeared in the West—to
Tvardovski's displeasure, as he insisted in a public statement. The poet had vainly sought to publish the poem legally in the Soviet Union but it circulated clandestinely in
Samizdat. In this poem the author renounced the convictions he had expressed in his poetry cycle, *Moravia*,[7] written between 1934 and 1936, in which he justified the collectivization then being imposed on the people and for
which he received the Stalin Prize. In this unpublished
new poem he describes how, during those earlier times, he
forsook his own father, an alleged "enemy of the people,"
in favor of Stalin, the "Father of the People":

> *He said: Follow me!*
> *Leave father and mother behind!*
> *Leave the temporal world behind you,*
> *Then you will enter Paradise!*

> *And we, who were proud of ourselves for not*
> *   believing in God,*
> *Because we had our own deities,*
> *We were the first ones to demand without*
> *   pity:*
> *Sacrifice mother and father!*

> *Forget the family to which you belong,*
> *Just remember one thing (no questions al-*
> *   lowed):*

All the love which you give to others
Necessarily lessens your love for the Father
of your People!

The task is clear and the duty a holy one.
And, while on the road, which leads to the
higher goal,
Denounce your brother, betray your friend,
If they should happen to spoil the game.[8]

The banishment of Tvardovski meant the loss of a key figure not only in Soviet literature, but even more so in the "legal" reform movement. His name is intrinsically bound up with the rise of the present literary elite in Russia, and he has played as important a role in their development as has Solzhenitsyn. Ever since 1953 Tvardovski, himself an active member of the Party and up until 1966 a delegate to the Central Committee, has sought a practicable compromise between the interests of the Party and the cultural and spiritual needs of the individual.

Valeri Kosolapov, who lost his position as editor in chief of *Literaturnaia Gazeta* in 1962 for having published Yevtushenko's poem, "Babi Yar," and thereby fell out of favor with the authorities, succeeded Tvardovski as editor of *Novy Mir*. It was widely feared that, following Tvardovski's retirement, *Novy Mir* would no longer remain what it had been, but that it would—although still considered to be on a higher level than the other contemporary journals—become more and more conformist and boring. Naturally when the dogmatists named the doctrinaire Konstantin Simonov as successor to the reprimanded Tvardovski in 1954, the last thing they had expected was that instead of Simonov changing *Novy Mir, Novy Mir* would itself turn Simonov into a liberal. And who could have predicted the development of the "Stalinist" Tvardovski when he assumed leadership of the newspaper in 1950? It is to be hoped that the traditional spirit of the newspaper will once again prove stronger than the influence of the dogmatists, and that in this instance too their success will prove to be a Pyrrhic victory.

In June of 1969 it was reported that four editors of *Junost* had been fired. Next to *Novy Mir, Junost* has always provided a type of forum for liberals, even though it could never concur with the opinions expressed in *Novy Mir*. The names of the dismissed editors—Yevgeny Yevtushenko, Vasili Aksenov, Viktor Rozov, and E. Vishniakov—indicate that this purge was just another feather in the cap of the dogmatists. These four writers were replaced by four others; one of them was Anatoli Kuznecov, whose appointment to the position of editor caused undisguised consternation because the rather "liberal" Kuznecov had been attacked more than once for his novels.

A few weeks after his appointment as editor of *Junost*, Kuznecov made headlines in the West following his successful attempt to escape from his guards in London and to seek political asylum there. Besides Valeri Tarsis (who had been deprived of his citizenship by the direct actions of the Soviet authorities), Mikhail Demin (whose bourgeois name was Trifonov), and Arkadi Belinkov, Kuznecov was the fourth (and the most famous) Soviet writer within three years to seek political asylum in the West. Mikhail

Demin, who had enjoyed a reputation in the Soviet Union as a successful, rather straight-line—and according to the censors, irreproachable—lyricist and prose writer, traveled to France during the summer of 1968 and never returned to the u.s.s.r. One month earlier the critic and writer Arkadi Belinkov succeeded in fleeing to West Germany. With his wife Natalia, this literary scholar—burdened with a severe heart condition—traveled to the United States where he died in May, 1970, leaving incomplete his work on a book about Solzhenitsyn. Born in 1921, Belinkov was very well-known in the Soviet Union—his successful book about the writer Yuri Tiniavov contributing to his firm and lasting reputation. Belinkov had spent thirteen years in Stalin's camps before he was rehabilitated in 1956. In a long declaration composed prior to his escape to West Germany, which he sent to the Union of Soviet Writers, Belinkov announced his resignation from the union, describing it as an "institution of a police state." He referred to the Soviet regime as "irredeemable and irreparable." It was also the "cruelest, most inhuman, and most merciless" regime in the history of mankind. In his letter Belinkov described the misery of freedom-loving intellectuals in the u.s.s.r. and the fear that forced the power system to persecute the best people in their land. The leadership feared everything, beginning with Solzhenitsyn right on up to the workers of Novocherkast who were shot to death, Jewish physicists, and the hungry farmers of the collectives.

Belinkov added:

> I am writing this letter in order to show that
> the Russian intelligentsia is alive, that it is

fighting, that it cannot be bought, that it has not yielded, that it is a force to be reckoned with.[9]

Shortly before his death, Belinkov wrote a letter to the P.E.N. Club in which he denounced those intellectuals of the West—

who call themselves liberals because they condemn the imperfection of Western democracy and rejoice over the successes of the socialist systems. In the past such intellectuals were called monarchists, obscurants, reactionaries, and pro-fascists. And although these intellectuals fight for progress in their own country, at the same time they unite themselves with the "most abominable reactionary forces." The danger and the bitterness of the real champions of freedom, namely the Soviet intellectuals, who had no choice but to surrender to persecution and who died in concentration camps, mean nothing to them. Rather, they seek to persuade them of the superiority and advantages of the Soviet regime. The progressive intelligentsia of the U.S.S.R. who see their greatest enemies in the Soviet dictators and fight against them, despise the "liberal" intellectuals of the West because they "pay their respects to these enemies, repeat their lies while shaking your hand, and destroy a de-

> *mocracy which they consider imperfect but which the Soviet opposition feels is an unattainable ideal.*[10]

Hardly a year had passed following Belinkov's flight when Anatoli Kuznecov, born in 1929, announced his resignation from the Writers' Union while in England. In one of his diaries which was smuggled out of the Soviet Union on microfilm, this significant writer described the activities of the censors and the secret security police, who accomplish their work by means of falsification, withholding information, the suppression of every free word, the stupefying of the spirit, and the corruption of one's conscience. Kuznecov went on to renounce publicly all his books which had appeared in the U.S.S.R. and which had been muzzled by the censor. In a letter addressed to the Central Committee of the CPSU he requested that body to relieve him of his Party membership.

> *After serious and lengthy consideration I have come to a complete renunciation of Marxism-Leninism. I feel today that this doctrine is completely and absolutely superannuated, rigid, and naïve. It is not in a position to solve the existing contradictions in today's society. Even worse, it has led to fearful social tragedies, it continues to do so today, and it threatens to lead to ever more tragic situations. It is impossible for me to continue as a member of the Communist Party, for it bases its policies on this doctrine."* [11]

For Anatoli Kuznecov, for Svetlana Alliluyeva, and for countless other members of the intelligentsia in present-day Russia there was no escape other than flight into foreign lands, into an uncertain and perhaps totally insecure future. They all had to emigrate under incomparably difficult conditions and surmount much more difficult obstacles than even former dissidents under the Russian czars were forced to face. When the Socialist Maxim Gorki (and also Lenin in 1905, for that matter) returned to Russia from his voluntarily chosen exile, he had nothing to fear. The decisions of writers and thinkers of that time to escape from the Czarist censorship was not a criminal offense, not even in the eyes of the rulers then in power. Were Kuznecov to decide today to return to the U.S.S.R. he would be assured of ten years in a concentration camp (as is well-known from the circumstances attending similar cases). Even in the twenties, indeed as late as the thirties, writers who had emigrated from Bolshevik rule could return without having to fear for their life and freedom as they now have to do in post-Stalinist Russia.

When has any regime made so great a habit—as Kuznecov described it—of forcing writers, artists, and scientists to turn informers, as well as employing every other means of suppression, in order to assure themselves, in this very tasteful manner, of their support?

Anatoli asked Kuznecov:

> *What would you say were you to learn that Lev Tolstoi had been an agent of the secret police, and wrote reports about every foreigner who visited his Yasnaia Polyana? Or*

that Dostoevski had betrayed his best friends? Would it still be possible to respect their best works, no matter how extraordinary they might be? I don't know how to answer this question. I can only say that Dostoevski and Tolstoi have not lived in Soviet Russia.[12]

EARLY SIGNS
OF FREEDOM

It will rise again, oh believe me, my
friend!
The morning star of bright success.
Russia will awaken from its sleep
And inscribe our names
On the ruins of the overthrown tyranny.
                              —A. S. PUSHKIN

While only a few years ago dissident individuals and various opposition groups suffered from a lack of any means of communication and absolutely no common "basis of operation," they stand today united to a certain extent, increasingly planning and acting together in accordance with a generally accepted strategy. According to Andrei Amalrik—with the exception of the national and religious opposition groups—at least three distinct currents can be identified within the opposing forces:

(1) The "true Marxism-Leninism"

(2) The "Christian ideology"

(3) The "liberal ideology" [1]

The "true Marxist-Leninists" believe in the utopian idea of the realization of a classless society. They accuse the present regime of having lost sight of the goals of the October Revolution instead of trying to put them into effect. They demand not only the reinstatement of the "internally directed democracy" but also political freedom for political dissidents, at least to the degree that such freedom is guaranteed in the Soviet Constitution and proclaimed in the Declaration of Human Rights.

Among the representatives of this "Marxist ideology," which is, in fact, basically a "reformed Communism" somewhat analogous to the Czechoslovakian version, Amalrik lists Petr Grigorenko, Ivan Yakhimovich, and the writer Aleksei Kosterin who died in 1968.

The "Christian ideology" according to Amalrik is not exclusively a theologicial or religious conception but primarily a political doctrine. It advocates the fundamental axioms of Christian morality in public life and may have been partially inspired by the ideas of the Slavophiles.[2] This group is made up mainly of leaders of the "Christian-Socialist Union," whose most important representative perhaps is Igor Ogurcov.

The "liberal ideology" proceeds from the conviction that the goals of the October Revolution are unrealizable. Its representatives (including, according to Amalrik, Pavel Litvinov and, with some reservations, the atomic physicist Sakharov) ultimately advocate a multiple-party system, in addition to a gradual approximation of the democratic society now represented in the West. At the same time, however, the members of this group place as their top priority the maintenance of social and state ownership. And, finally, as the so-called 14,000-word program states, the principle of a free-market economy, with the least possible amount of restriction, should be discussed in wide circles within the "democratic movement" and increasingly encouraged.

This brief introduction will only be able to describe those tendencies which are presently most visible within the opposition forces. The political and ideological boundaries between these various groups are very fluid, and they are complicated by the additional multitude of other political conceptions and possible goals. But it is for the most part those groups Amalrik has sketched which give the so-called "democratic movement" its direction and form. This movement, described as the repository of just about every opposition, antitotalitarian force, and group active in Russia today, is not a party, and in fact isn't even a strongly organized group. At the moment it has no central leadership, and only as late as 1969 did a detailed program appear within its ranks. The common goal to which all members strive in equal measure is the establishment of a Constitutional state based on the principles of human rights. Adherents of the "democratic movement" wholeheartedly support fundamental internal reforms and do not advocate revolutionary— that is, armed and violent—confrontations. One can easily distinguish between those who support the Constitution of the u.s.s.r. but fight against the present regime's extensive disregard of these rights, and those who question these rights themselves—that is, the basic principles of the Constitution. In other words, the former groups fundamentally support the Soviet order of state and society, whereas the latter wish to see it replaced by another political system. Lately, however, it seems that an increasing unity of political, economic, and social conceptions is beginning to take place, and there are many indications that this will lead to greater support at least for the demand of a multi-party system. This tendency was very clearly expressed in the "Program of the Democrats."

The champions of the "democratic movement" presently lack any meaningful contact with the masses of the population—the people who had formerly remained passive because they had at their disposal extremely few viable possibilities. (The national minorities provide the only exception to this, particularly the Jews, Crimean Tartars, and several religious communities, for the most part Baptists. In these cases the government feels itself threatened not by a few courageous intellectuals, but by a very well-organized mass movement, in which representatives of all, even the lowest, social levels are united.)

Just as their predecessors in the pre-Revolutionary intelligentsia did, the present-day freedom fighters complain about the *raskol* (gap or breach) between the actively fighting intellectuals and the great masses of the people. They seem to a certain extent convinced that the situation calls for an economic shake-up, or at least an economic stagnation, to help them establish the necessary ties with the average man on the street. Amalrik rightly points out that the revolution of 1905 would hardly have been conceivable had they not lost the war with Japan (1904-05) and that the revolution of 1917 probably would not have occurred except for the catastrophic results of the First World War in Russia. Nevertheless, Amalrik sees "many favorable signs that a yearning for a new ideology is fermenting within the greater part of the population, especially among the workers—a yearning that could be supported by the negative attitude toward the regime and its official policies." [3]

If one sought to justify the present attitude—not only that displayed by the opposing minority but the general posture of the people, one would arrive at few homogeneous facts, and these would be difficult to grasp. The main point, however, remains the same as ever: The regime has at its disposal every means of power, and the greatest of these is undoubtedly the secret police force with its information machine. This institution does not work solely with the weapons of force and psychological super-refinements, with the capital of fear or exploitation of human weaknesses and vulnerability, but also with a highly equipped and technically sophisticated laboratory. The regime also employs all the powers at its disposal to gain control of, or else debase, all means of communication which do not directly serve its interests. An obvious vacuum of information has resulted from these attempts, which up until now have been successful, although they are no longer as completely so as they once were. Because of this vacuum of information, even members of the intellectual circles of Russian society are often no longer capable of an alternative political and personal outlook. Hitherto their acknowledgment and acceptance of Communism resulted from the supposition that Communism and humanism were synonymous. Communism seems to them the single possibility of attaining equality, when by equality they understand justice. This conception of Communism has nothing to do with a violent "conversion"—for many of them it isn't even a messianic conception (although it is often included in the heritage of Russian messianism). The fact that this type of understanding of

Communism is widely held in Russia today is proved perhaps most clearly by the growing loss of actuality of the revolutionary ideas, at least in Eastern Europe.

The proverbial patience and the material unpretentiousness of the Russian people are wearing thin as the rulers attempt to put the people off with empty promises and bright visions of the future. In the end the current regime will not be able to contain its subjects indefinitely. And particularly not then should it ever cause a perceptible decrease in consumer goods. The rulers need only remember the uprisings in Novocherkask and other cities to be totally justified in their fear of this possibility. Should a similar event happen today, solidarity between the working classes and the intelligentsia would take place immediately, and it is not difficult to imagine what the results of such a union might be. This is another reason why the government is so concerned about economic development, which today seems to be regressing somewhat, and which Brezhnev repeatedly alludes to in his public remarks. For the first time in many years the irritation of the man in the street is apparent in Russia, especially in the face of an insufficient domestic-supply situation. And everybody is well aware that the concentration camps are filled with collective farmers who dared express "uncensored" feelings— that is, to criticize economic and other shortages.

There is nothing to indicate that the regime has gained any ground during the past decades; nothing has happened that would support its claim to absolutism. As a matter of fact, the measures of suppression and repression in the last few years have once again strengthened the fear felt among the intellectuals. This fear, however, does not lessen the antipathy and doubt they feel toward those who are responsible for it. The "pioneer" spirit that has remained alert and unflagging for many years, along with the assurance of victory and loyalty against the Party, has mellowed to an ever deeper disillusion and skepticism. A total satiety of the indefatigable but uninspired propaganda has existed for a long time. According to official Soviet announcements, more than 7,000 students were expelled from Ukrainian universities in 1968 alone,[4] and all for the alleged reason of ideological unreliability. In this instance, however, one must keep in mind the fact that many of these cases probably dealt with Ukrainian nationalists and their particular disturbances. But then again, this only emphasizes the difficulties the central powers in Moscow have increasingly faced, even in the non-Russian republics.

In the last few years three foreign events, in addition to the domestic and cultural-political convulsions, heightened the loss of confidence the masses felt toward the Party. These were:

(1)   The conflict with China

(2)   The policies concerning Israel

(3)   The occupation of Czechoslovakia

The first point is to a certain degree double-edged. On the one hand, the disagreements with China and the fear of a new war serve to strengthen the regime because patriotic Russians will defend their land, regardless of who rules it. Party and population merge at the point of patriotism; in such a case the regime is totally justified in relying even upon the intellectual elite for support. On the other hand, many Soviet citizens see in the open animosity between China and the u.s.s.r. not only a sign of the failure of the Chinese version of Communism but also a breakdown of the Soviet ideology. "Something has to be wrong with the doctrine," many argue, "if fifteen years ago leaders embraced each other for similar beliefs, under which they now fight each other."

Another factor which led to a further rift between the rulers and the intelligentsia was Moscow's position during and after the Six Days War between Israel and Jordan. The intellectuals were probably not alone in their distrust of the unilateral support of the Arabs and the disparagement of Israel (which went hand in hand with an anti-Zionist campaign, in truth and uncontrolled anti-Semitism). It was reported from many regions that during the war in June of 1967 not only representatives of the intellectual classes— who were often Jews themselves—but also a great number of the workers and collective farmers sided with the oppressed Israelis, despite the otherwise traditional anti-Semitism one usually finds in peasant circles. In several universities, there were reported incidents of money having been collected to aid the Israeli cause.

Most important, however, was the fact that the Six Days War—that is, the oppression of Israel at the time, even more than the subsequent Soviet "anti-Zionist" campaign— strengthened more clearly than ever the personal identity many Russian Jews felt with Israel. This was the actual beginning of the Zionist movement in the Soviet Union. Since then thousands of Soviet Jews have undertaken the arduous procedures for a journey to Israel despite innumerable obstacles and dangers. The authorities have surrendered to growing pressures and allowed thousands to emigrate; thousands of others, however, are still waiting for permission to do so. Some are waiting in prisons and "insane asylums," which so far have proved to be the only place their desire to leave the Soviet "paradise" in favor of their old homeland has brought them. This exodus, and the still unfulfilled requests to emigrate, has become a difficult problem for the Soviet regime, mostly because it demonstrates to the rest of the world more than the simple failure of its racial policies. It gives evidence of the failure of its social order.

Reactions to the occupation of Czechoslovakia have already been discussed as they appeared in *Chronika*. Even though these protests were heard only among a very determined and courageous minority, this fact alone indicates that such demonstrations and protests were symptomatic for the shame, the horror, and the disgust that this aggression on the part of the Kremlin occasioned in many parts of the Soviet Union.

One of the most conspicuous changes registered during the last few years among Soviet students is a growing political awareness, not only of world events but also an increasing concern over domestic policies. Today frequent questions betraying individual thought and an increased appetite and need for information have replaced the general ennui that used to reign in political discussions.

The goals and the wishes being expressed by this growing political conscientiousness not only differ from those of the so-called "new left" in the West; they are in total opposition to them. Early in the course of the liberalizing process in Czechoslovakia, the divergence between Czechoslovakian students and radical "leftists" in the West was clearly evident. The "progressive" youth, who were increasingly taking their place as an autonomous group in the Soviet Union, found most of the efforts of their Western contemporaries incomprehensible. Many members of the Soviet intelligentsia wanted what those in the West had, and what they themselves lacked: a parliamentarian democracy, sure guarantees of their civil rights, a free economy hampered by as few governmental limitations as possible, free and independent research without the current "politicization" of the universities. The Soviet intellectuals resist ideologizing of all areas of study, philosophically they often support the theory of personalism, and they celebrate the individual rather than collectives.

Their struggle against Stalinism is a result of the same historical experience which causes them to reject and abhor Maoism. The young Russian intellectuals are aware of both history and tradition, but both outside the official ideological doctrine. It is a combination of patriotism and an awareness of social responsibility that forces them to resist the system and in so doing to risk their lives, for in a system permitting no opposition the only way to accomplish one's ends is to risk one's very existence.

An inevitable result of all this is the drawing together of active opposition forces and politically unexposed intellectuals, in the face of the ever more flagrant contradictions between the interests of the Party and those of the people and the state. This has been demonstrated not only in the reactions to the trial against Ginzburg and Galanskov but also in the protests against the latest imprisonment of

Yesenin-Volpin, and even in the courageous behavior of the defendants in the latest political trials. Most recently the arrest of the biologist and geneticist Zores Medvedev has aroused general disapproval. Medvedev, a famous opponent of Lysenko, was involuntarily confined to an insane asylum in May of 1970 after several of his works appeared in *Samizdat*. His arrest was particularly disquieting because it was the first time since the Stalin era that a well-known natural scientist was persecuted in such a drastic manner— a member of a class that should sooner enjoy the protection of the authorities in the interests of research than members of other vocations, even more than their writers. In addition to courageous opponents, such as Solzhenitsyn, who were appalled at the arrest of Medvedev (*see page 395*), numerous well-known scientists (among them Sakharov and Kapica) spoke up against the arrest in a petition that not only demanded the immediate release of Medvedev but also demanded a revision of the conviction of Grigorenko. The pressure exerted by these groups was undoubtedly responsible for the release of Medvedev exactly four weeks after his arrest.

The fact that the otherwise letter-loyal president of the Academy of Sciences, Mstislav Keldysh, apparently supported these protests indirectly, shows that the rulers must soon seriously consider the possibility of opposition from previously loyal sectors, whose support and service they could rely on until very recently. The cracks in the current political machinery is even more clearly demonstrated in the occasional failure of its secret police organization. (*Chronika,* for example, cites instances in which KGB officials have taken the side of the opponents—that is, have moved into the ranks of those active in the "democratic movement.")[5] And finally, Andrei Amalrik maintains that the representatives of the "liberal ideology," advocates of a parliamentarian constitutional state, are to be found in positions very close to the seat of government.

Naturally, at first, only a small minority, driven by their passionate repudiation of injustice, stands up actively against a system of lawlessness and suppression. But the decisive factor is the manner in which this opposition is steadily gaining support and strength. Presumably, in a moment of temporary relaxation of the pressure exerted on them by the authorities, they will quickly expand and come into their own.

Up until now, at least in Russia, a small minority has always served as forerunner for every historical revolution. Even the intelligentsia of the nineteenth and early twentieth centuries did not provide an organized movement. They had no generally accepted program and were even less homogeneous in their methods and in their conceptions of ultimate goals than the present avant-garde of the Russian intellectuals. It was only in historically favorable moment that they succeeded in gaining the support of the masses and in overthrowing the power of the state. The intellectuals of today's opposition, who have sought their goals no less determinedly than their predecessors, are richer in painful experience and therefore more moderate in many respects. In them the rulers have recognized, if not a direct threat, at least a potentially dangerous adversary. Despite any temporary setbacks the democratic movement might suffer, the rulers appear incapable of putting an end to this growing opposition. In attempting to accomplish this, they are left with the single solution of reverting to the total terror of the Stalin years. But not only the fear of being completely isolated from the West keeps them from actively pursuing this course; more importantly, the danger of sooner or later becoming the victim rather than the perpetrator of such terrorizing tactics stands between them and their decision.

And, finally, one has to remember how quickly, considering the limitations of a totalitarian state, the development of the intellectual opposition took place. It is only recently that the fearlessness on the part of the participants has begun to triumph despite all forms of repression, and this fearlessness is one of the constituents of freedom.

Vladimir Bukovski states:

> *The essence of our struggle is the battle against fear—the fear that has imprisoned the people since the time of Stalin, the fear from which they have never yet been able to free themselves that, finally, allows the system to continue to exist . . . It is also the struggle against anxiety in which we expend our greatest efforts. And in this battle the most important thing is our personal example given to the masses.*[6]

By means of this example of personal integrity and unselfish daring, the civil and human-rights fighters in present-day Russia hope to establish a foundation outside their own ranks. One of their proclamations states:

Fortunately, the demand for human dignity is contagious, and a society in which responsible citizens, filled with the conviction of this dignity, grow from a minority to a majority—such a society is not an empty dream, but rather a real and reachable goal, even if it demands long and persistent efforts. The criteria for the priorities of this social order lie in that dignity which must be guaranteed to each individual member by that society and this not only includes the "right of life," but also the "right of conscience." [7]

DOCUMENTS

DOCUMENTS

Human Manifesto   YURI GALANSKOV

Don't trust the ministers, the leaders, the newspapers!
Stand up, you who are lying on the floor!
Look, in the cavernous sockets of the world
And see the little balls of atomic death,
   Get up!
   Get up!
   Get up!
O scarlet blood of rebellion!
Go out and destroy
The rotten prison of the state!
Step over the bodies of the frightened
And carry for the army of the hungry,
Black bombs—like plums—
On the plates of the public squares.

Where are they,
Those needed to stuff up the throats of the cannons,
To lance the boils of war

With the sacred scalpel of rebellion?
  Where are they?
  Where are they?
  Where are they?
Or don't they exist on this earth?
Over there, a handful of gold
Chains their shadows to the gun carriages.

Man has disappeared—a nothing, a fly.
He hardly stirs in the lines of books.
I am going out on the public square
And into the city's ear;
I'll shriek out my inner confusion.
Then I will find a gun
And press it firmly against my temple;
For no one shall trample the snow-white
Shreds of my soul.
People!
It's all right, let it be!
Stop trying to comfort me.
Imprisoned in your hell,
I find nothing to breathe.
Welcome baseness and famine!
But I, thrown to the ground
Spit on your inflexible city
Stuffed full of money and filth!

Heavens!
I don't know what I'm doing.

I need an exorcising knife.
Do you see how somebody
Has splashed the white with black lies?
Do you see how somebody
Chews upon the bloody flag.
And life is as frightful as a prison
Erected upon a pile of bones.
   I'm falling!
   I'm falling!
   I'm falling!
Just take your time growing old.
I will not feed on cadavers,
Like everybody else.
Nor shall I to satisfy my hunger
Reap fruits from graves.
I want none of your bread
Kneaded with tears.
I fall and rise again
Half delirious
Half asleep.
And I feel how
Humanity
Is flowering within me.

We have grown accustomed
When, in leisure hours
We stroll along the streets,
To seeing faces distorted by life,
Just as ours are.
And suddenly—

Like the rolling of thunder,
Like the second coming of Christ—
There ascended
Trampled and crucified,
The beauty of mankind.
It is I
Who calls for truth and revolt,
No longer ready to serve—
I shall rend your black chains
For they are but woven of lies.
It is I—
Though bound by the law
I'll shout out the human manifesto!
And may a raven peck out
A cross
On the marble of my body.

From PHOENIX, *1961. This translation is based on the German version by May von Holbeck in:* VORKAEMPFER DER FREIHEIT, *Frankfurt am Mainz, 1967.*

N. NOR

We are very few; we are very weak;
And you mock us from all sides.
You threaten us with exile,
With iron bars
And with the contempt of the people.
You tell us: "Give it up!
Bend your backs! Confess your guilt!

And sing the praises
Of our first-rate twaddle!"

We'd rather be few, we'd rather be weak!
We'll never acknowledge your nonsense!
We're sick unto death of it!
We need food for our minds—
For independent thought and deed!
We need joy and faith
And a clear understanding!

Yes, we'd rather be few; we'd rather be weak!
You could never control the growth of our numbers.
Your dark dreary kitchen
Has never known the aroma of fine, delicate fare,
Where salt and pepper and other sharp spices
Are hidden behind the pantry doors—
Your dreary kitchen reeks of murder
And stands on rotten wood!
We will splinter the planks beneath you!

So we'd rather be few!
     We'll wait! We'll believe!
And e'en should we fail,
     Our goal will be realized!

From phoenix, *1961. Reprinted in* grani, *No. 52, 1962.*

A. PETROV

Oh Romanticism! With your clouds and your blue.
The glowing beacon of Danko's heart—[1]
How much water and how much blood
Have flowed in the cellars of Lubianka.[2]

Oh Romanticism! With your clouds and your blue!
Soviet tanks are crawling through Budapest.
How much water and how much blood
Have flowed in the cellars of Lubianka.

Oh Romanticism! With your clouds and your blue!
They carve up our souls and wear them as socks.
How much water and how much blood
Have flowed in the cellars of Lubianka.

From PHOENIX, *1961. Reprinted in* GRANI, *No. 52, 1962.*

ARTIOMI MIKHAILOV

If you've never been in a concentration camp,
And you've never rescued yourself from a heap of corpses
If your best friend has never anonymously denounced you
And you've never rescued yourself from a heap of corpses
After having survived execution by nothing short of a
        miracle—

If you don't know the theory of relativity
And tensor calculus;
If you can't fly like the wind on a motorbike—
If you've never killed the girl you love on orders from
      another,
And don't understand how to build shortwave radios,
If you don't belong to some kind of Mafia,
And can't quite bring yourself to shout "Hooray" with
      the crowd—
If you can't save yourself within two seconds from an
      atomic holocaust,
If you can't live with five people in five square meters
      of space
And you can't even play basketball—
      Then you are not a man of the twentieth century.

From SFINKSY, *Moscow. This poem also appeared in* GRANI, *No. 59,*
1965.

Descent into Hell (Excerpts)   YURI STEFANOV

    I can't listen any more
    To that eternal song:
    "Oh Russia, my Russia—"
    For Russia is dead.

    Dead are the villages,
    The barns and the fields;

The strains of *Balalaika*
In the evening haze.

Dead are the hills,
The valleys are dead;
And so are the clouds
Which glowed in the sun.

Gone are the hamlets,
The trees and the grass;
Her enemies celebrate
For Russia is dead.

Oh God, my redeemer.
Give heed to my prayer.
I know that you share
My grief at this hour.

And you alone can
Show me the way—
That slope down the dark,
To see Russia again.

The slippery steps
I'll mutely descend—

I'll descend into hell,
To the grave of my land.

At that sacred site,
I will timidly swear:
Yours is my blood,
My body, my soul!

Rip my body, like
Linen, asunder!
And wipe away
Your desperate tears.

Then, renewed and renowned,
I will follow the star:
And having freed you,
I'll replace you in hell.

1963; from SFINKSY, *Moscow, 1965. Reprinted in* GRANI, *No. 59,*
1965.

The Phoenix   YEVGENY KUSCHEV

A profound purpose
Characterizes Man.
With eyes and with forests,

With flowers and weeds, and with all forms
    of thought.
We share our creator.

It was a long time ago
When the phoenix was born.
Who created the tiniest atom?
Was it God, or a dream?

There's a spirit behind any creation.
But where did hell originate?
But though hell scorch him as it will—
Man will always arise from the flames,
For immortal is his soul.

Therefore, Time, despite its rages,
Cannot separate life from death.
And ever the phoenix
Arising above the ashes—
Symbolizes our world!

Appeared in RUSSKOE SLOVO, *Moscow, and* GRANI, *No. 66, 1967.*

The Decembrists (Excerpts)   YEVGENY KUSCHEV

I have disturbing dreams.
Especially in December.

That's when I walk to the Senate Square[3]
And stand in square formation.

And I am wordlessly surrounded,
Quietly, motionlessly,
By Ryleev, Pestel, Bestuzhev,
Kakhovski, and Muravev.[4]

Then, closing in, like children,
They look in my eyes and ask:
"Is it true that the noose
Is all you've been bequeathed?

Is it true that only Nekrasov
And the poet of Bohemia
Have scraped away the blackness
And brought us into light?

And after more than a hundred years
Under the lash of the whip,
A spark of December smolders
In every Russian lad?

That hatred toward the hangman
Lives on as does our heir?"

And how can I make answer?
I weep, and I hold my silence.

Moscow, July 8, 1966

Appeared in RUSSKOE SLOVO, *Moscow. The German version was the work of E. Tarasova and D. Orlenin. In* VORKAEMPFER DER FREIHET, *Frankfurt am Main, 1967.*

For Aleksei Dobrovolski in Friendship and Love

LEONID SERGEEV

Whiter than a flock of swans
Winter lies around us.
I'm on my way and throughout the long and weary journey,
All I say is: "Lord, have mercy."

When I see a small church resting in the distance
I love to look toward heaven, cross myself,
And abandoning my soul in holy prayer,
Forgive my enemies everything.

Peace and harmony reign over my soul
In these bright and lucid hours;
But the cup, with its sharp and bitter hemlock,
Is already within my reach—its poison oozes out!

Living memories
Trouble my weak and weary mind.
Mute ghosts gather round me
And haunted by the shades of youthful years,
I stand dark and still, more dead than alive.

How bitter are the doubts
Which then benumb my soul!
Then the early peace is broken
And I am left with a passionate yearning
To sink down, deep down, into darkest hell!

But God in his mercy comforts me
And soon peace and light reign again in my soul;
As if, out of the immeasurable depths of heaven,
A friendly voice has answered me.

A whole new series of airy visions
Lend wings to my soul, refreshed and renewed.
The spring of poetry revive me
With living and life-giving waters!

Then my being explodes with joy and sweetness
And my weary heart begins to sing.
And I know I await no other destiny
Than to answer my God when he calls me away.

Only then will I finally know true peace
When I rest under the shadows of the grave;
I'll take my leave of this valley of sorrows
And joyfully, with a grateful prayer,
Will I receive the redeeming crown.

December 16, 1962, reprinted in GRANI, *No. 66, 1967.*

REPORT OF THE SMOG DEMONSTRATION

*The following report on the demonstration of the illegal
SMOG organization, held on April 14, 1965, was written by
a Moscow student. It was forwarded to the Western press
in December of the same year.*

On April 12, I found a notice in one of the buildings of
Moscow University (MGU), signed by the central committee
of SMOG, urging participation in the planned demonstration
on Mayakovski Square. During the next two days, additional
fliers and handbills dealing with the same topic appeared
repeatedly in the MGU building. They were torn down, but
constantly replaced.

These announcements occasioned lively discussions
among the students, who mentioned that such fliers had
also appeared in the Conservatorium, in several institutes,
on the bulletin boards of the Lenin Library, and on the
publishing houses of *Pravda* and *Molodaia Gvardia*. They
said that those students known to them as members of
SMOG had been summoned to the dean and were warned

that they would be expelled from the university if they appeared on Mayakovski Square. It was also common knowledge that the Committee for State Security, the Moscow Party Committee, as well as the Moscow and Central Committee of the Komsomol, knew of the planned demonstration and had issued the order to break it up.

Following a discussion with friends, we decided to proceed singly to the square, and to meet there at six o'clock in the evening. At the designated time, about two hundred people had gathered on the square, and more kept coming. Somebody made a short statement, the gist of which I was unable to grasp. Many of the people in the group felt that the speakers were members of the Central Committee of SMOG. The second speaker read a petition addressed to the Writers' Union. The petition demanded recognition of SMOG, the opportunity for free propagation and discussion of ideas, permission to set up a press, etc.

A few young people attempted to disrupt the reading and tore the petition out of the speaker's hands, but enraged individuals in the audience quickly restored order. The crowd continued to grow. Approximately nine hundred people had gathered by now, but something seemed to be bothering the organizers of the demonstration. They were waiting for someone who apparently had not yet appeared. The leaders became uneasy, and this tension was perceived by the mob.

At this point, a young man climbed up the steps of the monument and shouted: "If you're not cowards, and if Russian art means anything to you—follow me!"

He then proceeded to cross through the mob in the direction of Sadovaia. The greater part of the crowd—about

300 to 350 people—followed him. The rest remained at the monument where someone was now reading poems. Plainclothes men sneaked around the crowd whispering things to some of the demonstrators and threatening others. Two military cars equipped with loudspeakers attempted to disrupt the recital; but the crowd remained intact, and my friend and I stayed with it. A group of young people stepped off an approaching trolley and joined the demonstrators.

Those in front shouted: "Unroll the slogans!" Almost immediately, a three-meters-long sign was held up over the heads of the crowd. On a piece of wallpaper they had written, "Long live Leftist art!"

They had hardly managed to carry this thing three hundred feet before two unidentified chaps rushed over, and in their attempt to catch hold of it, tore the sign.

"Forward!" was the order coming from the head of the column and "Don't pay any attention to provocations!" We marched on.

Above our heads, additional slogans were raised: "Let's tear the brass buttons of ideas and themes off the Stalinist uniform!" "Fuck socialist realism!" "Freedom for Brodski, Osipov, Narica, Bukovski, and the others!" "Art free from ideology!" "We will be!"

Chekists [secret police agents] and emergency commandos in civilian clothes fell upon the slogan bearers, tore the placards from their hands, and tried to instigate a fistfight. But it was too late, for the crowd had by this time reached the offices of the Writers' Union.

Somebody managed to climb to the top of the steps where he repeated the text of the petition read just a short time ago. Two people then went into the Union building and when they returned, reported to 'the crowd that they had handed a copy of the petition to Ilin, the secretary in charge of the Moscow Section of the Writers' Union.

At this point, two of the emergency commandos, grabbed from behind the two who had read the petition and threw them down the steps, where two other commandos bound the hands of the petitioners behind their backs. Friends rushed to their aid, but it was apparent that many *Chekists* and other emergency commandos had also rushed over. Many demonstrators were arrested on the spot. The ringleader managed to break loose; but the *Chekists* hurled him to the ground, and dragged him off to a nearby wagon, beating him on the way.

Although severely beaten on the nose and the mouth, the leader managed to shriek out between fits of bloody vomiting: "Those who value art—help me!" The only answer he got was the scornful laughter of the *Chekists* and their assistants.

A group of MGU students tried to free him but were unsuccessful. In a confused rage, the leader kicked with his feet and tossed his head about, but six policemen carried him off and threw him into a wagon. We flung ourselves against this wagon and tried to break into it, but we were pushed aside. The wagon took off in third gear, and hurtled off to an undisclosed destination.

We were now forced to defend ourselves. A fistfight had broken out in front of the Union building. The trolleys couldn't get through. Belligerent demonstrators swarmed all over Herzen Street. The approximately two hundred students who remained were hopelessly outnumbered, for they also faced, in addition to approximately one hundred

Chekists, emergency commandos, riot police, regular police officers, and volunteers from the Writers' Union. About two hundred additional bystanders had gathered and remained neutral; they stood around, however, and heckled.

We managed to escape—not all, but many.

Several days later, the hearings took place, and those who were arrested were sentenced to no more than a few days in jail.

Six members of SMOG were expelled from the university, and many other students were put on probation. The important thing is that this was the first time in forty years that a literary-political demonstration was greeted with such an enormous show of support in Moscow.

This report appeared in POSEV, *December 3, 1965.*

THE MOSCOW TRIALS (1966-1968)

LETTERS FROM GINZBURG TO KOSYGIN

The following letter from Aleksandr Ginzburg addressed to Prime Minister Kosygin first appeared in the White *Book of the* Case *of Daniel and Siniavski, gathered together and edited by Ginzburg. The excerpts below are those which appeared in the journal* Ost Probleme. *The original text of the letter appeared in* Grani, *the first time in the West, in unabridged form.*

I am very familiar with Terz's short story entitled *The Trial Begins,* his collection of short stories entitled *Fantastic*

Stories, and his article *What is Socialist Realism?*, as well as Arzhak's short story entitled *Moscow Speaking*. I am also acquainted with a whole series of other works which, at various times, have aroused the displeasure of the KGB and were subsequently confiscated. I can see no reason for this animosity other than the fact that the authors in question avoided all banalities in their depiction of reality and in their depiction of literary characters. An example of this is Pasternak's *Doctor Zhivago*, an outstanding book that was deservedly awarded the Nobel Prize. (Its simultaneous confiscation by the KGB, incidentally, shows that it apparently stood on the top of their priority list.)

Possibly the actions of Siniavski and Daniel could have violated some voluntarily assumed obligation. The charter of the Soviet Writers' Union, of which they were both members, possibly could have contained a different interpretation of the principle "socialist realism" than that expressed in Siniavski's article. Possibly the short story *Moscow Speaking* could have been written in violation of some rule which was laid down in this charter. Also, I believe, the use of a pseudonym may be regulated in some manner by the writers' organization.

The violation of these obligations constitutes a definite offense. It is completely within the competence of the Writers' Union (if you happen to be a member of that organization) or within the competence of the CPSU (if you happen to be a member of the Party) or within the competence of any other voluntary organization, if after your entrance into the group you trespass against any of the rules of that particular organization. These actions, however, have absolutely no connection with the state. (Article 70 of the

Penal Code provides for crimes against the state.)

The fact that you were born in the Soviet Union does not deprive you of the right to think for yourself. The right to stand up for your own convictions and your ideas of what will benefit your country is not a monopoly of those who currently sit in positions of power. Siniavski and Daniel are entitled to be outraged over the crimes of recent years, to express their love for the past, and their own conceptions of the future of their land. The literary works of Siniavski in his native country—articles in *Novy Mir,* books about Picasso and the literature of the early Revolutionary War years, the introduction to a collection of Boris Pasternak's poems—furnish all the proof necessary for Terz's right to interpret socialist realism, for example, in his own way.

The only correct solution, which unfortunately has not yet been employed would be the following: to consider the case to be not before the Justice Department, but before our social organs—before organizations of writers, Party members, and the workers. Fortunately for literature, these organizations do not have control over a network of reform, and work camps, but simply over a well-thought-out and theoretically based system of social interaction.

Granted we no longer live in Stalinist times. But even today, the KGB is still a block that seriously hinders the evolution of social life-forms. A recent example of this is the "participation" of state-security police officers in the peaceful demonstration of December 5 (1965) at Pushkin Square. Attempts to unfold banners with the demand to open the trials of Siniavski and Daniel to the public, or with the slogan PAY ATTENTION TO THE CONSTITUTION, and attempts— nothing more—to say the same things out loud always ended with the fact that those who attempted these things were handcuffed and escorted to the nearest military department or to the headquarters of the Peoples' Police. Responsible members of the Moscow KGB staff watched all of this with a certain degree of satisfaction.

That is only the most recent, the very latest event. If, however, one were to look deeper into the matter, how can one then describe the arrest of Siniavski and Daniel and their three months of imprisonment as anything other than an interference in social life?

If the fact of their authorship has been proved and one prepares himself to convict them simply on the grounds of the contents of their works, then there is not the slightest necessity to keep them in custody until the trial. Even if one is of the opinion that their works violate Article 70 of the Penal Code, then all the rest of their activities (for example, the use of pseudonyms or the sending of the manuscripts abroad) would not be punishable by Soviet legislation. Imprisonment in solitary confinement for many months has deleterious effects on the human psyche, as I know from personal experience.

The arrest of Siniavski and Daniel, and the complete lack of publicity about their case—as in most of the KGB cases concerning anti-Soviet propaganda—make it impossible for the public to form its independent opinion about the actions of the accused, and to control in any way the legality of the KGB actions. It would be a sin, however, not to raise some doubt about this in this case.

Article 19 of the "General Declaration of Human Rights," passed by the United Nations in 1948 and ratified by the Soviet Union, reads:

> *Every man shall have the right to freedom of thought and its expression. This includes his right to maintain his opinion unharassed, and to receive and disseminate information and ideas by any means he chooses without consideration for state limitations.*

Don't these words have a direct relationship to the Siniavski/Daniel case?

I consider it my right and my duty to come to you with these questions. I am by no means convinced that they will not be interpreted as anti-Soviet. And there is ample justification for any doubts. I could be called to account and condemned because I used foreign sources of information. I listen to foreign broadcasts because, up until now, nothing has been published in our country concerning the case of Siniavski and Daniel, and because I am acquainted with the books of these authors and think them good, and because I participated in the demonstration on December 5, (it might occur to somebody to describe that demonstration as "anti-Soviet"), and because I have spoken out loudly about the very things I have written about in this letter. In 1937, in 1949, and indeed even in 1961, people have wandered behind prison walls for much less.

But I love my country, and I do not want its reputation to be blackened again by the uncontrolled actions of the KGB.

I love Russian literature and I do not want to witness yet again two representatives of this literature marching out under guard to chop down trees. I consider Andrei Siniavski an outstanding critic and prose writer.

A. GINZBURG

DECEMBER, 1965

MY ADDRESS: MOSCOW Z — 180

B. POLIANKA, 11/14

APT. 25

From OST-PROBLEME, *No. 25/26, 1966.*

LETTER TO AN OLD FRIEND

Dear Friend:

You asked me for my opinion about the trial of Siniavski and Daniel.

You were surprised that the tone of the foreign radio announcements concerning this trial is rather calm, although the case naturally affected the whole world more deeply, painfully, and more responsibly than did the infamous Pasternak affair in its time. But that is understandable. The silly incident with the Nobel Prize winner didn't really have anything to do with the principles of the Soviet society. The element of spiritual terror that played such a role in the story of Pasternak (I almost said in the Pasternak trial) was expanded in this case to a psychic terror. The manner in which the writers in this case were persecuted cannot be described allegorically; it is completely real, it is a rhetorical figure. Please excuse me when I use literary termini, but I feel they are justified by the sense and the tone of this trial.

The Siniavski trial was the first open political trial during the Soviet regime in which, from beginning to end—from the preliminary investigation to the final conclusions of the defendants—the accused pleaded not guilty and accepted the sentence in a manner in keeping with their personal dignity. The accused were both about forty—the optimal age for a defendant in a political trial. It was the first such trial to be held in over four decades. No wonder the eyes of the whole world were focused on it.

This was the first political trial since that against the Right social revolutionaries, already the legendary heroes of revolutionary Russia. The Right social revolutionaries were the only ones to walk out of the courtroom without having aroused pity, contempt, fear, or incredulity behind them . . .

If it were twenty years ago instead of today, Siniavski and Daniel would have been shot in some basement of the State Security Department or placed on the interrogative "conveyor belt," where the interrogators constantly relieved one another, but where the accused man had to stand in one place many hours and even many days on end until his will was broken and his opposition exhausted. Or else he would have been injected with a serum that weakened one's will power, one of the favorite methods practiced during the horrible public trials of the 1930's. If they never intended to hold an open trial and the accused was not "prepared" for one, he would be simply shot down in the corridor. The charges made against him would also have been quite different—Paragraph 58: treason against the fatherland, destructive activities, terror, sabotage.

Why weren't these paragraphs referred to during this new trial? Many things have changed, times have changed. One ought not to forget that Siniavski and Daniel composed their first works in 1956, right after the Twentieth Party Congress. Siniavsky and Daniel believed in the truth of what had just been said. They believed in it and wanted to reinforce it. From the standpoint of the Twentieth and the Twenty-Second Party Congresses, Siniavski's and Daniel's stories couldn't be condemned, even from the point of view of socialist realism" (something that not only Aragon but other Western Communists understood).

One ought not to forget that Siniavski and Daniel were the first to take up the battle after almost fifty years of reigning silence. Their example is magnificent, their heroism indisputable.

Siniavski and Daniel broke the despicable tradition of "repentance" and "confession." How did they accomplish this? How could they hold out so well to the end of the trial, without knowing whether their case would be supported in the West and whether their fate would even be followed there?

Remember the beginning of the trial. After those who were to take part in the trial were announced, and all the remaining formalities were over, including the naming of the judges, whose names, however, were never printed (so that it appeared that those who had agreed to participate in this trial felt they had done something they might be ashamed of and had therefore requested that their names not be made public, as was the general procedure applied to cases concerning the names of informers—there were unquestionably legal precedents for such a procedure), the defense moved that particular testimonies by the literary scholar V. V. Ivanov and the writers K. G. Paustovski and

L. S. Kopelev be included in the minutes. All three—Ivanov, Kopelev, and Paustovski—gave a literary analysis of the stories of Terz-Siniavski and Arzhak-Daniel. I might mention here that in the case of Ivanov we are talking about a linguist who enjoys a world-wide reputation in his field. He requested the court to allow him to participate in the trial as counsel for the defense. Finally, there were also two public plaintiffs—Z. S. Kedrina and A. Vasilev; any more significant figures among writers' circles managed to remain out of sight. According to the law, anyone can appear as counsel for the defense. As we know from the trials against swindlers and thieves, public defenders are permitted to participate.

The court overruled the request of V. V. Ivanov.

The court overruled the motion to include the testimonies of V. V. Ivanov, K. G. Paustovski, and L. S. Kopelev in the minutes. The tension increased.

The defense then requested the court to open the proceedings with the case against Siniavski in the hopes that he might be able to determine the tone of the trial. The court overruled the request of the defense.

The trial began.

The court had made a mistake. In Daniel they found they were facing a man completely capable and aware of his rights.

Daniel began with a retraction of one of the statements he had made during the interrogations. At that time he stated that he had given his manuscripts to Siniavski, and now he corrected the impression by affirming that he now remembered very well—the moment in question had taken place years ago—that he had passed on his manuscripts in Siniavski's house, but not in the presence of Siniavski himself.

Siniavski and Daniel were quite adept at keeping the trial on a literary level, within the realm of science-fiction and the grotesque, and they confessed to no charges of anti-Soviet activities. They demanded respect for the freedom of creativity and the freedom of conscience. The significance of the trial lay in this very point. Siniavski and Daniel behaved courageously, self-assuredly, and at the same time very carefully. They carefully considered every sentence and did not fall into the trap set up for them—not so much by the prosecutor as by the presiding judge.

Nothing would have been simpler than to have prepared a political speech and then to have delivered it, something along the lines of: Ever since I was a child I hated _____; I confess to having been a dissident in _____. (Variation: May the merciful administration forgive me!)

Nothing would have been simpler, and nothing would have been more detrimental. To assume such a position would have meant a victory for the prosecutor and the court and would at the same time have put the nation back into that unbearable situation when the author of the poem about that carefree bird[5] was condemned to a concentration camp as a parasite. They even wanted to make a case against the bird itself, since in it they perceived an accusation against the state and they would have considered the text as nothing more than rhetorical, bourgeois hackwork.

Siniavski and Daniel did not fall into this trap.

Actually, why is it precisely Siniavski and Daniel who are supposed to be the enemies of the Soviet regime rather than the prosecutor who, in reply to a question by the author, stated that he would not have allowed Siniavski's stories to be published in the homeland? Which one is it who commits the greater injustice to Russia?

Siniavski and Daniel denied any guilt in connection with anti-Soviet activities. How right they were! Any work of this description can only be beneficial.

Just think, old friend! The courage of Siniavski and Daniel, their integrity, their victory, also contains a drop of our blood, a drop of our suffering, of our struggle against humiliation and lies, against murderers and traitors of all kinds.

What is slander, anyway? We both remember the Stalin era; the concentration camps of an unprecedented, super-Hitlerian scale, Auschwitz without ovens, where millions of people perished. We know the moral corruption, the depravity of our government that feigns remorse and to this day does not want to tell the truth—even, for example, the truth about Kirov.[6] How long is this going to continue? Can there be a limit to the truth about our past beyond which it becomes slander? The human brain is not capable of inventing the crimes which were committed in those times. For this reason it would be better for the court to maintain the framework of purely literary discussion, as Siniavski suggested. It is much more pleasant for the court to discuss direct speech, poetic words, the grotesque, science-fiction. It's simpler that way . . .

The story by Arzhak-Daniel entitled *This is Moscow Speaking*, with its exceptionally successful Gogolesque subject, "Day of the Open Murders," can hardly be compared in a purely realistic context with the stenographic reports of the Twenty-Second Party Congress—in other words, with what was revealed in those reports. For we have had not one "open-murder day" but twenty years of open murder.

No, it would be much better to remain within the framework of a purely literary discussion. The presiding judge, L. Smirnov, the most prominent judge in the Soviet Union (this fact alone indicates just how strongly the government felt itself on the defensive at the start of the trial) preferred to choose the second alternative, and that was to determine the sentence on the basis of anti-Revolutionary agitation and propaganda, to throw the book at the defendants. Siniavski was condemned to seven years, Daniel to five, in a concentration camp.

Why was this particular trial singled out for the participation of the Chairman of the Supreme Court? . . .

L. Smirnov had been instructed to simulate democracy —to make a gesture of the type from which stemmed the surprising tricks they played against Tarsis, who had managed to cross the English Channel shortly before this trial began.

The speculation that Tarsis would condemn Siniavski from his new position in the West, and by so doing, would himself be considered and referred to as a paranoid, proved to be unfounded.

Moreover, the confirmation of a mental infirmity supported by health reports remains unconvincing not only in the case of Tarsis and Yesenin-Volpin, but also in the case of Chaadaev . . .

This trial, which the press assured was conducted "under the exact observance of all procedural norms," represented, in fact, a crude violation of those procedural norms.

If, on February 22, 1966, *Pravda* was compelled to hark back to the utterances Lenin made at the start of the Revolution to justify the severity of the sentence, then this in itself is already a lie. The whole world is changing, and it is only the dogmas of the Soviet law, intended for short-term application, that are not changing.

Smirnov did not conduct this trial simply to simulate democracy for the West. For all his many colleagues throughout the vast territory of the Soviet Union, this trial served as a seminar. It was a lesson for young lawyers facing the bar about the procedure one goes through to feign democracy. Even the necessity of such an imitation says a lot.

Siniavski and Daniel were convicted because they were writers and for no other reason. One cannot accuse a man of slander or anti-Soviet agitation, who has survived the Stalin era and has lived to tell about it.

The charge of anti-Semitism against Siniavski (harped on by Kedrina and quoted from newspaper articles during the trial) was just as classic. No one could believe such a thing. The obvious fabrication of this charge was so blatantly embarrassing that Smirnov ordered it to be excluded from the court records. The reason is a familiar one. Just when Stalin's statement in the 1930's about anti-Semitism representing the worst form of nationalism was being widely circulated, Stalin's henchmen murdered Michoels.[7]

Furthermore, the examinations which were made in connection with this trial occasioned not only private but even open protests, something that had not occurred since 1927. On December 5, 1965, university students, as well as faculty, demonstrated at the Pushkin monument.

In short, the court did not answer the questions as to

the guilt of Siniavski and Daniel. Confessions of the accused are too intrinsic an element in Soviet jurisdiction. Without such a confession, neither the court members nor the prosecutor nor the witnesses for the prosecution can comfortably wear the laurel wreath.

On the contrary, it is Siniavski and Daniel who, as early revolutionaries, have inscribed their names forever in golden letters on the banner for the freedom of conscience, the freedom of creativity, and the freedom of individuality.

By the way, while we're on the subject of gold letters, the witness for the prosecution, Vasilev, emotionally recalled those seventy-three writers who were killed at the front and whose names are engraved on the marble slab at the House of Writers. He accused Siniavski and Daniel in the name of those who had fallen.

If a witness for the defense had been allowed at this trial, he would have defended Siniavski and Daniel in the name of those writers who were tortured to death, murdered, or shot, who starved or froze to death in Stalin's concentration camps.

Pilniak, Gumilev, Mandelstam, Babel, Voronski, Tabidze, Yashvili—hundreds of names are included in this martyrology; these dead men, these victims of their time—a regiment of writers who could have been the pride of their country—raise their voices in defense of Siniavski and Daniel.

In accordance with the decision of the Twenty-Second Party Congress, all the victims of Stalin's tyranny were to be posthumously rehabilitated and their names inscribed on an obelisk. Where is this obelisk? Where is the marble slab in the Writers' Union upon which the names of those who were murdered in Stalin's times were to have been engraved in golden letters? There are three or four times as many of these names as those on the marble slab mentioned by the witness for the prosecution . . . Another important detail from this trial: Siniavski and Daniel did not want to involve anyone else in the case, and they managed to protect their friends from the undertow of the investigation. The absence of the application of inhumane techniques strengthened their will to fight and they were victorious.

Every writer wants to see his works published. Is it possible the court could not understand that an author needs the publication of his works as urgently as air to live?

How many have died without ever having attained this goal? Where is our *Doctor Zhivago?* Only half of Bulgakov's works have been published, and only a quarter of Platonov's. Despite this fact, they still rank as two of Russia's best writers. It is usually enough to die to have some of your works published, but Mandelstam was even deprived of that.

How can anyone reproach a writer for wanting to publish his works? And if a pseudonym is necessary, let there be a pseudonym. How else is a writer to succeed in getting published? No, Siniavski and Daniel are not hypocrites, they are fighters for the freedom of creativity, freedom of speech. To accuse them of hypocrisy is in itself the worst form of hypocrisy. No one has the right to call someone sitting in prison a hypocrite . . . The editorial in *Pravda*[8] reminds us of the worst years of the Stalin era. The whole tone of the article, its arguments based on quotations from Lenin, which were already worn out from constant use in the Stalin years—quotes about Kautski, about capitalist democracy, about the democracy of a proletarian dictatorship—in short, all the sophistry we mastered so well during the course of the past forty years—and the practical examples of that sophistry—are only too clear in our memories.

No one expected a "liberal sentence" from the court, but we did assume that the court would renounce bloody deeds and terror . . .

The sentence in the Siniavski-Daniel case plunges Soviet society anew into an atmosphere of terror and persecution. The Soviet government has done very little for the mutual rapprochement of East and West. Actions such as the trial against Siniavski and Daniel imperil even the existing relationship.

It seems to me we are suffering from an old disease which Petr Dolgorukov described so aptly more than a century ago:

> *Many of our compatriots say: "It is better not to tell foreigners the truth about Russia; we should hide the wounds of the fatherland from them.*

In our belief, these words stand in direct contradiction to a healthy logic, as well as to personal dignity, to love of one's fatherland, and to the opinions of truly enlightened men.

Apart from the deep disgust, at lies, felt by every decent and honorable man, that person who believes himself capable of deceiving everybody would have to possess an incredibly great degree of self-confidence. People who want to conceal and hide their wounds are like the critically ill who prefer to suffer and die quickly than call in a good doctor for help, one who could cure them and restore them to strength. For Russia, this doctor is publicity.

From the WHITE BOOK *in the case of Siniavski and Daniel. German edition: Frankfurt am Main, 1967.*

LETTER FROM LIDIA CHUKOVSKAYA
TO MIKHAIL SHOLOKHOV

. . . As far as outward appearances go, all the formalities demanded by law were observed during the proceedings held against the writers Siniavski and Daniel. This causes you to see a deficiency in this trial, but as far as I'm concerned, in this lies its very value. And despite this fact, I am now going to protest against the judgment of the court. Why?

For this very reason: It was against the law to bring Siniavski and Daniel before a criminal court in the first place.

Because a book, belles-lettres; a novella, a novel, a short story, in short, any literary work, whether good or bad, masterful or superficially written, full of lies or impeccable in its truth, is not subject to the jurisdiction of any court, civil or military, but rather is subject only to the judgment of that society to which it is submitted, one can and must bring an author, just like any other Soviet citizen, to account for any criminal deed—but not because of his books. Literature is not subject to criminal jurisdiction. One must oppose ideas with ideas, but not with camps and prisons.

And that, in fact, is what you should have declared to

your audience if you had really conducted yourself as a representative of Soviet literature on the speakers' platform.

Instead, you delivered your speech as a traitor of this literature. History will not forget your shameful speech.

And literature will revenge itself, just as it revenges itself against all who evade the heavy obligation it lays upon them. Literature will condemn you to the most extreme sentence there is for an artist—to artistic impotence. And no honors, no monies, no prizes either from the fatherland or international sources, will remove this judgment from your head.

Excerpt found in the WHITE BOOK *in the case of Siniavski /Daniel.*

SHOLOKHOV'S BARRACKS

The following letter, written by Yuri Galanskov and addressed to the writer Mikhail Sholokhov, was first published in Phoenix *in 1966. In it Galanskov refers to the speech Sholokhov delivered before the Twenty-Third Party Congress in which he sharply criticized the recently convicted writers Siniavski and Daniel, as well as all those who had in any way supported the accused. (See also the letter by Lidia Chukovskaya.) Sholokhov, born in 1905, is well-known even in the West as author of the novel entitled* Quiet Flows the Don. *However, for the last twenty years he has written nothing more. The fact that, of all people, this particularly mediocre novelist was awarded the Nobel Prize for Literature in 1965 not only infuriated Galanskov but also managed to arouse great dissatisfaction among the Soviet reading public, particularly among the intellectuals.*

In his speech to the Twentieth Congress of the Communist Party of the Soviet Union, Mikhail Sholokhov declared: "I want to say a few words about the role of the writer in the life of our society. Maxim Gorki's question can still be relevantly addressed to the artists of today: 'Whose side are you on, teachers of culture?' Stalin had a ready answer for this question: 'He who isn't for us is against us.' As early as the beginning of the twentieth century Lenin categorically differentiated between proletarian and bourgeois culture when he formulated the principle of party-mindedness in literature and defined the dependency relationship between an author and the purse."

A writer is, of course, as much dependent upon his purse as is any other person. But literature isn't. To make literature subject to such a dependency relationship would be the same thing as killing it, and in the same manner as this has happened to Soviet literature. Fortunately, the purse is not almighty. Very often it is just this purse that must succumb to the power of literature. All the significant literature of the nineteenth and twentieth centuries criticizing the ethical/political attitude of the ruling class not only did not disappear, but on the contrary prospered exceptionally well in that very society it fought against. And that is quite understandable. If we look, for example, at contemporary Russian literature, we come to the conclusion that the literature and the writers who currently enjoy the greatest popularity are those who oppose the regime and its power. We see this in the candid statement made by

Yevgeny Yevtushenko: "I am getting on well in the world thanks to the fact that I am not getting on well." That makes sense. The essence of it is simply that a run-of-the-mill literary careerist interests nobody. That individual, however, who gets on well in the world simply because he doesn't fit in is something totally different, something curious. And the world is full of oddballs and fools.

In conjunction with these thoughts concerning the dependency of literature on the purse, the reader might well consider the following: One example of how deep one can sink with his purse is the decision to award the Nobel Prize for Literature to Mikhail Sholokhov. The Russian intelligentsia, which was so unmercifully subjected to the political pressures of the Stalinist dictatorship, and which was physically decimated by it, will never forgive the Western cultures for this recognition of Sholokhov, a man who, because he enjoyed a greatly exaggerated and undeserved esteem, set into motion an activity that could only prove disastrous for the culture and the freedom of art in Russia.

As he further solidified his reputation at the Writers' Congress, Sholokhov expressed his feelings about the trial against Siniavski and Daniel with the following words: "Some people complain about the severity of the punishment and try to hide themselves behind humanistic phrases. I can see the political delegates of our beloved Soviet army in such a situation. How would they behave if someone in their division were to be exposed as a traitor? Our soldiers know very well that humanism has nothing in common with belly-crawling slime."

It is possible that the laws of a military tribunal are strict and that "our soldiers" know nothing more about humanism than that "it has nothing in common with belly-crawling slime." That might very easily be the case. But what did our orator really mean? Apparently Sholokhov pictures the Soviet state as being quite similar to military barracks and thus, in Siniavski and Daniel, he can see traitors who have been exposed suddenly in a division of this barrack-state—whereby he means, of course, in a division of the Soviet Writers' Union. Everything becomes very clear. In such a case "our soldiers" are unquestionably required to act in a consequential manner and are duty bound not to pattern their behavior along the lines set up by the directives of the law book—directives which at best correspond to the structure of democratic states—but rather they are required to pattern their behavior on the norms set up by the military code written specifically for barracks.

Sholokhov betrays himself by condescending to the comparison of the barracks atmosphere, and in this way he exposes himself in his personal psychology as a literary boor. Several dictionaries define the word "boor": "The sons of the soldiers in feudal Russia, who from the moment of birth, because of the principle of forced labor, belonged to the minister of war." It is not difficult to perceive—that Sholokhov pictures the whole of Russia as one huge reserve of such soldiers, wherein everybody from the moment of his birth belongs to the war department, and wherein the Soviet Writers' Union is just another subdivision of this "reserve." On the other hand, it is completely incomprehensible how one can accuse Siniavski and Daniel of being traitors. Siniavski and Daniel have never registered, or allowed themselves to be registered, as members of Sholokhov's "boors" and have never sworn allegiance to the laws

of the barracks; also, they have never sworn allegiance to the
military/political machinery that is even today being employed for the suppression of freedom in Russia.

Sholokhov, however, is not at all concerned with the
truth. For him, there is only one important thing, and that is
to accuse others of being traitors. Why? Probably because
the state prosecutor did not possess sufficient moral authority to do it himself. And so our Nobel Prize winner has
cast all the weight of his authority onto the scale and
delivered himself of a common testimony. In the beginning,
and very discreetly, he spoke of himself; he confided that
he "is a small part of a great and noble people, a son of the
mighty and beautiful motherland." The "small part" of
which he spoke was then elucidated. Above all, he attacked
the "repulsive monster" and vehemently cried out, assuming the role of an honorable man who had been disgusted
to the depths of his soul: "I am ashamed for those who
have slandered their fatherland and have dragged this, for
us the most holy thing, in the mud. They are immoral
people." The best, however, is yet to come. The "small
part" is ashamed for the whole progressive intelligentsia
who are "trying to protect our country." The "small part"
was doubly ashamed for the liberal writers who perform
"their duties" and "ask that the renegades be commited to
their care."

For, get this, "Our achievements are too dear to us, we
love the Soviet system too much, to be able to slander it
with impunity and cover it with mud." He actually said
that. The millions of people who were tortured and tor-
mented to death in Stalin's camps are too high a price for
Sholokhov's barracks, in which only one's toes can move

freely in one's boots, and that only because the guard can't see them. And after the defamation of two honorable men, after having insulted all courageous and honest men who have ever stood up for the defense of justice, the "small part," not entirely self-contented, rested on his laurels. Because the "small part" is probably convinced that he alone will not further the battle with the truth, he sought the help of—"the political delegates of the beloved Soviet army," and suggested a type of punishment for the discipline of the writers that the military tribunals reserve for traitors. But even that did not satisfy the "small part of a great and noble people," who announced: "Oh, these werewolves, these loafers with their guilty consciences, would not have escaped with impunity if they had been brought before, let's say, a revolutionary committee instead of a court, which would have handed down the sentences in accordance with the revolutionary conception of law."

They were not sentenced by a military tribunal; no revolutionary committee saturated with their own peculiar "revolutionary conception of law" condemned them to death. "And, just think, they still have the nerve to criticize the 'severity' of the sentence."

We should just think they still have the nerve to criticize! They are so bold as to criticize! Isn't that some sort of obscurantism? "I," said Sholokhov, "am one of those writers who, like every Soviet citizen, am very proud to be a small part of a great and noble people." You, citizen Sholokhov, are no longer a writer; for awhile there, you were a rather modest literate, but you ceased to be even that a long time ago. Now you are nothing more than a completely predictable political demogogue. You personify the degenerate practice of exercising your questionable authority in supporting and justifying a small group of literary parasites, such as Mikhalkov[9] and his like. And don't ring the bells of the greatness and honor of the Russian people. You are doing an equal injustice to both of them. The facts have shown that not one disparaging article in the official press (which, among other things, is completely dependent upon the purse) was successful in discrediting the accused. During the trial an interminable wave of letters in support of Siniavski and Daniel flooded the offices of the authorities and the newspaper editors. Every writer and every honest scholar felt himself compelled to speak up in defense of the accused. On April 5 many students joined forces with them during a public appearance in Pushkin Square. And do you know what all that means? Above all, it means that the floor has been pulled out from under the feet of people like you and that your only remaining contact with society is the machinery of suppression. In the end neither you nor the machinery will be able to find a place for yourselves, as soon as freedom is once again restored in Russia. The suppression machinery will be robbed of its power and purse, but you will be robbed of your money, honor, state and international recognition. And in this sense, your common accusation will neither be overlooked by your contemporaries nor forgotten by history.

The proceedings against Siniavski and Daniel accelerated the polarization of forces: Standards have gathered around one pole, and around the other—practically 180 degrees away—the anti-standards have gathered. But then again, was the Soviet Writers' Union ever based on standards?

The members of the Soviet Writers' Union do not have the slightest idea of the real possibilities of the Russian intelligentsia. The Soviet Writers' Union is none other than that division of the Sholokhovian barracks through whose help the "purse" buys literary talents and smothers them, nips them in the bud. In this way, during the course of several decades, it was able to cripple Russian literature completely, if not murder it outright. Only in the cases of several incorrigibles were they forced to resort to physical liquidation, and this only in the twenties, in 1937, and again in the 1940's.

Everybody knows what the physical elimination of literature means, but it is much more difficult to understand how the process of the crippling of one's conscience works. In this respect, Russia has shown herself to be a very original nation. This originality is shown in the fact that the writer, while fascinated by the ideals of Communism, can in no way accept the revolting Communist reality with its Stalinist camps and its general senselessness. The Communist concentration camps hinder him from singing the praises of the Communist ideals, but the Communist ideals do not allow him to criticize the Communist concentration camps. In this arena, therefore, he is torn apart—either he falls into a condition of artistic paralysis or he begins to deceive; in both instances he dies as a writer. All that is extremely simple. If, for example, Mikhail Sholokhov casts a quick glance over his past, he will have to admit that even he was not spared by this condition of artistic paralysis. This is probably the explanation for the interminable work on the second part of *Seeds of Tomorrow*, not to mention the miserable holes in the whole work.

Unfortunately, there are men in the West, such as the renowned Secretary of the European Writers' Organization, Giancarlo Vigorelli, who are inclined to believe that the underground literature in the Soviet Union is totally worthless; for such people, only published works have any value—"literature works in the light of day, with its victories and its defeats." Vigorelli would have done better had he devoted himself to questions about which he knew something. The Soviet Writers' Union and official publishing houses in present-day Russia humiliate both writer and literature; they destroy public taste and stupefy the readers. But luckily for Russia, the "official" works are read less and less, and even if they are read, the reader proceeds with great caution to protect his own taste against infection.

For the most part, it is the Russian and foreign classics, translations of current foreign authors and—ever since the 1960's—Pasternak, Akhmatova, Cvetaeva, Chlebnikov, Mandelstam, Bulgakov, Platonov, and others that are being read in Russia today; not because of the Soviet Union and official publications, but rather despite them, almost illegally, under fear of administrative and moral reprisal and often even under the threat of a court trial. As usual, the great majority of those authors named above are not officially published. In Russia, circulation of the best works of contemporary Russian literature reached unprecedented heights in individually executed copies during the 1960's. It is precisely this underground literature, whose access to official publication is denied—beginning with the writers of the 1920's and including the works of Siniavski and

Daniel—that has a great and intrinsic significance for our national culture. Literary Russia is like a sleeping queen who has hardly wakened; it has not yet succeeded in shaking off the feeble-mindedness of ideological hypnosis, and in putting a stop to the obedient clouding of eyes. The Secretary of the European Writers' Organization states: Don't pay any attention to it, only deceivers and literary speculators have anything to do with its Pyrrhic victories.

Authentic literature is wearily trying to pave a road in Russia; Western culture, however, fawns before Mikhail Sholokhov and awards him the Nobel Prize. Then Sholokhov turns up at the Writers' Congress and scolds. "I want to say to the bourgeois defenders of these libelous authors: Don't worry about the irreproachability of criticism in our country. We support and foster criticism, and it will be heard loudly and sharply during this Congress." If in fact you do "support and foster" criticism—not only in words, but in deeds—I shall take the liberty of counting on your help should my modest contribution to this criticism chance upon the bludgeons of the bureaucrats or the police.

I place my hopes completely and absolutely in your great renown as a model pupil, because I cannot count on anything else. In our country there are neither free newspapers nor free organizations nor free trials. I place my hopes in you, but deep in my heart I know very well that one cannot rely completely on your help. For this reason, I shall not in any event sign my real name to this article, but rather a pseudonym. Which pseudonym should I choose? I haven't even thought about it. Good, it will be

Yuri Galanskov. Of course, you realize that because of my poor health I have to avoid all administrative judicial persecution, and my mother's health is also too precarious for her to be able to bear such a thing. Unnecessary nuisances threaten me at work and at study, although naturally I know that every citizen of my native country has the right to work and to study—a right, by the way, that is guaranteed by the Constitution. I entertain the hope that you personally have no doubts about my good qualities as an honest citizen of our great Russia. Finally, I also think about Siniavski, for instance, who is at this very moment in a concentration camp, and how, with his exceptional intelligence, with his great talent as a literary critic, he has no opportunity to devote himself to literature or its criticism. Do you know that a writer in camp must perform heavy physical labor, like any common criminal; that he is kept constantly on starvation rations, and only after having served one half of his term does he have the right to receive two packages annually, each of which cannot exceed five kilos in weight? All this is very enlightened and humane, especially when one knows only that humanism "has nothing in common with belly-crawling slime." In camp it is impossible to devote oneself to the national problems of culture and politics, to the war in Vietnam, to revisionism, to disarmament, or to freedom, but I—I must tell you—am a convinced social pacifist and shun every form of force. I am also an "underground" writer, "underground" in the human sense, as Dostoevski used the word. But do you know what an underground writer is? The underground writer, who happens also to be a social pacifist, is not a millionaire. He doesn't even possess a typewriter, much less any money. He is either employed as a worker in order to earn a loaf of bread, or else he writes in the underground, but carefully, very carefully—almost fearfully—since he can be suddenly silenced.

Many times it seems as though this regime really wants to correct the mistakes it has made, but then it immediately commits some additional stupidity that makes one feel personally ashamed. You yourself understand how difficult life really is for an underground writer. But that's not enough: He must also write an article about the appearance of some idiot from the ranks of the esteemed model pupils—an appearance that threatens to retard the evolution of the national culture and push it back several decades. Finally, the underground writer is an example for his fellow citizens and a gentleman; therefore, he is not able to pass over in silence the derision aimed against his native country and its best sons.

I can also give you information about the address of my pseudonym: Moscow, Apt. 180, Golutvinski pereulok, m 7/9.

From PHOENIX, *Moscow, 1966; by* YURI TIMOFEEVICH GALANSKOV.

LETTER FROM THE SIXTY-TWO WRITERS

To: The Presidium of the XXIII Party Congress of the CPSU.
The Presidium of the Supreme Soviet of the U.S.S.R.
The Presidium of the Supreme Soviet of the RSFSR.

Honored Comrades!

We, the undersigned Moscow writers, request permission to post bail for the recently convicted writers Andrei Siniavski and Yuli Daniel. We would consider this permission as much an act of wisdom as of humanity.

Although we do not approve of the means to which these writers resorted when they published their works outside the Soviet Union, we cannot agree with the opinion that their actions were based upon an anti-Soviet aim or purpose. This is something that must be proved beyond a doubt in the face of such severe punishment. During the course of the trial such malevolence on the part of Siniavski and Daniel was not demonstrated.

On the contrary, the condemnation of writers because of satirical works represents an extremely dangerous precedent that can hinder the evolution of Soviet culture. Neither science nor art can exist in a land where paradoxical ideas are forbidden expression and subtle pictures are not allowed to be painted. The complicated situation in which we find ourselves demands expansion (and not contraction) of freedom for intellectual and artistic experiments. Looked at from this point of view, the trial against Siniavski and Daniel has today already produced greater damage than all the combined mistakes of Siniavski and Daniel.

Siniavski and Daniel are talented men who ought to be given the opportunity to make good their political mistakes and indiscretions. If someone posted security for them, Siniavski and Daniel could realize their mistakes all the more quickly and, once again in contact with the Soviet public, could create new works, whose artistic and ideological value would cancel out the damages done by their earlier misdirected accomplishments.

For these reasons we request that Andrei Siniavski and Yuli Daniel be released against our security.

This would serve the interests of our country, and moreover, the interests of the world. It also would serve the interests of the Communist world movement.

The members of the Writers' Union of the u.s.s.r.: (There follow sixty-two signatures of well-known writers and critics.)

This letter appears in the WHITE BOOK *in the case of Siniavski and Daniel.*

Excerpts from the Final Trial Statement by Vladimir Bukovski before the Moscow Municipal Court, September 1, 1967

. . . BUKOVSKI: I expected the prosecution would present a detailed analysis of the "disturbance" we made in [Pushkin] Square: . . . Who hit whom, who stepped on whose feet. This did not happen. The prosecutor said in his speech: "As far as I can see, the danger of this crime lies in its insolence . . ."

I happen to have before me the text of the Soviet Constitution: "In accordance with the interests of the workers and with the aim of strengthening the socialist system, the citizens of the u.s.s.r. will be legally guaranteed . . . the freedom to conduct street processions and demonstrations." We wouldn't need any freedom "to" if there weren't any freedom "against." We know that protest demonstrations are a powerful weapon in the hands of the workers; it is an inalienable right in all democratic countries . . .

A trial was held in Madrid against the participants in a May Day demonstration. They were tried under a new law which was recently passed in Spain and which demands a jail term of one and a half to three years—this for participation in demonstrations. I see a disturbing similarity between fascist Spanish and Soviet legislation.

JUDGE: Defendant, you are comparing things that cannot be compared; namely, the actions of the rulers of Spain and those of the Soviet state. The court cannot tolerate the comparison of Soviet policy with the intrigues and machinations of foreign bourgeois states. Keep your remarks relevant to the theme of the indictment. I object to the insulting tone of your words . . .

BUKOVSKI: You have no right to interrupt me. I have not strayed from the essential theme of my case. How can you talk of a democracy when we are constantly under surveillance? Why are we questioned about our acquaintances, about what we did two or three years ago, and the like? I acknowledge the important role the organ of the KGB plays in the battle for state security. But what do they have to do with this case? . . . Why did you have to prolong our case for seven months? I'll tell you why: in order to have enough time to invent some excuse that would successfully eliminate all traces of this embarrassing case. When they finally couldn't delay any longer, the proceedings against us were conducted so secretly that nobody could see through them and thus convince himself of their illegality. After four months our case was transferred from the state prosecutor's office to the KGB. This is a violation of procedure . . .

JUDGE: Defendant Bukovski, we are not interested in that. Stick to the subject of the indictment. Just what significance does all this you are saying have for the resolution of your case?

BUKOVSKI: I have already said that you have no right to interrupt me. The meaning is quite simple: Violations of the law have been committed during the investigation, and it is my duty to bring them out into the open. This is why I mentioned them here. We demonstrated for the observance of the law. We did not speak up against the law. We protested against an unconstitutional decree. Was this really an anti-Soviet demand? We are not the only ones who consider the decree unconstitutional. A group of representatives of the intelligentsia have presented a similar proposal to the Presidium of the Supreme Soviet of the U.S.S.R. . . .

JUDGE: Defendant Bukovski, we are lawyers here, and all those present in the courtroom have at least been through secondary school . . . Perhaps you will study law at Moscow University some day. If so, you will have the opportunity to discuss these questions on a higher level in the seminars there.

BUKOVSKI: No, I will not go there . . . If, however, everyone really does understand what I am talking about as well as you say, then it is even more incomprehensible why the prosecutor regards criticism of the law a crime . . . Freedom of speech and freedom of the press mean, first and foremost, the right to criticize. No one has ever forbidden someone to praise the government. If there are any articles in the Constitution concerning the freedoms of speech and press, then be good enough to have the patience to listen to criticism.

What countries forbid their citizens to criticize their government and to protest against its actions? Capitalist countries? Perhaps. No, we know that there are Communist parties in bourgeois countries whose goal it is to undermine the capitalist system. The Communist party was forbidden in the United States. The Supreme Court, however, declared the ban unconstitutional and restored the Communist party to its full rights.

JUDGE: Bukovski, that is totally irrelevant to the accusations made against you. We are not here to debate the legality of the laws; our duty is to see that they are carried out.

BUKOVSKI: You are interrupting me again.

JUDGE: I declare a five-minute recess.

BUKOVSKI: I didn't request a recess. I was almost finished with my concluding statement. You are interrupting the continuity of my statement. (The judge declared a recess.)

JUDGE: (after the recess) Defendant Bukovski, continue your final statement, but I warn you, if you continue to criticize the laws and the activities of the KGB, instead of giving an explanation of the case in question, I will have to interrupt you.

BUKOVSKI: There is still another aspect—the question of honesty and civic courage. You are judges. We are led to believe that you personify these qualities. If so, you will come to the only possible verdict in this case—that of "not guilty." I know this is very difficult.

PROSECUTOR: I should like to point out to the court that the accused is abusing his right to make a final statement. He criticizes the laws, discredits the activities of the KGB, and he is now beginning to insult you. A new crime is being committed here. As the representative of the prosecution, I must put a stop to this and I appeal to you to demand from the defendant that he talk only about the contents of the charges made against him. Otherwise, one could listen to interminable speeches of every description which serve no other purpose than to criticize the laws and the government.

JUDGE: Defendant Bukovski, you have heard the prosecutor's remarks. You will limit your remarks to the substance of the indictment.

BUKOVSKI: (to the prosecutor) You accuse us of having tried to discredit the KGB with our slogans, but the KGB has discredited itself to such an extent we need add nothing more. (to the court) I shall address myself to the charges. But the prosecutor will not hear what he would like to hear:

No criminal act has been determined. I do not for a second repent having organized this demonstration. I feel it accomplished what it was supposed to accomplish, and when I am free again, I will organize demonstrations as before, naturally in exact compliance with the law.

German translation from DER SPIEGEL, *No. 3, 1968.*

INTRODUCTIONS TO LETTERS AND TELEGRAMS TO PAVEL LITVINOV

The anthology of letters and telegrams sent to Pavel Litvinov provided the West with an informative testament to the growing opposition among all levels of society against the then current Soviet regime. Three documents of the original sixty-six communications—many of them telegrams—were lost. Therefore, sixty-three of these documents were published in the West; of those, eight are negative and two express an "undecided" viewpoint. The rest agree with Litvinov and his position; many outspoken in their opposition to the regime.

Litvinov forwarded the collection of letters and telegrams to Professor Karel van het Reve, then Moscow correspondent for the Dutch newspaper HET PAROOL. *It was published in Hamburg by Hoffman and Campe under the title* UNSOLICITED WITNESSES, *with an introduction by Karel van het Reve. We have translated several examples of the more typical letters. Out of consideration for their authors no names have been included.*

TO WORLD PUBLIC OPINION

The trial against Galanskov, Ginzburg, Dobrovolski, and Lashkova, which is currently taking place in the Moscow Municipal Court, is being carried out in violation of essential judicial norms of Soviet law. The judge and the prosecutor have transformed the proceedings into a blatant —and for our century hardly imaginable—mockery of the three accused, and they were aided in so doing by the participation of a certain kind of audience.

As early as the second day the proceedings assumed the character of the well-known "witch trials" as Galanskov and Ginzburg, despite their one-year imprisonment pending investigation and despite the pressures exerted by the court, refused to acknowledge any truth in the accusations Dobrovolski made against them, but rather attempted to prove their innocence of those charges. The testimonies given in favor of Galanskov and Ginzburg only succeeded in infuriating the court even more. Throughout the trial both the judge and the prosecutor encouraged Dobrovolski to make false accusations against Galanskov and Ginzburg. The defense attorneys were continually forbidden to ask questions. And the witnesses were not granted the opportunity to disclose in their testimonies the provocative role Dobrovolski was playing in this trial.

Judge Mironov did not once interrupt the prosecutor, the representative of the state. He permitted the defense, on the other hand, to say nothing more than that which was already determined and stated in the charge presented by the investigative organs of the KGB. As soon as anyone connected with the trial tried to disrupt the course of this sold-out performance, the judge cried: "Your question is out of order!" "That is irrelevant to the case!" "You may not speak!" These exclamations were directed at the accused (with the exception of Dobrovolski), at the defense lawyers, and their witnesses.

After the examination, the witnesses left the courtroom (or rather, were pushed out) completely defeated, if not in hysterics. The witness E. Basilova was not permitted to testify. She wanted to report how the KGB had pressed her emotionally disturbed husband, whose statement, which he had made when totally beside himself during the interrogation, was an essential piece of evidence for the prosecution. She was hurled out of the courtroom, accompanied by the exclamations of the judge and the howling of the audience, a din that drowned out all her words. P. Grigorenko then requested to be questioned as a witness, since he was in a position to explain to the court the origins of the money found in Dobrovolski's possession. (Dobrovolski maintained that Galanskov had given it to him.) Grigorenko's request was turned down on the grounds that he was allegedly insane (which is untrue). Topeshkina, a pregnant woman, wanted to explain some facts which would have proved the perjury of Dobrovolski's testimony: Under the howls of the audience she was forcibly expelled from the courtroom.

Following the recess the "court commandant," KGB Colonel Cirkunenko, prevented the witness L. Kac from reentering the courtroom. He told her: "If your testimony had been different, you would have been allowed to remain."

None of the witnesses were allowed to stay in the courtroom after their interrogation, and that despite the fact that they are required to do so under Soviet law. Appeals by the witnesses to Paragraph 283 of the Code of Criminal Procedure of the RSFSR were purposely ignored. The judge turned to witness V. Vinogradova and said straight out: "Under Paragraph 283 you may immediately leave!" The courtroom was filled with a carefully chosen audience—officials of the KGB and young militiamen, who were to give the trial the appearance of an open and publicly accessible hearing. These people shouted and insulted the accused and their witnesses under the general background of mocking laughter. Judge Mironov made no attempt to curb these violations of order. Not one of these boorish disturbers was ejected from the hall. In an atmosphere as tense as this, there can be no talk about the objectivity of the court, about justice or legality. The verdict was determined from the very beginning.

We are appealing to world public opinion, and primarily to Soviet public opinion. We are appealing to everyone in whom conscience and courage are still vital forces. Demand public condemnation of this farcical trial and the punishment of those responsible for it. Demand the immediate release of the accused. Demand a retrial under the exact observation of all judicial norms and in the presence of international observers. Citizens of our country! This trial is a stain on the honor of our state and on the conscience of every one of us . . . Not only the fate of the accused is in danger today—their trial is no better than the infamous trials of the 1930's, which have overwhelmed us with so much shame and so much blood that we have not yet managed to recover. . . .

Larisa Bograz
Pavel Litvinov
January 11, 1968

LETTER FROM TWENTY-FOUR STUDENTS TO PAVEL LITVINOV

Dear Pavel Mikhailovich:
We began to see things clearly two years ago when

Siniavski and Daniel were convicted and we realized the crying injustice of our governmental organs and the cruelty of individuals who dared to trample upon artistic freedom and human rights. Our grandfathers and our fathers after them were shot, died in camps, and were personally subjected to all the horrors of Stalinist reaction. We can imagine how terrible it is to live when all around us silence and terror reign supreme. For this reason the thinking generation of the 1960's calls upon all decent people to support the bold step which you both have taken, and to add their signatures to your letter. He who keeps silent sins against his conscience and against Russia. And Russia has to pay dearly for this: the blood of its most intelligent and most gifted sons, from Osip Mandelstam to Aleksandr Ginzburg. We want to see the publication of Brodski's verses, of the stories of Romisov and Zamiatin, the poetry of the late Mandelstam, and the prose of Pasternak. We want to see an international court of law investigate the case of the four writers on the principle of international law, and we want to see a severe punishment meted out to those judges who have placed themselves above the norms of socialist justice . . .

Only by acting in accord can we hope to accomplish anything. Otherwise, the times will only get worse: terror, reaction, innocent sacrifice. For we are responsible for all that happens in the world; even the best works of our literature teach us that. We cannot condone the fact that Tolstoi, Chekhov, Kuprin, and Blok are so narrow-mindedly interpreted, and that Dostoevski, Bunin, Cvetaeva, Pasternak, and others have been written off the school curriculum. Our schools have tried to raise reliable watchmen—stubborn blockheads who have sweated primarily over Party history and the principles of historical materialism. We cannot keep silent when demagogy, journalistic lies, and deceit reign all around us. We are only sorry for our parents. Therefore we request that this letter be circulated so that our comrades and those who share our opinions learn of it, and so that a just decision will be reached about the fate of the convicted writers.

We hope that, despite everything, we are not alone and that the voices of decent men will be heard by us and our comrades.

A GROUP OF TWENTY-FOUR STUDENTS
(MOSCOW, JANUARY 13, 1968;
SIGNATURES, ADDRESSES)

Pavel Mikhailovich!
I want to express to you and Larisa Daniel my admiration for your courage in the struggle for human dignity and justice, and at the same time add my support to your protest.

The number of those who understand and support you is many hundred times greater than the number of those who actually express their support in letters to you.

Very sincerely yours,
(*initials*)
Moscow, January 17, 1968

Dear and highly respected Pavel Mikhailovich!
Dear and highly respected Larisa!
Thanks for reviving my faith in mankind with your

courageous and honorable actions. As a result of your deeds, you have aroused noble thoughts, feelings, and efforts in the hearts of many.

Dear Larisa, I pray for your husband, for Andrei Siniavski and the others. I am almost positive that my letter will not reach you, but nevertheless I could not forbear writing to both of you.

All decent people are with you.

With deepest respect,
(*signature*)
Moscow, February 1, 1968

Greetings, dear comrade Litvinov!

We, the pupils and students of Moscow, have been inspired by your actions.

We are one with you in complete solidarity.

We believe that the truth will triumph.

We are with you!

A GROUP OF SOVIET CHILDREN

LETTER FROM I. A. YAKHIMOVICH TO SUSLOV

Ivan Yakhimovich (born in 1930), the chairman of a collective farm, sent a letter to the Party Secretary M. Suslov in which he protested the conviction of Galanskov, Ginzburg, etc., in January of 1968. Because of this letter he lost his position. Along with Grigorenko and Marchenko, Yakhimovich had also expressed his sympathy to the Czechoslovakian Embassy in Moscow for the policies of the Prague reformers in July, 1968. Together with Grigorenko, Yakhimo-

vich later spoke out in favor of the return of all Soviet troops from Czechoslovakia.

On March 25, 1969, he was arrested near Riga not long after he had addressed a moving proclamation to the groups and individuals with whom he stood in close contact. Eighteen persons published a protest against the arrest of the former kolkhov chairman. A few weeks later, in April of 1969, Samizdat published a "White Book Concerning the Case of Yakhimovich" which contained six documents in toto. Yakhimovich was tried on April 18, 1970, in Riga, declared mentally ill, and confined indefinitely to an insane asylum. (He was finally released on May 3, 1971.)

Up until a few years ago the official press had portrayed Ivan Yakhimovich as a glowing example of a kolkhov leader and a model Soviet citizen.

I have not got sufficient information at my disposal to be able to judge the guilt of those persons subjected to reprisals, but I am convinced about one thing, and this I know: This kind of justice, which took place in the Moscow Municipal Court between the eighth and twelfth of January, 1968, has done great harm to our party and to the cause of Communism, in our land and all over the world.

We have celebrated the glorious anniversary of the Revolution, praised ourselves for our accomplishments in economic questions, science, and technology; the UNO has proclaimed 1968 as the Year of the Defense of the Rights of Man—and we are giving trump cards to the enemies of Communism in their battle against us. It's absurd. We were naked, hungry, and helpless, but we won—because we wanted to free men from injustice and violence. We can lose everything despite our rockets and atomic bombs, if we forget the essence and the meaning of the great Socialist October Revolution. Ever since the time of Radischev, trials against writers have aroused only disgust in the eyes of liberal, progressively thinking people. What are our leaders thinking when they gag Solzhenitsyn, make a joke of Vosnesenski, and "punish" Siniavski and Daniel with forced labor?

One ought not to subvert the confidence of the masses in the party, one ought not to speculate with the honor of the state, even if a certain leader does want to put an end to *Samizdat*. There is only one way of emasculating *Samizdat*: to establish democratic rights instead of suppressing them, to act in accordance with the Constitution instead of violating it, to realize the principles of the Declaration of Human Rights . . .

I consider the persecution of youthful dissidents in a country whose total population is half composed of people under thirty an extremely dangerous policy, almost adventurism. Our future will not be determined by hypocrites, by a nation of yes-men (Oh, God, how they have multiplied!), not by mamma's boys, but by the rebels who are the most active, most daring, and most idealistic members of our young generation . . .

The Moscow Municipal Court permitted gross violations in legal procedure. Terechov, Judge Mironov, and the court commandant Cirkunenko ought to be punished in the appropriate manner, primarily because they acted like fools and abused their power. One cannot establish justice if one violates the laws. We will never again permit anyone to prostitute our Soviet courts, our laws and our rights . . .

I live in the provinces where every house with electricity is matched by ten without, where in winter the buses do not run, and the post arrives weeks late. When the news (about the Moscow trial) finally reached us by radio, you can easily imagine what kind of seed you sowed in our country. Be good enough to have the courage to correct the mistakes you have made, before the workers and the peasants take matters into their own hands!

I do not want this letter to be ignored, for the cause of the Party cannot be a private affair, a personal cause, or even less, an unimportant concern.

I consider it the duty of a Communist to warn the Central Committee of the Party. I demand that all members of the Central Committee be informed about the contents of this letter.

With Communist greetings,
I. A. Yakhimovich
January 22, 1968

From DER SPIEGEL, *No. 13, 1968.*

PETITION BY FORTY-SIX RESIDENTS
OF NOVOSIBIRSK

To: *The Prosecutor General of the Supreme Court of* RSFSR: *Rudenko*

Copies: *The Chairman of the Presidium of the Supreme Soviet of the* U.S.S.R.: *N. V. Podgorny*

The Prime Minister of the U.S.S.R.: *A. N. Kosygin*
The Secretary-General of the Central Committee
of the CPSU: *L. I. Brezhnev*
The attorneys B. Zolotuchin, D. Kaminskaia
The Editorial Office of Komsomolskaia Pravda

The absence of an even approximately coherent and complete report from our newspapers about the substance and course of the trial of A. Ginzburg, Yuri Galansko, A. Dobrovolski, and V. Lashkova, all of whom were convicted under Article 70 of the Penal Code of the RSFSR, has at one and the same time disturbed us and forced us to seek information concerning these trials from other sources—namely, in foreign Communist newspapers. What we have been able to learn has driven us to doubt whether this political trial was conducted in accordance with all the norms required by law, such as the principle of an open trial. This situation is alarming.

Our sense of civic responsibility forces us to declare very emphatically that we consider it inadmissible to conduct trials which are, in fact, closed to public scrutiny. We are disturbed by the fact that injustices are in fact being committed behind the closed doors of the courtroom and that unfounded sentences based on illegal accusations could have been handed down. We cannot permit the judicial mechanism of our state to escape once again from the control of the general public and allow our country once again to be plunged into a state of despotism and lawlessness. For this reason we maintain that the verdict of the Moscow Municipal Court in the case of Ginzburg, Galanskov, Dobrovolski, and Lashkova must be annulled, and we demand that this case be retried with complete attention paid to the fact that the public must be accurately informed about the proceedings and that the legal norms be observed to the letter, which would mean that all evidence must be unfailingly publicized in the press.

In addition, we demand that those persons who have acted in violation of the public nature of the court and of the norms which are prescribed by law for the conduct of a trial be called to account for their actions.

46 SIGNATURES

Taken from POSEV, *No. 7, 1968.*

The following is the text of a leaflet circulated widely throughout Moscow, protesting the occupation of Czechoslovakia. It is entitled Let Us Think for Ourselves.

What would happen if it should suddenly occur to a few of our zealous successors of Stalin and Beria to appeal, let's say, to our Chinese, Albanian, or similar brothers for help?

What would it be like if tank and parachute troops were suddenly to turn up overnight in our cities? And their soldiers were to begin to persecute the heads of our party and government, to close down the editorial offices of newspapers and radio stations, and to shoot those people who might dare oppose such actions—all in the name of the defense and the rescue of the ideals of Communism, or at least their conception of these ideals?

Not only the overwhelming majority of Czech and

Slovak Communists, but also all the Italian, French, British, Swedish, Norwegian, as well as the Rumanian and Yugoslavian Communists—in short, the great majority of Communists in the whole world—and among others, the leaders of seventy-eight out of a total of ninety parties which have, up until now, supported the CPSU in its struggles with the Chinese Communist party, are all convinced that it is precisely Czechoslovakia that, since January of 1968, has been the first really to begin to put the Marxist ideas into action, and that in all of our writings, whenever they speak about "counter-revolutionary danger" and a "revival of revisionism," not one single word of truth is to be found . . .

How would it be if in the streets of our cities Yugoslavian, Rumanian, Czechoslovakian, or East German tanks and propagandists wanted to begin, with the aid of machine guns, to prove that even all this means nothing more than a show of fraternal aid and proletarian solidarity? Let us think about all these things and let us consider who has actually and ultimately been injured by what happened on August 21st, and who has actually profited by it.

Taken from POSEV, *No. 2, 1969.*

LETTER BY NATALIA GORBANEVSKAYA

To the Editors-in-Chief of the Newspapers: Rudé Právo, Unità, The Morning Star, Humanité, The Times, Neue Zürcher Zeitung, The New York Times, The Washington Post, *and all other newspapers of the world that publish this letter:*

Dear Sirs:

I hereby request that you publish in your newspaper my letter about the demonstration in Red Square in Moscow on August 25, 1968, since I am the single participant of that demonstration who is for the time being still free. Konstantin Babicki, linguist; Larisa Bogoraz-Daniel, philologist; Vadim Delone, poet; Vladimir Dremliuga, worker; Pavel Litvinov, physicist; Viktor Fainberg, art critic; Natalia Gorbanevskaya, poet, all took part in the demonstration.

At twelve noon we gathered around the steps of the execution platform and unfolded our banners: "Long Live a Free and Independent Czechoslovakia" (written in Czechoslovakian), "Shame on the Occupiers," "Hands Off CSSR (Czechoslovak Soviet Socialist Republic)," "For Your Freedom and Ours." Someone immediately blew a whistle. From all sides of Red Square, members of the KGB (secret security police) in civilian clothes rushed toward us. They maintained a guard along the Red Square while waiting for the departure of the Czechoslovakian delegation from the Kremlin. As they hurried past they shouted to one another: "These are all dirty Jews. Let's skin the anti-Soviets!" We remained peacefully sitting and did not defend ourselves. They ripped our banners from our hands. They knocked out a few of Viktor Fainberg's teeth and left his face a bloody mess. They beat Pavel Litvinov in the face with a heavy book bag. They tore a small Czechoslovakian flag from my hand and ripped it to pieces. They shouted to us: "Get lost, shitheads!" But we continued to sit there. Several minutes later, cars drove up and all of us except me were forced into them. I had my three-month-old son with me, so they did not immediately fall on me. I remained seated on the execution block for about another ten minutes. Then they beat me in the wagon. They also brought my baby to military headquarters. For a period of six hours I was not allowed to comfort him.

Several of the passers-by, and members of the crowd that had gathered around, were arrested with us—people who had wanted to express their sympathy for our cause. They were released later that evening. During the night all those arrested were interrogated, since they were all accused of having violated the laws governing group agitation and according to which they had seriously disturbed the public peace. One of us, Vadim Delone, had already been given a suspended sentence according to the same paragraph of the Penal Code of the RSFSR, because he had participated in the demonstration that took place on Pushkin Square on January 22, 1967. I was released following the interrogation, only because I had two small children to care for. I was repeatedly summoned for testimony during the following days. I refused to say anything about the organization and conduct of the demonstration because it was a peaceful demonstration that did not disturb the public peace. On the other hand, I did make statements about the coarse and illegal behavior of the people who had arrested us, and I am still prepared to bear witness to that before world public opinion.

My comrades and I are happy that we had the opportunity to participate in this demonstration, that we succeeded, at least for a moment, in breaking through the stream of unbridled lies and cowardly silence, in order to show that not all the citizens of our land are content with the application of violence being carried out in the name of the Soviet people. We hope that the Czechoslovakian people have already or will soon receive news of this demonstration. Our belief that the Czechs and the Slovaks will not picture the Soviet people in their minds solely as the occupiers of their country lends us strength and courage.

From the NEUE ZURCHER ZEITUNG, *September 13, 1968.*

EXCERPTS FROM THE FINAL STATEMENT
MADE BY PAVEL LITVINOV
BEFORE THE MOSCOW MUNICIPAL COURT
ON OCTOBER 11, 1968

. . . Our innocence is obvious and I cannot consider myself guilty. But it is just as obvious that the sentence will read: guilty. I knew that even before I decided to go to Red Square. I was convinced that the KGB people would provoke me, and I knew where such a provocation would eventually lead. I read my sentence in the eyes of that man who continually shadowed me. And in spite of all this I went to Red Square . . .

As a Soviet citizen I was compelled to raise my voice against the recent actions of the government, actions which appalled me. As he handed me the records of the interrogation to be signed in the precinct, one of the police officers said: "You're crazy; you would have done better to keep quiet and lead a peaceful life!" It may be that he was right, and we are indeed crazy. Our arrest was illegal . . . Even the prosecutor said that we had spoken up against the policies of the Party or the government, but not against the socialist order. Possibly there may be people who feel that our policies, and particularly our political mistakes, are a logical result of our state and social system. I am not in agreement with this supposition. I believe that the prosecutor is also not in agreement. Otherwise he would have to admit that the crimes of the Stalinist years were also a result of our social and ethical system.

[P. Litvinov proceeded to say that the prosecutor had twisted the meaning of Article 125 of the Constitution when he maintained that the rights and freedoms which are guaranteed in it may be exercised only in the interests of the state.] But it is precisely in the interests of socialism and its founders that these rights and freedoms have to be guaranteed to the people. . . . [At this point Litvinov was interrupted by the prosecutor—these remarks had obviously nothing to do with the case.] On the contrary, they have everything to do with it. Who can possibly judge what is and what is not in the interests of socialism? Perhaps the prosecutor, who spoke with so much enthusiasm—yes, even with tenderness—about those who beat and abused us? For this reason he is an expert in the field of law? But it is exactly that which is so threatening. One assumes that it is precisely these people who must know what socialism and counter-revolution are.

And that is what strikes me as terrible; it is for this very reason that I went to Red Square. I have fought against this, and I will spend the rest of my life fighting against it with all the legal means I have at my disposal.

From POSEV, *No. 11, 1968.*

PETITION BY P. GRIGORENKO
AND I. YAKHIMOVICH TO THE
CITIZENS OF THE SOVIET UNION

The campaign of self-immolations which began with the
Prague student Jan Palach on January 16, 1969, out of protest against the interference in the internal affairs of the
Czechoslovakian Socialist Republic has not abated. Still
another—for the time being at least, the last—living torch
flared up in Wenzel Square in Prague on February 21.

This protest, which has taken so horrible a form, is primarily addressed to us, the Soviet people. The uninvited
and absolutely unjustifiable presence of our troops has
called up this type of anger and tumult from the Czechoslovakian peoples. The death of Jan Palach did not shake
all the workers of Czechoslovakia without reason. We all
share the guilt for his tragic end, just as much as we share
the guilt for the death for all other Czechoslovakian brothers who take their own lives. Inasmuch as we condone the
invasion by our troops, justify it in some way or simply hold
our silence, we are contributing to the fact that additional
living torches will be set ablaze on the squares of Prague
and other cities. The Czechs and Slovaks have always
thought of us as brothers. Are we then really going to allow
the word *Soviet* to become a synonym for *enemy*?

Citizens of our great land! The greatness of a country
does not consist in the strength of its troops which invade a
small, freedom-loving people, but rather in its moral
strength.

Are we going to look on silently in the future as our
brothers die? It is already clear to everyone that the pres-

ence of our troops in the territory of the CSSR lies neither in the interests of the defense of our homeland nor in the interests of our allied socialist states.

Do we then not have the courage to admit that a tragic mistake has been made, and that we must do everything in our power to rectify it? That is our right and our duty!

We are calling upon all Soviet citizens, without acting hastily or without thought, to demand with every means at their disposal that the soviet troops be recalled from Czechoslovakia and that interference in their internal affairs be prohibited! Only in this way can the friendship between our two peoples be re-established..

Long live the heroic Czechoslovakian people!
Long live the Soviet-Czechoslovakian friendship!

PETR GRIGORENKO
IVAN YAKHIMOVICH
Moscow, February 28, 1969

From POSEV, *No. 4, 1969.*

OPEN LETTER FROM ANATOLI JAKOBSON

On August 25, 1968, seven individuals—Konstantin Babicki, Larisa Bogoras, Natalia Gorbanevskaya, Vadim Delone, Vladimir Dremliuga, Pavel Litvinov, and Viktor Fainberg— gathered on Red Square, where they climbed up on what used to be the executioner's block and unrolled scrolls with the following inscriptions: "Long live a free and independent Czechoslovakia!" (written in the Czech language), "Shame on the Occupiers," "Hands off Czechoslovakia,"

"For your freedom and ours!"

Everyone in our country who wanted to know the truth learned of the demonstration; the Czechoslovakian people learned of it; in fact, the whole world learned of it. If Gercen (Herzen) single-handedly rescued and preserved the honor of Russian democracy a hundred years ago when, from his residence in London, he spoke up for freedom for Poland and attacked those powers which were trying to destroy that freedom, then these seven demonstrators have without a doubt rescued the honor of the Soviet people. The significance of the demonstration of August 25 should not be underestimated. Many humane and progressively thinking people considered the demonstration a bold and honorable deed, and believe that the step which inevitably led to the arrest of the participants and to revenge against them was an unwise act of force and not in keeping with the ultimate goal. We heard the word "self-arrest" used in the sense of "self-immolation."

Even if the demonstrators had had no time to unroll their slogans, indeed if no one had ever even learned of this event, I believe the demonstration would still have been meaningful and justified in any case. Steps of this description cannot be measured by the rules of normal politics, according to which every single event must be aimed at a direct, concretely conceived result, a cold and lifeless objective. The demonstration of August 25 was not just another manifestation of a political battle—incidentally, the prerequisites for such a thing are completely lacking here— but rather, a manifestation of a moral battle. It is impossible to evaluate even approximately the results of such a movement. One can assume that truth is necessary for truth's sake and no other reason, that each individual will refuse to compromise his own human dignity in the face of evil, even if it is not within his power to prevent such evil.

Lev Tolstoi said: ". . . Deliberations concerning the effect on the world if we were to behave in one manner as against another should not serve as standards for our behavior and our action. Man has at his disposal another, completely unmistakable resource—namely his conscience, by which means he knows that when he follows its dictates, he is doing what he must do." From this stems the moral principle and the behavioral standards of one's "inability to remain silent." That does not mean that all those people who sympathize with the demonstrators have to follow them into the streets; and it also does not mean that every moment is ripe for a demonstration. It does mean, however, that everyone who shares the convictions of the heroes of the twenty-fifth of August has to seek out for himself the moment and type of his protest, for each must rely upon his own faculties. There is no generally applicable rule for this. Only one thing is commonly understood: The "judicious silence" can lead to a disastrous mistake, namely to a revival of Stalinism.

Ever since the condemnation of Siniavski and Daniel— that is, since 1966—not one single arbitrary act of despotism and force on the part of the administration has gone unchallenged. That is an honorable tradition, the beginning of the self-liberation of man from degrading fear, from participation in evil-doing.

ANATOLI JAKOBSON
Moscow, September 18, 1968

This first appeared in POSEV, *No. 9, 1969.*

ANNIVERSARY DECLARATION

On August 21st of last year a tragic event occurred: armed troops from the Warsaw Pact countries invaded our ally Czechoslovakia. The purpose of their action was to divert this country from its newly chosen democratic path. The whole world had observed with high hopes the developments in Czechoslovakia. It seemed, after that previous January, as if the socialist idea, which had been brought into disrepute during the time of Stalin, would finally be rehabilitated. The tanks of the Warsaw Pact countries destroyed this hope. On this sad anniversary we declared that we are no more in support of such a decision that threatens the future of socialism than we have ever been. We declare our solidarity with the Czechoslovakian people and by doing so hope to prove that socialism with human attributes is possible.

Sorrow for our own homeland, which we want to see great, free, and happy, has dictated these lines. We are convinced, however, that a nation suppressing another nation can be neither free nor happy.

Ju. Vishnevskaia	A. Levitin (Krasnov)
T. Baeva	L. Petrovski
I. Gabai	L. Pliusch
N. Gorbanevskaya	G. Podiapolski
Z. M. Grigorenko	L. Ternovski
N. Emelkina	I. Yakir
M. Djemilev	P. Yakir
V. Krasin	A. Jakobson
S. Kovalev	

Appeared in POSEV, No. 9, 1969.

WRITTEN IN OPPOSITION TO THE DECREE OF SEPTEMBER 16, 1966

To: *The session of the Supreme Soviet of the* RSFSR

Copies: *The Politburo of the Central Committee of the* CPSU, *the Presidium of the Supreme Soviet of the* U.S.S.R., *the Prosecutor General of the* U.S.S.R.

Comrade Delegates:

We, a group of Soviet citizens, consider it our duty to express our position with respect to the decree of September 16, 1966, "Concerning the Inclusion of a Supplement to the Penal Code of the RSFSR." In our opinion there is no cause in the real political life of our country that would necessitate the inclusion of Articles 190/1 and 190/3 in the Penal Code of the RSFSR. The adoption of such laws at the present time seems to us to be an unjustified step increasing anew the danger of judicial misuse, of violation of socialistic legality, as well as the creation of an atmosphere of suspicion and denunciation. Article 190 allows the possibility of subjectively judging the testimony of any particular person, of declaring it to be an out-and-out lie, and of qualifying it as slander against the Soviet state and social order. We are convinced that Articles 190/1 and 190/3 are in direct contradiction to the Leninistic principles of socialistic democracy, and if they are ratified by the session of the Supreme Soviet of the RSFSR, they could constitute an obstacle to the realization of those freedoms which are guaranteed by the Constitution of the U.S.S.R.

Among the signatories were:

Academician Astaurov

Academician Zeldovich

Academician Kunianc

Academician Leontovich

Academician Skazkin

Academician Sakharov

Academician Tamm

Academician Engelgardt

Author Kaverin

Author Nekrasov

Author Dombrovski

Composer Shostakovich

Author Voinovich

Film Director Romm

A group of Bolsheviks (twenty-one names in all). (Note: several names were illegibly written.)

From POSEV, February 10, 1967.

LETTER FROM V. I. KUZNECOV
TO THE EDITOR OF IZVESTIA

The case of the artist Kuznecov is typical of innumerable instances. Because of his nonconformist views, which he publicly proclaimed on two different occasions, Viktor Kuznecov was arrested in November, 1966 and confined to an insane asylum; however, he was released two months later. On March 20, 1969, he was arrested a second time and brought to trial for the "propagation of anti-Soviet writings." (The works of Siniavski, Daniel, and other writers, along with the draft of a new Constitution, were found in his possession.) On July 16, 1969, following a secret trial, Kuznecov was committed to a "special psychiatric clinic." These institutions owe their infamous reputation to the foregone conclusion that those imprisoned in them are used in medical experiments.

On March 13, 1965, my husband, V. I. Kuznecov, spoke up during a dispute at Moscow University (MGU) His attitude displeased many of those present. During the autumn he was twice summoned before the KGB and warned that, according to Article 70 of the Penal Code, he must reckon with one of two alternatives: either be brought to trial or be committed to an institution for the mentally ill.

Thereafter, punishment caught up with my husband. It all started on October 26, 1966, when he was laid off from his job because of the cancellation of the extra artist's position. "Cancellation of the extra artist's position!" For God's sake! And finally, November 1st at six o'clock, he was apprehended and brought in a police car, under the protective escort of a police officer and a nurse, into the Moscow Area Hospital for Nervous Disorders on March 8th Street.

The admission card stated: "V. N. Kuznecov, born in 1936, residence in the Armand settlement, number 16, is admitted for the purpose of consultation and clarification of the diagnosis. Diagnosis number 300.

Doctor (Voicechovich)"
And it was completely covered with violet stamps.

Since when are people dragged out at so early an hour in the morning only to be subjected to a diagnosis? Since when are people transported in police cars for the determination of a diagnosis? The confused and astounded doctors in the hospital hadn't the slightest idea of what they were supposed to do. Finally somebody decided to telephone, and indeed (whom else!) they telephoned the chief of the police district of Rayon in the city of Pushkina. Since when is a psychiatrist, such as Dr. M. Ja. Koltunova, dutybound to appeal to the chief of the police precinct, A. M. Deev, in order to determine whether or not she should keep in her hospital the recent admission for examination? Since when have the psychiatrists come under the control of the police?

Moreover, another slip of paper was attached to the admission card with the following text: "Kuznecov, Viktor Vasilevich. He expressed crazy ideas about influence and relationships. Feels himself badly treated by relatives. Separated from his wife, since he suffers from a crazy notion about mutual relationships. Feels himself badly treated at work. Reacts in a sick manner when someone in his presence tries to speak. Makes critical remarks against the government. Criticizes the most diverse governmental measures. Changes his position with an erratic notion of having been falsely treated in the service."

Since when are pages of such meaningless and fabricated nonsense provided at the moment of admission for the determination of a diagnosis? This is already a diagnosis, decided upon even before the examination. One need only read: "Separated from his wife, since he suffers from a crazy notion about mutual relationships."

I, the wife of V. N. Kuznecov and the mother of two children, declare: THAT IS A LIE, just as all the rest of it is—lies. From the beginning to the end—all lies. I believe that all of this was instigated by the KGB, that all of it is a gross misunderstanding, that all of it is a lamentable echo from the times of the personality cult. FREE MY HUSBAND.

I request that you publish this statement.

V. I. Kuznecov
Pushkina, Moscow
Armand Settlement #16
December 15, 1966

From POSEV, *May 12, 1967.*

ANATOLI MARCHENKO ON
CONCENTRATION CAMPS

The worker Anatoli Marchenko, whose reputation has be-
come established in the West because of his approximately
400-page camp report entitled My Testimony (Moi Pokazan-
ija)*, was first incarcerated in camps and prisons from 1960*
to 1966 as a "political prisoner." He was arrested a second
time on July 29, 1969, for alleged violations of the pass laws
and was sentenced to an additional year at hard labor in a
camp. Actually, it is probable that this conviction rests
much more on the contents of a letter he wrote in which he
supported the Czechoslovakian program of reform. As a re-
sult of his allegedly "anti-Soviet" book, My Testimony, *which*
had appeared around this time in the West, Marchenko was
convicted on August 20, 1969, shortly before his scheduled
release, to an additional two years in a concentration camp
after a secret trial.

To: *The Chairman of the Red Cross of the* U.S.S.R.,
        G. A. Miterev;
        Minister of Public Health of the U.S.S.R., *S. V.*
        Petrovski;
        Director of the Institute for Nutrition of the
        Academy of Sciences, A. A. Pokrovski;
        Patriarch of All Russia, Aleksi;
        President of the Academy of Sciences of the
        U.S.S.R., *M. V. Keldysh;*
        President of the Medical Academy of Sciences of
        the U.S.S.R., V. D. Timakov;

> Director of the Institute for State and Law,
> Chikvadez;
> Rector of the Moscow State University, I. G.
> Petrovski;
> First Secretary of the Board of Directors of the
> Writers' Union of the U.S.S.R., K. Fedin;
> Chairman of the Journalists' Union of the U.S.S.R.,
> Zimjanin;
> The Writers: K. Simonov, R. Gamzatov, R. Rozh-
> destvenski, Y. Yevtushenko

Copies: To the United Nations Committee for the Protection of Human Rights
To the International United Nations Conference
for Human Rights

You should be aware of the following:

Many thousands of political prisoners are currently being held in prisons and camps in our country. Most of them were convicted in trials which were not open to the public. As a matter of fact, public proceedings were almost nonexistent, with the single exception of those trials concerning war crimes and war criminals. In all instances, the fundamental principal of jurisdiction, an open and public trial, was violated. In this manner society could not and cannot control compliance with the law or the scale of political reprisals.

Political prisoners are treated in the same manner as criminal prisoners, and in many respects even worse. For political prisoners, the minimum punishment is confinement in a strict state camp; the minimum punishment for those convicted of a criminal offense, on the other hand, consists of confinement in moderate or even mild state camps. Criminals may be released after they have served two thirds and sometimes only one half of their sentence, but again, political prisoners must serve out their sentence to the letter, to the bitter end . . .

The group of political prisoners is comprised for the most part of people who had, up until their arrest, performed useful services for society: engineers, workers, men of letters, artists, scientists. In camp they are subjected to "indoctrinizational procedures"—forced labor. In this way the camp administration renders work a form of punishment: The weaker prisoners are forced to perform difficult physical labor, and men of intellectual occupations are called upon to accomplish heavy physical labor that is totally foreign to their natures. Not completing the work schedule is considered an offense against the rule and serves as an excuse for various administrative punishments, beginning with a prohibition against visitors and going so far as to include incarceration or even solitary confinement.

One of the favorite reprisals against political prisoners is the attempt to wear them down through starvation. Board requirements have been so minutely curtailed that inmates constantly suffer from hunger. The daily ration in a camp consists of 2,400 calories (the daily requirements of a seven to eleven-year-old child), and with it a fully grown, physically overworked man must content himself day in and day out over a period of many years, often between fifteen and twenty-five.

The greater part of the caloric requirement is met in daily ration of black bread (700 grams). Fresh vegetables, butter and many other necessary nutritional elements are never allotted to the prisoners. As a matter of fact, such commodities (as well as sugar) are not even allowed to be purchased in the exchange stands within the camp. While I am on the subject, prisoners must purchase their food as well as their clothing in the camp out of the meager recompense they are granted in return for their work. (Of that, however, 50 percent is withheld for the upkeep of the camp: for the barracks, equipment, fences, watchtowers, etc.) And from what is left of these wages, after the various deductions have been made, the prisoner is permitted to spend no more than five rubles a month in the exchange stands. But even this right, which amounts to spending seventeen kopeks a day, can be denied the prisoner if "a rule is broken." Thus, for instance, the historian Rendel (who received a ten-year sentence for having participated in an illegal Marxistic organization) lost his purchasing right for two months because he brought supper to the barracks for one of his fellow inmates who happened to be too ill to go to the canteen. The imprisoned writer Siniavski was similarly disciplined because he spent a few minutes conversing with his friend, the writer Daniel, while the latter was serving out a temporary incarceration within the camp.

As a result of so-called violations against the camp regulations, including among other things, the nonfulfillment of the work schedule, a prisoner can be subjected to a severe reduction of his daily rations. These can be reduced as low as 1,300 calories a day (the daily requirement for a one to three-year-old child). Such disciplinary actions, for example, were exercised against the writer Daniel and the engineer Ronkin during the late summer of 1967.

Strict state camps do not permit prisoners to receive care packages from their relatives; the camp administration permits reception of such care packages only as an incentive, or as a reward for good behavior (that is, contrition, denunciation, and collaboration with the authorities), but even this is denied until at least half of one's sentence has been served, and then no more than four packages a year are allowed, and each package must weigh less than five kilograms.

In this way the administration maintains an insurmountable weapon of physical repression against the political prisoner—a completely systemized starvation. The results of the application of this system are undernourishment and complications caused by vitamin deficiency.

The constant lack of sufficient food forces some of the prisoners to such extreme measures as the killing of crows, or, if he is particularly fortunate, a dog, for immediate on-the-spot consumption. In the fall of 1967 one prisoner in the camp division at Dubrovlag died after having eaten too many raw potatoes all at once, potatoes which he had been able to "organize" in the infirmary. An even more horrifying starvation reigns in the prison at Vladimir and in the camps under special regulations, where a considerable number of political prisoners are being held. In contrast to the constant hunger that is endured, the other "indoctrination measures" appear much less insidious. Nevertheless, several of these indoctrinational measures ought to be mentioned at least. The reception of visitors is strictly forbidden, heads are shaven bald, the wearing of one's personal clothes is forbidden (including warm under-

wear in winter), creative work is hampered if not forbidden, as well as the observance of religious rituals . . .

The deprivation of their rights has driven prisoners to
horrible and harmful protest actions: to hunger strikes, to
self-mutilation, to suicide. Thus there have been instances
of a prisoner purposely entering the barbed-wire zone in
full daylight, knowing he will be shot by the guards "for
attempted escape."

I don't know if any other part of the world (with the
exception of our own country) employs a similar treatment for political prisoners in the 1960's—the legal deprivation of rights, legal starvation, and legal forced labor.
I am convinced that this condition is only possible in our
situation because nobody (with the exception of those
employed as organizers and executors of this system) knows
anything about it. If only the masses were informed about
this, just think what unlimited possibilities for protest
against such treatment of Russian political prisoners would
be available for concerned people outside the u.s.s.r. For
the time being, our own political prisoners are the only
ones who read about the protests in newspapers and can
recognize the incredible hypocrisy of the situation: the immeasurable contradiction between the propaganda "for the
outside world" and the practice here at home . . .

I request that you:

demand that the situation of the prisoners be publicly
examined;

demand that the "analyses of camps and prisons" be
made known to the public through general publication,
and try to set up some special regulations for the imprisonment of political prisoners;

demand that the personnel of the Stalinist concentration camps, as well as those who have demonstrated cruelty and inhumanity against prisoners during the past few years, be immediately relieved of their "educational work"; that they be brought to court and be tried in open and public proceedings.

It is our duty as citizens, the duty of our human consciences, to put a stop to outrages against humanity. These outrageous crimes do not begin with the smoking chimneys of the crematoria, nor with the steamships bound for Magadan and loaded to overflowing with prisoners. These crimes begin with the apathy and indifference of the individual citizen.

ANATOLI MARCHENKO
ALEKSANDROV, VLADIMIR
27 NOVINSKI STREET
April 2, 1968

From POSEV, *No. 6, 1968.*

STATEMENT BY A. I. SOLZHENITSYN IN DEFENSE OF ZARES MEDVEDEV

AND SO WE CONTINUE TO LIVE: A healthy man is accosted by two policemen and two doctors without either a warrant for his arrest or a medical justification. The doctors declare that the man is crazy, the policemen shout: "Stand up! We are an organ of force!" His arms are bound, and they take him to a madhouse.

This can happen tomorrow to any one of us. As a matter of fact, it has just happened to Jaures Medvedev, a geneticist and publicist, a man with a sharp, subtle, brilliant intelligence and a good soul (I know personally of his disinterested help given to many totally unknown and dying people). And just the diversity of his abilities is supposed to be sufficient proof that he isn't normal: "A split personality"! It is precisely his sensitivity to injustice and ignorance that is supposed to demonstrate his sick deviations: "insufficient adaptation to the social environment"! If you don't think the way you should, you aren't normal! Those people who have no trouble adjusting to anything all think alike. And we have no way of combating this— even the appeals of our best scientists and writers fly back like peas thrown against a wall.

If only this were the first case! But this type of thing has become the rule with us, this illegal doing away with a person that does not concern itself with questions of guilt because people are ashamed to give the real reason. Several of those who have been persecuted are very well-known; the majority, however, are totally unknown. Servile and unscrupulous psychiatrists define the concern about social problems, overflowing enthusiasm as well as extensive cold-bloodedness, exceptional talents as well as the total lack of any talent, as "mental illness."

Meanwhile, the simplest consideration of these things ought to protect us from them. In his time nobody touched a hair on Chaadaev's head—but to this day we continue to curse the excutioners of those days, more than a century later. It is high time we realized that the forced confinement of free-thinking, healthy people in an insane asylum is spiritual murder. It is a variation of the gas chamber, only more cruel; the tortures of its victims are more malicious and more prolonged. These crimes, just like the gas chambers, will never be forgotten, and all those who are involved in them will be condemned eternally, as long as they live and then after their death. Even in the midst of despotism and crime one must observe the limits beyond which a man becomes a cannibal.

The arithmetic is wrong that maintains one can live simply by relying on power alone and constantly ignoring the objections of one's conscience.

A. SOLZHENITSYN

June 15, 1970

Taken from RUSSKAIA MYSL', *Paris, July 2, 1970.*

GRIGORENKO ON THE RIGHT TO VOTE

To: *The members of the local election commission of the Lenin district in Moscow (11 Timur-Frunze Street) The editors of* IZVESTIA *and* MOSKOVSKAYA PRAVDA

In an effort to spare your registration agents useless work, I hereby declare that I will not appear at the election polls.

My reasons:

(1) There are no elections for the Soviet people. There is only a show of hands for one single candidate who is designated by the current rulers. This single candidate un-

questionably will be "elected," independently of the election turn-out. This "election" is important only to the rulers, for they use it to demonstrate to the rest of the world that "the entire population is behind them." I have no desire to participate in such a farce and will only cast my vote in those instances where my voice has some authority.

(2) Our delegates have no real power, not even a genuine franchise. At the very most, they only have the opportunity to voice their approval or consent, in contrast to the political power of the well-co-ordinated and well-skilled governmental leadership. And under the current Constitution, a delegate—regardless of the level and position he may assume—has never yet dared to criticize the despotism of our rulers. Weren't there times during which uncountable millions of innocent people were exterminated, among them a considerable number of delegates "elected by the people"? From my own personal experience, I can vouch for the meaning and significance of the unimpeachability our delegates can attain. In 1964 I was arrested by the KGB for the simple reason that I advocated the reinstatement of the Leninist principles in the life of the Party as well as of the state. I was not brought to trial, obviously because they feared the truth I would have been able to say if brought before the court of law. Without any legal proceedings at all, I was confined to a psychiatric prison, discharged from the army, and demoted from the rank of general to that of private.

My petitions to the authorities and offices of the administration of justice remained unanswered. Not one single delegate deigned to answer me, though I have addressed myself to every representative of the Supreme Soviet of the u.s.s.r., including those to whom I gave my support.

Judge for yourself whether I can participate in such an election farce, whose only purpose is to express confidence in a regime seeking to eternalize its own powers by means of political despotism.

P. GRIGORENKO
MOSCOW, G-21
KOMSOMOLSKI-PROSPECT,
14/1, APT. 96
March 16, 1969

From POSEV, *No. 6, 1969.*

AN APPEAL FROM REPRESENTATIVES OF THE CRIMEAN-TARTAR PEOPLE TO THE PEOPLE OF THE WORLD

The following is an appeal of the Crimean Tartars who were accused of having collaborated with the Germans in 1944 and had, as a result, been deported to Uzbekistan.

Ten elected leaders of the Crimean Tartars, among them Rollan Kadyev, the well-known expert in physics, as the main defendant, were sentenced on August 1, 1969, to imprisonment in the work camps with terms ranging from one and a half to three years. During a special trial held on April 29, 1969, the engineer Gomer Baev was also sentenced to two years in a work camp. The arrest and conviction of these Crimean Tartar leaders occasioned a wave of

*protests and demonstrations in which many Russians also
participated. The most prominent demonstrator was the
Major General of the army, Petr Grigorenko, who was himself arrested in Tashkent, Uzbekistan, on May 7, 1969,
while actively supporting the interests of the Crimean Tartars, and was confined to an insane asylum as allegedly
mentally disturbed in February of 1970.*

In 1944, our entire race was slanderously accused of
treason against the Soviet fatherland and was forcibly
evicted from the Crimea.

At that time all able-bodied men found themselves at
the front, and those older men and adolescents who were
strong and healthy enough were employed in the work
brigades. During the course of one single day—May 18—
200,000 defenseless women, children, and invalids were
driven from their huts by NKVD troops, loaded on transport
trains and carried off under guard to reservations. This
journey to Central Asia lasted about three weeks—the
wagons were unventilated, there was insufficient food and
no satisfactory clothing. After the end of the war our men
were likewise transported to this area. As a result of this
inhuman deportation and of the unbearable conditions
under which we had to live, more than half of our total
population died in misery. At the same time our national
autonomy was annulled, our national culture destroyed;
our monuments were demolished and the graves of our
ancestors were defiled and left undistinguishable on the
face of the earth.

In the course of the next twelve years we lived under
conditions not much different from exile; we were subjected

to discrimination and even our children, who were born in this exile, bore the mark of "traitors," and, as always, we were forbidden to return to the Crimea. Slanderous literature was published against us, widely circulated, and to this day some of it continues to be read by the Soviet public. Following the Twentieth Congress of the Communist Party of the Soviet Union, we were officially released from the status of exiles, but not, however, from the accusation of treason against our country. From 1957 to 1967, we sent hundreds of collective and individual letters to the Central Committee of the CPSU, as well as to the Presidium of the Supreme Soviet of the U.S.S.R., demanding an end to these injustices. After stubborn and persistent requests on several occasions, representatives of our people were repeatedly received by Party and government leaders Mikoyan, Georgadze, and Andropov in Moscow. On each occasion we were promised the prompt consideration and resolution of the Crimean Tartar question, but instead, these meetings resulted only in additional arrests, deportations, dismissals from our jobs, and expulsions from the Party.

Finally, on September 5, 1967, the Presidium of the Supreme Soviet of the U.S.S.R. issued a decree that absolved us from the charge of treason; in this decree, however, we were no longer designated as Crimean Tartars, but rather as "citizens of the Tartar nationality who previously lived in the Crimea." In this manner the decree determined our status as deportees and exiles from our homeland and abolished our existence as a nation. The actual significance of this decree was not at first correctly understood by everyone. Immediately after its publication several thousand of our people tried to return to the Crimea; once again, however, they were forcibly transported back to the reservations. The following protest, which was sent to the Central Committee of the CPSU in the name of our people, remained unanswered, as did the appeals of representatives of the Soviet public who supported us.

Persecutions and court actions were the only answer we received from our rulers. Since 1959, as a result of these trials, about 2,000 of the most active and most courageous representatives of our people were sentenced to an average of seven years, although they had all, without exception, acted strictly within the framework of the Soviet Constitution. The repressions against us have greatly intensified during the last few years. On April 21, 1968, Crimean Tartars who had gathered in celebration of Lenin's birthday were dispersed by troops and the militia in the city of Chirchik; more than 3,000 people were arrested that day. In May, representatives of our people arrived in Moscow for the purpose of presenting the Central Committee of the CPSU with a document demanding the return of our people to the Crimea. On the sixteenth and seventeenth of May, almost all of our delegates were arrested and brought under guard to Tashkent. At the same time, four representatives of our intelligentsia were sentenced to deprivation of their freedom in Tashkent. Every day dozens of our people were summoned to the local authorities where blackmail and threats were employed in an attempt to force them to renounce their demands to return to the homeland. They circulated lies about us, saying we wanted to return to the Crimea in order to drive out those people now living there. This is not true. We are a peaceful people; we have always lived peacefully among the many peoples of the Crimea, and we will always do so. We threaten nobody; we are kept under the constant threat of national destruction, however. Whàt they are doing to us falls completely and absolutely within the sphere of genocide.

In the course of our struggle, a total of about three million signatures have been sent by our people on petitions to the Soviet government. This means that every adult Crimean Tartar has signed no less than ten such petitions. But 300,000 persons have repeated their pleas ten times over in vain. Not one state or Party political agency has ever answered us even once, and not one Soviet newspaper has even thought about our struggle.

Therefore, we are turning to the peoples of the world.

We are turning to all peoples of the Soviet Union, just as a small independent people turns to its allies. We are turning to all peoples of the world, and primarily to those who have learned from experience what national inequality and oppression means.

We appeal to all people of good will in the hope that they will assist us.

Help us return to the land of our fathers!

This letter is signed by representatives of the Crimean Tartar people who are responsible by mandate to fight in the name of their people and with all legally available means for the return to their homeland.

ZAMPIRA ASANOVA *(doctor)*

ROLLAN KADYYEV *(physicist)*

RESHAT BAJRAMOV *(mechanic)*

MURAT VOENNYI *(construction worker)*

ZERA CHALILOVA *(teacher)*

MUSTAFA IBIRSH *(engineer)*
ELDAR SHABANOV *(chauffeur)*
ASHE BEKIROVA *(teacher)*
RAMAZAN MURATOV *(worker)*

There follows a total of 118 signatures.

Taken from CHRONIKA TEKUSCICH SOBYTIY, *1968; reprinted in* POSEV, *1969.*

LETTER FROM THE INTELLECTUALS
AND WORKERS OF KIEV

The following open letter comes from the Ukraine and bears a total of 139 signatures belonging to mathematicians, technicians, writers (among others Viktor Nekrasov), artists, lawyers, engineers, doctors, workers, students, and merchants. The letter is undated, but it is assumed that it was written in February of 1968.

In the trials mentioned below, held in 1965-66 in Kiev, Lvov, Ivano-Frankovsk, and other cities in the Ukraine, the defendants were for the most part Ukrainian intellectuals who had continually demanded that their constitutionally guaranteed rights be granted, as well as continually advocating the free applicaton of the Ukrainian language and the preservation of their cultural heritage. They were sentenced to rather severe prison terms for having circulated "anti-Soviet propaganda." The young journalist Viacheslav Chernovil, mentioned in the letter below, gathered together a great amount of important information con-

cerning these trials in his book Lycho Z Rozumu, *published in Paris in 1967. For having written and "illegally circulated" this book, Chernovil was sentenced in 1967 to eighteen months in a work camp.*

To: The Secretary General of the Central Committee of the
         CPSU: *Leonid Brezhnev*
      The Prime Minister of the U.S.S.R.: *Aleksei Kosygin*
      The Chairman of the Presidium of the Supreme Soviet of the U.S.S.R: *Nikolai Podgorny*

Honored Comrades:

We have come to you with a question that distresses various circles of Soviet society. During the course of the last few years, political trials against young people belonging to the ranks of the creative and scientific intelligentsia have been held in the Soviet Union. These trials have disturbed us for many reasons, but mainly because we cannot remain indifferent to the fact that during the course of many of these trials the laws of the land have been violated. For instance, all the trials that took place in Kiev, Lvov, and Ivano-Frankovsk in 1965-66, as a result of which more than twenty persons received convictions, were not open to the public. This, of course, is in direct violation of the rights clearly and unambiguously guaranteed in the Constitution of the U.S.S.R., the constitutions of the various Soviet Socialist Republics, and the penal law. Moreover, the secretive character of these trials made possible the violation of justice during the interrogations.

We are of the opinion that the decision to conduct secret trials is not in keeping with the decisions of the

Twentieth and Twenty-Second Party Congresses concerning the reinstatement of legality . . . The principle of publicity requires not only open trials but also extensive and truthful accounts of them in the press. After all, one of Lenin's postulates states that the general masses should assimilate such knowledge and should have the opportunity moreover to draw their own conclusions and judgments from it. . . But our newspapers carried no mention of the political trials being held in the Ukraine. Also, the short announcements appearing in the press about the political trials then being held in Moscow aroused nothing more than confusion and dissatisfaction among their readers because of the press's condescending tone and underestimation of the general level of intelligence rather than providing accurate information concerning the course of events during the trials.

. . . There is also another situation that bodes only disaster for our country. In many instances the accused were reproached with statements or opinions which could in no way be described as anti-Soviet and which were, in fact, nothing more than criticisms of isolated events in our social life, or criticisms of notorious regressions from socialist ideals, or sometimes even violations of the officially proclaimed legal norms.

As an example, the journalist Viacheslav Chernovil was brought before the district court in Lvov simply because he gathered together some informational materials and submitted them to official organs, materials that pointed out the illegal and judicially farcical nature of the political trials held in the Ukraine during 1965 and 1966 . . . But despite the fact that the charges against Chernovil could not

be proved, all the demands of the prosecutor were nevertheless fulfilled by the court, and the young journalist was
sentenced to three years deprivation of freedom.

All these and many other facts suffice to demonstrate
that the political trials contrived during the last few years
represent a suppression of political dissidents, a strangula-
tion of civilian activity and social criticism—normally essential for the health of any society. They demonstrate an
increased revival of Stalinism, exactly what I. Gabai, Yuri
Kim, and Petr Yakir so energetically and courageously
warned the Soviet scholars, scientists, and artists against
in their proclamation to the people. In the Ukraine, where
violation of democracy is intensified by the distortion of
the nationalist question, symptoms of Stalinism are more
clearly and more primitively evident.

We consider it our duty to express our deep concern
over these events. We are appealing to you to exercise your
authority and your competence to insure that the courts
and the organs of defense follow the Soviet laws to the
letter, that the existing problems and differences of opinion
in our social-political life be solved along given ideological
guidelines, and that they not be passed on to state prosecutors and secret police forces.

139 signatures

From NEUE ZURCHER ZEITUNG, *November 2, 1968.*

PETITION IN THE CASE OF YESENIN-VOLPIN

To: *The Minister of Health,* U.S.S.R.
           The Prosecutor General of the U.S.S.R.

Copy: Chief Psychiatrist, City of Moscow

We have learned that the great Soviet mathematician Aleksandr Sergeevich Yesenin-Volpin, a well-known specialist in the field of mathematical logic, has been forcibly confined to the Psychiatric Hospital No. 5, Stolbovaia, seventy kilometers from Moscow, without prior medical examination and without the knowledge or consent of his relatives.

The forcible commitment of a gifted and entirely able-bodied mathematician to a hospital for seriously disturbed mental patients, and the conditions to which he has been subjected in such an institution as this, are having particularly deleterious effects on his mental attitude and his health, and insult his personal dignity.

From the standpoint of the humanitarian goals of our legislation and particularly from the standpoint of the public-health services, we consider this a coarse violation of medical and legal norms. For this reason we request that you intervene as quickly as possible in this matter and put into motion those measure which will allow our colleague to resume his work again under normal conditions.

Signatures:

Member of the u.s.s.r. *Academy of Sciences and Lenin Prize winner, P. S. Novikov*

Corresponding member of the u.s.s.r. *Academy of Sciences, Lenin and State Prize winner, I. M. Gelfand*

Corresponding member of the u.s.s.r. *Academy of Sciences and State Prize winner, Lazar A. Liusternik*

Corresponding member of the U.S.S.R. *Academy of Sciences, Andrei A. Markov*

Corresponding member and State Prize Winner, Dmitri E. Menshov

Corresponding member of the U.S.S.R. *Academy of Sciences and Lenin Prize winner, I. R. Shafarevich*

Lenin Prize Winner, Professor, Doctor of Physics and Mathematics, Vadim I. Varnold

Lenin Prize Winner, Professor, Doctor of Physics and Mathematics, Vadim I. Arnold

State Prize Winner, Professor, Doctor of Physics and Mathematics, Aleksandr Kronrod

Lenin Prize Winner, Doctor of Physics and Mathematics, Yuri I. Manin

State Prize Winner, Professor, Doctor of Physics and Mathematics, N. N. Meiman

Additional signatures of Professors and Doctors of Physics and Mathematics follow:

F. F. BAKSHTEIN	D. A. BOCHVAR	V. A. YEFREMOVICH
LIUDMILA KELDYSH	A. A. KIRILLOV	V. A. KONDRATEV
A. G. KUROSH	E. M. LANDIS	A. M. LODMICH
A. YA. POVZNER	N. V. ZVOLINSKI	I. I. PIATECKII-SHAPIRO
V. P. PALAMODOV	JU. M. SMIRNOV	S. V. FORMIN
G. E. SHILOV	A. M. YAGLOM	I. M. YAGLOM

Sixty-five additional signatures follow those already given, all from scientific workers and members of the faculty of Mechanics and Mathematics of the Moscow State University; a total, therefore, of ninety-five signatures.

March 9, 1968

Please send your reply to the attention of the signatories above at the following address:

THE LOMONOSOV STATE UNIVERSITY IN MOSCOW

DEPARTMENT OF MECHANICS AND MATHEMATICS

Taken from POSEV, *No. 4, 1968*

A LETTER FROM THE WRITER A. KOSTERIN TO THE CENTRAL COMMITTEE OF THE CPSU

The writer and long-time Communist Aleksei Kosterin (1896-1968) spent seventeen years of his life in Stalin's concentration camps, the "death camp" at Kolima among others. The diary of his daughter, Nina, is well-known. In it she describes the arrest of her father and of other members of her family. Active as a partisan, Nina Kosterin was killed at the beginning of the war. Her diary was published in Novy Mir.

Kosterin, who had worked on and off for several newspapers, including Izvestia, Trud, *and* Gudok, *was an active member of the civil-rights movement. He became involved particularly with the attempts of the deported Crimean Tartars to regain their rights. He was also one of the signers (along with Petr Grigorenko, Ivan Yakhimovich, and two other Soviet citizens) of a letter encouraging the Czechoslovakian regime to continue its course of reform, even against Soviet opposition. Kosterin's burial in Moscow on November 14, 1968, for which about three hundred people had gathered, resembled a public demon-*

stration against the dictatorship of the regime. Petr Grigorenko, a close friend of the writer, delivered the famous eulogy, which ended with the words: "There will be freedom and there will be democracy!" The texts of the seventeen other speeches, none of which were any less critical, managed to reach the West before they were confiscated by officials in the Soviet Union.

To: The Politburo of the Central Committee of the
CPSU

Copies: The Editor of Pravda for Publication
The Party Regional Committee—Frunze
The Party Committee MO SSR—For Your Information

Honored Comrades:

During the past few months I sent several letters to my appropriate Party headquarters, as well as to the Central Committee of the Party, in which I criticized a series of negative events occurring in the public, as well as private, life of the Party. I insisted that relevant questions be openly discussed so that it would be possible to decide quite peacefully whether and where I am supposed to be wrong, or, in the event I am actually right, whether and where I might find assistance; and to come to a decisive conclusion concerning the appropriate courts of the Party and the state in this matter.

I do not think that anyone can deny me my incontestable right as a Party member, as defined in the Party

Statutes of the CPSU. The fact that the very opposite has actually occurred, not only contradicts the above-mentioned statute; it is also totally incomprehensible to the simple and healthy human understanding.

I was informed that a judgment concerning my letters of October 17th of this year was being .deliberated by a Party Committee of the Moscow division of the Writers' Union. Health precautions prevented me from participating in the meeting. My doctor categorically forbade me to participate in discussions which would involve considerable nervous strain so shortly after having suffered a heart attack. And since the questions to be discussed were so perfectly clear and unmistakable, I felt that they could be discussed even in my absence. Therefore I decided not to attend. It has since been learned, however, that my letters never were discussed with respect to their contents. Instead, they were laid aside in a totally unjustified manner as being against Party interests and anti-Soviet, and because I dared to write these letters, I was summarily expelled from the Party.

. . . What has here been perpetrated against me is not accidental nor does it fall within the framework of normal activities. The Politburo of the Central Committee itself pays no attention to the Party laws and does not act in accordance with them. In direct contradiction to the decisions of the Twenty-Second and Twenty-Third Party Congresses, the rehabilitation of the name and inhuman deeds of Stalin was "quietly" but very persistently pursued. Civil rights in their practical administration became increasingly reminiscent of Stalinist methods.

Today, as in Stalin's time, freedom of speech, press,

convocation, meetings, and demonstrations exist only on paper in the form of the declarations expressing them in the Constitution. In practice, however, those who want to avail themselves of their constitutional rights are locked up; those who dare to protest such despotism are expelled from the Party, driven away from their places of work, placed under the constant surveillance of KGB agents, and —in an attempt to gag them—no methods, however repulsive, are ignored.

Just as in Stalin's time, a whole series of small nations and peoples are being subjected to infuriating persecutions, discrimination, and a decimation that comes close to being described as genocide.

The spirit of Stalinism is also very visible in foreign policy. A particularly blatant example of this is apparent in the events surrounding Czechoslovakia. Without the slightest consideration for the true interests of our country and for the movement of world Communism, the highest Party and state leadership in the U.S.S.R. did not hesitate to push the world toward the brink of catastrophe . . . Out of their own narrow-minded interests they have brought down, not only upon our land but also upon the world Communist movement, an incomparable moral injury.

These alarming conditions even reign over the Party. Chosen and gathered together according to Stalinist standards, this Party apparatus imposes itself in brotherly solidarity upon every person who dares to express even the smallest doubt about the infallibility of the policies being pursued, or who maybe decides to criticize someone—it doesn't matter whom—in the Party or state leadership.

In our current Party, deliberations are not permitted

and second thoughts are forbidden. You can expect to be expelled from the Party for making suggestions that result from individual thinking not specifically sanctioned from "above." Only that person can survive in this Party who considers his continuation in it as security for his personal well-being.

As a sign of my protest against these blatant violations of the Party Statute, and with the wish of freeing myself from Party discipline that robs me of my freedom of thought, I hereby resign from the Communist Party of the Soviet Union and return my Party identification card #8293698.

A. KOSTERIN
October 24, 1968

From POSEV, *No. 2, 1969.*

AN APPEAL BY IVAN YAKHIMOVICH

The days of my freedom are numbered. On the eve of arrest I appeal to those people whose names are treasured in my memory and my heart—hear me out! . . . I am compelled to talk about myself because a flood of lies and hypocrisy will soon stream from the courtroom. I am compelled to talk about myself because my fate is the fate of my people and my honor is their honor.

Under Article 183 of the Latvian Penal Code, I am accused of having deliberately circulated falsehoods slandering the Soviet State and the socialist system. The maxi-

mum penalty is three years deprivation of freedom. . . .
Bertrand Russell! You are a philosopher, so perhaps you
can recognize more quickly what the basis of these accusations are . . . What laws have I broken? The Constitution of the Latvian Soviet Socialist Republic and the
Declaration of Human Rights allow every individual to
write and distribute whatever he wishes, to demonstrate,
etc. . . . Whom does my freedom threaten? And why is it
essential to deprive me of it? . . .

Comrade Aleksandr Dubcek! When on August 25
[1968] seven people gathered with the slogans "hands off
Czechoslovakia!" and "For your freedom and ours!", they
were beaten until they bled; they were called "anti-Soviet
slanderers," "yids" and other things. I could not be with
them, but I was on your side, and I will always be on your
side as long as you serve your people honorably. "Remain
firm, the sun will come up again . . ."

Aleksandr Isaevich [Solzhenitsyn]! I am happy that
I had the opportunity to read your works. May you be
granted "the gift of the heart and the wine."

Pavel [Litvinov] and Larisa [Daniel]: We welcomed
your gladiatorlike courage. "Hail Caesar, we who are about
to die salute you!" We are proud of you . . .

Farmers of the collective farm "Juana Gvarda": I have
worked with you for eight years. That is long enough to
get to know a person. Judge for yourselves, and place
your judgment in the service of the truth. Don't let yourselves be deceived.

Workers of Leningrad, Moscow, and Riga! Dock
workers of Odessa, Liepai, and Tallinn! To save the honor
of your class, the worker Vladimir Dremliuga went to Red

Square to say "No!" to the occupiers of Czechoslovakia. He was thrown into jail . . . Under the pretense of having violated the police residence regulations, the worker Anatoli Marchenko was thrown into jail. His letter exposed the hyprocrisy of the heads of state, their interference in the internal affairs of the CSSR. Before that he languished six long years in the work camps of Mordvinia where he lost both his hearing and his health.

Who but another worker will help a worker? One for all; all for one!

Comrade Grigorenko, Comrade Yakir! You are fighting stolidly for the truth. May life preserve you for the just cause!

Crimean Tartars! He who robs a whole people of their homeland, he who slanders a whole people from the infant to the old man, he proves himself the arch-enemy of all peoples. For your homeland, for the autonomous Crimean Tartar Soviet Socialist Republic! For your sons and daughters who have been thrown in jail! For your rights which have been trodden underfoot! . . .

I turn to the people of my own nationality—to the Poles, wherever they are living and wherever they are working. Do not keep silent when injustice occurs. "Poland is not yet lost as long as we are living." [10]

I turn to the Latvians, whose state has become my homeland and whose language I know as well as Polish and Russian. Do not forget that thousands of your fellow countrymen are pining away in the labor camps of Mordvinia. Pay strict attention to the fate of everyone who, for political reasons, has been deprived of his freedom . . .

Academician Sakharov, I have heard about your

"Thoughts." I regret that I was not able to write you my opinion on the subject. The fault is mine . . .

Communists of all countries, Communists of the Soviet Union! You have one sovereign, one ruler—the people. But the people is made up of living beings, of concrete destinies. When human rights are violated, especially when this is done in the name of socialism, in the name of Marxism, there can be no alternative viewpoints. At such a time your conscience and your honor must be your guides.

Communists, ahead! Communists, move forward!

Soviet power is itself in great danger, particularly when people are robbed of their freedom because of their convictions, for then it will not be long before it too (the Soviet power), loses its freedom.

The mighty of the world are strong because we are on our knees. It's time to stand up!

I. A. YAKHIMOVICH
March 24, 1969

From RUSSKAIA MYSL', *May 29, 1969.*

PROTEST AGAINST THE ARREST OF YAKHIMOVICH

We were shocked to learn of the arrest of Ivan Antonovich Yakhimovich and of the letter which he wrote shortly before his arrest. For those who know him personally and know how often and with what results he spoke up against the lawlessness now reigning in our land, there is not the slightest doubt that the penal authorities are attempting to do away with a man of impeccable honor and exemplary valor, a man who we are convinced is innocent.

We will never condone reprisals which try to encroach upon the legitimate rights and dignity of our fellow citizens. We will never accept the arrest of Ivan Yakhimovich without protest. We consider it our duty therefore to declare that, without exceeding legal bounds, we will stop at nothing and do everything imaginable to prevent an infamous act of violence against Ivan Yakhimovich.

T. BAEVA *(employee)*

D. VASILEV *(lawyer)*

I. GABAI *(philologian)*

V. GERSHUNI *(worker)*

A. LEVITIN-KRASNOV
    (religious writer)

A. LAVUT *(mathematician)*

JU. MALEV *(philologian)*

B. RAKITIANSKII *(physicist)*

I. RUDAKOV *(worker)*

N. EMELKINA *(employee)*

S. KOVALEV *(biologist)*

V. KOZHARINOV *(worker)*

V. KRASIN *(economist)*

G. SAMOCHINA *(teacher)*

V. TIMACHEV *(geologist)*

M. YAKIR *(employee)*

P. YAKIR *(historian)*

I. YASHINOV *(oceanographist)*

From POSEV, *No. 5, 1969.*

PETITION TO THE SECRETARY GENERAL
OF THE UNITED NATIONS

The following mimeographed petition addressed to the United Nations—or, rather, to the Secretary General of the United Nations—is the third of five appeals from the so-

called "Initiative Group for the Protection of Human Rights in the Union of Soviet Socialist Republics" which dispatched them between May of 1969 and January of 1970 to the direct attention of the Commission on Human Rights. Under instructions from U Thant, which were issued in compliance with a request from Malik, the Soviet delegate to the United Nations, subsequent acceptance of petitions by the Secretary General of the United Nations was curtailed. In accordance with U Thant's directions, no written supplications could be accepted which were not sent to the headquarters of the United Nations in New York City by means of "normal mail or telegrams." Of course, it is self-evident that the "normal" postage path for petitioners in totalitarian states, such as the u.s.s.r. *where the whole postal operation is under the control of the censor, must be a hopeless undertaking.*

Amnesty International was mainly responsible for the future delivery of these petitions.

To the Honorable Secretary General:

In May of this year we appealed to the United Nations Commission on Human Rights, informing them of the innumerable, blatant violations of human rights in the Soviet Union. Not only in that letter but in the more detailed ones that followed, we stated that the principles proclaimed in many of the articles of the Declaration of Human Rights are being violated in our country; that this infringement consisted of the persecution of individuals solely on the grounds of their personal convictions. We have no idea how the Commission on Human Rights reacted to our plea. We do know, however, that in our country these statements have resulted in reprisals for their authors. In June, the Leningrad worker Vladimir Borosov was forcefully confined to a nerve clinic; in July, the engineer Genrich Altunian from Carkov was arrested; in September, the famous religious author and former prisoner of Stalin's camps, A. E. Krasnov (Levitin), as well as the Crimean Tartar worker, Mustafa Dzhemilev, were arrested; moreover, Oleg Vorobev was committed to a psychiatric clinic.

The remaining authors of the petition were summoned before the secret-police interrogating committee, because they considered our plea to the United Nations a particularly treasonous crime against the state. Meanwhile reprisals against dissidents continued undisturbed in many parts of the land.

We beg you to employ the full weight of your authority as Secretary General of the United Nations, as well as your personal influence, in speaking up against the violation of human rights in our country and making sure that this question is set before the U.N. Commission on Human Rights for discussion.

Silence on the part of the international judicial organizations serves only to strengthen the possibility that those who have further reprisals in mind will continue unhindered. We ask you to let us know what measures you have put in motion.

MEMBERS OF THE INITIATIVE GROUP:

TATIANA VELIKANOVA	LEONID PLIUSCH
NATALIA GORBANEVSKAYA	GRIGORY PODIAPOLSKI
VIKTOR KRASIN	TATIANA CHODOROVICH
ALEXANDER LAVUT	PETR YAKIR
YURI MALCOV	ANATOLI YAKOBSON

There are an additional thirty-six signatures

ENCLOSURES:

Letter to the public in connection with the arrest of A. E. Levitin-Krasnov; letter from the religious groups addressed to the world ecclesiastical court concerning the arrest of A. E. Levitin-Krasnov; letter from the citizens of Charkov concerning the arrest of G. Altunian; letter addressed to the public concerning the arrest of M. Dzhemilev from the Crimean Tartars.

September 26, 1969

From POSEV, *No. 11, 1969.*

WHAT IS THE INITIATIVE GROUP?

The complete text of the letter, excerpts of which are reproduced below, was delivered in May of 1970 to APN *in Moscow and Reuters in London by the "Initiative Group for the Protection of Civil Rights in the Union of Soviet Socialist Republics."*

. . . The Initiative Group has neither a program nor a charter, nor any organizational structure. We have no formal obligations. None of us are obliged to participate in any special document composed by the Initiative Group or to sign such a document; each is free to act in accordance with what he feels to be right when he takes a stand in his own name. Each one of us is free to leave the group. The entire group decides on the acceptance of new members. So far we have not felt it necessary to increase the number of our group.

The Initiative Group is composed of people who are bound together by certain common opinions. All of us—believers and nonbelievers, optimists and skeptics, people of Communist and non-Communist persuasion—are united by the feeling of personal responsibility for that which occurs in our country, by the conviction that recognizing the absolute worth of the individual is the basis of normal life in a human society. This also forms the basis of our efforts to defend human rights. We see social progress primarily as the progress of freedom. All of us share also the intention to act openly, in the spirit of legality, regardless of our personal convictions about particular laws.

We believe that every one has the right to make different political demands, and this corresponds to the Declaration of Human Rights and the laws of our state. Nevertheless, the Initiative Group itself is not concerned with politics. We do not suggest any positive solutions having to do with problems of state administration; instead, we simply maintain: You may not violate your own laws. We do not pursue our own politics, but we do not want to condone the policies of persecution against dissidents.

The task of the Initiative Group is to provide opposition against lawlessness and despotism.

The Initiative Group does not believe that it speaks against the state when it criticizes the actions of the authorities. A limitation of those activities of the state which are aimed against human rights is just as necessary—and in no way aimed against the state—as is the prohibition of murder and acts of violence (which, in the same way, represents no reduction in human rights).

To describe our activities as anti-Soviet is to assume that the violation of human rights is one of the basic precepts of the Soviet state order.

There are people who reject the violations of our rights taking place in our country, but at the same time condemn those who openly speak out against the violation of these laws because they believe that protests will drive the rulers to even greater severity and to increased reprisals.

We remember that the rulers in our land employed the most unmerciful suppression exactly in those times when no one "provoked" them. Actually a favorable atmosphere for repression is created simply by the lack of opposition, by that undignified submissiveness with which we inwardly sanction the violation of our rights. Silence aids evil and spoils men because it leads to hypocrisy and cynicism. Society needs publicity, needs public opinion. This hinders extremism and acts of force, not only those stemming from above but also those from below.

In our country, those who turn to the outside world are reproached with having done some harm to the reputation of our fatherland. The reputation of a nation, however, does not suffer from exposures, but rather much more from those deeds which must be exposed. Unfortunately, there is no other way to denounce publicly the violations of rights now occurring in the Soviet Union than this—to inform the rest of the world about them. In this way some information, however infinitesimal it might be, reaches at least some of the Soviet citizens. Furthermore, it is not out of the question that our leadership—though only incidentally and in specific cases—may consider the public opinion of the outside world . . .

People say to us: Why do you turn to the UNO and not to your own government? We emphasize that it was not the Initiative Group that began the discussion of the violation of civil rights in the U.S.S.R. In recent years individual citizens and groups of people have sent hundreds, if not thousands, of declarations and proposals in which they denounced despotism; in so doing they have written to all Party and governmental courts and the social organizations of the Soviet Union. All in vain.

We are by no means convinced that our proposals to the UNO represent the only right way—and even less, the only possible way—to act. We are trying to do something in a time that we feel forbids doing nothing. The Initiative Group is convinced that various civic actions of many people serve a purpose and that inactivity is senseless . . .

We have appealed five times to the Human Rights Commission of the United Nations Organization. Up until now the commission has not reacted to our proposals. It is possible that there are reasons for this which we do not know about. With this letter we want to explain why we do not consider our proposals pointless.

The Initiative Group for the Protection of Human Rights in the Union of Soviet Socialist Republics

T. VELIKANOVA	L. PLIUSCH	P. YAKIR
S. KOVALEV	G. PODIAPOLSKI	A. YAKOBSON
A. LAVUT	T. CHODOROVICH	

From POSEV, *No. 11, 1970.*

Thoughts on Constitution Day

VALERIA NOVODVORSKAYA

The author of the following poem, a nineteen-year-old Moscow student, distributed it as a flier on Constitution Day, 1969, in the Congressional Palace of the Kremlin. She was arrested by KGB officials and in April of the following year was committed under court order to an "insane asylum."

I thank you, Party, for everything:
What you have done and continue to do.
For granting us this poisonous hatred
I thank you, Party, for everything.

I thank you, Party, for making it so
That lies are blooming all around us;
Betrayal is swinging its two-edged sword,
And apathy reigns as sovereign power.

I thank you, Party, for lies and deceit,
For cleverly organized smear campaigns,
For crackling gunshots on Wenceslas Square
For all the lies that continue to come.

For ultramodern housing complexes
Supported by the crimes of the past;

For torture chambers where the whole world
Falls to pieces in the absence of light.

You alone, Party, are responsible
For our resentful lack of faith
In the remnants of the old formulae
Now floating in the surrounding fog.

I am very grateful to you, Party,
For the bitterness and confusion
For that crippling, criminal silence.
I thank you, Party, for everything.

I thank you for that heavy burden,
For the destruction of sacred truth,
For the shots of approaching battles—
I thank you, Party, for everything.

Original version appeared in CHRONIKA TEKUSCICH SOBYTIY, *Moscow, No. 13, 1970, reprinted in* POSEV, *July, 1970.*

THE ANTI-STALINISTS

Letter to the Presidium of the Advisory Meeting of the Communist Parties in Budapest

During the past few years a series of political trials took place in our country. Underlying these trials is the fact that by violation of their basic civil rights people were being condemned simply on the grounds of their personal beliefs. Blatant violations against the law were apparent in these proceedings where the greatest wrong lay in the exclusion of the public.

The public, however, is not willing to endure further such violations against the law; the disgust engendered by these trials, and the protests against them, increase with every new one. A mountain of letters was sent by individuals, as well as collectives, to the justice, administrative, and Party authorities. These letters remain unanswered. Those most active in the protests, however, were relieved of their jobs and were summoned before the KGB where they were threatened with arrest. The most shocking form of revenge finally' was forced confinement to a psychiatric clinic. These illegal and inhuman acts cannot lead to positive results. On the contrary, they increase the tension and sharpen the disgust.

We consider it our duty to point out that several thousand political prisoners, about whom hardly anyone knows, are being held in camps and prisons. They find themselves subjected to inhumane conditions, forced labor with reduced rations—the daily amount of which is left completely to the discretion of the camp administration. After having served their terms they are subjected to despotism beyond the control of the courts and are often subjected to illegal persecution; they are deprived of free choice regarding place of residence and must submit to official surveillance. Under these conditions a free man becomes an exile.

Furthermore, we want to direct your attention to the discrimination practiced against national minorities, as well as the political persecution of those people who fight for racial equality. This is particularly evident in the case concerning the Crimean Tartars.

We know that many Communists in the outside world and in our own land have repeatedly and eloquently objected to the political persecutions of the last few years. We are asking the participants of the Advisory Meeting to consider the danger that has developed from disregard for human rights in our country, and to consider this problem in its entirety.

ALEKSEI KOSTERIN (*writer*)
PAVEL LITVINOV (*physicist*)
PETR YAKIR (*historian*)
ILIA GABAI (*teacher*)
ANATOLI LEVITIN-KRASNOV (*religious writer*)
YURI GLAZOV (*linguist*)
LARISA BOGORAZ-DANIEL (*philologian*)
ZAMIRA ASANOVA (*doctor*)
VIKTOR KRASIN (*economist*)
BORIS SHRAGIN (*philosopher*)
YULI KIM (*teacher*)
PETR GRIGORENKO (*construction engineer, formerly Major General*)

February 24, 1968

From POSEV, *No. 3, 1968.*

CALL TO THE REPRESENTATIVES OF ART AND SCIENCE (CONCLUSION)

We appeal to you people of creative labor, people in whom our nation places its absolute trust. Raise your voices in protest against the approaching danger of new Stalins and Yezhovs. Your conscience must bear the fate of future Vavilovs and Mandelstams. You are the heirs of the great humanistic tradition of the Russian intelligentsia. The courageous behavior of the modern and progressive intelligentsia of the West serves as a good example of this.

We are well aware that the conditions under which you must work are such that an act of courage is inevitably demanded simply for the fulfillment of your duty as citizens. There is, however, no other choice: either courage or cowardly participation in foul deeds; either a risk or an alliance with the Vasilevs and Kedrinas; [11] either the renunciation of certain privileges or the climbing on the bandwagon in the company of such unprincipled hack-writers as those who work for *Izvestia* or *Komsomolskaya Pravda,* writers who morally have taken it upon themselves to slander openly those people who have already been done away with.

We remind you once more that people are suffering under the cruel conditions of the state forced labor camps, people whose only crime was that they dared to think. Every time you keep your silence you lay the cornerstone of a new trial. A new 1937 could eventually dawn, and all because of your silent consent.

I. GABAI

YU. KIM

Taken from POSEV, *No. 3, 1968.*　　　　　P. YAKIR

MORALITY AND PERSONALITY IN HISTORY

This is an excerpt from the address to the Institute of Philosophy in Moscow by the philosopher and writer G. S. Pomerantz, December 3, 1965.

Where is the ghost of Stalin leading us? Some comrades are still holding on to the impression of their youth, when they rose up under the scorching fire of machine guns and dragged the soldiers along with them with the words: "For the Fatherland, for Stalin!" It seems to them that the slogan "For Stalin!" still means the same thing today as it did in 1943. In 1943 I myself shouted "For the Fatherland, for Stalin—onward!" In 1943 "For Stalin!" meant "against Hitler." History left us with no other choice. History placed a whole generation in the position of Pangloss,[12] to whom the officers had given the choice of being hanged or running the gauntlet. The officer remained unmoved regardless of Pangloss's objections to the first as well as the second alternative. This is not a laughing matter when it represents the real difference between life and death. Ehrenburg relates in his memoirs that Nikolai Ivanovich Bukharin went off to Paris in 1937 without the necessary permission. There he spent a few days wandering about the streets, breathing the air of freedom, telling nobody about what he was doing. Then he returned to Moscow, despite the fact that he pretty much imagined what he could expect to find waiting for him. The logic of war would have forced him to expose Stalin at that time. But by then Stalin had already seized power with his merciless grasp; to accuse Stalin would have meant to accuse the Soviet system, but it was exactly that Soviet system which was one of the most powerful obstacles in the path of fascism. And not because Stalin didn't have any use for Hitler—maybe he thought very highly of him—but the situation was decreed by the logic intrinsic to the system and this was stronger than Stalin's personal will. Besides, one was not allowed to perform any surgical operations, one was not allowed to touch the Soviet system, not even with the intent to improve it, because of Hitler. Bukharin was thus forced to keep silent—just as he was forced later to speak.

That's how it was twenty-five years ago. But *now* the slogan "For Stalin" no longer means to fight against Hitler, against fascism; "Hitler is kaput." Stalin, too, is dead and exposed for what he was. Be it good or bad, an unmasked idol can never be restored to its former throne. It's easy enough to publish some kind of resolution, but such a resolution would be no more effective than Nicholas I's resolution concerning the complaint of a landowner whose daughter married against her father's will: "The marriage is to be annulled; young so-and-so is to be considered a virgin." Stalin, who proved himself a despot and a murderer, can never again be considered worthy of respect, let alone love. To revive respect for Stalin even though everyone knows what he did, would mean introducing something new, namely, to re-establish respect for denunciation, for tortures, and for executions. Stalin himself never tried such a thing; he preferred hypocrisy.

To re-establish respect for Stalin would mean to raise up a moral monster alongside our flag. Such a thing has never been done before. People have acted outrageously but the flag has remained unstained. We have inscribed upon it the words for which it is a symbol: "An association in which the free development of each individual is the condition for the free development of all." Marx, Engels, Lenin have all stood in front of that flag—people who had many human weaknesses, but who remained people, despite them. One could say of them (to quote one of Marx's favorite axioms): "I am a man, nothing human is alien to me." Stalin can no longer keep his position next to them. That would be to drag the flag through the mud. One has to be able to separate Stalin's anti-fascist war from the meaning of that war itself. The heroic accomplishment of the people during the civil war of 1812 are no less great because a "bald fop, an enemy of work, who happened to be accidently illumined by the beams of fame" stood at that time at the head of state. The people's feats of heroism during the great anti-fascist war will not be lessened by the fact that Stalin happened to be the head of state.

Some people fear the threat of an approaching nihilism, an ideological vacuum. But a prosaic and pedestrian culture is not capable of filling this vacuum. It collapses like a house of playing cards. One of the most important reasons for the present vacuum is the conflict between religious and scientific world views. The thousand-year-old ethical integrity of mankind existed in the form of a code, in the various religions of the world. The scientific world view shattered the world religions, but was incapable of creating images of moral beauty to replace the old ones; they could not equal the attraction of a Buddha or a Christ. That seems to be totally outside the sphere of science. It is rather the task of poetry and a process which cannot be steered, a very long process that could take several centuries to evolve. For this reason the world Communist movement has already actively aimed its main thrust against religion; under the influence of events it has moved to another form of contact with religion, to the dialogue, about which so much has been written in "Problems of Peace and Socialism." This dialogue with the various cultures of the world, cultures which can boast of Bach, Rubens, and Dante, seems to me to be a worthier course than the restoration of the cult of a despot and murderer. By means of this dialogue, we can unite the strength of the entire intelligentsia and bring true enlightenment to the people—the true meaning of culture, that one ought never to confuse with mere outward symbols, be they aesthetic or religious. This true culture, this true intellectuality—this is one of the most important paths for the overthrow of the contemporary "vacuum."

LETTER BY LIDIA CHUKOVSKAYA TO IZVESTIA (ON THE FIFTEENTH ANNIVERSARY OF STALIN'S DEATH)

To the Editor of *Izvestia:*
. . . While recently looking through a newspaper, I happened to find a short poem. It begins with a heartrending question:

> *The debt of days gone by,*
> *That endless debt—has it really been paid?*

and it ends with the comforting words:

We repaid that bill with more money
And more tears than it was ever worth.

What moved me was the consolation these last few lines afford . . . There is one responsibility one cannot escape from—and still he can't meet it. It is blasphemy to write about a paid-off debt in the same paragraph with our recent past. How and with what can we balance out the tortures and the death of one innocent man—and there were millions of them!—how much per head? And who has the right to say the account has been settled? It would be much better if we never undertook such a task! For there isn't anyone who has the resources to pay such a debt simply because humanity has never learned how to bring the dead back to life.

And who is to pay for the betrayed faith we had in those memorable words, the words that taught us: "In our country no one will be arrested without just cause"? Who is to pay for the faith we had that if Ivan Denisovich and his like are sitting behind bars, then they must indeed be enemies? We must admit that the provocation machines functioned magnificently in the past on the radio, in the press, and in meetings. They functioned so accurately and efficiently that sometimes even decent people bitterly persecuted the innocent. Wives renounced their husbands, children their fathers, and friends their closest comrades. But these betrayers were themselves victims of a sort, victims of organized lies . . . With what, therefore, could we possibly pay for this mass destruction of peoples' souls, the prostitution of the pen and the word? It seems to me the only way to "pay" for such outrages, if it's possible to pay at all, would be by means of integrity, the whole truth. But the truth was lost somewhere along the way; the hangmen's lust of the Stalinist era is once again skillfully hidden behind a wall of haze and insufficient information. And this fog continues to thicken before our very eyes.

The thirst after the most basic, elementary justice remains unsatisfied. The widows of the dead were informed that their husbands were arrested without cause and therefore are to be posthumously rehabilitated in the absence of any incriminating evidence. Those prisoners who were fortunate enough to survive have also been informed about this lack of evidence. They have returned. But where are they who are responsible for all this? Those who fabricated the evidence of a crime against millions of innocent people? . . . Who are these people, where are they, and what are they doing today? Who, where and when, has ever totaled up the crimes they committed quietly, systematically, and with total impunity day in and day out over a period of years? And these criminals, what have they been told and by whom?

It seems no one has told them anything. For had they done so, it would not have been possible that the man who bears the guilt of the death of poets is currently occupied in the publication of poems; that a writer who produced nothing other than denunciations should take his place as chairman at solemn meetings; that a white-haired respectable old man who is responsible for the deaths of Vavilov or Meierhold[13] in the past should collect a pension for his dutiful actions . . . A fog even deeper than we thought conceals all this!

The poem says we have wept enough over the bill. It's

true—we have wept an ocean of tears. But these tears have been shed secretly on our pillows . . . There is a Railroader's Day, a Flier's Day, a Tanker's Day—but where is the memorial day for all those who were innocently tortured to death? Where are the common grave sites, where are the monuments bearing the names of those who perished, where are the cemeteries to be visited by relatives and friends on that memorial day who come to lay flowers and wreaths on the graves, and more importantly, no longer to weep in secret? And finally, where are the lists of those who ordered the denunciations, of those people who carried out these orders, of those who . . . but enough of this! At the grave site, silence and sorrow are more appropriate.

No, I am not talking of revenge, I am not advocating the retaliation of a tooth for a tooth. Revenge does not appeal to me. I am not talking about criminal justice, but rather, of social justice. The informers, the executioners, the provocateurs unquestionably have earned the death penalty, but our people do not deserve to be fed on executions.

Clear thought, and not additional executions, ought to grow out of the deaths of the innocent. Truth and integrity should replace old horrors.

I should like to see a thorough examination made of every screw in every machine that transformed the vitality and activity of a man in the prime of life into a cold corpse. I want to see this machine loudly and publicly condemned. We should not write off the bill and ease our conscience with the comforting stamp "paid in full," but rather, we should earnestly and meticulously unravel the knot of cause and effect. Strand by strand . . . Those millions of peasant families, honest and hard-working people who, under the rubric of "Kulaks" or "Kulak hirelings," were driven north to their doom—millions of citizens who were sent off to prisons and camps, and sometimes directly into the next world, as "spies," "saboteurs," and "delinquents." Whole races of peoples were accused of treason and were driven out of their homeland into exile.

How have we managed to arrive at such an unprecedented misfortune? What led up to this complete defenselessness of people before the machine that annihilated them? What led to this unprecedented unification and fusion, to this mutual evolution of the state security organs with the state judicial organs which were set up to protect the laws in the first place (and which were themselves victims of a servile blindness for years) and finally with the press, which persecuted and slandered its victims in a regular, mechanical, and monotonous manner? Where and how has this fusion taken place, which is by far one of the most dangerous of all chemical or scientific reactions known to man? How was it possible? This is virgin ground for the historian, the philosopher, the sociologist, but primarily for the writer. It is the most important task facing us today—a task that will tolerate no procrastination. Speed is of the essence. We must call upon all the people, the young and the old, to take up this gigantic task, to devote themselves to the overthrow of the past. Only then will all the paths to the future become clearer. Moreover, the current trials over the word would never have taken place had we tackled this problem when we should have . . . Indeed, in those days we attributed a great honor to the word. People were even executed for it.

> *We were young, we were proud,*
> *Our youth was hard as steel,*

There was no misfortune in the whole world
That we couldn't overcome,
And no war from which we
Would not walk away the victors.
And there was nothing
For which we were not blamed.

These lines represent a double falsification of the truth. First of all, there was indeed a misfortune which we could not overcome and from which we could not have rescued our country. This misfortune was Stalinism. But as far as the guilt goes, which one apparently seeks to place on someone today, I should like to know the following: Who is doing it, where and against whom? We never hear anything about the guilt that one could apply today to the crimes of yesterday . . . We assimilated, we agreed: "Yes, everything that has happened is a thing of the past." And we never took one step further. In the meantime one simple and clear result grew out of all that "happened to us," something that we all knew from the beginning, although we now have to perceive it and assimilate it anew. A century ago, Gercen (Herzen)[14] repeated this train of thought day after day in his *Kolokol:* "Without a free word there are no free people, without an independent word there is no powerful nation capable of internal reform." "Only loud and open speech can satisfy man," wrote Gercen. "Only the outspoken conviction is sacred," wrote Ogarev.[15] For as far as they were concerned, silence was a synonym for slavery, for the "bowing of one's head." Herzen wrote of the "conspiracy of silence": "Muteness supports despotism."

The legal proceedings of recent years, and particularly

of the past few months, evoked a resounding opposition from people of various ages and occupations. The shameful memory that we as a people share for what we were years ago and for our apathy in the face of that earlier oppression is expressed in our intolerance toward the current violations of the law. As we, members of today's older generation, look over the shoulders of these young defendants, we see the ghostly dance of human shadows. Between the lines of the manuscript that should be, but is not allowed to be published, we recognize the faces of the writers who did not live to see the day when their manuscripts would be turned into books. And behind today's newspaper articles, we can still see all those yesterday men, those parliamentary whips and the heralds of the executions.

May the word then be liberated from all chains, regardless of the names by which they are known. Silence must disappear, for it has always supported tyranny.

Memory, on the other hand, should remain eternal and indestructible in spite of the supposedly settled account. For memory is one of man's most precious possessions, without which there can be neither conscience nor honor, nor intellectual creativity. In the figure of a great poet memory is personified . . . The memory of the past is a reliable key to the present. And in the light of all this, are we to tear up the bill, to allow the past to become overgrown with the weeds of confusion, of lost opportunity and of stupidity? Never! Even if our memories should fail us, the current trials over the word and the dry crackle of contemporary newspaper articles would still convey to us the familiar stench of past ashes.

But today is today, not yesterday. The "conspiracy of

silence" has come to an end.

LIDIA CHUKOVSKAYA

February, 1968

Taken from POSEV, *No. 8, 1968.*

OPEN LETTER TO THE CITIZENS OF THE
SOVIET UNION

The author of the following open letter is assumed to be the officer of the atomic submarine fleet, Gavrilov, who was arrested in May of 1969 because of "anti-Soviet activities." The author dedicates a long passage—untranslated below because of lack of space—to Sakharov's memorandum, which he supports in principle, though he considers the demands made by Sakharov as being too mild to be really effective.

Emphatically opposing the rulers, the progressive minority has had to suffer inevitable defeats in their battle at all times and in all places because of the lack of actual organization and unity in their actions. Society quickly forgets its leaders, and has nothing to do with the best of her members.

Siniavski, Daniel, Vladimir Bukovski, Viktor Chaustov, Viacheslav Chernovil—the list could be continued indefinitely—have all languished in prison cells; Leonid Gubanov and Aleksandr Yesemin-Volpin in their insane asylums.

Zolotuchin, the attorney who dared defend Ginzburg, was expelled from the Party. And all of this took place between 1965 and 1968. In this way, judges and state prosecutors, assessors, eager doctors, and political functionaries managed to achieve their personal ambitions, limited only by the extent of their efforts and abilities. Thus did society demonstrate its shortcomings.

The protest of Siniavski and Daniel, which found its expression in the total condemnation of the horror of Stalinism through methods of artistic creativity, certainly did not seem any more illegal than violations made manifest in illegal judicial convictions or perhaps in the political despotism of the guardians of order and silent routine, all of which took place within the atmosphere of general and absolute silence of the people. But such a protest as this does not qualify as political, even though that's what the honorable judges wanted to prove. It is rather to be considered as an expression of inner uneasiness . . . It is far from being a conscious political struggle in the name of progress. The sacrificial wrestling match Solzhenitsyn engaged in with the stubborn censor, who suppresses philosophy, sociology, economic literature, and art—the author purposely avoids mentioning politics because today that is something lying beyond the competence of the people—had clear goals in mind, but as an isolated action it was doomed to failure . . .

These protest actions have one thing in common: They are all disorganized and isolated from one another in their execution. While the number of victims continues to rise, the cause of justice, humanity, and intellectual freedom has not advanced one single step. On the contrary, we have become the impotent witnesses to the brutal suppression of the

Czechoslovakian process of democratic growth, and that before the whole world. Such defeats suffered by the progressive forces of our country seem a logical result of the catastrophic lack of organization. There is not yet any nucleus around which these splinter groups can unite, no social force which might be capable of turning ideas into actions, of opposing evil, and finally conquering it.

Who is to blame?

The historical experiences of mankind have more than sufficiently proved that there is no single social-economic formation (including the socialist one) that can point to an absolutely irreproachable organization of economic, social, and political relationships among its members, so that improvements, revisions, reforms, or revolutions really become superfluous. What was subordinate yesterday demands equality today, and tomorrow shall force its way to leadership. A society that wants to progress is constantly forced to revise the currently valid social forms; its cornerstone must be a constant balance between the interests of the individual and the demands of society. If this type of harmony is lacking, opposition and struggle are inevitable. And this very thing often enough has been recorded in blood historically . . .

The Communist party has approached the realization of the revolution in full possession of the trust and the support of the people, and has [carried through] the execution of its program, as well as the construction of socialism in our land, in a clear and realistic evaluation of the circumstances. One might have been justified in expecting that, during the early years of applying the basic Marxist theory, and then later, following the death of Lenin, of applying the Marxist-Leninist theory, one could have judged and decided the contradictions in all areas of socialist society between individuals and society by means of a timely, scientific, and humane manner. But after the suppression of its internal and external enemies, the Communist party has proceeded to harass the people whom it promised liberation from slavery and despotism. The number of prisoners is steadily growing, especially the number of prisoners who are the progressive representatives of the Party. The victims of these illegalities are for the most part exceptional military leaders and scientists, as well as representatives of the creative intelligentsia. Their names have not been forgotten: Babel, Bliucher, Vishia, Vavilov, Gamarnik, Kosior, I. Kataev, Kvitko, Kolcov, Kulish, Kurbas, Levidov, Mandelstam, Markish, Meierhold, Postyshev, Tzhicki, Tulup, Tuchatchevski, Tretiakov, Yakir, Yasienski, and many others, the enumeration of which would fill pages—not to mention the tens of thousands of less prominent representatives of socialist society. In the period between 1937 and 1939 alone, more than a million Party members were arrested, half of the total Party membership at the time.

These Party policies were continued during the postwar years. Whoever dared to think was either tortured to death or executed behind the walls of the NKVD, or was exiled in concentration camps. Those who dared to protest fell by the thousands under the fire of machine guns. He who presumed to be discontent paid for his presumption with inhuman slavery. He who rose up against the despots was liquidated in the sealed cars of transport trains, or was drowned in the flooded holds of transport ships. The taking over of methods used during the time of the class wars, and their application against the people themselves, led to the physical annihilation of more than 14 million people, which, according to A. Sakharov, equals the total population of Czechoslovakia. Are these not fascist methods? And are they not crimes against the socialist order?

Today, once again, we find ourselves on the threshold of what has gone before. Once again, a growing inner fermentation is being consciously suppressed with the same despicable methods, and once again, the progressive representatives of our nation are forbidden to speak. It has caused increasing violations of Soviet law and the Constitution by members of the Committee for State Security, by members of the justice department, the State Prosecutor General, and the courts. Arrests, house searches, terrorist measures and hearings, illegal confinements in insane asylums, summonings for criminal charges for artistic and creative activity, expulsion from the Party, discharge from the services, and deprivations of livelihoods, etc., are common. Once again, a policy of complete subordination is being dictated to the philosophers and sociologists, to representatives of science and the arts, indeed to the whole country.

Under the obliging framework of a biased press, political unanimity, and social equality of rights and justice, paths are being prepared for the rebirth of Stalin's political heritage. Hidden behind the progressive Marxist-Leninist ideology lies a criminal activity directed against the people, against the whole socialist encampment, indeed even against the whole world. And what are the goals? . . . Having once assumed unlimited powers, it never occurred to the Communist leaders—and of course at the time it was terribly difficult to foresee—that the progressive principle of total power, which at first seemed absolutely necessary, already concealed within itself many contradictions and the seeds for its own self-destruction. The spirit of socialist society declares that everyone enjoys equal rights, but in that same spirit, power-hungry, ambitious sychophants, and unscrupulous people with common intentions, egoists, began to infiltrate the political Party apparatus. In addition, an artificially but highly cultivated atmosphere of fear against accusations and on-the-spot fabricated reprisals contributed a great deal to the situation. The dictatorship of the Party itself provided an additional contribution, and it became known as the dictatorship of the working classes. That the activities of the Party corresponded entirely to the interests and the efforts of the working classes, and therefore of the whole people, and that this was the only way it could operate, was considered self-evident. In this way conditions were gradually created for the Party—an organ [made up of] the people and the revolution, and personifying progress—to become an organization of power that exercises its activities, of course, in the name of the people, but completely independently of the will of the people. Servility and formalism stand in the foreground, personal gain comes before the interests of the state, and demagogy, egoism, corruptibility, open bribery, and nepotism flower lavishly on all levels of the power apparatus. This state of affairs logically demands the establishment of special working procedures and methods for the protection of such a magnificently, lastingly built structure. As a result of these alterations in reality, an equality based on rank and position came into being, instead of general equality. The laws

forfeited their general applicability in favor of those holding the power. An unproclaimed goal was attained.

A hegemony of power was born and grew in strength,
and it created the conditions for the formation of a privileged elite, which in its turn raised itself economically as
well as judicially above the level of the common people, and
indeed not at all because of any particularly outstanding
intellectual abilities. In this way they—the elite—inflicted
not only a great moral injury on the people, but also an
economic and political disservice to the state. The creative
activities of the masses, the collective intelligence of the
people, their spiritual freedom, and the powerful possibilities
of socialist reforms fell into the clawlike grip of the demagogic rulers . . .

It was inevitable that the aspects of our reality discussed above should lead to an inert, passive attitude on the
part of the great majority of people when compared to the
social interests of the state. This too has happened, and what
is more, the educated sector of our population has completely turned away from politics and left it to the servile
admiration of the followers of such methods and practices
of leadership . . .

The author is convinced that the explanation given
above in no way does justice to the extremely complicated
circumstances of our nation. He wanted to remind you once
again, however, of the horrors of the Stalinist purges, which
shall never be allowed to recur. That would be a crime. "It
is not important who, but it is important what, has won,"
wrote the Russian revolutionary P. L. Lavrov, a contemporary of Marx. "The essential thing is the triumphant idea.
If the idea looses its meaning, the Party too loses its reason

for being, and then all that is left are questions of personal power . . . And the great, the immortal words will have to wait for new people, who will return to them their meaning, and in whom the work can be renewed and personified."

RUSSIA IS WAITING FOR NEW PEOPLE!

GENNADI ALEKSEEV, (Communist)

Tallinn, September 22, 1966

From POSEV, *No. 1, 1969.*

WHAT IS "SOCIALIST REALISM"?

ANDREI D. SINIAVSKI

. . . All of our art, as well as our whole culture and government, is fundamentally teleological. It is subordinated to the highest purpose lending it nobility. Our whole aim in life is to accelerate the coming of Communism.

. . . The privilege of having such long-distance goals has been denied to lower forms of life. Animals bite because they bite, and not simply out of an intention to bite. They do not think about tomorrow, about possessions, and not even about God. They live on without even having to face any particularly complicated problems. Man on the other hand desperately needs something that he has not got. And in an effort to find our way out of this dilemma, we devote ourselves to hectic activities. We transform the world into our own image, and we reduce nature to an object. Aimless rivers are turned into paths of trade and communication, "useless" trees are turned into paper that ultimately bears the printed directive.

Our thinking is no less guided by an ultimate goal. Man comprehends the world by attributing to it his own peculiar finality. He asks: "Why is the sun necessary?" and answers: "To provide light and warmth." The animism of primitive peoples represents the first attempt to explain the senseless chaos surrounding them and to subordinate the indifferent universe into service for human life.

Up until now science has not provided a satisfactory answer to the question that bothers even children: "Why?" A hidden and distorted finality is perceived within all those causal relationships which it sets up itself. Instead of saying: "The monkey's destiny is to resemble man," science maintains that man descends from monkeys.

But regardless of wherever man may find his origins, his appearance and his destiny are inseparably bound up with God. He is the highest conception of purpose which is imaginable—if not to our understanding, then at least to our desire for certainty about His existence. He is the final purpose of all that is and all that is not, and this purpose is eternal and without a goal. He is purpose personified. For what goal could the highest and only purpose have?

There are periods in history during which the presence of this purpose is apparent—when the search for God surpasses all minor passions and when He begins openly to draw mankind unto himself. In this manner the Christian culture was born, a culture that captured the final purpose in perhaps its most inaccessible sense. A while later the epoch of individualism proclaimed the freedom of the person—and worship of this freedom as being the highest of all purposes took the form of the Renaissance, humanism, the superman, democracy, Robespierre, and many others. Today we have entered the era of a new world system, the era of socialism.

A blinding light emanates from this new height. "This world, which we have imagined, is more material and corresponds more to human needs than does the Christian Paradise," wrote the Soviet writer Leonid Leonov about Communism.

Words fail us when we try to describe this new world. The enthusiasm it arouses takes our breath away. We find only negative comparisons in our zeal to describe the glory that awaits us. In this Communist world there will be neither rich nor poor, neither gold nor war, neither prisons nor boundaries. Also, there will be no disease, maybe even no death. Everyone will eat and work as much as he wants and the work will bring joy instead of suffering. As Lenin promised, our toilets will be made of pure gold . . .

The modern spirit is incapable of imagining anything more beautiful and more splendid than the Communist ideal. The best it can do is rejuvenate the old ideals of Christian love and the freedom of the individual. At the moment, however, it is not capable of offering a new purpose . . .

The teleological nature of Marxism is expounded primarily in the articles, exposés, and works of its most recent theorists who have discovered clarity, strength, and the direct style of military orders and economic decrees. One can cite as an example Stalin's judgment about the significance of ideas and theories (in the fourth chapter of the *Short Course of History of the Communist Party of the Soviet Union*): "Various types of general ideas and theories are conceivable. There are old, worn-out ideas that serve the interests of the outdated forces of society. It is their function to hinder the development and progress of society. There are also new, progressive ideas and theories, however, which serve the interests of progressive forces of society. Their purpose is to facilitate the development and the progress of society . . ." (*Short Course of History of the Communist Party of the Soviet Union* approved by the Central Committee of the CPSU, 1938, page 111.)

Here every word of the idea is subordinated to the ultimate goal. Even that which does not contribute to the forward march of mankind toward this purpose has some significance: It acts as an obstacle of evolution. (Apparently Satan had a similar function at one time.) "Idea," "superstructure," "base," "natural law," "economics," "forces of production"—all these abstract, impersonal categories have suddenly taken on life, assumed a concrete form, appeared as gods and heroes, angels and demons. They created their own purposes and out of the lines of philosophical treatises and economic handbooks they made themselves heard, like the voice of a great religious mystery: "The superstructure will be produced by the base so it can serve the base . . ." (J. Stalin: *Marxism and National Questions*.) . . .

The whole history of human thought consists only in preparing the way for the appearance of historical materialism—that is, Marxism, the philosophy of Communism. It stands before our eyes today as the highest and only purpose of creation, as beautiful as eternal life and as inevitable as death. And we fling ourselves toward it, having left all barriers behind us and having rejected everything that might have been able to halt our frantic course. Without regret we have freed ourselves from faith in another world, from the love of our neighbors, from the freedom of the individual and other prejudices, which are fairly worn out and above all, much more miserable than the ideal that recently has been dangled before our eyes. In the name of the new religion, thousands of martyrs have sacrificed their lives for the revolution and have outshone the heroic deeds of the first Christians with the example of their sufferings, their courage, and their holiness.

We have sacrificed more than our lives, our blood, and our bodies to our new god. We have also offered him our snow-white souls and have stained them with all the filth of the world . . .

So that prisons should disappear forever, we have erected new prisons. So that the boundaries between nations should become a thing of the past, we have surrounded ourselves with a Chinese Wall. So that labor should become a recreation and a pleasure in the future, we have instituted forced labor. So that not one additional drop of blood should be shed, we have killed and continue to do so without end.

In the name of the highest purpose, we have had to sacrifice everything we had and were forced to resort to the same means our enemies employed: to proclaim the omnipotence of Russia, to publish lies in *Pravda* (Truth), to set a czar on the empty throne, to re-establish officers' epaulettes and tortures . . . Sometimes it seemed as if there were only one final sacrifice to be made for the total triumph of Communism: the renunciation of Communism.

Lord, Lord, forgive us our trespasses!

Finally, it has gone to the point that our world is created in the image and likeness of God. Admittedly we have not yet reached Communism, but we have come very close to it. We get up, weary with exhaustion, look around us with bloodshot eyes and do not see what we hoped to see . . .

The results have never approached the goal that we initially set up. The means and efforts which were spent on its attainment transform its countenance and that often to a point beyond recognition . . .

When Western writers reproach us for our lack of the freedoms of creativity, of speech, etc., they are speaking out of their own conviction and belief in the freedom of the individual, which is, of course, the basis of their culture, but which is alien to the concept of Communist culture. A convinced Soviet writer, a genuine Marxist, would not only reject such reproaches, he would find them totally incomprehensible. What kind of freedom can a religious person demand from his God? No more than the freedom to praise Him all the more.

The Christians of today, who have renounced their spiritual fast by accepting individualism, with its free elections, its free enterprise, and its free press, sometimes go so far as to misuse the expression that Christ is supposed to have bequeathed us: "freedom of choice." This suggests the appearance of an illegal borrowing from the parliamentary system, to which they are all well accustomed, but which nevertheless has nothing in common with the kingdom of God, be it only for the reason that one does not elect prime ministers or presidents in paradise. And even if one were to admit that God is unendingly merciful, he nevertheless gives us only *one* freedom of choice: to believe or not to believe, to be with him or with Satan, to go to heaven or to go to hell. Communism offers approximately the same right: He who does not choose to believe can remain in prison—something no less evil than hell.

But for him who believes, for a Soviet writer who sees in Communism the goal (purpose) of his own existence and that of all mankind (and if he doesn't believe that, there is no place for him either in our literature or in our society), such a dilemma could never arise . . .

Who, if not the Party and its chief, could be in a better position to know what kind of art we need? Especially since it is the Party that leads us to the highest purpose in accordance with all the norms of Marxism-Leninism, since it is the Party that lives and works in constant contact with this God. In the person of the Party and the person of its chief, we therefore possess the wisest, most experienced, and most competent leaders for all questions concerning industry, linguistics, music, philosophy, painting, biology, etc . . . In him we have at one and the same time our highest army, as well as our highest head of state and our high priests. To doubt his words is as grave a sin as to question the will of the creator.

These are the aesthetic and psychological concepts which one must unquestionably know if one is to penetrate the secret (mystery) of socialist realism.

From NEUES FORUM, *Vienna, June, 1966.*

SOLZHENITSYN'S LETTER TO THE FOURTH
CONGRESS OF SOVIET WRITERS

Since I do not have any access to the speaker's podium, I ask that the Congress discuss the following questions:

(1) The no longer tolerable oppression, to which our literature has been subjected for decades and which the Writers' Union should no longer condone.

This censorship, which is not provided for in the Constitution and is, therefore, illegal, and which is never called by its real name, exercises its control over our literature under the obscure name of Glavlit. It affords uneducated people the opportunity to impose arbitrary measures against the writers. A relic of the Middle Ages, this censorship resembles Methuselah in the sense that it continues to exist almost into the twenty-first century. Although an ephemeral thing, it tries to exercise its power over eternal things and to differentiate between good and bad books.

As writers we have been denied the right to be the first to explain our judgment about the moral life of man and society, as well as to illuminate in our own way the social problems or the historical experiences which have so deeply affected our country. Works that might express the thoughts that have matured with the people, which might be able to exercise at a given time and in their own peculiar manner their influence over the spiritual life or over the social conscience, are either forbidden or distorted by the censorship, and that on the basis of considerations which are petty, egotistical and, from the national point of view, short-sighted.

Outstanding manuscripts by young authors, still completely unknown, are currently rejected by editors solely on the grounds that they "will not be successful." Many members of the Writers' Union, and even many of the delegates to this Congress, know how they themselves were compelled to bow before the pressures of the censorship and to compromise in regard to the structure and the meaning of their works. They have altered chapters, pages, paragraphs, and sentences; they have made them insipid for the purpose of seeing them published, and in this way they have irremediably destroyed them. If one observes the intrinsic uniqueness of literature, one cannot help but notice that these alterations are detrimental, if not fatal, to good works, but in the bad, they are hardly perceivable. The better part of our literature appears in mutilated form.

Fortunately the labels bestowed by the censorship ("ideologically harmful," "a depravity") are very short-lived. They are changing constantly and are disappearing before our very eyes. Even Dostoevski, the pride of world literature, could at one time not be published in the Soviet Union and those of his works available today are not completely authentic. His works were banned from the classroom, made inaccessible for reading, and his person was reviled. For how many years was Yesenin looked upon as a "counter-revolutionary" and Mayakovski considered an "anarchist," a political "hooligan"? For decades the immortal poetry of Akhmatova was defamed as being "anti-Soviet." A timid first edition of the dazzling poems by Tsvetsova, which came out about ten years ago, was declared a "gross political error." Only after a delay of twenty to thirty years were Bunin, Bulgakov, Platonov, Mandelstam, Voloshin, Gumilev, and Kliuev returned to us. It is also inevitable that Zamyatin and Remizov will eventually be recognized. And the decisive moment comes after the death of an uncomfortable writer, because then he will sooner or later be returned to us, complete with an "explanation of his errors." For a long time the name of Pasternak could not be pronounced out loud. Now that he is dead, his books are published and his poems are even quoted at official ceremonies.

These deeds bear sad witness to the bulk of Pushkin's words: "They are only capable of loving the dead."

The belated publication or "acceptance" of an author, however, can never replace either the social or the artistic losses suffered by our people as a consequence of these outrageous delays and the suppression of artistic conscience. In the 1920's particularly there were writers such as Pilniak, Platonov, and Mandelstam who called attention early on to the beginnings of the personality cult and the peculiar traits of Stalin's character; but these writers were eliminated and silenced instead of being listened to. Literature cannot develop within the categories of "permitted" and "not permitted." Literature that is not the very air contemporary society breathes today can say nothing about its sufferings and its fears, cannot warn against moral and social dangers in time. Such literature does not deserve the name of literature; it can only be described as surface make-up. Such literature losses the confidence of its people. Its books do not deserve to be read; they are only wastepaper.

Our literature has lost the leading role it played in the world toward the end of the last century and the beginning of this one, and it has lost the brilliance of experimentation that distinguished it in the 1920's. To the entire world the literary life of our country today seems immeasurably poorer, flatter, and more common than it actually is or than it would have appeared if it were not confined and if its paths were not blocked. The loser in this case is our country, especially in the eyes of world public opinion, and the loser is also world literature itself. If the world had possessed all the fruits of our literature without any restrictions, if it were enriched by our own spiritual experience, then the whole artistic evolution of the world would run a different course; it would find a new stability, it would reach a new artistic threshold.

I move that the Congress demand and attain the abolition of that censorship—both open and secret—that concerns artistic production; I move that the Congress release the publishing houses from their obligation to obtain the authorization to print before they actually publish a work.

(2) The duties of the union toward its members are not clearly formulated in the statutes of the Writers' Union ("Protection of copyrights" and "Measures for the protection of other rights of writers"). It is embarrassing to admit that for a third of a century the union has neither defended any other "rights" nor even once defended the copyrights of its members.

During their lifetimes many writers have been subjected to abuse and slander in the press and from various speakers' rostrums without having the possibility of making a pertinent reply. Moreover, they were compelled to endure suppression and personal persecution (Bulgakov, Akhmatova, Pasternak, Toshchenko, Platonov, Alexandr Grin, Vassili Grossman). Far from guaranteeing its members the possibility of defending and justifying themselves in its publications, far from speaking out in their defense, the leadership of the union, on the contrary, always took its position at the head of the persecutors. Writers who were the crown jewels of our poetry in the twentieth century were expelled from the union, always assuming they had been allowed in to begin with. And even more, the leadership of the union cowardly abandoned to their misfortune all those for whom persecution ended in exile, concentration camps, or death (Pavel Vasilev, Mandelstam, Artem Veseli, Philniak, Babel, Tabidze, Zabolotski, and others). The list must be cut off with the words "and others"; after the Twentieth Party Congress we learned that the obedient union had abandoned more than six hundred innocent writers to their fates in prisons and camps. Meanwhile the list has grown even longer. Our eyes have never finished reading this list, which remains rolled up, and they never will read it to the end. It contains the names of young prose writers and poets, whom we have known accidentally through personal encounters; people whose talent was crushed in the camps before it had the chance to bloom; people whose works have never got any farther than the walls of the state security service in the days of Yagoda, Yezhov, Beria, and Abakumov.

There is no historical necessity for the newly elected leadership of the union to share the responsibility for the past with its predecessors.

I move that all guarantees for defense which the union grants to those members who are subjected to slander and unjust persecution be clearly formulated in Paragraph 22 M of the union statutes, so that a repetition of illegal actions will be rendered impossible.

If the congress does not remain indifferent to what I have said, I will also request that it consider the interdictions and persecutions which I myself have experienced:

(1) About two years ago the state security authorities confiscated my novel, *The First Circle*, and thus prevented me from submitting it to the publishers. As a result, it was published in a "closed" edition during my lifetime, against my will and without my knowledge, so that it could be read by a chosen but not further described public. My novel was made available to literary officials but was kept from the majority of the writers. I have not been able to hold any open discussions of the novel within writers' associations. I am not even able to prevent misuse and plagiarism.

(2) Together with this novel, my literary papers, which I have been collecting for the past twenty-five years—things that were not intended for publication—were taken away from me. Now, tendentiously chosen excerpts from these papers have been circulating in a closed edition among the same groups. The play, *Feast of the Conquerors,* which I memorized and wrote in verse while still in the concentration camp, where I was known by four different numbers (at a time when we were left to die, when we were forgotten by society, and when no one outside the camps spoke up against these persecutions)—this play, which I have now left far behind me, is being ascribed to me as my very latest work.

(3) For three years now, a campaign of irresponsible slander has been conducted against me, despite the fact that I fought as a battery commander all through the war and possess military decorations. Now I hear that I supposedly served this time as a criminal, or had surrendered to the enemy (I was never a prisoner), that I "betrayed"

my fatherland and "served the Germans." This is the way rumor now accounts for the eleven years I spent in camps and in exile, after having been arrested for criticizing Stalin. This slander is being circulated in secret meetings and instructions by people who hold official positions. In vain have I tried to fight against the slander by appealing to the Writers' Union of the RSFSR and to the press. The Union leadership did not deign to answer me and not a single newspaper printed my reply to the slanderers. In the past year, on the contrary, slanderous remarks emanating from speakers' rostrums have been more intense and more vicious. In making them, the perpetrators are using material in my confiscated library, albeit in a distorted version, and I am faced with no possibility of replying.

(4) My story, *Cancer Ward* (twenty-five pages), which has been recommended for publication by the prose department of the Moscow writers' organization, cannot be published either by chapters (rejected by five journals) or in its entirety (rejected by *Novy Mir, Zvezda,* and *Prostor*).

(5) The play, *The Reindeer and the Little Hut,* accepted by the "Sovremehnik" Theater in 1962 has not yet been approved for performance.

(6) The screenplay, *The Tanks Know the Truth;* the play, *The Light That Is in You;* and several short stories (*The Sincere Brush* and the series, *Small Pieces*) have not been able to find either a producer or a publisher.

(7) My stories published in *Novy Mir* could never appear in book form. They were rejected everywhere (Soviet Writers' Publisher, the state literature publishing house, and the Ogoniok Library). Thus they remain un-

known to the majority of the public. In November, 1966, nine out of eleven scheduled meetings or radio broadcasts were canceled at the last moment. Even the simple act of giving a manuscript away for "reading and copying" is currently defined as a crime (just five centuries ago the old Russian scribes were permitted to do this).

In this way my work has been completely smothered, gagged, and slandered.

Does the Fourth Writers' Congress have any intention whatsoever of taking up my defense against such a blatant attack on my rights as an author and my other rights as a human being? It seems to me that this decision is not without significance for the literary future of many delegates.

I will of course remain calm because I shall continue to fulfill my duty as a writer under any circumstances and because I will be able to fulfill these duties more successfully after my death in a more unchallenged manner than was permitted me during my lifetime. No one can bar the road of truth. For this road I am ready to suffer death. But when will we ever learn that it is unwise to ban the works of an author as long as he is still living? That was never an honorable page in the annals of our history.

ALEKSANDR SOLZHENITSYN

May 16, 1967

From OST PROBLEME, *No. 12, 1967.*

SPEECH BY G. SVIRSKI DELIVERED BEFORE THE MOSCOW SECTION OF THE WRITERS' UNION

. . . Through an official act of government our collective farms have been granted the privilege of deciding for themselves what is to be cultivated or bred. There were also economic reforms in industry. Many people feel themselves being drawn into public life. Only the Writers' Union has remained untouched by this healthy and natural process.

Every political writer has a personal sense of responsibility. A Communist writer has, in addition, a sense of responsibility toward the Party. He must answer for what he writes. But he has been deprived of his right to answer to the people for what he writes in his works. He has been humiliated and robbed of his particular inalienable right to appear before his fellow countrymen in the form of his most intimate and most sacred thoughts without the assistance of any hypocritical court presuming to decide anything and everything for him and to initiate deletions wherever they wish . . . The uncontrolled manipulation of texts, the elimination of whole chapters, have become the rule. No matter which author one might approach in connection with this encroachment on the part of the censor, someone will interrupt him: "Ah, that's nothing! Wait till you hear this!" . . .

When one does hear all this, especially if one has experienced it for himself, one is inevitably reminded of a tank attack that Tvardovski described:

> . . . *Lying in the trench*
> *Terrified before the blindly approaching crush*

DOCUMENTS 463

Your heart almost stops beating.
A tank, after all, has no eyes . . .

But is Glavlit [the highest censor authority] really as deaf and as blind as all that? It must at least see those people upon whom it puts its screws, and probably very clearly. Is there then any logic or legality to be discovered between what is allowed and what is forbidden? What are its targets? Have we perhaps entered a field of annihilating fire? As we all know, Solzhenitsyn hasn't been published for years now. And neither have the works of Aksenova-Ginzburg[16] and other Communists who have returned from Beria's prisons and told of what they endured there. Time has clearly proved that this is an undignified and equally senseless procedure. . . .

How they criticized Aksenova-Ginzburg when her book was published in the West—an occurrence as equally unexpected by the author as by the authorities. How infamously Semichastni gave vent to his feelings in his speeches about her! It wasn't even possible for us to judge such a book at all fairly . . . Moreover, the work by the Communist Aksenova-Ginzburg still stands on the list of forbidden books in our country, despite the significance it has attained throughout the whole world.

I have mentioned the camp theme for the very reason that today it is suppressed with particular animosity. And who knows how much is stricken from the books which are allowed to be published? Everything that even hints at the elimination of the fatal consequence of the personality cult is burned out with a glowing iron; this has even gone so far today as to eliminate every hint that the personality cult ever existed. The demand for the truth, even a word of truth, has become the most dreaded enemy of Glavlit . . .

What do they say to writers, both Communists and non-Communists, when they attempt to defend their works? What do they say when there is no pertinent reply? Throw it away without any explanation? It's always the same thing: "This is not the right time," "Circumstances do not permit," "You have to wait," "Wait till . . ." Just wait . . .

And so we wait. We wait one year, two years, ten years. And all of a sudden we realize that not everything is forbidden. Not every author is advised to "wait." On the contrary, a lot of prose and poetry that are directly related to Stalin's personality cult are not only not forbidden, but rather, they are published in huge editions . . .

The poet S. Smirnov, according to the view of *Literaturnaia Rossia,* came forward from a lofty, patriotic standpoint. We can read these words in that journal. What does he proclaim then from his lofty standpoint? Maybe that which appeared in the tenth number of the 1967 edition of the journal *Moskva?* Even if these verses dedicated to Stalin are familiar to you, one should not abstain from repeating them here:

> *Even the trumpets greeted him joyfully.*
> *Our Captain who, in all those trying years*
> *When he stood as our model and our teacher*
> *Never left his post.*
> *Praying for deliverance, we looked to him,*

And revived; we made of him
A beaming icon for troubled times.

Abandon yourselves, comrades, to these insulting, obsequious verses:

Towering over all who command
He moves on—but not alone,
For the crowd of trampled souls
Surrounds him, their Crown of Thorns,
      (APPLAUSE IN THE HALL)

What's that supposed to mean? Stalin sent millions to their graves, and the people, according to Smirnov, should have enthusiastically woven wreaths out of the dead and trampled souls? (APPLAUSE IN THE HALL)

That is no typographical error on the part of Smirnov. It is also no mistake. It is an aimed attack against the Party decisions. And even more, it is barefaced mockery and derision . . .

Lenin said that one shouldn't lie even to his enemies. In our country we lie to our friends. How much have we lied during the past few years! We lied about Pasternak, and Solzhenitsyn, about Voznesenski, Yevtushenko, Yevgenia Ginzburg, and Bulat Ckhudzhava. False accusations were made, saying that these writers were not patriots, that they showed consideration for retrogressive elements . . . There was nothing we didn't lie about. We have become so accustomed to lies that we don't even pay any attention to the shadow of probability. And finally, into this web of lies we also have trapped our writers, who are compelled to tell lies under the disguise of a "higher discipline." Pure hypocrisy shines through the slogans "Don't look back," "Don't open old wounds," "Don't keep bringing up the past." A. Bek— simply don't point to him; Y. Yevtushenko—don't touch him; E. Malcev—just don't dare; but S. Smirnov—please! . . . Smirnov was very well aware of the situation (who among us isn't?) and knew how to make the most of it—all that had to do with the forbidden books of serious writers, with forbidden chapters, with the paragraphs that were edited out, all that had anything to do with the original notes of his colleagues in the Writers' Union—when he wrote with biting cynicism in the same poem:

> *Write the words which must be written,*
> *Don't fall victim to cowardly fear!*
> *Good—nothing to complain about here—*
> *Better to end up in a bier!*
> *Right now nothing is forbidden.*

Are there no forbidden themes for Smirnov, Zakrutkin, and for those who hang around with them . . . ? It is better to let yourself be beaten. Better to say nothing! . . . We call ourselves internationalists. In what kind of a position are we putting our comrades—the Communists of Italy, France, and all foreign Communists, who are forced to justify us in the eyes of their completely and totally informed readers? . . .

Unscrupulous people might perhaps say that I am now focusing attention on Stalin and the past. But—let's ignore these unscrupulous people, for awhile. As you see, I am talking about today's literature, about the very real danger facing us today, about those people who no longer make the effort to hide the fact even from themselves that it is not a question here of individuals, but rather a question of law and despotism. That is why there is such cruel persecution of books which certainly make no mention of Stalin or of the camps, but which analyze the machinery and psychology of despotism or else are concerned with the living conditions of our daily life. Allow me to take one single example, my own. I did not want to talk about myself, but excuse me, it really is quite painful.

Thirteen years ago, in 1954, I wrote my novel called *State Examination*. It is about the fate of cybernetics between 1949 and 1953, about the resolute scientists who protected their science against calumnies, about the scientists, who, in the end, put Sputnik into orbit around the earth. For thirteen years this book has been denied publication. It was even scratched by the censor from the list of books approved by the Soviet Writers' Publishing House—postponed, just like other works, which only proves the well-known arbitrariness of the officials. And who is responsible for this? Nobody! In the Propaganda Department of the Central Committee there is a sign: "Make your demands heard at the publishing house!" And then the publisher says: "Go to Glavlit." The elimination of books dealing with current problems and current events is a particularly dangerous symptom. It means that thinking men have become superfluous. A thinker living under despotic conditions is automatically a potential dissident . . .

Perhaps the time has come when we should stop bowing down to the demands of those who forbid everything they see and in so doing have brought the high calling of Communism into discredit. It is high time to wage war against those who have no thoughts about their people and who don't care about the international movement, against those who do continuous damage to the dignity and the prestige of our country. (APPLAUSE)

Taken from POSEV, No. 9, 1968.

LETTER FROM LEONID PLIUSCH, ENGINEER IN KIEV, TO THE EDITOR OF KOMSOMOLSKAYA PRAVDA

I have before me this year's February 28th issue of your newspaper, as well as the letter of protest from Aleksandr Ginzburg's mother against that slanderous article—in her own words—appearing in your journal on January 18, 1968. What this all represents is a confrontation between the censored press with its "fawning servility" (according to Marx) and the uncensored Samizdat publications. The problem arises of whom to believe. An impartial investigation would be difficult to conduct, for who has ever had access to the minutes of the Ginzburg and Galanskov cases? All that remains is the path of circumstantial evidence. I shall attempt to explain in this letter why I do not trust the official sources of information in this question.

Argument 1

For a long time now our press has no longer deserved our confidence. Bombastic articles based on rumors about

the "enemies of the people," announcements about "innocently suffering heroes of the Revolution and the Civil War,"
drum rolls about the "flourishing of the villages," and confused thoughts about the millions of peasants who died
during the artificially caused famine in the 1930's in the
Ukraine (at least that is how the Revolutionary and Civil
War hero, Admiral Fedor Raskolnikov, described this event)
next to "portraits" of the "Gestapo agent" I. B. Tito, insignificant excuses aimed at the Yugoslavian Communist party,
the persecution and defamation of Pasternak that hastened
the death of this author; the furious witch hunts during the
days of 1963 when one culture campaign followed the other,
praises for the speech of "our true" contemporary N. S.
Khrushchev, next to the niggardly insinuations and gibes
concerning the uneducated "Voluntarists" and other similar
defamations; lies about the "anti-Semite Siniavski," who supposedly even hated Chekhov (I have read the *Grapho-
manen* and have become unbiasedly convinced of the slander inherent in these calumnies against this author), and
finally the malicious falsehoods which appeared in the
journal *Perec* against Dzhiuba, one of our best Ukrainian
critics. Even honest thoughts are clothed by our press in
such deficient expressions that the reader begins to doubt
them right from the start (for example the "unilateral
polemic" against Steinbeck). The list of the disclosed, as
well as the still-hidden, lies of our press is unending: here
botched-up praises of tyrants and their fawning; there
filth heaped upon the works and persons of our best citizens
and, in addition, brilliant falsifications of history (for example, the "wonderful" conversion of the traitor of the
Ukrainian people, B. Chmelnychky [17] . . . into a hero of

these same people), etc. This flood of lies, that started at the close of the 1920's, is never completely exhausted, not even during the "thaw" occurring somewhere between the Twentieth and the Twenty-Second Party Congresses when Khrushchev attempted to strike a balance on the foundation of half-truths.

Samizdat stands in direct opposition to this flood.

Are there any grounds to trust and believe the letter from Ginzburg's mother, the "Appeal to World Conscience" by L. Bograz and P. Litvinov, the "Appeal to the Creative Minds in Science, Culture, and Art" by Gabai, Kim, and Yakir? (Yakir, the son of the eminent army officer who was slandered and finally martyred in Stalin's prisons?) My opinion is yes! Or are they too "insufficiently informed" or "incorrectly informed by bourgeois propaganda"? Or have they perhaps been bought by the NTS, the CIA, the BBC, or the "Voice of America"? I hope you do not go so far as to believe such absurdities! If these were all untruths, then the KGB and its subsidiaries would gleefully initiate a campaign of slander against them. Not even appropriate laws along the lines of the infamous Paragraph 190 in the Penal Code of the RSFSR are needed for that. Courage is not for sale.

Argument 2

If the trials against Ginzburg and his friends were legal, then one need hardly have feared to conduct them publicly. Ovcharenko, in fact, declared that "representatives of undertakings and organizations to which the accused for their part were connected" were present during the proceedings. Litvinov and Yakir, however, assure us that these "representatives" were simply "hired hands" and nothing more. And I believe them and not Ovcharenko, because in 1965 I witnessed with my own eyes analogous trials against so-called "Ukrainian Nationalists" and had the opportunity to hear for myself the fantastically nonsensical "explanations" of the court officials about the "open-and-closed" character of that sort of courtroom procedure.

Had the trial been a legal one, *Komsomolskaia Pravda* would have published the letter from Ginzburg's mother and presented the facts, which would have coincided with those of Yakir or Litvinov. Facts such as these concerning the house searchings and the minutes of the trial, which L. I. Ginzburg wrote about, could not possibly have been denied, for then her letter would have defeated its own purpose.

But alas, the times have passed in which the Bolsheviks could proudly proclaim: "We do not fear the truth because it works for us!" Their illegitimate successors (the legitimate successors and heirs were all annihilated by Beria in Stalin's prisons), these October Thermidorians, fear the truth. The most they are capable of are: correctly edited, arbitrarily pieced-together quotes. Only with the truth could they have convinced us and the world that the trial was legal and just. Those times are gone in which a naïve Feuchtwanger could successfully witness a trial against Radek, Piatakov, Sokolnikov,[18] and others, and actually believe in such a farce. (Later on, and for the rest of his life, he could never forgive himself for having done so.)

Argument 3

The mendacity of the article itself is obvious to an eye unclouded by past experiences. The paper maintains that

Ginzburg and Galanskov were "paid agents of the NTS," that they had "silently conspired" as the agents of an anti-Soviet organization are wont to do. And the same paper maintains in the same article that their "creations" have appeared in the West *under their own names*. Conspiracy? Is that even imaginable in this case? During their forty-year Thermidor they haven't even learned how to lie correctly!

Because of "bourgeois propaganda," Ovcharenko did not dare to give the names of the people who had signed the "Telegram from the Fifteen," addressed to Litvinov and Bogoraz-Daniel; names which included, for example, Bertrand Russell, Igor Stravinski, Priestley, and others, but he did not hesitate to alter the sense of Yuri Galanskov's concluding statement, in which Galanskov said that he did not want to glorify himself. There was apparently one single instance when Ovcharenko told the truth: "These names mean absolutely nothing to the Soviet readers." True, and in exactly the same manner as just a few years ago the name of Bulgakov meant nothing to young readers, and as remains the case today with names such as Ivanov-Razumnik and many others. I pity those readers who did not know that the great writer Solzhenitsyn lives and works in Russia, the author of the novels *Cancer Ward* and *The First Circle,* and of the shorter pieces, *Candles in the Wind, The Reindeer and the Hut.* I also feel sorry for those who signed the letters recently published in this year's February 28th issue of *Komsomolskaia Pravda.* They just don't understand anything. They will probably be as ashamed of themselves someday as those people are today who marched along with the huge mobs and "angrily" demanded the death of their co-fighter Lenin. They should not be written off as mere supporters of a tyrant without examination, but should be looked upon more as successors of that little lady who brought wood to the funeral pyre of Jan Hus. May God grant that they be cured of their "holy ignorance." For then there will also be no more funeral pyres. And I am sorry for those who do not know, and do not want to know, what is happening in their native country today. In his letter to Stalin, Raskolnikov wrote that the people would judge him for what he had made out of our Revolution. I hope that the time will come when Stalin and his lackeys will be mercilessly judged according to the laws of our land. And in the same manner as these twisters of the truth, you too, editor of *Komsomolskaia Pravda,* will be judged according to the laws of honor. By these laws, you have already earned the contempt of all decent men, as lackeys and false witnesses of our times.

LEONID PLIUSCH, *Mathematician, Engineer*
Kiev

P.S. In an attempt to guard against any possible calumnies from your paper, I am sending copies of this letter to persons in whose integrity I have the utmost confidence.

From POSEV, *No. 3, 1969.*

SOLZHENITSYN TO THE WRITERS' UNION

A few days after his expulsion from the Writers' Union, A. I. Solzhenitsyn directed this open letter to the Secretariat of the Soviet Writers' Union.

With the speed of a fire brigade you shamelessly violated your own statutes and expelled me in absentia from the Writers' Union. You didn't deign to send me a summons by telegram, you did not even grant me the four hours it takes to travel from Ryazan and be present at the meeting. You have shown openly that the "decision" preceded the "discussion." Was it more convenient for you to invent charges in my absence? Were you afraid you might be required to grant me ten minutes to reply? I have no other choice than to substitute this letter for those ten minutes.

Wipe the dust off your watches—they're slow. Draw back the heavy drapes you have become so fond of—you do not even suspect that it's already morning. The stifling, dreary monotony of those times when you expelled Akhmatova in the same determined manner has long since passed. The time of intimidation and rigidity when you could single out Pasternak is also long since past.

Is this shame not enough for you? Do you want to make it even greater? The time will come when each one of you will try to erase his signature from today's resolution. Blind leaders leading the blind, you do not even realize how zealously you pursue that very thing which you yourselves have renounced. This is a critical time for our gravely ill society, but you are proving yourselves incapable of suggesting anything constructive or anything good for it; you know nothing more than a malicious vigilance, and your only concern is to inhibit and not let anything go through.

Your ponderous tomes swarm with your lifeless superficiality—you have no arguments, just a show of hands and dispositions. Neither Sholokhov nor all of you together dared answer the famous letter of Lidia Chukovskaya, this master among Russian essayists. Instead she should be abandoned to the bureaucratic pincers—how could she be so bold as to read an unpublished book? Once the "court" decides not to publish somebody—then get ready, choke yourself, cease to exist! Don't let anybody read something you wrote.

They have already considered expelling Lev Kopelev, a front-line veteran who, although innocent, has already served ten years. Now he's supposed to be guilty, because he spoke up for the persecuted, because he disclosed some secrets he learned in a conversation with an influential personality, because he revealed an "official secret." Why do you carry on such conversations, the contents of which must not be made public? Weren't we promised fifty years ago that there would never be any more secret diplomacy, no more secret conversations, no more secret, incomprehensible appointments and transfers, that the masses were to be informed of all matters and make up their own minds about them?

"The enemy will overhear"—that is your eternal and unvarying excuse. "Enemies"—they are still a convenient justification for your functions and your existence. As if there were no enemies around when they promised complete openness. But what would you do if you didn't have "enemies"? You probably couldn't live at all without "enemies." Your sterile atmosphere would turn to a hatred which cannot surpass racial hatred. In this way the sense of a common, united humanity is lost—and only serves to accelerate its ultimate defeat. If the Antarctic ice should melt tomorrow and we were all to suffer the lot of a drowning humanity—who would you then approach with your "class struggle"? Not to mention the time when the remaining bipeds wander aimlessly about a radioactive earth until they die.

For this reason it is high time to consider that we are all people—first and foremost. The feature that distinguishes humanity from the animal world is our ability to think and to speak. And naturally, people must be free. If they are put in chains, they become as animals.

But true, free word, its openness—that is the first prerequisite for the health of any society, even our own. But he who does not want this free word for our country doesn't really care for his fatherland; all he thinks about is himself. He who does not want to see this free word in his fatherland also doesn't want to heal it of its diseases; rather, he suppresses them, keeps them concealed where they are left to fester.

ALEKSANDR SOLZHENITSYN
November 12, 1969

Taken from DIE WELT, *November 17, 1969.*

THE REFORMERS

Handbill from the "December Fifth Movement." This flier appeared in Moscow in 1966

Citizens!

The "December Fifth Movement" is a political organization and not an anti-Soviet fraternity. The "December Fifth Movement" is an idealistic movement under whose auspices Soviet citizens ought to fight for and defend the rights which are guaranteed to them in the Constitution of the u.s.s.r.

Ten years after the Twentieth Congress of the Communist party of the Soviet Union, renewed attempts are being undertaken to rehabilitate Stalin, the man whose very name has become a synonym for despotism and lawlessness in the minds of all decent people.

The democratic public ought to turn its attention to the fact that the decisions of the Twentieth and the Twenty-Second Party Congress have not been followed and that the promises which were made to the people during these Congresses remain unfulfilled today.

Neo-Stalinism—that is, the attempt of the "Stalinist hawks" to restore "the good name of the leader" under variously acceptable disguises—has come into being because scientific examination of the problems closely related to the personal dictatorship of Stalin lead us to the conclusion that it is impossible to control the Party line in the most important questions of politics, ideology, and economics, from which we can unhesitatingly deduce that the total system must be radically revised.

It seems, as if by decision of the Twenty-Second Party Congress, to put into effect several reforms which are necessary for the country. In particular, this congress promised a new and more democratic constitution (up until 1964 Khrushchev was chairman of the Constitutional Committee, followed by Brezhnev). But who has heard even the slightest hint of a new Constitution?

The exact opposite occurred. The Draconic law passed on September 16, 1966, represents a most atrocious illegality and an obviously unconstitutional procedure!

Our country is standing at the crossroads. Looking at it from the ethnic point of view, the very mention of Stalin's name as the instigator and organizer of all victories sounds like a blasphemy. All our economic, scientific, and military accomplishments were achieved, not thanks to Stalin, but in spite of him. Everyone should be convinced of this. For example, it was proved incontrovertibly in the letter from E. Genri to Ehrenburg; the old Bolsheviks spoke a lot about this in the IML during their consultations on the drafts of the third volume of the *History of the Communist Party of the Soviet Union,* and this was also the theme of the book by Nekrich.

But people cannot stop Stalinism with words alone! Workers and Farmers, Intelligentsia and Youth! The "December Fifth Movement" is a movement for the defense of legality. Our slogans are: "Honor the lawful order!", "The State for the People and not the People for the State!", "Abolish anti-Democratic laws!", "Stalinism will not pass!"

We cannot count on a serious victory in any area based upon an insufficient or incomplete de-Stalinization. Only democracy and democratic institutions can guarantee a normal and balanced development of the nation and the people.

Demand the guarantee of civil freedoms and the immediate adoption, following an appropriate plebiscite, of a democratic constitution.

To hesitate means to commit a crime!

Read this handbill, pass it along to others, act!

All legal methods are our weapons in this democratic battle.

THE DECEMBER FIFTH MOVEMENT

From posev, *January 21, 1967.*

CONCERNING THE
MULTIPLE-PARTY SYSTEM

This essay appeared in 1965, in the uncensored journal
Kolokol, *published by the illegal Marxist group called the*
"Union of the Commune-ists" (those living on communes)
in Leningrad.

If one analyzes the construction of burocratically governed
states—regardless of whether they belong to a socialist order or stand outside the block (as Algeria, VAR)—it soon
becomes evident that they all have a common characteristic: the lack of a legal political opposition, or an opposition
party. Although the multiple-party system exists formally
in countries like Poland, the German Democratic Republic,
Czechoslovakia, Bulgaria, and even in the People's Republic of China, these parties are all united in one block. They
all acknowledge the role of the Communist party as leader,
they turn up at elections with a common list of candidates,
and the delegate positions for parliament and the individual Soviets are nominally distributed on an appointment
basis among the Party leaders. In practice, however, it
seems that the Communist party lets the other parties have
as many seats as it—the Communist party—deems correct.
The number of members in each party is likewise deter-

mined by the Communist party. This is the way bureaucracy maintains the multiple-party system they inherited
from capitalism—all in order to deceive the masses. It has
been converted into a fiction and is controlled by a single
party in the same way that it is controlled in the u.s.s.r.

Why does bureaucracy always incline so heavily toward a one-party system? Mainly, this was caused by the
novel situation of the bureaucratic class. In the capitalist
system, power actually lies in the hands of the capitalists.
An exchange of the highest state officials, as happens for
example in the United States of America when Republicans
replace Democrats, generally doesn't even touch the interests of the capitalist circles. In a bureaucracy, on the
other hand, the actual positions of power lie in the hands
of those officers who are, in accordance with their nature,
not the least bit interested in separating themselves voluntarily from that power or from the privileges associated
with it. And it is for exactly that reason that bureaucracy
makes use of the one-party system. Experiences with fascist
countries, however, have shown that the one-party system
leaves the door wide open for despotism. Even in many
Western Communist parties, voices are raised in favor of
a genuine multiple-party system as the single guarantee
against the personality cult (see, for example, *Problems of
Peace and Socialism,* No. 9, 1963, a speech by P. Togliatti
before the Plenum of the kpi). Even in our country, many
are beginning to realize that the presence of a legal opposition party—though not in a position to overthrow the
bureaucracy—could effectively control its despotic rule and
keep it within limits. With respect to this, the ideologues
of bureaucracy are trying somehow to justify this self-

discrediting system and to portray it as the perfect political mechanism.

Let's look at their reasoning. As their basic theoretical argument, they refer to the fact that the Party represents the avant-garde and progressive part of the working class, and that with the creation of more parties, a split would take place within this avant-garde. An argument such as this would break down if satisfactory criteria permitted this class to decide for itself exactly who would justly pass as the representative of progressive ideas and who would not. The facts show, however, that every politically active representative of a class—let's say of the proletariat—no matter what Party he might belong to, whether Communist, Anarchist, or Socialist—will look upon the ideas of his Party as being particularly progressive. The class as a whole, however, judges the parties from an entirely different standpoint and is inclined to express solidarity with this or that party simply on the basis of how energetically it supports that class in its struggles with the other parties. In addition, one must mention that the composition of any party very often does not correspond to its class character. In many bourgeois parties the majority is not composed of the bourgeoisie, but the party nevertheless remains a bourgeois one. From this we can see that a party is to be considered a weapon in the political struggle but is not to be considered the avant-garde of a class. Past experience teaches that it is useful for all classes (except the bureaucracy) to possess several such weapons, because they can exercise a definite pressure through support, or refusal of that support, against those parties making use of their name. In the opposite case of a one-party system, the party always escapes from the control of its class.

As a second argument, the advocates of a one-party system refer to the unanimity of the ultimate goals of our society. Even if there were such a thing, which there isn't because of bureaucratic rule, it would in no way lead to a one-party system. Different parties do not necessarily have to advocate different goals. They could very easily strive toward the same goal, although at the same time suggesting different paths to its possible realization (as is the case with the Republicans and Democrats in the United States). The class, or rather the society, will discover the ways best suiting it. Regardless of whatever solutions to a question the party—or more correctly, the leader of the party—may happen to suggest, however, it can always admit to being imperfect in those instances when the party leadership acts out of the most genuine motives. But in the one-party system, where the person making the mistakes usually is not held personally responsible for them, the general line of the party generally consists of retroactively correcting any mistake that might be made. In all of this we have not said one word about the fact that the leaders intentionally ignore the will of the working classes, something which occurs more often than not.

One could raise the objection that an extension of internal party democracy, and the continuance of various fractions within the framework of a party, would suffice to create a choice between various possible paths. Then, however, it is either one or the other: Either the members of various backings arrange themselves according to the general party discipline, in which case the minority fraction always would be dissolved because it is unpopular with the party majority, or there exists no generally accept-able party discipline and the fractions transform themselves into different parties, which are then united by nothing more than a common name. At this point we have already reached the area of our discussion concerning the form, not the content, of such systems.

As the third argument in favor of a one-party system, the phantom of anarchy and disunion is brought up. If one wants to take a logical position on this point, it must be ex-plained that only the head of state has the right to influ-ence the *status quo* in the land while the masses are not even allowed to express their opinions about the govern-mental measures being taken. If considered from this point of view, naturally every type of democracy is destructive and inadmissable. And yet opposition parties have existed in many lands and continue to do so today. Although they have often enough been successful in overthrowing the gov-ernment, they have never hindered a normal economic de-velopment and have not occasioned any chaotic situations. When the struggle between parties led to the downfall of political stability, as happened in France in 1947-48, it had nothing to do with a multiple-party system, but rather with the violence with which the class conflict was carried out.

In contrast to that, the system of one single party in-evitably leads to the liquidation of basic democratic free-doms and makes possible wholesale reprisals, violations of the law, numerous secret trials in which the final judgments are based on denunciations and confessions obtained through torture. This system has been able to transform our country into a concentration camp of gargantuan dimen-sions.

Moreover, the Party leaders have done a great deal of harm to the Soviet sciences and art in declaring themselves the infallible authority in all areas of human creativity. The attacks against cybernetics, the repression of progressive accomplishments in the fields of biology and chemistry, the brutal administrative pressure exerted against writers and artists—which has increased during the most recent years—remind one of the darkest epochs of the Middle Ages. Simply because it makes such vulgarities possible, the one-party system does not rescue the nation from sudden evolutionary setbacks and the general line of the Party has long since become the target of derision for all Soviet citizens. Of course, it is naturally possible within a multiple-party system that a demagogue could entice a certain group of citizens to follow a false direction. The one-party system, however, makes it possible to force an entire people, by means of threats and insinuations of reprisals and under the scrutiny of the KGB, to set out along a wrong path.

There are no arguments in defense of the one-party system that could withstand serious criticism, and such arguments contradict the Marxist conception of a socialist society. The members of the commune-ists must clearly demonstrate that a genuine democratization of the bureaucratic regime is impossible under the continuation of a legal opposition; that is, without some form of a multiple-party system.

VOLGIN

From KOLOKOL, *Leningrad, No. 4, 1965. In* POSEV, *No. 4, 1968*

TO PROCRASTINATE OR TO ACT

A MEMORANDUM FROM ESTONIAN SCHOLARS

This memorandum is in reply to that by A. D. Sakharov entitled "Thoughts Concerning Progress, Peaceful Co-Existence and Intellectual Freedom."

Sakharov's memorandum is divided into two parts: "Dangers" and "The Foundation of Hope." In it he provides an analysis of the past, the most alarming problems of the present are raised, honorable goals are prescribed, and the means of accomplishing these goals are suggested. The basic precepts of this article will certainly be welcomed by all decent and thinking men in our community.

In this essay we will not discuss those areas in which we agree with Sakharov, but rather draw attention to those points where we are of a different opinion and where we have a few thoughts to add. Sakharov's place in a learned world is particularly evident in his train of thought. He places unjustifiably great hopes in scientific methods, in economic measures, in the good will of the leaders of the community, in the healthy understanding of man; he sees the basic causes of the world crisis as lying outside the borders of our society . . . And in this lies Sakharov's greatest error; he shares the basic prejudice of the times. He sees the causes, draws forth external, material solutions, and re- nounces internal, intellectual, political, and organic methods.

In this connection we shall point to three factors which are at once both the goals and the means to that goal.
1) *The moral-philosophical factor*

The political convulsions of the twentieth century led to the putting aside of Christianity as the basic ideological power within our community, and led to the destruction of the moral values of society. The new materialistic ideology did not replace these lost values (something which it was totally incapable of doing). What resulted was a moral vacuum. This vacuum led to a personality-split in society. On the one hand, we saw the external hypocritical appear- ances of morality, the hypocritical morality of the collec- tives; on the other hand, the internal, furtive, egotistical, and to human beings, intrinsic underlying morality. That created a society with an external mechanical solidarity, but which, in reality, was made up of individuals who were anti- social, who mistrusted their neighbors, were afraid of them, and who felt themselves insignificant and alone in the face of the gargantuan machinery of the state. In a society that has disintegrated in this way, regrettable occurrences— about which Sakharov is justifiably concerned—are inevita- ble. Moreover, these events are an organic part of such a society.

At this point we must ask the following question: Aren't we making the demonic figure of Stalin and his de- voted assistants responsible for too many things? Society as a whole bears a direct responsibility for these events: Didn't it provoke all the excesses of the personality cult by its indolence, apathy, servility, ignorance and, finally, by its own cruelty? An idol is inconceivable without idol worshipers. And something else: If a new Stalin should appear, it is possible that the same thing would happen right all over again from the beginning. As a people, we possess not only the moral-psychological prerequisites for this, but also the direct social basis. Only the raising up of the ethical standard of our society, an intensification of conscious civic actions, the arousing of a personal feeling of responsibility can hope to withstand effectively such a bloody Bacchanalia.

To accomplish this, the creation of a new system of moral values is of top priority. Our whole nation must either work out a new moral-philosophical system for itself or assume an already existing one. In any event, they must look for it and find it. Such a system does not yet exist. But he who seeks, finds.

2) *The social-political factor*

   A. *Domestic*

At the present time our society finds itself in a precarious political balance; it is unstable and insecure. A strong personality could assume power at any moment, could erect a neo-Stalinist regime, plunge the nation into a new depths of lawlessness and suppression, and then the figure of 10 to 15 million victims, given by Sakharov, will be significantly increased. Political (and not only intellectual) freedom and activity for the individual citizen are weapons against neo-Stalinism. A liberation of the whole population is not possible without its active participation. Right now society needs an extensive movement toward democracy as urgently as it needs air to breathe. The right of the minority to express their opposition must be legally established. The activities of those in positions of governmental power must be placed under public control. The positions of power are not the birthright of the ruling bureaucracy. The Supreme Soviet must be a neutral forum and not a dictatorial machine. The franchise must be built upon the foundation of a multiple-party system.

The leading personalities of our community—its most honorable and courageous representatives—who have been deprived of their freedom because they had the courage to think for themselves, create and hold independent opinions, and then had the courage to express these convictions, must be immediately released, beginning with the writers Daniel and Siniavski and including the participants in the demonstration that took place August 25, 1968, on Red Square against the occupation of Czechoslovakia (Pavel Litvinov, Dremliuga, and others).

The racial question is subject to a just settlement: The right of various nationalities to a sovereign and independent government must be guaranteed. The privileged position of single classes must be revised. All levels of society and all classes must be granted equal rights. The pretense has existed too long now that the ideal of political freedom is foreign to our people, that they know only material interests. And even if this does apply to a certain portion of the population, it is then the responsibility of our intelligentsia not to have any part of such ignorance but instead to lead the people toward an understanding of democratic ideals, and to elevate its ethical-political standards. A democratic community is the only genuine school for the learning of humanism. . .

Twelve years have passed since the Twentieth Party Congress. We are waiting and asking our government for liberating reforms; we are even willing to wait and to ask a little longer. In the end, however, we will demand and we will act! And then they won't be sending tank divisions to Prague or Bratislava any more, but will have to station them in Moscow and in Leningrad!

B. Interstate

More than anything else, we are obligated to exercise self-criticism in judging the role we ourselves play in the world. For we are the ones responsible for the doctrine of a belligerent, aggressive Communism! The doctrine of peaceful co-existence was dictated less from humanitarian considerations than from the fear we felt for our own security at the demands arising from industrial and economic fluctuations. Was it not our country which in the period between 1939 and 1949 "annexed" a total area of 700,000 square kilometers and established military-political control over eight countries in Europe alone with the total area of 1,274 million square kilometers? During the same period, the national area of the other allies remained virtually unchanged. This fact may provide a pleasant gratification to the illusions of power of some of our right-wing patriots, but nevertheless it contributes absolutely nothing to the relaxation of international tensions and cannot be considered as a morally untainted event.

We have to renounce the senseless annexation or territory, the widening of state power, and the aggressive course of events; we must contribute to the creation of a girdle of neutral countries surrounding our borders and placed under the surveillance of the UNO; we must make peace with the other countries; and we must shift the greater part of state power away from the construction of a war machine to the creation of cultural and economic values. Inasmuch as we bear not only half but the greater portion of responsibility for the tensions in the world, we are obligated to take the first and most important steps toward relaxing these tensions!

3) *The material-economic factor*

An economic development, be it ever so lackluster, can not by itself miraculously improve society and root out the evil in it. If one is determined to re-educate the people, it cannot be accomplished simply through the stomach. A world with a full stomach will never become a lamb. If our goal is to create a highly moral man, then the material-economic factor forms a supplement to the first two factors. It becomes their logical result. Our economists must be granted the opportunity for free research in the widest sense of the word and the opportunity for renouncing the prototypes in order to discover the most appropriate economic forms to satisfy best the needs of all members of the community, not merely those of the state. To orient the population in the direction of material demands as a goal in itself is a great political error. Material needs are in the end only justified as means employed to arrive at moral goals, the ideal of good. Such an ideal is very rare indeed in this world of power politics and evildoing.

As a summation, we consider the following points necessary as a supplement to the suggestions made by Sakharov. It is necessary:

1. to settle not only the tensions between inimical countries, but to form closer ties with them;

2. to establish not only coexistence and cooperation, but also reconciliation;

3. to wage war not only against physical hunger, but to satisfy man's moral hunger as well;

4. to set up not only laws governing the press and the flow of information, but additional laws which guarantee the political freedom of the individual;

5. not only to check and expose Stalinism, but to wipe it out entirely;

6. to establish not only an amnesty for political prisoners, but also to complete their rehabilitation and the guarantee that no one will henceforth be persecuted because of his personal convictions;

7. to initiate not only a superficial economic reform program, but to set up fundamental economic revisions; and most importantly, not only to overcome the dissension with other countries, but also to alleviate the alienation felt between the various domestic states with respect to one another.

In closing, we appeal to the leading personalities of our nation: Do not limit yourselves to scientific and technical improvements, to pleasant illusions, to the arousing of rosy hopes! Create new, generally acceptable moral values! Work out new and generally acceptable political and economic ideals!

Give us a program of action and let us act for ourselves, even if our hopes and our requests for reforms should prove to be folly. And, finally, live up to your positions and lead us when it is historically necessary to do so.

NUMEROUS REPRESENTATIVES OF THE TECHNOLOGICAL INTELLIGENTSIA OF ESTONIA.

From FRANKFURTER ALLGEMEINE ZEITUNG, *December 18, 1968*

SUGGESTIONS FOR REFORM
BY THREE SOVIET SCIENTISTS

The Soviet physicists A. Sakharov and V. Turchin, as well as the historian R. Medvedev, addressed a letter to the heads of government in which they outlined a draft for democratizing their country. The outline is very similar to the corresponding demands the Czechoslovakian scientists made in the summer of 1968.

To: *The Central Committee of the* CPSU, *L. L. Brezhnev*
The Prime Minister of the U.S.S.R., *A. N. Kosygin*
To The Presidium of the Supreme Soviet of the U.S.S.R., *N. V. Podgorny*

Comrades:

We appeal to you in a question of the utmost importance. Our land has accomplished much in the development of production, in education and culture, in the essential improvement of living conditions among the workers, in the creation of new social affiliations between men. These accomplishments have a historical significance: They have exercised a deep influence on the world situation as a whole and have created a solid basis for a further build-up of

Communism. There are also serious problems and failures, however.

In this letter we will state and discuss in detail a point of view which can be briefly summarized in the following points:

1. There is today an urgent necessity to decide upon a series of measures for the further democratizing of the social life of our country. This necessity stems partly from the close relationship of problems concerning the technological and economic development of our country, and from the scientific administrative methods being applied to questions of freedom of information, publicity, and competition. This necessity also stems in part from other domestic and foreign political problems.

2. Democratization should contribute to the maintenance and reinforcement of the Soviet socialist order, the socialist economic structure, our social and cultural accomplishments, and the socialist ideology.

3. Democratization, which will be carried out under the leadership of the cpsu in close cooperation with all levels of society, should maintain and reinforce the leading role of the Party in the economic, political, and cultural life of our society.

4. Democratization should be carried out step by step in order to avoid possible complications and mistakes. At the same time, it should be basic, far-reaching, and logical, and should be carried out in accordance with a carefully conceived program. Without a fundamental growth of democracy, our society will not solve the

problems now facing it, and will not be able to evolve in a normal manner.

There are reasons for assuming that the standpoint expressed in the above theses will be shared to a certain degree by a significant sector of the Soviet intelligentsia and avant-garde of the working classes. This viewpoint is also reflected in the opinions of students and young workers, as well as in numerous discussions of smaller groups. But we consider it expedient to represent this point of view within the framework of a letter in hopes of arousing a comprehensive and open discussion of the most important problems. We are seeking a positive and constructive attitude which will be acceptable to the leadership of the Party and the state, and which should reduce misunderstandings and unjustified fears . . .

The remains of the Stalinist era are having a negative effect on the economy, directly through the hindering of an economic approach to the problems of organization and administration, and indirectly, through a general reduction of creative potential in all fields. Under the conditions of the second Industrial Revolution, creative work is becoming ever more important for the national economy.

In this connection, we must also speak about the mutual relationships between the state and the intelligentsia. Freedom of information and creativity are prerequisites for the activity and the social function of the intelligentsia. The efforts on the part of this intelligentsia toward a widening of these freedoms is legitimate and natural. The state, however, is trying to suppress these efforts by employing all possible restrictions, including administrative pressure, job firings, and even judicial persecution. This all gives rise to tensions and mutual distrust, as well as complete lack of understanding, and makes fruitful cooperation impossible between the Party and the state apparata on the one side, and the intelligentsia—the most active and, for society, the most valuable group—on the other. Under the conditions of a modern industrial society, in which the role of the intelligentsia becomes increasingly important, such dissension can only be described as suicidal.

A large number of the intelligentsia and youth of our country recognize the necessity of democratizing and of a careful step-by-step implementation of this trend, but they cannot understand and justify antidemocratic measures. How can one justify the fact that people are put into prisons, camps, and insane asylums simply because they expressed their opposition in a way that was totally and lawfully within the realm of ideas and convictions? In many instances, this had nothing to do with opposition, but only with an attempt to get information or to hold courageous and unprejudiced discussion of important social questions. It is absolutely inadmissable to imprison a writer because of what he has written. One is equally unable to understand and justify such absurd and scandalous steps as the expulsion of the most significant and most popular writer [Solzhenitsyn] from the Soviet Writers' Union, a man who has shown himself to be deeply patriotic and humanistic in all his works. Equally incomprehensible is the dispersement of the editorial board of *Novy Mir,* which had gathered around itself the most progressive elements of the Marxist-Leninist forces.

For these reasons it is also imperative to speak again

about ideological questions. Democratization and a surfeit of information and competition will return the dynamic and creative element to our ideological life—sociology, art, and propaganda—and will purge the bureaucratic, ritualistic, dogmatic, pompous, hypocritical, and mediocre style that reigns in these areas today.

A course of democratization will set aside the dissension between Party and state apparatus and the intelligentsia. Close cooperation will replace the present mutual lack of understanding. Such a course will occasion a wave of enthusiasm, such as was prevalent in the 1920's. The best intellectual forces of the country will be mobilized for the solution of economic and social problems.

The introduction of democratization is a difficult process. Its normal development could be threatened by individualistic and anti-social forces, or by the supporters of a consolidation of power and fascist demagogues, who could make use of the economic problems of our country, the mutual lack of understanding between Party and state apparatus—on the one hand—and the intelligentsia—on the other—as well as nationalistic and bourgeois tendencies present in certain circles of our society, in the accomplishment of their own goals. For this reason we must be completely clear about one thing: that for our country there is no other viable alternative to a complete democratization and that we have to solve this difficult assignment ourselves.

Introducing it through initiative and control of the highest organs will make this democratic process possible according to plan, with a rearrangement of all levels of Party and state apparatus under a new chain of command that differs from the present one in its great openness and freer discussion of all problems. The majority of functionaries, who were born and raised in a modern and highly developed country, undoubtedly will be able to adjust to this style and quickly recognize its advantages. The filtering out of a small number of incompetents will only facilitate the task.

In the following program draft, we are suggesting a series of measures which could be accomplished in the course of four or five years:

1. Explanation to the highest Party and state organs concerning the necessity of a wider democratization, as well as length of time required and methods needed for its introduction.

2. Limited circulation of information within Party organs, departments, and administrative authorities about the state of the nation and of theoretical works concerning social problems which are of such a nature as to justify keeping them partially classified. Gradual relaxation of limited access to these materials until such restrictions have been completely eliminated.

3. Extensively planned organization of industrial bodies which exercise broad autonomy in questions concerning production planning, technological processes, raw-material supply, and sale of products, finances, and personnel. A spreading of these rights to smaller production units. Scientific appointment and intensive research concerning the form and degree of governmental control.

4. Cessation of interference with foreign radio broadcasts. Freer sale of foreign books and newspapers. Admis-

sion of our country to the international copyright convention. Gradual relaxation and expansion of international tourism throughout the world within a period of three to four years. Facilitation of the post and other measures for broadening international communications, especially to the member nations of Comecon.

5. Establishment of an institute for the research and evaluation of public opinion. Publication of the results of this research (limited at first, but later complete) concerning public opinion on various domestic and foreign-policy questions, and of other sociological materials.

6. Amnesty for political prisoners. Arrangement for obligatory publication of the minutes of all political trials. Social control of all prisons, camps, and psychiatric clinics.

7. Introduction of measures to improve the functioning of the courts and of the office of prosecutor general, as well as abolition of their autonomy with regard to executive power of the state, local influences, prejudices, and personal relationships.

8. Abolition of the obligatory inclusion of nationality in passes and official formulas. Uniform passport system for the inhabitants of cities and villages. Gradual elimination of the system of official passport checks, which should be carried out simultaneously with the removal of economic and cultural inequalities in the various regions of our country.

9. Education reform: Promotion of higher levels for primary and secondary schools. Heightening of the living standards of teachers, increase of their autonomy and of their rights to experiment.

10.   Passage of a law concerning press and information. Concession of new press organs for social organizations and citizens' groups. Complete elimination of the censor in every form.

11.   Improvement in the education of leading cadres to control modern techniques of administration. Introduction of apprenticeships. Improvement in the information available to all cadres as well as a reinforcement of their right to autonomy, experiments, free expression of opinion, and the practical application of these opinions.

12.   Gradual introduction of real choices among several candidates for the elections of Party and Soviet organs in every district, even in the primaries.

13.   Expansion of the rights of the Soviet organs, expansion of the rights and the responsibility of the Supreme Soviet of the U.S.S.R.

14.   Restoration of the rights of those nationalities deported under Stalin, and of their national autonomy, as well as permission to return to their native homes.

15.   Measures governing publication, including greater access to the works of leading organs commensurate with the interests of the state. Establishment of scientific consultation teams, among the leading organs of every area, to which highly qualified specialists in the different disciplines should belong.

This plan is naturally to be considered as a draft and a suggestion. Clearly, it must be supplemented by plans for economic and social measures, to be worked out by experts.

In addition, we emphasize that democratization alone cannot pretend to solve all the economic problems facing it, but can form a favorable atmosphere for their solution. Without the creation of such an atmosphere, the economic and technical problems will never be solved . . .

A series of correct and necessary foreign-policy actions undertaken by our government is not properly understood because citizens are not completely informed about them. A few years ago there existed cases of imprecise and partisan information which, of course, never encouraged their trust. An example of this is the economic aid to underdeveloped countries. Fifty years ago the workers of war-torn Europe provided aid for the starving peoples in the Volga area. The Soviet people are not egotistical and hardhearted, but they must be convinced that our responses in aid will be used for actual rescue work and the solution of pressing problems, not for the erection of pompous sport stadia or the purchase of American automobiles for local officials. The present-day world situation, the challenges and problems facing our country, demand extensive participation in economic aid for underdeveloped countries, along with other countries. Verbal appeals are not sufficient to make the public understand these questions and all the complications associated with them. What we really need is explanation and instruction, and this, once again, presupposes complete information and democratization.

The Soviet foreign policy is basically a policy of peace and cooperation. The lack of total information, however, spawns discontent and tensions. In the past there were certain negative aspects of Soviet foreign policy—symptoms of Messianism and exaggerated ambition—which suggested that imperialism alone was not solely responsible for international tensions. All these negative aspects of foreign policy are•closely allied to problems of democratizing the Soviet and remain so in a complicated relationship.

One source of growing unrest is the lack of any democratic discussion concerning such questions as weapons aid to other countries—for example, Nigeria, where a bloody war is now going on and about whose origins and development the Soviet public knows very little. We consider the resolution of the Security Council of the United Nations concerning the Israeli-Arab conflict a correct and reasonable one, though perhaps a little too insubstantial on several points. Nevertheless we are also disturbed by the question of whether or not our position goes beyond this document and is itself somewhat one-sided. Is our position concerning the status of West Berlin realistic? Is it always realistic to extend our influence to areas far beyond our borders, regardless of the tension in Sino-Soviet relations and of the serious problems in the economic-technological development of our country? Such a "dynamic" policy may perhaps be necessary, but it ought to agree not only with the basic principles of our country but also with its real possibilities.

We are convinced that the single realistic policy for the Atomic Age is a course intensifying international cooperation; persistent efforts toward possible closer cooperation in the scientific-technical, economic, cultural, and ideological areas; the renunciation, total renunciation, of weapons that have a potential for mass annihilation.

We are taking this opportunity to express our opinion about the expediency of one-sided or generalized explanations given by the atomic powers, which renounce their being the first to employ atomic weapons.

Democratization will encourage better understanding of foreign policy by the public and will help to purge all negative elements from this policy. As a result, it will also wrest a "trump card" from the hands of those opposed to the democratic movement.

What is in store for our nation if it does not follow the course toward democracy?

As the second Industrial Revolution develops, it will fall behind the capitalist nations and gradually become a second-class provincial power (history has parallel examples of this); the economic problems will increase; the relationship between Party and state apparatus and the intelligentsia will only become more tense; a split between the "left" and the "right" threatens to occur; the racial question will intensify, and the slowly dying movement for democratization will assume ever more nationalistic characteristics among the individual republics of the Union. These possibilities become even more threatening if one adds to them the danger of a growing totalitarian nationalism in China (something which we have been accustomed to regard as a temporary phenomenon in the long-range historical view, but which we shall have to consider as extremely serious in the next few years). Against this danger we can only maintain our position if we widen our existing economic and technical distance from China or at least keep it at the current level, increase the number of our friends in the world, and offer co-operation and aid as an alternative to the Chinese people. This impresses itself upon us if we consider the superiority of this potential enemy's population in contrast to our own, its militaristic nationalism, the length of our common borders, and the small, weak settlements we have so close to their borders in the Far East. An economic standstill, a reduction in the rate of development, and a continuation of an unrealistic and overambitious foreign policy in all continents could only have catastrophic results for our country.

Honorable comrades!

There is no other solution to the problems now facing our country but a course of democratization, to be carried out by the CPSU in accordance with a carefully conceived plan. A turn to the right—that is, a victory for those forces which advocate a stronger administration, a "tightening of the screws" cannot solve the problems; it would only intensify them and lead our country into a tragic dead end. A passive attitude of waiting would ultimately have the same result. The only option we have today is to set out on the right path and to initiate the urgently needed reforms. In a few years it could be too late. We must recognize this situation as it affects the whole country. Every person who is aware of the causes of these problems and the path toward their solution has a duty to point out this path to his fellow citizens. The understanding of the necessity and the potential for a gradual move toward democracy is the first step along the road to its fulfillment.

A. D. SAKHAROV

V. F. TURCHIN

R. A. MEDVEDEV

March 19, 1970

First German translation in the NEUE ZURCHER ZEITUNG, *April 22, and 24, 1970*

REFORMISM

ANDREI AMALRIK

. . . Not only does every Soviet citizen feel that he is living in greater security and enjoying more personal freedom than he did fifteen years ago, but indeed the director of an industrial enterprise now has the right to decide for himself matters that previously were not within his province, and the writer or theater director operates within a much wider area than he did before. The same can be said about almost every aspect of life in our country. This has given rise to yet another ideology in our society, possibly the broadest one—the "ideology of reformism."

This doctrine is based on the view that a certain "humanization of socialism" will occur through a replacement of the current inert and oppressive system by a dynamic, liberal one. This will be achieved through gradual changes and piecemeal reforms, as well as the supplanting of the old bureaucratic elite by a more intelligent and more reasonable group. In other words, this theory is based on the belief that "reason will prevail" and that "everything will be all right."

That is why it is so popular today in academic circles and, in general, among those in comfortable circumstances, who hope that others will also come to accept the view that it is better to be well-fed and free than to be hungry and enslaved. I believe that all American hopes for the Soviet Union are derived from this naïve point of view. We know, however, that history—and Russian history in particular—has never been a story of the continuous victory of reason and that the whole history of mankind has not followed an unbroken line of progress . . .

In my opinion, the trouble lies not so much in the minimal degree of freedom available to us as compared to what is needed for a developed society, or that the process of liberalization, instead of being steadily accelerated, is at times perceptively slowed down, retarded, or reversed. The problem seems far more rooted in the fact that the very nature of the process makes us doubt its ultimate success.

Liberalization presupposes some purposeful plan, gradually put into effect "from above" by means of reforms and other measures, and meant to adapt our system to contemporary conditions while leading it toward radical regeneration. As we know, there has been—and still is— no such plan; no radical reforms have been, or are being, carried out. There are only isolated and uncoordinated attempts at emergency repairs by occasional, and short-range tinkering with the bureaucratic machine . . .

Liberalization, however, could assume a "spontaneous" form. It could come as a result of constant concessions by the regime to the demands of a society that had its own plan, and as a result of constant efforts by the regime to adapt itself to the storm of changing conditions all over the world. In other words, the system would be self-regulating; difficulties in foreign and domestic policy, economic problems, etc., would constantly forewarn the ruling elite of changing conditions.

We find, however, that even this is not the case. The regime considers itself the acme of perfection and therefore has no wish to change its ways of its own free will or, still less, by making concessions to anyone or anything.

The current process of "widening the area of freedom" could be more aptly described as the increasing decrepitude of the regime. . . .

From "Will the Soviet Union Survive 1984?"

TOWARD A REVISION OF CRIMINAL PROCEDURE

YURI GALANSKOV

Yuri Galanskov wrote this essay, excerpts of which are presented below, while imprisoned in a work camp. It was most probably written toward the end of 1969 and at the beginning of 1970, but did not appear in the West until the summer of 1970.

. . . Events such as the hunger strike of February, 1968, or the "Letter from the Six" [19] or the general hunger strike supporting Aleksandr Ginzburg have been made known sooner or later through chance circumstances in our country and beyond its borders. When one considers the state of our nation, this situation takes on particular significance. The Western press and, even more importantly, the Russian-language radio broadcasts originating in the West, are informing the masses about cases of governmental despotism and excesses of our leadership. They explain the details of its social nature and present to the organs of the state the absolute necessity of putting urgently needed measures into immediate action. In this manner they have overcome the natural laziness, and conservatism of the bureaucracy for its natural tendency is to maintain an official formalism, to postpone actions, and to keep problems unsolved. Thus the Western press and radio broadcasts fulfill the task of an organized opposition, which is lacking in Russia today, and help advance our national development. Unfortunately, the West is selling itself short with the concessions it makes to the appetite for sensationalism and with the temporary political compromises it enters into; also, it does not demonstrate the persistence needed in the handling of questions which, for us, are vital.

During the years of the Stalinist dictatorship, when the Western intelligentsia could have supported us with such opposition, it was more shocked than helpful to us. It was appalled by the cruelty of evil and by the extent of our tragedy, but lacked the spiritual determination and moral force necessary to counter effectively the eruption of diabolical forces. It proved itself deficient in principle by entering into political compromises and making pacts with its own conscience. Behind the dramatic news stories concerning Russian concentration camps, the Western intelligentsia did not hear the moaning from the other side of the barbed wire. And no sensationalism has helped us to protect our own intelligentsia from psychic deterioration. In the same manner, none of the startling announcements about events in China could pretend to assuage the national tragedy of that country—a tragedy that threatens to plunge the whole world into a general catastrophe. But the West ought not to reassure itself too easily with conjectures about a probable Sino-Soviet clash.

. . . The Secretary-General of the Communist party in

Italy, Palmiro Togliatti, peremptorily posed an important question in a memorandum published in *Pravda* in 1964. The Italian Communists could not comprehend how the regime of suppression and limitation of democratic and personal freedoms and rights introduced by Stalin continued to exist in Russia. The question remains unanswered. But if this question leaves the Communists in the West without an explanation and, at worst, annoyed, for us it is a question of life or death. For us, the regime of suppression and limitation of democratic and personal freedom means the suppression of political and economic activities of the national forces; it smothers and strangles every creative initiative, destroys belief in one's fellow man, and robs one of all hope. The confusion of a man who has lost his belief, having been crushed under the remains of broken hopes—that is the dissolution of the "crystal ball" of his philosophy of life and the desecration of his soul. That is the danger threatening Russia from within . . .

We need the freedom to push forward the development of our national forces.

We need the freedom to put into action all those mechanisms which are necessary for the fulfillment of this task.

We need the freedom to fulfill our obligations toward Russia and toward life itself.

There is land, and then there is the Russian land that nourishes you and whereon you stand. If today, on this very land of yours, men sit behind barbed wire—men who have followed the dictates of their consciences and remained true to them—then you have to be aware of the fact you are responsible for this Russian land and for life on this land.

. . . Italians, Frenchmen, Englishmen, Americans, Austrians, Japanese, etc., are asking the Communists of Italy, France, England, America, Austria, and Japan: What kind of a social order are you offering us in which all political freedoms are denied, in which opposing thoughts have been forced into the paths of unofficial and illegal actions, so as to facilitate the reprisals against them and to bring people behind barbed wire and in front of machine guns? Wherein parties are forbidden but in which even the members of a "Union of Commune-ists" have to sit behind barbed wire? You offer us a social order that divides a mother from her child (the trial of Larisa Bograz-Bruchman is a case in point), a father from his children (Konstantin Babicki), a husband from his wife (Pavel Litvinov), and condemns them to exile because of a simple protest demonstration.

"By no means" will be the reply of the Western Communists. "We condemn such policies and will have nothing to do with them. Our Communism will be different, we will guarantee all political and creative freedoms, and will be tolerant toward political dissidents.'' Then the Communists of the West will be asked: "And how are we supposed to believe that? You yourself maintain that it is the actual practice that forms the criterion for the accuracy of a theory. Practice shows, however, that the two greatest Communist nations (China and the Union of Soviet Socialist Republics) have followed, and continue to follow, a policy that you yourselves have condemned and continue to condemn. Moreover, practice shows that these two greatest Communist countries find themselves on the brink of a war that could easily annihilate both the Russian and the Chinese peoples. You talk about problems and mistakes, but how can you prove to us that Stalinism and Maoism do not represent the essence of Communism? How can you prove to us that your Italian, French, or Engish Communism will not become a national tragedy for the Italian, French, or English peoples? You want to convince us that Communism is capable of assuring democratic and personal freedoms to a greater degree than the Western World does? You Communists have this Western system, toward the destruction of which all your activity is directed; you have all the organizational and technical possibilities to carry out this activity. You have your parties, your presses, your bookstores, and you enjoy all political freedoms, but in Russia a group of young Marxists who call themselves the "Union of Commune-ists," rots in a camp. . . .

You condemn such policies, you have nothing to do with them. You maintain that a regime of repression and limitation of democratic and personal freedoms does not lie within the spirit of Marxism itself. You maintain that such a regime is simply the result of problems and mistakes. You maintain that the CPSU is capable of overcoming its mistakes and of putting an end to a suppressive regime. If you are going to assure us of all that, however, then you ought to make the following demands from the CPSU:

1. Complete and general amnesty for people who have been condemned because of their political or religious convictions and

2. Revision of criminal procedure as far as it is based on political or religious discrimination.

Since you are the partisans of the CPSU, you bear the moral and political responsibility for all this. However, if you try to escape from this responsibility, if you want to overlook the criminal policies of the CPSU with the excuse that you have no desire to meddle in the internal affairs of a fraternal party, then we will accuse you of amorality and a lack of political principles. And we will tell the voters without hesitation that a regime of suppression of democratic and personal freedoms does indeed lie at the heart of Marxism, being a necessary result of the political practice of Communism. We will declare you outlaws, force you underground, and keep you behind barbed wire and in front of machine guns for as long as the CPSU keeps all political dissidents in Russia behind barbed wire. Thus not only their political popularity but the very existence of Western Communist parties depends directly upon the domestic and foreign policies of the U.S.S.R. Every debasement of the domestic policies of the CPSU necessarily leads to an intensification of the contrasts, to theoretical disputes, and to political disunity within the international Communist movement.

From POSEV, *No. 7, 1970.*

THE CPSU AS THE RULING CLASS
IN SOVIET SOCIETY

B. V. TALANTOV

Boris Talantov (1903-1971) was a member of a highly religious family. Both his brothers were priests who were killed during the persecution of the Church under Stalin. Talantov was a mathematician and held a position as teacher in Kirov (Viatka) until 1954. His poor health led to his premature retirement. Late in life he intensively supported the clergy, the Church, and the community during the persecution of the Church. Like Levitin-Krasnoz, Talantov did not limit himself in his last year to religious opposition alone, but was also actively engaged in the so-called "democratic movement." On September 2, 1969, Talantov was sentenced in Kirov to two years in a concentration camp for having violated Paragraph 190/1 of the Penal Code, regardless of the fact that his heart condition rendered him too weak to withstand any sort of imprisonment. During June, 1969, in a letter addressed to the Supreme Court of the U.S.S.R., *forty religious supporters protested the arrest of Talantov. On January 4, 1971, the civil-rights fighter died in a prison near Kirov.*

The following excerpts from his essay about Soviet society appeared in Samizdat. *It was first published in the West in 1969.*

. . . In earlier times the ruling classes extended the exercise of their power to cover all areas of politics and administrative rule, and even somewhat the area of private enterprise. The experiences gained by the whole world, as well as the Soviet Union, teach that private enterprises in agriculture and crafts, and in the greater areas of the public-service fields, are more than a match for state enterprises. (They offer the general consumer greater services and advantages at lower prices.) These branches of the economy have driven to a new low the socialization of the agricultural means of production (forced collectivization) in particular, but also the socialization of the means of production of the handcrafts industry in the whole area of service industries (trade, transportation and crafts). The total socialization of the means of production forces the citizen of the u.s.s.r. into a relationship of absolute dependency upon the government, for he has no other possibility of earning a living except for employment in state-controlled enterprises.

All state-controlled enterprises, however, are governed by members of the Communist party. So the dependency upon state industries means absolute dependence upon the Communist party. And economic dependency carries with it spiritual dependency. As far back as you care to go, every ruling class took pains to graft its ideology and its philosophy of life onto the people it ruled. The cpsu uses this absolute dependency of all citizens to impose upon them its own ideology and philosophy of life. This goes far toward explaining the wide acceptance of atheism in our country. Every person who wants a job—and especially if it is a question of a well-paid position—must acknowledge himself an atheist and give his complete support to the Soviet ideology, for otherwise he simply would not be hired or would lose his current position. As a direct result of all this, the official ideology is forced upon the masses not only by means of official administrative pressure but also by means of economic deprivation. Until now such methods of pressure have never been employed by any ruling class.

And thus the cpsu lives on—thanks to its total control of all means of production—by means of its monopoly over the disposing of these products, as well as its hold on every private enterprise, regardless of area, to spread its influence in the sphere of politics and government, but even more, to dominate all areas of economic activity as well as the spiritual life of the people. Because of this all-encompassing power position of the Communist party, a general spiritual slavery reigns in the u.s.s.r., for every person who wishes to earn the barest requirements for existence must acknowledge his support of the Party ideology. What is the basis for this unlimited sphere of influence that the Communist party enjoys in the Soviet Union?

The responsible positions in government, in administration and in the courts are without exception reserved for Party members, who, for their part, are subordinate to the corresponding Party committees. Inevitably this means that the government, the administrative, and the judicial branches, all stand essentially under the direct influence of a Party committee. Thus the highest and most unlimited power in the u.s.s.r. naturally lies in the Central Committee of the Communist party or, more precisely, with the Secretary-General of the cpsu. . . .

The unlimited power position of the Communist party in the u.s.s.r. is firmly supported by the fact that the right to possession of the key positions in government, administration, and the courts, is in fact a monopolistic privilege of the cpsu.

And upon what does the uncontrollability of the cpsu rest? The foundation for it is guaranteed in the fact that the workers do not have the slightest opportunity even to express their demands or their protests against the despotism, illegalities, and violations committed by Party members, and this because there is no service that is not absolutely controlled by the cpsu; the press, as well as the radio, is completely in the hands of the Central Committee's power monopoly. Millions of innocent people could be silently eliminated by the organs of the State Security Police (KGB) in the U.S.S.R. with the help of this domination by the Central Committee. And this sad historical experience shows us just how endangered human life can be when the radio and the press fall into the hands of a ruling class. For the most part, this is incorrectly understood by the rest of the world. And for this reason the cries of A. Solzhenitsyn and P. Yakir and the others urging a battle against the censor, calling for freedom of speech and freedom of the press, should be supported by all decent men in our country and especially by all faithful Christians . . . In direct violation of appropriate laws and the Constitution, extensive use of secret instructions and secret orders is practiced by the administration and by the justice department. As a preventive measure against organized protests, all Soviet citizens are kept under surveillance by an immense army of spies in the service of the KGB. Since 1965 this army of plain-clothes informers has significantly increased in number. For the enlistment of these spies—and in this respect today does not differ from the times of Ezhov[20]—extortion, threats, and bribery are routine enticements. Generally these informers behave quite unashamedly! They receive unearned wages and are quickly promoted to glowing careers in the service. Within the framework of this surveillance all private correspondence is not only extensively controlled but often is confiscated or delayed. One illustration of this attempt to thwart communication is the interference with foreign radio broadcasts, which has been going on since 1967. In this manner, broadcasts from Peking, the BBC and Die Deutsche

Welle were all disrupted in Kirov (the city formerly known as Viatka). Demagogy, slander, perjury and faithlessness, blackmail and naked force are among the practical tools employed by the CPSU; lies appear to be the final nadir to which truth has descended in the choice of methods for the control of people. For this reason the majority of U.S.S.R. citizens do not believe anything that is written in the Soviet press or broadcast over the Soviet radio.

The Communist Party of the U.S.S.R. trains its members in the conviction that, as members, they stand head and shoulders above non-Party members and have the right to reign over them as some sort of supermen. At the same time, a blind subordination to his superiors is impressed upon our party comrade. In their governmental methods, in their overbearing consciousness of exclusive superiority with respect to other people, in their greed for material advantages and in their desire to rule, and not in the least because of their hate for any religion, the Soviet Communists reveal themselves to be the followers of Nietzsche though disguising their claim to power with Marxist phraseology. As employers they imagine themselves the spokesmen and protectors of the interests of workers. So what remains as the final result of the October Revolution is one ruling class having replaced another even more cruel and power-hungry class . . .

So wherein lies the strength and wherein the weakness of the Communist party of the Union of Soviet Socialist Republics?

The strength of the CPSU lies in the all-encompassing, unlimited, and uncontrollable power that enables it to keep the masses under its pressure of duty and guilt, and permits at any time a sudden repression of any protest.

The weakness of the cpsu lies in the fact that its official ideology is no longer acknowledged by wide masses of the people and can only be maintained by means of an organized application of power in economic and administrative pressure. There is no longer anyone formerly excited by the idea of a paradise for the working classes, about whom it would be said today:

> *The Communists are deceiving us with an earthly paradise, which they dangle before us as the mirror of the future but which we will never see; however, they themselves are making great efforts to build a paradise for themselves in the present.*

Fifty years of experience show clearly and uncontestably the dearth of Soviet followers of Marxism. The doctrines of the gradual wasting away of religion, the state, and classes of exploitation in the face of the results which socialization of the means of production has brought about, strike us as error ridden. It is now perfectly clear to everyone that a community cannot be maintained without a government and administrative authority. The socialist reconstruction of society only leads to a reshuffling from one ruling class to another. It is clear that internationalism continually and inevitably transforms itself into nationalism. As great as the power of the Communist party of the u.s.s.r. may be today, its end seems just as inevitable and predictable as the fact that the life of the Party ideology has run its course because it began to apply the brakes to progress as a reactionary measure.

In its all-encompassing, boundless uncontrollability the power of the CPSU leads to the moral deterioration of its members on one hand, and, on the other, fosters antagonism toward the servile masses who stand outside the Party. The great majority of the people today see in the leaders of the Party—regardless of how hard they might try to pass as representatives of the people—nothing more than the leaders of a ruling class that is increasingly quite out of touch and indifferent toward the masses.

Stalin, with an eye to the consolidation of his power and his ambitious targets of conquest, began an intense campaign for the propagation of "Soviet patriotism" by emphasizing that the Russian people were supposed to lead the other races of the Soviet Union in the role of an "older brother." In this manner he made the Russian people a weapon of repression over the rest of the Soviet Union. This tyrannical chauvinism is still being quietly propagated today under the mask of "Soviet patriotism." And making use of this mendacious chauvinism, the "father of the people" revenged himself mercilessly and cruelly against those peoples who had incurred his wrath. In 1940 innumerable Poles, Lithuanians, Latvians, and Estonians were deported into the northern forests of the U.S.S.R. where countless numbers of them found an early grave. In 1944 the Crimean Tartars and other autonomous Soviet Republics were wiped out in a flash. Anti-Semitism was repeatedly instigated by those in high governmental positions. The CPSU suppressed every attempt of a national movement toward independence and equality. In this way, and in this way alone, does "Soviet patriotism" expose itself for what it actually is.

Human society is searching for new social and political

goals. Today the creative spiritual strength of the champions of humanity must be concentrated on the evolution of ideas to replace those of the official Soviet Marxist-Leninist Stalinism, the fragility of which has already been recognized and admitted by everyone.

Kirov, March, 1968

From posev, *No. 9, 1969.*

A FREE PHILOSOPHICAL TREATISE
(EXCERPTS)

A. S. YESENIN-VOLPIN

. . . What should we say about the obvious error of so-called historical materialism, which sees in economically originated relationships the basis for all other relationships, particularly the basis for moral and legal relationships?

This interpretation cannot be applied, for instance, to Soviet society, in which a strong state authority can transform an agrarian economic system into an industrial one. In so doing, how can this authority maintain its position as the "superstructure over the economic basis"?

The Marxists rely on sophisms and use them in their attempt to conceal this paradox, or rather, this self-deception. These sophisms are well-known. I only want to say that if they themselves believe in their theory, then their own blindness will destroy them. I have the impression that they are not so stupid as to misunderstand this, especially since their theory has long since become a very comfortable "carriage shaft." Will they be able to convince their successors of this? I do not want to prophesy.

With their Marxist classification of philosophical systems into "clerical," "bourgeois," "proletarian," etc., they turn out to be as blind as moles. Do they really fail to comprehend that the difference between materialism and idealism, for instance, is primarily a question of the intellect, that it depends upon a more or less distinct inclination for analytical thinking, and that it has nothing at all to do with the social origin of the thinker? (In all this I am naturally neglecting the fact that this origin can have left its marks on the thinker, which could always be overcome by sufficiently critical perseverance.) Perhaps they [the Marxists] want to appear blind deliberately; such an approach is not exactly stupid. Their first teachers—Marx, Engels, and Lenin—were not philosophers primarily and therefore this oversight could have occurred without their immediately noticing it. If so, then the demagogic line might later have gained the upper hand. In any event, their attempts to approach these problems sociologically had a definite value, which ought not to be overestimated, however . . .

I am against moralistic norms which are interpreted as dogmas—regardless of what they might consist of. But there are natural norms, the unnecessary violation of which disturbs me to a greater or lesser degree.

The most important thing is to be honest, i.e., not to lie and not to be a traitor. At times this demands courage, something inherent in the individual. The rest then follows by itself . . .

Neither a state nor a culture should have control over

the convictions of its individual members!

I have expressed my opinions on most of the questions. I should be very glad if this manuscript were to be published in the West. In Russia, it is not possible.

I give my permission to publish it without any alterations in Russian, as well as English, German, French, and Italian.

I am not concerned about the consequences.

I have written this in great haste. I have neither reread nor proofread any of this, because I had to hand it over as quickly as possible.

I do not claim to be the most intelligent person in Russia. Much of this is not new, but in Russia, every student who has come to a philosophical skepticism through his own thinking can consider himself a Columbus. (Incidentally, Columbus was not a great man.)

There is no freedom of the press in Russia, but who would say that there is no freedom of thought here?

July 1, 1959
*Mosco*w
VOL' [PIN]

Taken from VESENI LIST, *New York, 1961; German translation in* OST-PROBLEME, *No. 22-23, 1967.*

CULTURE AND MAN, AN EDITORIAL
FROM THE UNCENSORED JOURNAL

RUSSKOE SLOVO

. . . During the years of the Soviet leadership the intelligentsia has increased considerably. Its ranks have been expanded by representatives of peoples who earlier had great difficulties in getting an education, but who eventually have come to comprise the majority of its members. With the growth of the intelligentsia, however, the young man of to-day is, after his graduation from some institution, very often nothing more than a highly qualified craftsman. He knows his field but displays an inexcusable ignorance of every-thing that does not somehow belong within the sphere of his narrow "professional province"; he is completely lacking in civic conscientiousness and independent thought, and at the same time he is very often a boor in everyday life—he drinks, he curses, and he leads a profligate life. It is not our intention to judge these people; despite their various ethical deficiencies, they can develop into very valuable workers and they do possess a native intelligence, a healthy mind, and a good heart. But such intellectuals cannot be educators or teachers.

For this reason the cultural revolution is a necessity dictated by life itself in an attempt to intensify humanistic education in harmony with the given strength of our peo-ple, for this is the only thing that can broaden the horizon, arouse the aspirations for truth in the individual, educate him toward the elevation of his spiritual qualities, and so teach each one to understand his fellow-man and remain true to himself. It is absolutely essential to transmit a knowl-edge of Russian and foreign classics to our youth, especially since our schools, with their sterile classification and stereo-typed predictability, rather than arousing an interest in literature have only succeeded in fostering an aversion to literature during the last few years. It is especially essential to foster an interest among our youth in philosophical problems and historical questions, for without a knowledge of these things we won't even be able to understand ourselves.

It is also imperative that a wave of moral purification should begin and take up the battle against debauchery, alcoholics, and hooliganism. If we continue to fight these social problems with commands, bureaucratic techniques, and newspaper articles, we will only succeed in attaining what we now have, but the essence of the problem, "the root of the evil"—this debilitating ignorance that has violent effects on the human character and ultimately leads to an aversion against morality—will not be overcome. For the complete elimination of these abnormal phenomena in our society, the heroic enthusiasm of our youth is essential, the elevation of their characters toward honorable deeds, as well as the development of a social awareness, of integrity, of a love for truth and a lack of fear. There is never any excuse for lying—no one should ever utter a word in which he himself does not believe, nor should he ever support something that he himself cannot accept. One must be courageous and brave—it is a disgrace for a man to be a coward, a hypocrite, or a traitor! It is a disgrace for a woman to be a coward, an opportunist, and a deceiver—such a woman does not deserve to be a wife and mother! They are not human beings, but rather, contemptible misfits; they are not citizens, but spiritual degenerates . . . We must fight against egotism, narrow-mindedness, and avarice with every weapon at our disposal; life means to give one's self completely to others—as if we were sacrificing ourselves for them—as Pasternak said.[21]

Life is an eternal flame, devotion, enthusiasm. A coward, a swindler, an egotist, a miser, and a liar do not know how to value life; instead, they spend their time anxiously worrying about it.

What we have just discussed is a philosophy of life and a real culture; the dissemination, expansion, and preservation of a world view—that is what it means. It would be an inexcusable and absurd form of pedantry to attempt to prescribe the form such a revolution should take from this point; a revolution is a revolution simply because it bursts through all formulas, rules and dogmas . . .

At least for the time being, free discussions, friendly conversations, as well as a basic and extensive study of Russian and foreign cultures, should be an important element in the methods of the Ryleev Club—a socio-literary, cultural, historical community based upon humanistic convictions. May its wonderful motto[22] benefit the cause of a moral and cultural rebirth of man, citizen and patriot.

From GRANI, *No. 66, 1967.*

PERSONALITY AND SOCIETY

P. SMIRNOV

The following document, excerpts of which are reprinted below, appeared unabridged in Posev. *It circulated within the U.S.S.R. as a* Samizdat *publication.*

. . . This is not the place to examine why Christianity, which was called upon to establish a kingdom "not of this world," has proved itself incapable of establishing a just society "in this world." But nevertheless this failure does support a historical fact: had there never been a Christianity, man would never have discovered that society was unjustly established, no one would have thought of "equality" and "brotherhood." Only their fellow countrymen qualified as brothers for the Jews, and for those heathens who had been initiated into the "mysteries," only the likewise "initiated" qualified as their brothers.

Thus it is a question of standards—man must have some common rule with which he can measure equality. Christianity says that all are equal "before God." But the declarations of moral bankruptcy made by the "Christian countries" have led to a denial of God. This denial began with the spiritual revolution of the Renaissance, which led directly to the French revolutions and ultimately to the Russian Revolution.

But if one denies that common measure, according to which "all are equal," only a mere assumption remains: All men are "simply" equal in their relationship to one another. But is that really true? Ought one perhaps to interpret it another way—namely, that all are equal "with regard to the state," since one common standard of measure has been replaced with another? Is it an accident that the French Revolution gave rise to Napoleon, the Russian to Stalin, and the Chinese to Mao, and that in these three cases the "leader" as an individual person personified the impersonal state? Actually, if all are equal "with regard to the state," in an abstract sense, then the logical conclusion of the thought is that all are in fact "equal" with the "leader"; they all serve him in the same manner—either as fodder for the cannons or game for the forced-labor camps.

We do not want to suggest that Napoleon, Stalin, and

Mao are the only tyrants modern history has known. They are simply significant because in their countries the citizens' lack of rights was always accompanied by their rulers' cry of equality. We mentioned a lack of rights; one must, therefore, consider again the concept of "law" and attempt to define it more closely.

Law is primarily a defense of possession, and as such it has come down to us today from the practice of ancient Rome. But what type of possession is meant here? That is the pivotal question: One can only speak of "equality" when every individual has the real possibility of at least governing *himself*, when he has control over his own body, his thoughts, and his convictions.

If the law decides, however, that the state has, to a certain extent, priority over the disposition of me, then there no longer can be any equality.

For the state is an abstraction that inevitably must be personified in some sort of apparatus, and often simply— as we have already said—in one leader. He creates the law in the most personal manner. In this sense Marxism offers a very accurate definition when it says that law is a class law in the sense that "class" connotes a group possessing power and control over other groups. This very exercise of control distinguishes the ruling class for all others, and this class naturally formulates the law in defense of its own interests . . .

As far as equality goes, with regard to the state, it is a matter of deceit, perhaps even of self-deception; from a simply physical point of view, not everyone can belong to the power apparatus and this apparatus is consequently ruled by a small number.

How can one realize therefore the "natural" desire for equality, which is by no means natural, but rather something that has evolved slowly and torturously in the course of thousands of years?

If one renounced the common standards of comparison, be it God or the state, then all that remains is a return to the indefinite assumption that as men we are all "simply" equal. If we assume that, then what is our individual value? From the scientific physical or chemical standpoint, the value of a man is very low indeed: He is weaker and more sensitive than a tractor, and it doesn't even pay to make soap out of him as Hitler learned during his reign in Germany.

Are we then to conclude that we are all equal and are all of very little value? If one has no "common standard for comparison," then one can no more dispute such an assumption than he can dispute its opposite, that man represents the highest value in the world.

History has objectively demonstrated that in mankind's mutual relationships with one another nothing can objectively hope to guarantee the value of man. Its single guarantee is of a subjective nature, and takes the form of the mutual agreement that maintains that the next person is just as unique and valuable as I am. . . .

Just let a single member of such an ideal society refuse to adhere to this rule and set himself above it, and already equality has been destroyed.

If an individual man does not recognize the equal value of others, he will inevitably try to rob them of some of their possessions and ultimately try to rule over them.

We must admit that a large number of people do not

suffer in the least from this estrangement, from this lack of "control over their own persons." On the contrary, the great majority of people are passive and happily renounce their personal responsibility, gladly turning it over to some "Grand Inquisitor," asking only that they be nourished and amused in accordance with another old Roman principle: *panem et circenses.* Roman diversions during the last period of the Empire consisted mostly of the mutual murder of professional fighters—gladiators—or the torturing of "enemies of the people" with wild animals; and, as a matter of fact, it all took place in fabulously arrayed and decorated arenas (some of them even "air-conditioned"). We might accept this historical example as an indication of what very often serves to delight the masses. The conviction of the equal value of the next person does not simply "come into being." It demands a lengthy preparation, and it disappears with a surprising swiftness, as the example of Germany during the recent past might demonstrate . . .

An ideal democracy is a general aristocracy wherein each person acknowledges the same, highest value in the next. There is no such society, there never has been, and there probably never will be. To assume that there could be would mean wasting one's time in hopeless illusions or evolving a coarse demagogy . . .

There probably will never be total equality for the simple reason that people are not equally endowed—and besides education, biochemical, genetic, and other factors are responsible for this. But it is important and possible to protect society, as far as it goes, from the "pharaohs" and the "machines." Even if the state curtails personal freedom by depriving its citizens of some of their rights to "self-control," it soon proves necessary to protect even these still-remaining meager rights against the efforts of big and little candidates striving for the position of dictator.

For this reason one has to renounce his illusions and satisfy himself with a compromise: that state is good in which the necessary element of the exercise of power is kept at a minimum and the highest priority is given to service in defense of the "value" of each individual citizen.

It is not the goal of a realistic political program to proclaim the impossible equality of millions of people who, with respect to their talents, energies and desires, are not at all equal, but rather to acknowledge and to insure the equal "value" of these people. Once again we have collided with the old contradiction: How can there be an equal value of man if one acknowledges the initial assumption of inequality? It's clear that the expression "equality" has two meanings. We must try to define it more exactly . . .

If one speaks of the "value" of a man, one has to search for some intrinsic definition of man. Such a task, however, is by no means simple, especially since we have thrown away the earlier "common standards of measure." If one casts away the definitions which hold man to be an "image of God" or a "small wheel of the state," then one has to look for another definition. Perhaps then the fact remains as one of the not totally unacceptable criteria that every man, even a savage who still lives under Stone-Age conditions, is aware of himself to a certain degree, that he "sees himself" as if in a film—sees himself in how he lives, behaves, and thinks. This awareness of one's self is actually that which we mightly call "conscience" . . . It is clear that the substance of what is "allowed" and what is "forbidden" evolves through phases which are partially (but not completely) determined by economic factors.

It is still important to determine that every man possesses an awareness of what is allowed and what is forbidden, even if this takes on a completely distorted form ("everything is allowed which is of use to me"), and that means that he is aware of himself. We now can assume that one can make this phenomenon the basis of one of the possible definitions of man: Man is a being with a conscience— that is, an awareness that his actions are either "good" or "bad." . . . We say that a cannibal is a savage because we act differently and "know" that he behaves "badly." The single basis for this judgment is the education we have cultivated for many generations, an upbringing that has taken centuries to attain its goal, and in its turn can be instantly forfeited. (Once again we can point to Germany under Hitler as an example.)

For this reason the actual concrete task of establishing a society is a negative one. One cannot permit this awareness, which has cost us so much effort, to be lost again. One cannot permit the value of man to be set any lower than the level at which he found it . . .

"Freedom, equality, brotherhood," within their limits of attainment, are not the gift of a revolution that has been ended once and for all, and according to which, everything automatically will be wonderful. It is rather a Sisyphus-like task that suffers no interruption . . .

Many have pointed out already the fact that the Russian word *pravda* formerly meant truth as well as justice . . . Without law or its strictly ordained framework, however, there is no justice. Every exception renders law a dead letter and leads society back into its former wild condition. And it is absolutely unimportant which "ideological" excuses are offered (some portion of the population has to be starved because it may be "dangerous"). The right of life (*my* life) is forfeited from the very moment in which I permit any category of man—or even individual persons—to take this right away, even if it is done in the name of an ideal society. For in such a way this ideal society will become a repulsive deception . . .

In a modern developed society the right to life means the right to work. Out of the right to live spring all the other rights such as the right to education, to medical attention, etc. . . .

In the underdeveloped societies, he who received his nourishment from another person becomes that person's slave or at best his servant. This is the foundation of a patriarchal society.

Thus a society that demands the spiritual subordination of its citizens as compensation for the guaranteed instruction it offers will stand psychologically no higher than its slaves. At best, it stands as a patriarchal society.

One can only speak therefore about the existence of a right to education when the educated person has the real opportunity of making use of the fruits of his efforts (for learning is no easy task) wherever possible and according to his desires. Naturally one cannot avoid a compromise here either, for society, too, expects a return on the expenses incurred for this education. But in this case it is better to make a mistake in the direction of "greater freedom" than in the direction of an exaggerated defense of the "interests" of the state. It is obvious—even from the stand-

point of the simplest scientific advancement—that painfully
exact control, the suppression, or the underestimation of this
or that area of intellectual activity lead inevitably to colos-
sal losses for the state itself. And one should not let himself
be deceived by the difference between the humanitarian
and natural sciences. Linguistics, for example, are fated to
play an ever greater role in the formation of the laws governing information. An effective application of computer technology, however, depends upon the knowledge of these laws
in a very high degree. Moreover, the consideration of the
natural sciences as the end goal leads to the forgetting of
a simple truth, namely, that every discovery can serve both
a good as well as a bad purpose. Oppenheimer described
this danger with the words: "science without conscience."
The scientific discoveries prove absolutely nothing when
one applies them to the human level of society. Hitler's V-2's
in their time were the height of rocket technology. Fortunately the Jewish scientists who were successful in fleeing
from Germany managed to reach America safely; it was
therefore not Hitler who promoted the production of the
first atom bomb. The fact that the first atom bomb was
created in America, however, no more demonstrates the advantages of capitalism than the V-2's demonstrated the advantages of Nazism.

Thus the measuring standards for the advantages of
this or that society lie elsewhere. We feel that they lie in
the value society guarantees its members and this not only
includes the "right to life" (although this does signify the
first necessary step of evolution) but also the "right of conscience."

If one renounces one's right of judgment concerning

what is good or bad, if one considers it as nothing more than an unnecessary "relic," then the value of the human being will be reduced to a mere illusion, to nothing. For this reason the single guarantee for the value of each individual person and for the foundation of a state consists of a system by which a reasonable standard of personal freedom is at best united with the "interests of the state." This single guarantee consists of an untiring defense of a human being's value—one's own being as well as that of the other person—and, moreover, it must be defended by persons for whom the word "value" is not an empty noise.

For the time being, there are very few citizens in any society who are aware of this relationship. If there are too few of them, then we have totalitarianism—the moral equivalent of a Stone Age—even in the midst of the miraculous accomplishments of modern technology. Fortunately, however, the demand for the value of man is contagious; and a society in which responsible citizens possessing this very conscious demand have grown from a minority to a majority, is no empty dream but a real, attainable goal, even if its attainment demands long-drawn-out and persistent efforts. This is the true ideal of that "permanent revolution" to which humanity is called.

From POSEV, No. 7, 1969.

The following is an excerpt from the speech delivered by the Ukrainian writer Ivan Dzjuba (born in 1931) marking the twenty-fifth anniversary of the massacre at Babi Yar. For several years Dzjuba had been one of the leading edi-

tors of the journal Vitcyzna, *the organ of the Ukrainian Writers' Union. In 1965 he wrote an article about integrity in creative research that has become well-known. Since then he has been practically forbidden to publish anything else. His works, however—the most famous of which is his book* Internationalism or Russification?—*circulated extensively in the underground, and some of them have appeared in the West or in Czechoslovakia. During the mass arrests of Ukrainian intellectuals in 1965-66, Dzjuba was interrogated by the Party and the secret security organs, but was released, most probably because he suffered from acute tuberculosis. In 1969 he was expelled from the Ukrainian Writers' Union. The expulsion, however, was annulled after Dzjuba made a statement in which he renounced any connections with his foreign publishers and actually attacked them.*

AGAINST CHAUVINISM

I. DZJUBA

. . . As a Ukrainian, I am ashamed that there is anti-Semitism here, just as in other nations; that the shameful and, for mankind, undignified phenomena we call anti-Semitism exist here . . .

The road to true and honest brotherhood does not lie in self-forgetfulness, in rejection of ourselves and in adaptation to others, but rather in being ourselves and respecting others. The Jews have a right to be Jews, and the Ukrainians have a right to be Ukrainians, not only in the formal, but in the full and profound sense of the word. Let the Jews learn their history, their culture, and their language, and be proud of them. Let the Ukrainians learn their history, their culture, and language, and be proud of them. At the same time, let them learn each other's history and culture, as well as the history and culture of other nations, and let them realize their value as individuals and the individual value of others. Let them realize that they are brothers. It is difficult to accomplish this, but it is better to strive for this than to shrug one's shoulders and climb onto the bandwagon of assimilation and adaptation—that will result in nothing more than boorishness, blasphemy, and veiled human hatred, for us.

We should devote our whole beings to the battle against the civilized forms of human hatred. At the present time there is nothing more important for us than this, for, without such opposition, all our social ideals will lose their significance.

This is the duty we owe to millions of victims of despotism; this is the duty we owe to the better men and women of the Ukrainian and Jewish nations who have urged us to mutual understanding and mutual friendship; this is the duty we owe to our Ukrainian homeland in which we all live together; this is the duty we owe to humanity.

I. DZJUBA
September 23, 1966

From PROBLEMS OF COMMUNISM, *No. 5, 6, 1968.*

EVERY POWER MUST FALL . . .

A. LEVITIN-KRASNOV

The essay "V Cas Rassveta" ("At the Hour of Dawn"), excerpts of which appear below, was published in the Moscow underground journal Tetradi Socialisticeskoi Demokratii *(Notebooks of Social Democracy). The author, Anatoli Levitin (Krasnov is a pseudonym), is a former priest and, to use his own words, "religious writer." He was sentenced in 1949 to seven years in a prison camp and was released in 1956. Levitin-Krasnov is the author of numerous religious articles which circulate secretly in the* U.S.S.R. *One of the most remarkable documents is a letter to Pope Paul VI that Levitin is supposed to have sent to Rome via regular mail (!) shortly before his latest arrest. Among other things, the author referred to the growing number of believers to be found among the younger generations of Russians. With Vadim Shavrov, Levitin-Krasnov composed a three-volume work (to this day unpublished in the* U.S.S.R.*) about the persecution of the Church during the early years following the Bolshevik take-over:* Ocerki Po Istorii Russkoi Cerkovnoi Smuty.*

Recently Levitin-Krasnov has also lent his support to the non-Church-affiliated opposition and has signed his name to many protest documents. Following the arrest of the mathematician Boris Talantov, he applied himself as energetically and persistently to the cause of this man's release as he did in the case of Petr Grigorenko. On September 12, 1969, Levitin was arrested in Moscow. In an appeal addressed to the World Council of Churches seven Soviet citizens describing themselves as "faithful orthodox Christians" protested the arrest of the writer. Two of the signatories were co-workers on Phoenix *who became well-known during the political trials and persecutions in 1966—Vera Lashkova and the* SMOG-*poet Julia Vishnevskaya. In a declaration addressed to U Thant, forty-four persons voiced their objection, and finally an additional forty members of the civil-rights movement informed the "Soviet Public and the World" about this injustice.*

"We still do not know," admits the declaration, "what he [Levitin] is accused of, although it is not difficult to imagine that he has been called to account for the statements he made in defense of human rights currently being trodden underfoot in our country. He spoke up against the persecution of the Church . . . in defense of all those imprisoned . . . he was always prepared to come to the aid of the persecuted . . . we know for a fact that this man has never, orally or in writing, slandered either his country or his people. All his untiring efforts were devoted to the battle for the freedom of the spirit, for the liberation of our people from the curse of the Stalinist past." [23] *On August 19, 1970, the Western press reported the unexpected release of Levitin. Several months later, however, he was again arrested and sentenced on May 20, 1971, to three years in a work camp for anti-Soviet propaganda."*

. . . Friedrich Nietzsche (a brilliant and profound thinker despite the fact that he was an evil man) once said: "In order to overcome decadence, one must himself become decadent." Decadence (as an overdeveloped sensitivity for the tragedy of life) represents an inescapable stage in the evolution of mankind—and in the creativity of this thinker. One cannot simply exculpate oneself from decadence, but rather must buy oneself in it, make it a part of oneself, and only then overcome it. (A philosopher who does not comprehend the tragedy of this world is not a philosopher but a frivolous billy goat.)

Marxism, too, represents an inevitable stage in the history of mankind, which man again cannot simply ignore. So what is Marxism really? "Marxism is the philosophy of class conflict." And just as class conflict is unquestionably an unalterable fact, so is it unthinkable and impossible simply to cast Marxism to the winds. Moreover, as Sergei Bulgakov[24] stated, among economic philosophies Marxism is the only authentically scientific economic doctrine. A philosopher and historian who is not familiar with Marxism is also a frivolous billy goat (because he is ignorant of the profound dissonances in world history). And despite all this, Marxism is still one-sided and insufficient. If we take as an example the first chapter of *Das Kapital,* what immediately grips the reader is the harmony and the simplicity of the great scholar (value—surplus value, that's all). If we now turn to the second volume, however, we find that the whole conception plunges into bias. Marx himself leaves no stone unturned (profit as the price we must pay for production completely outweighs the value of that production). This is, however, completely understandable: the first volume is pure mathematics; the second volume, on the other hand, is real life (wherein the real relationships are now subordinated to algebraic signs, and mathematics finally proves itself superfluous).

In the first volume, then, Marxism is essentially the

algebra of class conflict. A second volume should have been added—one in which reality is subordinated to mathematics. Reinterpreting Nietzsche I could say: "In order to overcome Marxism, one must himself become a Marxist." I am not only no Marxist; I am the exact opposite of a Marxist. The opposite of a Marxist is a Christian. Marxism is the philosophy of a great stage of human history, the stage of class conflict. With the disappearance of classes, it, too, will be exhausted. Christianity, however, will never be exhausted. Marxism explains only one side of life—the philosophy of economic systems. Christianity, on the other hand, explains all occurrences of life in relation to its totality. Christ said: "I am the way, the truth and the life."

In the article entitled "The Brazen Step," I have attempted to sketch the functions of rulers in the era of socialist democracy. These functions can be summarized in the following manner:

1. to protect the borders of the u.s.s.r.,
2. to administer the economic life of our nation,
3. to wage war against capital criminals (among which, of course, one must also consider spies, traitors, and parasites).

This war, however, ought to be waged within strictly legal limits and under public scrutiny.

As the reader has doubtless realized, the functions of a governmental authority, as I have just described them in the era of socialist democracy, are still very extensive, although they are already considered as a type of "half-rule." In an environment of complete freedom of conscience in all areas of public and private life, such common employments as those of the slanderer, the informer, and the spy will disappear completely, and such shameful phenomena as tale-bearing, hypocrisy, cowardice, and fear to admit to one's own opinion will likewise disappear. National talents will experience a heyday, and a renaissance of art, science, and philosophy will dawn. Religion and the church, liberated from all external chains, would take up a duel on equal footing with the atheistic creed and, we believe, would have to emerge victorious after an open, brilliant, and honorable battle in the minds and hearts of man.

I firmly believe that a powerful socio-religious move-ment would evolve under such conditions and would bring about an ethical renewal of our nation. This would be the rebirth of that type of man about which the Austrian social democrat Friedrich Adler so enthusiastically wrote, whom the best minds of mankind have prophesied. And only this type of movement would be capable of rendering govern-ments ultimately superfluous.

Only after all the common instincts so abundant in man have been suppressed and the individual is finally master of his passions, instead of their unwilling plaything—then, and only then, will the state become superfluous. The state can-not fall by itself, for such powerful fortresses do not simply disappear into thin air. There is also another reason why the state will not simply die out: it is the structure that has propagated the materialistic ideology, [an ideology] which has so obviously proved unable to renew the individ-ual person morally. Rather, a great spiritual revolution must precede the fall of national power. A great ethical resurrection of the national masses can only result from a powerful socio-religious movement affecting every level and bringing about a spiritual world revolution. Such a great spiritual world revolution will alter the face of the earth. At that time the state will be transformed into a scientific research institute concerned with the administration of economic activity. At that time will be realized the vision of Karl Kautsky, the man who described socialism as "organization in the field of industry; anarchy in the field of ideology." It is significant that Kautsky emphasized this in the 1880's, and it is also a telling fact that there has never been any contradiction of this, not even from Lenin. All of this, however, is the concern of the distant future, but the future matures in the lap of the present, and it is absolutely necessary therefore that we exert ourselves, that we devote our lives to that future.

From TETRAD, *Moscow, No. 8, 1965.*

OPEN LETTER FROM SOLZHENITSYN TO THE MINISTER OF STATE SECURITY, YURI ANDROPOV

For many years I have remained silent in the face of the despotism of your co-workers: the censorship of my entire correspondence, half of which was confiscated; check-ups concerning the people I correspond with, who are spied upon by their co-workers and administrative organs; surveillance of my house; harassment of my visitors; installation of a tape-recording device in my town house, as well as in my garden; tapping of my telephone conversations; an unremitting propaganda crusade against me, emanating from speakers' platforms when these were turned over to your cohorts.

But after what happened yesterday I can no longer remain silent. My vacation home in the village of Rozhdestvo, in the rural district of Naro-Fominsk, was empty; according to my calculations, those people who had been spying on me knew I had gone. Because of a sudden illness, however, I returned to Moscow and asked my friend Aleksandr Gorlov to drive out to my garden plot and fetch a spare part for my automobile. The doorknob on my cottage would not turn, and voices were heard from within.

Gorlov entered and demanded that the intruders present their identification. In the small room, which hardly holds three—much less four people—Gorlov found ten people in civilian clothes. Upon the command of their leader: "Into the forest with him and shut him up!" they bound Gorlov and pushed him out, held his head down while they dragged him into the forest, and there beat him up. At the same time, others ran along another path through the bushes and carried packages, papers, various other things—maybe even parts of the equipment they had brought along—to their waiting automobiles.

Gorlov put up an energetic fight, shouted, and managed to gather a group of witnesses about him. Neighbors and passers-by hurried to his aid when they heard his screams; they barred the path against the miscreants and demanded to see their identification cards. One of them then produced a red I.D. (*udostoverenije*), and the neighbors moved aside. The miscreants dragged Gorlov, whose face had been disfigured and whose suit was torn, to their car. "Nice methods you've got," he said to his escorts. Their answer: "We're on special assignment, so anything goes."

After having shown his identification to the neighbors,

Captain Ivanov—he mentioned this name himself—immediately brought Gorlov to the military headquarters of Naro-Fominsk, where the officers on duty respectfully greeted "Ivanov." "Ivanov" then demanded that Gorlov sign his name to an explanation of the event. Although he had been badly treated, Gorlov stated in writing the purpose of his journey and all the circumstances surrounding it. When he had finished, the leader of the group that had beaten up Gorlov demanded that he, Gorlov, sign a statement assuring that he would never mention what had happened at the cottage. Gorlov categorically refused to do so.

They then drove back to Moscow, and during the drive the leader of the group of bullies impressed upon Gorlov the following statement: "If Solzhenitsyn ever finds out what happened at his summer house, you can be sure you won't escape untouched. Your vocational career (Gorlov is a doctoral candidate in technical sciences and is currently preparing the defense of his dissertation; he is presently employed at the GIPROTIK Institute) will not be continued, and also there won't be any more dissertation for you to defend. It will also have repercussions on your family, on your children, and—if necessary—you will be arrested."

Anyone familiar with our way of life also knows how such threats are carried out. Gorlov, however, did not give in to him; he refused to sign the document, and for so doing he is now being threatened by the criminal courts.

I demand from you, Mr. Minister, public reading of the names of all those who participated in this raid, the punishment prescribed by law, and an official public explanation of the incident. If all this is not forthcoming, I am forced to conclude that those who participated in the raid were acting under orders—your orders.

A. SOLZHENITSYN
August 13, 1971

Enclosure:
To: The Prime Minister of the U.S.S.R., A. N. Kosygin

I am sending you a copy of my letter to the Minister for State Security. I hold him personally responsible for all the despotic acts therein described. If the government of the u.s.s.r. fails to call Minister Andropov to account for these actions, I shall expect an investigation.

A. SOLZHENITSYN
August 13, 1971

From die welt, *August 16, 1971.*

NOTES

INTRODUCTION

1. For further information, see the two outstanding presentations made by G. Simon and M. Bourdeaux, in which the reader will discover an extensive selection of documents having to do with the religious opposition in the U.S.S.R. See Gerhard Simon, *Die Kirchen in Russland: Berichte, Dokumente* (Munich, 1970); Michael Bourdeaux, *Patriarch and Prophets: Persecution of the Russian Orthodox Church Today* (London, 1970).

2. See *Pismo G. Vladimova v Prezidium 4-go Vsesoiuznogo S'ezda Sovetskich Pisateleei, P*, No. 4 (1968) 16.

3. See *Otkrytoe Pismo Redaktoru, Literaturnoi Gazeta, Process Chetyrech (Trial of the Four)*. This white book edited by P. Litvinov is expected to appear in 1971 in an English translation in England and the United States. A Russian edition is currently being prepared by the Alexander Herzen Foundation in Amsterdam. An abridged Russian edition appeared in 1971 under the imprint of the Posev Publishing House.

4. KGB is *Komitet Gosudarstvennoi Bezopasnosti* (Committee for State Security). This is the name given to the secret political police in the U.S.S.R. in 1954. Previously it was known by the following designations: VCK, GPU, OGPU, NKGB, MGB, MVD.

5. In rare instances one might find direct references to *Samizdat* in the official press and literature. Thus, for example, the journal *Nauka i Religija (Science and Religion)* mentioned a book by a certain B.S.B., which was circulating by hand—that is, in manuscript or typescript form. This book was published in 1962 under the title *Religija i Sovremennoe Soznanie (Religion and Current Awareness)* through the underground. *With Every Indication Of Anger, Nauka i Religija* No 8, p. 35 (1969), observed that the author, a former engineer, was generally known to be an adherent of the religious philosophies of V. Solovev and S. Bulgakov.

THE FIRST THAW

1. A. Karanin, "Otkrytoe pismo Evgeniju Evtusenko," *Feniks* (1961), reproduced in *Gr*, No. 52 (1962), 182.
2. See *Pr.* (March 11, 1953).
3. See *L'Express* (Paris, March 14 and 21, 1963). The quotation appearing in the text came from *O-P*, No. 10 (1963), 318 f.
4. A. Solzhenitsyn, *V Kruge Pervon* (Zurich, 1968), p. 320.
5. I. Ehrenburg, "Ottepel'," *Znamia* (Moscow) No. 10 (1954), 14-87.
6. V. Panova, "Vremena Goda," *NM*, No. 11 (1953) 3-101; No. 12, 62-158.
7. L. Zorin, "Gosti," *Teatr* (Moscow) No. 2 (1954) 3-45.
8. I. Ehrenburg: "O Rabote Pisatel'ia," *Znamia*, No. 10 (1953), 160-183.
9. V. Pomerancev, "Ob Iskrennosti v Literature," *NM*, No. 12 (1953) 213-245. The quotation appearing in the text came from *O-P*, No. 10 (1954) 418.
10. See *LG* (December 16, 1954).
11. Zhdanovscina is the period between 1946 and 1953. This name was derived from that of the "culture pope," Andrei Zhdanov, who determined the guidelines of a dogmatic and chauvinistic cultural policy from 1946 until his death in 1948. Zhdanov advocated the "reinstatement of Party principles" in all areas of science and culture. During the Zhdanovscina, innumerable intellectuals of various fields were persecuted, especially the alleged "Zionists" and the Jewish "rootless cosmopolitans." These years can be described as the most fruitless of post-Revolutionary Russian cultural history.

DE-STALINIZATION AND THE SECOND THAW

1. Komsomol is *Kommunisticeskii Soiuz Molodezi* (Organization of Communist Youth).
2. Svetlana Alliluyeva, *The Last Year* (New York, 1969).
3. A. Karanin, "Otkrytoe Pis'mo Evgeniiu Evtusenko," *Gr*, No. 52 (1962) 182.

4. Y. Yevtushenko, "Stanciia Zima," *Okiabr* (Moscow) No. 10 (1956).
5. See *Voprosy Literatury* (Moscow) No. 2 (1963). The quotation appearing in the text came from *O-P*, No. 10 (1963) 317.
6. V. Dudintsev, "Ne Chelebom Edinym," *NM*, No. 8 (1965) 31-118; No. 9 (1965) 37-118; No. 10 (1965) 21-98.
7. See J. Ruehle, *Literatur und Revolution* (Cologne, 1960) p. 142.
8. Nikolai Vavilov was the most important Russian authority on classical genetics (Mendel-Morgan Law). From the year 1930 he was subjected to increasing difficulties, since the official line maintained that the Mendel-Morgan Law contradicted the concept of dialectical materialism. Vavilov's chief opponents were Ivan Michurin and Trofim Lysenko. Lysenko particularly championed the so-called Milieu Theory, which classified externally acquired characteristics as hereditary. Vavilov was arrested as an ideological opponent and died in a concentration camp on January 26, 1943. The scientist was posthumously rehabilitated in 1955. Readers are urged to refer to Jaures Medvedev's *"Biologiceskaia Nauka i Kul't Licnosti"* now circulating in *Samizdat* in the u.s.s.r., reprinted in *Gr*, Nos. 70 and 71 (1969); German version, *Der Fall Lysenko* (Hamburg, 1971).
9. *Literaturnaia Moskva* (Moscow, 1956).
10. A Kron, "Zametki Pisatel'ia," *Literaturnaia Moskva*, II, 780
11. See *LG* (March 13, 1957).
12. *"Za Tesnuiu Sviaz' Literatury i Isskustva s Zizin'if Naroda,"* *Pr* (August 28, 1957 *et al*).

THE PASTERNAK AFFAIR

1. See *LG* (October 25, 1958).
2. See *KoPr* (October 28, 1958).
3. See *Pr* (November 2, 1958).
4. See also S. d'Angelo, *"Der Roman des Romans,"* *Osteuropa* No. 7 (1968) 489-501.
5. B. Pasternak, *Ueber Mich Selbst: Versuch Einer Autobiographie* (Frankfurt am Main, 1959).
6. See G. Ruge, *Pasternak* (Munich, 1958) p. 104

7. See H. Schewe, *"Es Gibt Schicksale in Peredelkino," Die Welt* (September 17, 1966).

THE SEARCH FOR NEW VALUES

1. Yevtushenko's poem appeared in *LG* (September 19, 1961). Babi Yar is a ravine near Kiev where nearly 40,000 Jews of Kiev were murdered by Hitler's ss troops on September 29 and 30, 1941— that is, on Rosh Hashana, the Jewish New Year.
2. N. Mandelstam, *Hope Against Hope* (New York, 1970). The quotation appearing in the text is Max Howard's English translation.

THE 'CAMP' LITERATURE

1. A. Tvardovski: *"Za Dal'iu Dal'," Pr.* (April 29, 1960). The quotation appearing in the text was taken from the translation by Wilhelm Loeser in *O-P*, Nos. 25, 26 (1960) 111.
2. K. Ikramov/V. Tendriakov, *"Belyi Flag," Molodaia Gvardiia* (Moscow) No. 12 (1962) 122.
3. M. Mikhailov, *Moskauer Sommer 1964* (Bern, 1965).
4. Yuzek Aleskovski, *Pesnia o Staline.* The quotation appearing in the text was taken from the translation by S. Stankovich.
5. A. Solzhenitsyn, *"Odin den' Ivana Denisovica," NM*, No. 11 (1962) 8-74.
6. Well-known character from Tolstoi's novel, *Voina i Mir (War and Peace).* Karatayev symbolizes the eternal good qualities of the peasant: compassion, piety, and the capacity to suffer.
7. See *LG* (November 22, 1962).

THE NEW CAMPAIGN

1. *"Tvorit' Dlia naroda, Vo Imia Kommunizma," Pr.* (December 22,

1962).
2. Ibid.
3. Ibid.
4. Ibid.
5. "Ob otvetstvennosti Chudoznika Pered Narodom," Pr. (March 9, 1963).
6. Ehrenburg's memoirs appeared under the title Liudi, Gody, Zizn' between 1960 and 1963 in NM.
7. See V. Ermilov's attack against Ehrenburg in Iz (January 30, 1963).
8. Y. Yevtushenko, "Naslednik Stalina," Pr (October 21, 1962).

THE GROWING EMANCIPATION
OF THE INTELLECTUALS

1. "Ot Redakcii," NM, No. 9 (1965). The quotation appearing in the text was taken from O-P, No. 25-26 (1965) 772.
2. See K. Mehnert, Der Sowjetmensch, (Stuttgart, 1958), p. 232.
3. See "Polen," Warsaw, No. 10 (1967). The quotation appearing in the text was taken from O-P, No. 22-23 (1967) 627.

THE CULTURAL AND POLITICAL
DEVELOPMENTS FOLLOWING
THE FALL OF KHRUSHCHEV

1. See KoPr (October 23, 1964).
2. A. M. Rumjancev, "Partiia i Intelligenciia," Pr (February 21, 1965). The quotation appearing in the text was taken from O-P, No. 6 (1965) 166-170.

BEGINNING OPPOSITION

1. *KoPr* (December 23, 1955).
2. Ibid. (January 4, 1956).
3. Ibid. (December 16, 1956).
4. Ibid. (December 28, 1956).
5. See G. Hillman, *"Selbskritik des Kommunismus. Texte der Opposition," Rowolt's Deutsche Enzyklopaedie,* Vol. 272-273 (Hamburg, 1967) 208.
6. According to various sources, including those which P. Litvinov gathered together in his White Book concerning the January, 1968 Trial (*Process cetyrech*), Dobrovolski was sentenced at that time to six years in a work camp, but was pardoned after having served the first three. Official documents published in *Posev* and dating from October 6, 1967, however, state that the length of the term as originally stated in the verdict was no more than three years.
7. See *P* (June 25, 1965).
8. See *Iz* (September 6, 1959).
9. See *KoPr* (October 30, 1960).
10. Ibid. (May 31, 1959).
11. *"Literature i Zizn',"* (Moscow) November 23, 1960.
12. See *LG* (September 24, 1964).
13. See *KoPr* (February 21, 1964).
14. A detailed report about Samefir with numerous references to Soviet newspaper announcements appeared in *P,* No. 6 (1968) 13-17.
15. See also A. Wolgin, *Hier Sprechen Russen* (Mainz, 1965), p. 468 f.
16. Ibid., p. 484.
17. See *Le Monde* (August 8, 1962), also the article by A. Boiter, "When the Kettle Boils Over," *Problems of Communism,* (No. 1, (Washington, 1964) pp. 33 ff.
18. "Socialist" revolution is the name given to the actual and legitimate February Revolution of 1917, which was instigated and initiated by the Russian intelligentsia and supported by workers, peasants, and soldiers. The "October Revolution," which saw the Bolshevik minority seize power and overthrow the government of Kerensky, was in reality only a well-prepared *coup d'état.*

SAMIZDAT

1. Reprinted in *Gr*, No. 58 (1965) 95-193.
2. See *Iz* (September 2, 1960).
3. Article 70 of the Penal Code of the RSFSR: *Anti-Soviet Agitation and Propaganda.*

    "Agitation or propaganda for the purpose of undermining or weakening the Soviet power or that which entails the committing of single, particularly dangerous crimes against the state; the circulation of slanderous lies which serve to damage the reputation of the Soviet state and social order for the same purposes, as well as the dissemination, production or storage of literature having to do with the same purposes will be punishable by a six-month to seven-year deprivation of freedom or exile of two to five years.

    "The same activities, if they are committed by a single person who has previously been convicted of particularly dangerous crimes against the state, or if they are committed during the time of war, will be punished with a three- to ten-year deprivation of freedom."

    See "Ugolovny Kodeks RSFSR" (Moscow, 1970) 36.
4. See *Vecernyaya Moskva* (Moscow) June 3, 1965.
5. Reprinted in *Gr*, No. 52 (1962) 86-190.
6. Ibid., p. 179. The quotation appearing in the text was taken from the translation of A. Steininger.
7. Ibid., p. 164.
8. Ibid., p. 87.
9. Ibid., p. 124.
10. Ibid., p. 140 f.
11. Ibid., p. 125.
12. Ibid., p. 128.
13. Ibid., p. 178.
14. See *KoPr* (January 14, 1962).
15. Ibid.
16. See *Molodoi kommunist*, No. 1 (Moscow, 1962); German version in *O-P*, No. 5 (1962) 134.
17. Reprinted in *Gr*, No. 59 (1965), 9-77.
18. Ibid., p. 28.

19. Ibid., p. 27.
20. Ibid., p. 9.
21. See *Gr* No. 61 (1966), 14.
22. See *KoPr*, June 20, 1965.
23. See *Gr* No. 61 (1966), 12.
24. Yu. Kublanovski, "Otryvok is Poémy Arlekin," ibid., 20.

WRITERS UNDER PURSUIT

1. M. Narymov, "Nespetaia Pesnia," *Gr*, No. 48 (1969), 5-113.
2. For the text of the letter, see *Gr*, No. 51 (1962) 9 ff.
3. See *Daily Telegraph* (London), July 29, 1970.
4. V. Tarsis, *"Palata* No. 7," *Gr*, No. 57 (1965) 9-110; German version: *"Botschaft aus dem Irrenhaus"* (Frankfurt am Main, 1965).
5. See Chr, No. 11 (1969); reprinted in *P*, *"Tretii Special'niy Vypusk 1970,"* p. 32 (additional installments in *P*, I., II., III., IV).
6. V. Tarsis, loc. cit., *Gr*, No. 57 (1965) 67-68.
7. See also G. Stukov, *"Poët—"Tuneiadec"—Josef Brodski,"* from *Josef Brodski, Stitchotvoreniia i Poemy* (Washington, New York, 1965).
8. A. Yesenin-Volpin, *"Svobodnyi Filosofskii Traktat"* (*"A Free Philosophical Treatise"*), from *Veseniy List* (*A Leaf of Spring*) (New York, 1961) pp. 110-171.
9. VINITI *is Vsesoiuznyi Institut Naucnoi i Techniceskoi Informacii* (All-Union Institute for Scientific and Technical Information).

THE "CAUSE CÉLÈBRE": SINIAVSKI AND DANIEL

1. The following editions are the most complete: N. Arzhak (Yu. Daniel), *Sbornik Proizvedeniy* (New York, 1966); *Fantasticeskiy mir Abrama Terca* (New York, 1966).
2. From *Belaia Kniga Po Delu A. Siniavskogo i Yu. Danielia* (Frankfurt am Main, 1966). The quotations appearing in the text were taken from the German edition: *Weissbuch in Sachen Sinjawskij/*

Daniel (Frankfurt am Main, 1967) p. 282—henceforth designated as *White Book.*

3. Boris Pasternak, *Stichotvoreniia i Poemy; Vstupitel'naia Stat'ia a. D. Siniavskogo,* pp. 9-62 (Moscow, Leningrad, 1965).
4. *White Book,* p. 400 ff.
5. *White Book,* p. 52 ff.
6. Ibid., p. 59 ff.
7. Ibid., p. 44 f.
8. L. Waldimirow, *Die Russen Privat* (Vienna, Munich, Zurich, 1969) p. 169.
9. *White Book,* p. 48.
10. See *Iz* (January 12, 1966).
11. See *LG* (January 22, 1966).
12. *White Book,* p. 392 f.
13. See *Die Welt* (July 28, 1967).
14. See *"Pis'ma Politiceskich Zakliucennych Sovetskim Deiateliam Kul'tury,"* P, No. 6, p. 12 (1970).
15. A Marchenko, *Moi Pkazania* (Frankfurt am Main, 1969).
16. For the actual wording of the letter, see *P,* No. 1 (1970) p. 15 f.

THE STRUGGLE INTENSIFIES

1. *Glavlit is Glavnoe Upravlenie po Delam Literatury i Izdatel'stva* (Central Administration for Literature and Publication), the main censorship office in the u.s.s.r.
2. See *Gr,* No. 63, 9 f.
3. Article 190, paragraph 1: "The systematic oral dissemination of deliberate lies, which serve to discredit the Soviet state and social order, as well as the manufacture or circulation of literary works for the same purpose, whether printed or in some other form, will be punished with a three-year deprivation of freedom or forced-labor up to one year, or with a fine of no more than 100 rubles." Article 190, paragraph 3: "The organization of, or active participation in, group demonstrations which blatantly disturb the peace or which result in action related to the blatant non-observation of lawful instructions of the representatives of the state, or disturbances which hinder the scheduled departures of

transportation facilities, the scheduled completion of work in governmental and social institutions, or businesses, will be punished by a three-year deprivation of freedom or with a forced-labor term up to one year or with a fine of not more than 100 rubles." (From *Vedonosti Verchovnogo Soveta* RSFSR, (Moscow, September 22, 1966).

4. *Delo o Demonstracii na Puskinskoi Ploscadi 22 Janvaria 1967 goda. Sbornik Dokumentov pod Redakciei Pavla Litvinova* (London, 1968).

5. See *Molodoi Kommunist,* No. 2 (1969) 88 f. Bukovski's authorship of this letter was also proved elsewhere: in a letter that Vadim Delone sent to the Editor in Chief of *Literaturnaia Gazeta* and *Komsomol'skaia Pravda* in reference to the January Trials of 1968. See *P,* No. 3 (1969) 54 ff.

6. See text in *NRS* (April 6, 1968).

7. See *Il Girono* (Milan) December 19, 1967.

JOURNALS OF SOCIAL CRITICISM

1. Reprinted in *Gr,* No. 66 (1967) 3-34.

2. Kondratiy Ryleev (1795-1826), Poet and friend of Aleksandr Pushkin. Ryleev was executed in 1826 as one of the leaders of the Decembrists (he belonged to the "Northern Alliance").

3. *Narodniki* means Nationalists, or rather, "those who go to the people"; also called Populists. It was a movement of actual "socialist peasants" inspired by A. Herzen (Gercen) as well as by various Slavophiles during the last third of the nineteenth century (1860-1890). Their spiritual heroes were P. Lavrov and N. Michailovski. The *narodnike* actively polemicized against the Marxists, whom they reproached for having denied the role of personality in history and having ignored the interests of the peasants, among other things.

4. The Russian word *dekabristy* comes from *dekabr'* and means "December." The Decembrists earned their name after the unsuccessful revolt of December 14, 1825, when a group of nobles demanded a constitution and refused to swear allegiance to Czar Nicholas I. Five of the Decembrist leaders were sentenced to

death and executed in 1826. One hundred twenty-one were exiled to Siberia. The main goal of the Decembrists was a constitution, but they also strove for the elimination of serfdom. In 1821 the Decembrists split away from the more moderate "Northern Alliance" under A. Muravev and the more radical nationalistic "Southern Alliance" under P. Pestel'. Both groups had set up program drafts for a future form of government. The representatives of the Northern Alliance advocated a constitutional monarchy; those of the Southern Alliance championed a republic and the simultaneous inclusion of all East-European (Slavic) peoples.

5.   E. Kusev, "Dekabristy," *Gr*, No. 66 (1967) 27.
6.   Partially reprinted in *Gr*, Nos. 63, 64, 65, 67 (1967); Nos. 68, 69 (1968); No. 75 (1970).
7.   *"Organizacionnye Problemy Dvizeniia za Polnoe i Vseobscee Razorunzeni i Mir vo Vsem Mire,"* *Gr*, No. 64 (1967) 167-174.
8.   O. Mandelstam, *"Cetvertaia Proza,"* *Gr*, No. 63 (1967) 20.
9.   See text in *Novy Zurnal* (New York, 1966) No. 83, 185-227.
10. A. Siniavski: *"V Zascitu Piramidy,"* *Gr*, No. 63 (1967) 114-139.
11. A. Dobrovolski, *"Vzaimootnosenie Znaniia i Very,"* *Gr*, No. 64 (1967) 194-201.
12. IML is *Institut Marksizma-Leninizma pri CK KPSS* (Institute for Marxism-Leninism of the Central Committee of the CPSU).
13. *"Obsuzdenie Maketa 3-go Toma Istorii* KPSS *v Institute Marksizma-Leninisma pri* CK KPSS *s Ucastiem Starych Bolsevikov; Konspekt,"* *Gr*, No. 65 (1967) 129-156.
14. *"Rossisskii Put' Perechoda k Socializmu i Ego Resul'taty,"* *Gr*, No. 68 (1968) 137-156; No. 69 (1968) 134-153.
15. See *Gr*, No. 63 (1967) 7 f.

THE JANUARY TRIAL, 1968

1.   For text see NRS (April 7, 1968).
2.   See *The Times*, (London) January 9, 1968; NZZ, January, 1968.
3.   NTS is *Narodno-Trudovi Soiuz Russkich Solidaristov* (Peoples' Labor Alliance of Russian Solidarists), founded in 1930. In accordance with its statutes, the NTS unites various groups of people

with different world views, but was primarily inspired by the Russian philosophers N. Berdiaev and I. Il'in and also influenced by the teachings of Christianity. As its socio-political goal, the NTS aims at a parliamentarian democracy and a mixed, partially socialized economic system. Its most important theorist is A. Levicki. Particularly since the end of the war, this organization has grown and continues to gain adherents in the underground NTS in the U.S.S.R., which currently poses a grave threat to the Soviet leaders.

4. Brocks-Sokolov traveled around the U.S.S.R. in the service of the NTS and was arrested there by the KGB. Unable to bear the extreme pressures to which he was subjected, Brocks-Sokolov decided to denounce the four defendants publicly during their trial and thus improve his own position.

5. See NRS (June 6, 1968).

6. Text in NRS (March 2, 1968).

7. See *Le Nouvel Observateur* (Paris) March 6, 1968, 18 f.

8. See *KoPr* (January 18, 1968); *Iz* (January 16, 1968).

9. See *LG*, No. 13 (1968).

10. Text in *P*, No. 6 (1968) 7.

11. Galanskov's wife and mother sent a petition to the NVD (Department of the Interior) in March, 1970, drawing attention to the fact that the prisoner could neither eat nor drink and that he was hardly able to move. See text in *P*, No. 5 (1970) 2 f.

12. See *P*, No. 8 (1970) 5 f.

A FLOOD OF REBELLION

1. See K. van het Reve, *Nicht Geladene Zeugen* (Hamburg, 1969) p. 13.

2. See NRS (March 10, 1968).

3. See *P*, No. 8 (1968) 15.

4. See NRS (March 2 and 7, 1968).

5. Ibid. (June 7, 1968).

6. Ibid. (March 2, 1968).

7. See *Iz* (January 16, 1968).

8. RSFSR is *Rossiiskaia Socialisticekaia Federativnaia Sovetskaia Respubliks.*

9. See *P*, No. 4 (1968) 8.
10. In 1937, Stalin's purges reached their zenith. This year saw the mass annihilation of the officers of the Red Army, whose victims included, among others, the famous General Iona Yakir, the father of Petr Yakir. Then fourteen, Petr Yakir was brought to a concentration camp, and not released until after his rehabilitation in 1956.

THE RULERS' REVENGE

1. *"Resplatnaia Medicinskaia Pomosc,"* from *Natalia Gorbanevskaya —Stichi* (Frankfurt am Main, 1969) pp. 141-171.
2. See *Chr*, No. 1 (1968); PII. (1969) 8.
3. A. Amalrik, *Prosuscestvuet li Sovetskii Soiuz do 1984 Goda?* (Amsterdam, 1970). The quotation appearing in the text is taken from the German edition, *Kann die Sowjetunion das Jahr 1984 Erleben?* (Zurich 1970), p. 27.
4. See "Moskva," No. 10 (Moscow, 1967). The quotation appearing in the text was taken from *O-P*, No. 25-26 (1968) 624.

ANTI-STALINIST SPOKESMEN

1. Text appears in *P* (September 16, 1966).
2. See *P*, No. 11 (1970) 3.
3. A complete collection of materials concerning the Nekrich affair, including the book itself, appeared in the German edition, *Nekritsch/Grigorenko—Genickschuss*, edited and introduced by Georges Haup (Vienna, 1969).
4. See *Voprosy Istorii KPSS* No. 9 (Moscow, 1967) 127 ff.
5. "The act of concealing the historical truth is a crime against the people." Letter to the editor of *Voprosy Istorii KPSS*, from *Genickschuss, et al.*, 234-269. (Article is written in German.)
6. Ibid., p. 302.
7. Ibid., p. 310 f.
8. The novel appeared under the title: *Sofia Petrovna* in *Novyi*

Zurnal, No. 83 (1966) 5-45; No. 84 (1966) 5-46. A German translation (entitled *Ein Leeres Haus*) appeared in Zurich in 1967.
9. See *P,* No. 6 (1969) 7.
10. Pis'mo P. I., *"Jakira v. Redakciiu "Kommunist," Za Prava Celoveka* (For Human Rights) (Frankfurt am Main, 1969) p. 30.
11. See *P,* No. 7 (1969) 7.
12. See *Pr* (December 21, 1969).

THE ROLE OF SAKHAROV,
THE ATOMIC PHYSICIST

1. A. Sakharov, *Rasmysleniia o Progresse, Mirnom Sosuscestovovanii I Intellektualnoi Svobode* (Frankfurt am Main, 1968); German edition, *Gedanken ueber Fortschritt, Friedliche Koexistenz and Geistige Freiheit* (Frankfurt am Main, 1968).
2. See also the noteworthy letter by the Priest Sergei Zeludkov, in which he takes exception to the problem of intellectual freedom: *"Krazmysleniiam ob Intellektual'noi Svobode. Otvet Akademiku A. D. Sakharovu,"* from *Vestnik Russkogo Studenceskogo, Christianskogo Dvizeniia* (Paris, New York, No. IV 1969) 46-57.
3. See *Voprosy Filosofii,* No. 5 (Moscow, 1919) 147.
4. See *Rude Pravo* (Prague, July 10, 11 and 12, 1968).
5. In the meantime the mathematician Igor Safarevich joined the Human Rights Committee. The writers Aleksandr Solzhenitsyn and Aleksandr Galich, as well as the physicist Boris Cukerman (who has since emigrated to Israel), were named "correspondents" of the committee.
6. See *The Times* (November 16, 1970).
7. See *"Neprimimost'k Burzuaznoi Ideologii, Pr* (November 23, 1970); *"O Rabote Partiinogo Komiteta Fiziceskogo Instituta Imeni P.N. Lebedeva Akademii Nauk* u.s.s.r., *Partiinaia zizn',* No. 21 (Moscow 1970) 8-10.
8. See p. 197 f.
9. Revol't Pimenov (born in 1931), a student of mathematics, was brought in 1949 to an insane asylum, following his resignation

from the Komsomol. He was released a short time later, was permitted to continue his studies at the Leningrad University, but was temporarily suspended from that institution. Because of "anti-Soviet agitation" (he had written various articles about the Hungarian Revolution, among other things, and had organized an allegedly anti-Soviet student group), the mathematician was at first sentenced to six years, but the term was later extended to ten years deprivation of freedom. He was paroled in 1963 and permitted to continue his studies at the university, on condition that he finish his doctoral dissertation within the year. In 1969 he finished his dissertation and on October 22, 1970, the scientist-scholar was exiled under Paragraph 190/1 for a period of five years.

CHRONIKA

1. See *Pr* (April 11, 1968).
2. See *Chr*, No. 5 (1968); *P*, I., 54.
3. See *Chr*, No. 7 (1969); *P*, II., 20.
4. See also Radio Free Europe Research Report of June 3, 1970.
5. See *Chr*, No. 13 (1970) nzz (June 28, 1970). In the meantime first two numbers of *Ischod* have been published in *P*, VII. The first two numbers of *Vestnik Ukrainy* (*"Ukrainsky Visnyk"*) appeared in Paris and Frankfurt am Main.
6. See *Chr*, No. 5 (1968); *P*, I., 42.
7. See *Chr*, No. 7 (1969); *P*, II., 14.
8. Ibid., p. 34.
9. See *Chr*, No. 13 (1970); *P*, IV., 25 ff.
10. See *P*, III., 55.
11. The verdict against Krasin was later challenged by the prosecutor. In September, 1971 Viktor Krasin was allowed to return to Moscow.
12. Ivanov, however, was prematurely released after serving eight years.
13. A reproduction of the illustrations appeared in *P*, No. 6 (1970) 3-11.
14. Together with his wife, Kochubievski was permitted to emigrate

to Israel following his release from the camp in November, 1970.
15. See *Chr*, No. 8 (1969), *P*, II., 35.

THE LENINGRAD TRIALS

1. See NZZ (January 6, 1966).
2. Sel'ga, *"Suslov M. A.,"* *P*, No. 1 (1968) 12 f.
3. V. S., *"Lavirovanie ili Povorot?"* Ibid., 11 f.
4. See *Expressen*, (Stockholm), July 8, 1970.
5. See *Chr*, No. 1 (1968); *P*, I., 12.
6. See *"Vserossiiskii Social-Christianskii Soiuz Osvobozdeniia Naroda,"* *P*, No. 1 (1971) 38 ff.
7. Perception, which assumes desire (Latin: *voluntas*), instead of intellectualism or emotionalism, to be the essence of understanding, psychology, or metaphysics (according to Schopenhauer). F. Toennies was the first to introduce the concept of "voluntarism" in philosophy; the term was then applied in particular by F. Paulsen and W. Wundt.
8. See *Chr*, No. 1 (1968); *P*, I., 12.
9. See *"Otkrytoe Pis'mo Pisatel'ia Al. Petrova-Agatova Borisu Polevomu,"* excerpts of which appear in *P*, No. 6 (1970) 10 ff.

THE 'DEMOCRATS' PROGRAM

1. *Programma Demokraticeskogo Dvizeniia Sovetskogo Soiuza* (Amsterdam, 1970).
2. Ibid., p. 54.
3. Ibid., p. 72 f.
4. Ibid., 73 ff.

DISSIDENTS IN THE ARMY

1. Oleg Penkovski, *Geheime Aufzeichnungen* (Munich-Zurich, 1966).
2. For further information about Grigorenko, see pp. 170 ff.
3. See *Iz* (March 21, 1970).
4. See *International Herald Tribune* (Washington) June 13, 1969.
5. *Narodnaja volja* means "the will of the people." This was a radical terror-organization, originally led by the *narodnike*, that became particularly active toward the end of the nineteenth century. They were responsible for many acts of terror and violence, including the one that claimed the life of Czar Aleksandr II in 1881.
6. Interview with UPI of January 12, 1968. See *P*, No. 2 (1968) 17.
7. See *New York Times* (October 24, 1969).
8. See *Chr*, No. 10 (1969); *P*, III., 36.

ANDREI AMALRIK AND THE DISCUSSION ABOUT THE FUTURE OF RUSSIA

1. A. Amalrik, *Nezelannoe Putesestvie v Sibir'* (New York, 1970); German version, *Unfreiwillige Reise nach Sibirien* (Hamburg, 1970).
2. Title of the German edition: *Kann die Sowjetunion das Jar 1984 Erleben?* (Zurich, 1970).
3. See *The Observer* (London), November 15, 1970.
4. Other similar insinuations were mentioned in the *Washington Evening Star* (November 26, 1969) and in *Der Spiegel* (Hamburg, March 16, 1970). In both instances Amalrik complained to the editors of these journals in letters. See *The Times*, December 3, 1969; *Survey*, No. 74-5 (London, 1970) 311 ff. (an extensive dossier of just about every essay and letter Amalrik wrote was published in this issue of the *Survey*.)
5. Petr Y. Chaadaev (1793-1856). Chaadaev was a religious and historical philosopher, and advocated, primarily in his *Lettres Philosophiques* and *Apologie d'Un Fou*, a closer cultural relation-

ship between Russia and Western Europe, in particular; he championed the reunification of the Russian Orthodox Church with the Roman Catholic Church, however. On the basis of such nonconformist statements, Nicholas I declared Chaadaev insane. (In fact, Chaadaev, who has had a lasting affect on Russian intellectual history, was never confined to a mental institution; rather, he maintained a "political" salon in Petersburg where many of his famous contemporaries met.)

6. See *Survey*, No. 74-5 (1970) 108.
7. See *Die Welt* (November 28, 1969).
8. See *Daily Telegraph* (July 29, 1970).
9. See A. Amalrik, loc. cit., 42.
10. See *Chr*, No. 13 (1970); *P*, IV, 19.
11. See *Chr*, No. 13 (1970); *P*, IV, 40 f.
12. S. Zorin/N. Alekseev, *Vremia ne Zdet* (Frankfurt am Main, 1970).
13. That is, the defamation campaign that was instigated against Pasternak, could have accelerated the outbreak or the deterioration of his fatal case of cancer.
14. This portion of the letter by Petro-Agatov is indeed available in the West, but it has not yet been published.

THE DEFENDERS OF CZECHOSLOVAKIA

1. Text in NRS (September 13, 1968).
2. A. Marchenko, *Moi Pokazaniia* (Frankfurt am Main, 1969); German version, *Meine Aussagen* (Frankfurt am Main, 1969).
3. A. Marchenko, loc. cit. p. 5.
4. See NRS (September 18, 1968).
5. A. Marchenko, loc. cit., 416.
6. See *Die Welt* (August 15, 1969).
7. Ibid. (August 21, 1969).
8. See *Washington Post* (September 29, 1969).
9. Self-immolation of political opponents has been practiced in the U.S.S.R., and primarily in the Ukraine, for many years now; longer, in any event, than in Czechoslovakia or Western Europe.
10. N. Gorbanevskaya, *Polden'* (Frankfurt am Main, 1970).

11. Ibid., p. 135 f.
12. Ibid., p. 128.
13. Ibid., p. 328.
14. Ibid., p. 325.
15. Ibid., p. 336 f.
16. Ibid., p. 340.
17. Ibid., p. 325.
18. Ibid., p. 441 ff.
19. See *Moskovskaia Pravda*, (Moscow) October 12, 1968.
20. N. Krupskaia, *Vospominaniia*, vol. 2, pp. 28-30 (Moscow, 1927).
21. See N. Gorbanevskaya, loc. cit., p. 493.
22. Natalia Gorbanevskaya was released on February 22, 1972.

GENERAL GRIGORENKO:
SYMBOL OF OPPOSITION

1. See *International Herald Tribune* (April 2, 1970); *Christ und Welt* (April 10, 1970); *P*, No. 4 (1970) p. 4 ff.
2. See *P* (October 13, 1967).
3. Ibid.
4. See *P*, No. 4 (1969) 55.
5. See *P*, No. 1 (1969) 8.
6. "*Ot Initiativnoi Gruppy Po Zascite Grazdanskich Prav v USSR v Komitet Prav Celoveka Ob-Edinennych Nacii,*" *Za Prava Celoveka* (Frankfurt am Main, 1969) 5.
7. Text in *P*, No. 5 (1970) 5.
8. During the course of the past few years SMOG groups have formed in these and in other countries which actively support the cause of the Soviet freedom-fighters. Members of these organizations also were arrested in the fall of 1969 in Moscow after they had distributed flyers in which they demanded the release of Grigorenko. Two Italian students decided to undertake similar actions in January of 1970 and were immediately sentenced to one year in a work camp, but were subsequently pardoned.
9. Text in *P*, No. 4 (1970) 3 f.
10. For text of the letter, See English version in *Survey*, No. 77

(1970) 175 ff; Russian version in *P*, V, 35 ff. See also Sergei Razumnyi's article about Soviet prison psychiatrists, which was published in *Samizdat* in 1970. For the text, see *P*, No. 2 (1971) 29 ff. V. Bukovski sent a letter to the World Health Organization in January, 1971, as well as to a number of Western psychiatrists, requesting them to investigate the question of prison psychiatrists in the U.S.S.R. At the same time he sent a series of informative documents—primarily explanations from several political prisoners currently being held in such institutions—to the West. See *P*, No. 3 (1971) 5 ff.

11. See *P*, No. 4 (1970) 10.

THE SOLZHENITSYN CASE

1. See *P*, 00 f.
2. A. Solzhenitsyn, *V. Kruge Pervom* (Zurich, 1968).
3. See NZZ (March 30, 1969).
4. A. Solzhenitsyn, *Rakovyi Korpus* (Frankfurt am Main, 1968).
5. See NZZ (July 20, 1969)
6. Ibid.
7. See P, No. 4 (1968) 17.
8. See *P*, No. 3 (1968) 18 f.
9. See *P*, No. 8 (1968) 10; NZZ (July 20, 1969).
10. See NZZ (July 20, 1969).
11. Ibid.
12. See *O-P*, No. 12 (1967) 358.
13. See *P*, No. 3 (1968) 20.
14. See *O-P*, No. 25-26 (1968) 596.
15. See *P*, No. 11 (1968) 39 f.
16. See *P*, No. 10 (1969) 10.
17. See *Sunday Telegraph* (London) December 15, 1968.
18. See *LG* (November 26, 1969).
19. See *The Times* (December 1, 1970).
20. Text in *P*, No. 12 (1970) 3 f.
21. Because of technical difficulties connected with the printing of Solzhenitsyn's new novel, *August 1914*, the first volume of a planned historical trilogy, further information is not available

(Russian: *August 1914,* Paris, 1971. German: entitled *August 1971,* Munich, 1971; Neuwied-Berlin, 1972).

THE ALIENATION BETWEEN THE ADMINISTRATION AND THE WRITERS

1. See *Osteuropa,* No. 5-6 (1967) 625.
2. See *O-P,* No. 22-23 (1967) 625.
3. A. Voznesenski, *"Ne Pisetsia,"* NM, No. 7 (1969) 105. The quotation appearing in the text was taken from the translation by Galina Berkenkopf.
4. Yu. Levitanski, *"Novyi God na Dunai,"* N.M., No. 9 (1969) 151. The quotation appearing in the text was taken from the translation by Galina Berkenkopf.
5. See *KoPr,* No. 151 (1967).
6. A. Tvardovski, *"Po pravu pamiati,"* P, No. 10 (1969) 52 ff.
7. Strana Muraviia, A. *Tvardovski—Poemy,* (Moscow, 1950) pp. 5-92.
8. Quotation taken from the translation by Maria G. Rasumowski.
9. See *P,* No. 8 (1968) 6.
10. See *Ami,* No. 1 (Jerusalem, 1970) 47 ff.
11. See *Die Welt* (August 5, 1969).
12. Ibid.

Chapter 29   EARLY SIGNS OF FREEDOM

1. A. Amalrik, loc. cit. p. 14 f.
2. The Slavophiles unquestionably represented the most important political-theological current in Russia in the nineteenth century. Their effects are still being felt in the twentieth century. The most important representatives of the Slavophiles were A. Chomiakov (1804-1860), the brothers I. and P. Kireevski (1806-1856), 1808-1856, respectively, the brothers K. and I. Aksakov (1817-1860), 1823-1886, respectively, and Yu. Samarin (1819-

1876). While the very homogeneous first-generation Slavophiles were greatly influenced by Hegel (his philosophy of history), Herder and even Schelling, the members of the second-generation Slavophiles were primarily influenced by Dostoevski. The most famous representatives of this second generation were N. Danilevski (1822-1885) and the young V. Solovev (1853-1900). The later Slavophiles particularly adhered to a strongly pronounced Russian Messianism.

3. A. Amalrik, loc. cit., p. 16.
4. See *Pravda Ukrainy* (Kiev) January 21, 1969.
5. See *Chr*, No. 12 (1969); *P*, IV (1970) 11 f.
6. See *Survey*, No. 77 (1970) 145.
7. P. Smirnov, *Licnost' i Obscestvo*. Reprinted in *P*, No. 7 (1969) 43-49.

DOCUMENTS

1. Danko is a revolutionary folk figure from the early tale by Maxim Gorki entitled 'Starucha Izergil.' In order to save his people, Danko sacrificed himself. He tore his heart out, but brightly blazing as the flaming symbol of brotherly love, it continued to banish both darkness and danger until it was carried away and extinguished by a faint-hearted fellow.
2. The Lubianka is the main office of the KGB headquarters in Moscow (formerly also the main office of the Ceka). An infamous prison is maintained in its cellars where executions were carried out in earlier days.
3. On December 14, 1825, the Decembrist revolt was put down by shooting in the Senate Square in Petersburg.
4. The executed Decembrist leaders.
5. The reference is to a famous poem by A. S. Pushkin.
6. Sergei Kirov (1886-1934). Kirov was a Party Secretary in Leningrad. His assassination (probably instigated by Stalin himself) provided the prelude to the first great purge.
7. Solomon Michoels, Director of the Jewish Theater in Moscow and Chairman of the Board of the Jewish Anti-Fascist Committee. Michoels was murdered in 1948 by the secret police as a

victim of the anti-Zionist campaign.
8. *Pr* (February 22, 1966).
9. Sergei Michalkov (born in 1913), hack writer, composer (along with El Ragistan) of the Soviet national anthem.
10. Beginning of the Polish national anthem.
11. Public prosecutor in the trial against Siniavski and Daniel.
12. Character out of Voltaire's novel, *Candide*.
13. Vsevolod Meierhold (1874-1942), actor and director. In 1920 he was the Peoples' Commissar for Education. He was also the founder of the Meierhold Theater in Moscow, which was closed down in 1938. Meierhold was a victim of the Stalinist purges. It is assumed that he died in 1942 in a concentration camp.
14. Aleksandr Gercen (Herzen) (1812-1870), an important social-revolutionary writer and thinker. In his youth Gercen was an adherent of the so-called "Westler"-idea (the Russian counter-movement to the Slavophiles). Gercen was Russia's first political emigrant. In 1947 he left his native country and from then on lived primarily in London, where he published the political journal *Kolokol* (*The Bell*).
15. Nikolai Ogarev (1813-1870), strategist of the Russian revolutionary movement. He was a friend of Herzen's, with whom he was temporarily involved in London while working on the journal *Kolokol*.
16. Yevgenia Ginzburg (Y. Aksenova-Ginzburg), born in 1905. She is the mother of the writer Vasili Adsenov. In 1937 she was arrested as a Trotskyite and spent the next eighteen years in prison camps. Her book about her years in prison was published in *Samizdat* under the title *Krutoi Marsrut* (*The Road of My Life*). A German edition was published in Hamburg in 1967, *Marschroute eines Lebens*. Legal publication of this significant piece of "camp" literature is still prohibited in the u.s.s.r.
17. Bohdan Chmelnychkyi (c. 1595-1657), Hetman of the Zaporogian Cossacks. As a leader of the Cossack rebellion of 1648, Chmelnychkyi defeated the Poles. In the treaty of Perejaslav (1654) the Hetman swore allegiance to the Russian Czar Aleksei and thus returned the Ukrainians to Russian control. For a long time they had been ruled by the Poles.
18. These people were old-Communists and Party leaders who, in the course of Stalin's purges of January 1937, were sentenced

by a kangaroo court as Trotskyite conspirators—that is leftists —and, together with some other unfortunates, were either executed or left to die in prisons.

19. A letter of March 1969, in which the political prisoners Ginzburg, Galanskov, Daniel, Ronkin, Kalnynsh, and Moshkov demanded improved prison conditions. The letter was addressed to the deputies of the Supreme Soviet of the U.S.S.R. See text in NRS (June 28, 1969).

20. Nikolai Ezhov succeeded G. Jagoda as Peoples' Commissar for Internal Affairs in 1939. One of the bloodiest chapters of Soviet history is named after him: the Ezhovschina (1936-1938). This was a period of gargantuan purges and the "Moscow Trials," the time when Stalin's despotic and all-encompassing tyranny had its beginnings. Ezhov "disappeared" in 1938, after L. Beria took over his position. The circumstances surrounding his death are still not clear today.

21. B. Pasternak, *"Svadba," Znamia*, No. 4 (Moscow, 1954).

22. The reference is to the famous poem by K. Ryleev: "Grazdanin."

23. See *P*, No. 11 (1969) 3 f.

24. Next to Petr Struve and Nikolai Berdiaev, Sergei Bulgakov (1871-1944) was the most important leader of the "Vechi" (Turning-Point) movement. This was a nonsocialist Russian reform movement based on the idealism of Kant and Hegel, as well as the religious philosophy of Solovev. A political economist by vocation, Bulgakov had been a Marxist in his youth. Later he became an orthodox priest and, next to Berdiaev, the most important Russian religious philosopher of this century.

INDEX

INDEX

Abramov, F., 36
Akademgorodok, 169
Akhmadova, Bella, 82-83
Akhmadulina, Bella, 101, 269
Akhmatova, Anna, 34, 45, 119
Aksenov, Vasili, 72, 289
Alekseev, Gennadi. *See* Gavrilov
Alekseev, N., 237-238
"Alliance of the Soldiers for Political Freedom," 225
Alliluyeva, Svetlana, 39, 41, 284, 293
  Just One Year, 124-125
All-Russian Christian-Socialist Union for the Liberation of the People (VSCHON), 205-210
Altunjan, Major Genrich, 197, 198, 221-222
Amalrik, Andrei, 116, 169-170, 210, 229-237, 295-298, 306, 505,-507
  Involuntary Trip to Siberia, 230
  "The Normans and the Russians of Kiev," 229
  "Will the Soviet Union Survive the Year 1984?," 230-237
Amateur radio, subversive, 95-96
Andropov (secret-police chief), 224, 542-545

Anthology of Soviet Pathology, 107
Anti-Semitism, 57-58, 201-202. *See also* "Babi Yar"; Israel, U.S.S.R. policies concerning
Antokolski, Pavel, 270
"Appeal to World Public Opinion," 24
  See also Daniel, Larisa; Litvinov, Pavel.
ARI, 108
Army, dissidents in the, 221-227
Arzhak, Nikolai. *See* Daniel, Uri
Asmus, V., 51
Avangard, 112
Avangard Russkogo Isskustva. *See* ARI
Avantgarde of Russian Art. *See* ARI
Averochkin (lawyer), 208

Babel, Isaac, 33
Babicki, Konstantin, 251-253, 255-257
"Babi Yar" (Yevtushenko), 57 n.l, 58, 72
Bachmin, Viacheslav, 174

Baeva, Tatiana, 251, 255
Baklanov, Gregori, 67, 277
Banner, The, 49
Batsev, Vladimir, 112, 135
Belgorodskaya, Irina, 245-246
Belinkov, Arkadi, 289-292
Bell, The, 204-205
Berdiayev, Nikolai, 208
Berdiayev Circle, 208
Berggloe, Olga, 37
Blok, Aleksandr, 33
Blue Bud, The, 91
Bograz, L. *See* Daniel, Larisa
Bolsheviks, Bolshevism, 33, 37, 77, 79, 108-109, 145, 148, 207
Bom, 107
Boomerang, 103
Borisov, Vladimir, 196
Borodin, Leonid, 209
"Bratsk Station" (Yevtushenko), 147
Brezhnev, Party Secretary Leonid, 83, 85, 140, 174, 260, 281
Brodski, Josef, 115, 119, 120
Bukovski, Vladimir, 25, 27, 106, 127-128, 137-141, 307, 358-362
Bulgakov, Mikhail, 23, 33, 84
Burlacki, F., 286
Burmistrovich, Ilia, 197

Call to the World (Daniel, L. and Litvinov), 155-156
Cancer Ward (Solzhenitsyn), 67, 267-269, 271-274, 281
Central Committee, of CPSU, 69, 86
Chaadaev, Petr, 11, 229, 231 n.5

Chakovski, Aleksandr, 24, 156, 157 n.10, 275
Chalidze, Valeri, 189
Chaustov, Viktor, 136-137
China, U.S.S.R. conflict with, 301-302
Chr. See Chronika
"Christian ideology," 295-296
"Christian-Socialist Union," 296
Chronicle of Current Events. See Chronika
Chronika, 169, 191-202, 205-208, 225-226, 236, 242, 247-249, 303, 305-306
Chukovskaya, Lidia, 61, 129, 275, 277, 344-345, 433-440
  "Open Letter to Mikhail Sholokov," 177, 344
Chukovski, Kornei, 125, 174
"Citizen, The" (Grazdanin), 145
"City of Ccholars," 169
Classic Russian literature, publication sale of, 78-79
Cocktail. See Koktejl
Committee for State Security. *See* KGB
"Commune-ists, Union of the," 480-485
Communist Party, Congress of the Twentieth, 39, 42, 55, 91-92
  Twenty-Second, 61, 129
  Twenty-Third, 85-86, 174
Communist World Conference, 178-179
"Concerning the Integrity of Literature" (Pomerancev), 35-36, 227
"Concerning the Work of a Writer" (Ehrenburg), 35

Constitution, of the U.S.S.R., 25, 212-213, 297

Constitution Day, demonstration of December 5, 136-139, 141-142

White Book concerning, 137

"Correlation between Religion and Understanding, The" (Dobrovolski), 148

CPSU, 82, 86, 212

"Cradle of the Revolution." *See* Leningrad

Crimean Tartars, deporation of, 19, 260, 263-264, 399-404

Cul, 112-113

Cvetaeva, Marina, 23, 33, 111

Czechoslovakia, invasion and occupation of, 99, 170, 179, 181-194, 226, 238, 241, 301, 303-304, 374-384

Daniel, Aleksandr (son of Uri), 201-202

Daniel, Larisa (Mrs. Uri), 24, 27, 151-152, 161-162, 168, 251-254, 256-257, 263

"Appeal to World Public Opinion," 130

Call to the World, 155-156

Daniel, Uri (pseud. Arzhak), 19, 23, 27, 34, 51, 86-87, 115, 118, 123-135, 146, 157-158, 283, 328-358

White Book of Daniel and Siniavski trial, 127-129, 328-345

Danilov, Nikolai, 243

Day of Poetry, 57

"December Fifth Movement," 136, 477-479

Decembrists, 144 n.4, 145

"Decembrists, The" (Kuschev), 144-145, 320-322

Decembrist uprising, 112

Declaration of Human Rights, 25, 191-192, 198, 213, 215

Delone, Vadim, 115, 137-138, 141-142, 251-253, 255-256, 258

White Book concerning Delone and Kuschev, 142

Demichev, Party Secretary Peter, 82, 270

Demin, Mikhail, 289-290

"Democratic movement," 297-298

"Program of the," 211-219, 226

Democratic Republics, Union of, 213

Denisovich, Ivan, One Day in the Life of (Solzhenitsyn), 65-67

Dergunov group, 210

"Descent into Hell" (Stefanov), 317, 329

Djilas, Milovan, "The New Class," 149, 208

Dobrovolski, Aleksei, 20, 93 n.6, 135-136, 151-157

"The Correlation between Religion and Understanding," 148

Doctor Zhivago (Pasternak) 22, 49-52, 115

Dostoevski (writer), 78-79, 111, 294

Dremlyuga, Vladimir, 251-256, 258

Dubrovlag, 131, 157, 209

Dudintev, Vladimir, 82
  Not by Bread Alone, 43-45
Duvakin, Viktor, 124, 128-129
Dzemilev, Mustafa, 265
Dzjuba, Ivan, 534-536

Egorychev (party secretary), 86
Ehrenburg, Ilia, 37, 52, 148, 270
  "Concerning the Work of a
    Writer," 35
  Men-Years-Life, 72
  The Thaw, 34-35
Emigré publications, 25, 102
Eremin, D., 128
Eres. See Heresy
"Estonian Scholars, Memorandum
  of the," 18
Exodus, 194

Fainberg, Viktor, 243, 251-252
February Revolution of 1917. *See*
  Socialist revolution
Fedin, Konstantin, 271, 274
Feltrinelli, Giangiacomo, 49
Feniks, 93, 103-107, 109, 136, 141,
  146-149, 151, 154
Fetisov, A., 195
Fetisov Group, 195
Fifth Congress of Soviet Writers,
  132
Fig Leaf, 91
Figovy List, 91
First All-Union Congress, 76
First Circle, The (Solzhenitsyn),
  33, 175, 267-268, 274

Five Point Manifesto, 189
Fonar, 107
"For Aleksei Dobrovolski in
  Friendship and Love" (Ser-
  geev), 322-323
Fourth Congress of Soviet Writers,
  269-271, 285-286
"Fourth Prose, The" (Mandel-
  stam), 147
"Fragment from the Poem 'Harle-
  kin'" (Kublanovski), 113
Free Philosophical Treatise (Yes-
  enin-Volpin), 120-121
Fresh Voices, 91
"From Distant Reaches" (Tvar-
  dovski), 62-63

Gabai, Ilia, 135, 137, 165, 168,
  179, 264
Galanskov, Yuri, 20, 25, 27, 134,
  136, 146-147, 149, 151-158,
  161, 164, 201, 203, 283, 345-
  356, 507-512
  "Human Manifesto," 106, 311-
    314
Galich, Aleksandr, "Silence is
  Golden," 109
Gavrilov (army officer; pseud.
  Alekseev, Gennadi), 212, 440-
  447
  "Letter to the Citizens of the
    Soviet Union," 225
Gaydenko, P., 169
Gelfand, I., 169
Gendler, Yuri, 243
Genri, Ernst, 148

Gercen (Herzen), Aleksandr, 204, 211, 251

Ginzburg, Aleksandr, 20, 27, 102, 126, 128-129, 151-159, 161-162, 164, 200-201, 283
    White Book of the Case of Daniel and Siniavski, 328-345

Gogin, Viacheslav, 58

Golomstok, I., 128-129

Golovin, Yevgeny, "Song of the Old Party People," 108

Goluboy Buton. See Blue Bud, The

Gorbanevskaya, N., 104, 167, 251, 257, 375-378
    Noon, 252, 258

Gorki, Maxim, 34, 293

Gorki, University of, 242

Gr. See Grani

Grani, 25, 102, 116

Granin, Daniel, 45

Grazdarin (poet), "The Citizen," 145

Greene, Graham, 131

Grigorenko, Major General Petr, 118, 135, 141-142, 152-156, 168, 175, 221, 242, 244, 253, 259-266, 296, 380-381, 397-399

Grigorenko, Zinaida (Mrs. Petr), 263-264

Gubanov, Leonid, 127

Guests, The Zorin, 35

Gumilev, Nikolai, 33-34

"Heirs of Stalin, The" (Yevtushenko), 72

Heresy, 91

Herzen (Aleksandr) Foundation, 25-26

History of Bolshevik Russia, The (von Rauch), 208

History of the Communist Party of The Soviet Union (Nekrich), 148-149

"Human Manifesto (Galanskov), 106, 311-314

Hungarian uprising, 45-46, 92-93

Ideological Commission, 69, 82

Ikramov, K., *The White Flag,* 64

Ilin (army lieutenant), 223-224

Ilyichev, Leonid, 69-71

Ilyichev (Chairman of Ideological Commission), 82

"In Defense of Pyramids" (Siniavski), 147

Ingold, Felix Philip, 267-268

"In the Hour of Dawn" (Levitin-Krasnov), 143

"Initiative Group," 198-199, 262-263, 421-425

Institute for Marxism-Leninism (IML), 175

Involuntary Trip to Siberia (Amalrik), 230

Iofe, Olga, 174, 190

Ischod. See Exodus

Israel, U.S.S.R. policies concerning, 301-303. *See also* Anti-Semitism

"It's Impossible to Write Any More" (Voznesenski), 284-285

Ivan Denisovich, One Day in the Life of (Solzhenitsyn), 267-268
Ivanov, Nikolai, 200 n.12, 209
Ivanov, V., 125
Ivanov, Yuri, 200-201
Ivinskaya, Olga and Irina, 51
Izvestia, 94, 123, 128, 156, 164-165
Iz. See Izvestia

Jachimovich, Ivan, 242
Jakir, Irina (daughter of Petr), 263
Jakir, Petr, 153, 165, 168, 178-179, 236-237, 253
    "Open Letter," 178
Jakobson, Anatoli, 134, 179, 250-251, 381-383
January Trial, the, 151-156
    White Book of, 153
Junost, 86, 289
Just One Year (Alliluyeva), 124-125

Kapica, Petr, 81, 174, 186-187
Kaplan, Fanny (Dora), 223
Kaplun, Irina, 174
Karanin, A., 31, 42
Karasev, Vladimir, 248
Karjakin (writer), 269
Karpinski, L., 286
Kataev, Valentin, 174
Kaverin, Veniamin, 37, 46, 269, 274
Kazachstan. See Cancer Ward

Kazakova, Rumma, 82-83
Kedrina, Zoya, 125, 128
Keldysh, Mstislav, 304
KGB, 27, 102, 119, 136, 142, 205, 223, 226, 231, 251-252, 261-263, 267, 305-306
Khrushchev, 39-42, 46-48, 50, 55, 61-62, 66, 70-72, 81-84, 94, 116, 238, 259, 267
Kiev, Letter from the 139 Citizens of, 18-19
Kim, Yuli, 165, 168
Kirov, Party Secretary S., 223
Kirsanov, Semion, 37, 45
Kochetov, Vsevolod, 82
Kochubievski, Boris, 201, n.14
Koktejl, 107
Kolcov, Mikhail, 33
Kolokol, 204-205
"Kolokol" Group, 203-205, 209
Kolyma, "death" camp at, 231
Kommune Members, Union of the, 203-204
Kommunist, 177-178
Komsomol, 40, 46, 50, 58, 92, 94
Komsomolskaya Pravda, 91, 106, 112, 156, 286
Kopolev, Lev, 125, 175-176
KoPr. See Komsomolskaya Pravda
Krasin, Viktor, 199, n.11
"Krasnopvcev-Rendel Group," 94, 210
Kravchinski, Sergei, 259
Kron, Aleksandr, 45
Kosolapov, Valeri, 57, 288
Kosterin, Aleksei, 242, 260, 296, 410-414
Kosygin, Aleksei, 126, 260
Kosyrev (army officer), 225-227

Kovshin, V., 107

Kozhevnikov (writer), 271

Kublanovski, Yuri, "Fragment from the Poem 'Harlekin' ", 113

Kuleshov-Bezbarodko (Count), 144

Kuschev, Yevgeny, 137-138, 141-142, 144-145
"The Decembrists," 320-322
"The Phoenix," 319-320
White Book concerning Delone and Kuschev, 142

Kvachevski, Lev, 24, 243

Kuznecov, Anatoli, 232, 246, 289, 293-294

Kuznecov, Eduard, 103

Kuznecov, V. I., 386-388

Lantern, The. See Fonar

Laskova, Vera, 20, 135-136, 151-156

Leaf of Spring, A. (Yesenin-Volpin), 70

"League in the Struggle for Political Rights," 225

Lenin, Leninism, 77, 93, 184, 203, 223, 257, 266, 292-293

Leningrad, as intellectual center, 227

"Leningrad Trials, the," 190, 203-210

Leningrad, University of (LGU), 203-205, 209

"Letter to the Citizens of the Soviet Union" (Gavrilov), 225

"Letter to a Comrade," 176

Letter of the 99, 169

"Letter from the Sixty-Two Writers," 356-358

"Letter to Yesenin" (Yevtushenko), 143

Let Us Think for Ourselves, 374-375

Levin, Ju. I., 123

Levitanski, Yuri, "New Year on the Danube," 285

Levitin- Krasnov, Anatoli, 18, 537-542
"In the Hour of Dawn," 143

LG. See Literaturnaya Gazeta

"Liberal ideology," 295-297, 306

Liberman, E., 76-77

Lifsic, M., 36

Listen. See Cu!

Literary Moscow, 45-46

Literaturnaya Gazeta, · 57, 128, 156, 275

Lituraturnaya Moskva. See Literary Moscow

Litvinov, Pavel, 24, 27, 137, 142, 151-153, 163, 168, 173, 224-225, 241, 251-258, 263, 277, 296, 363-369, 378-379
Call to the World, 155
White Book on January Trial, 153

Litvinova, Tatiana, 277

Lubianka, 316 n.2

Lysenko (biologist), 76, 82

Malchev, Juriy, 198-199

Mandelstam, Nadezhda (Mrs. Osip), 58-59

Mandelstam, Osip, 23, 33-34
    "The Fourth Prose," 147
Marchenko, Anatoli, 131, 156-
    157, 389-395
    My Testimony, 244-245, 389
Markov, G., 82
Marshak, Samuil, 119
Marx, Marxism, 43, 50, 203, 292
"Marxism-Leninism, the true," 295-
    296
Masterskaya, 107
Mayakovski, Vladimir, 33, 111-
    112
Medvedev, Roi, 177-178, 187-
    189, 493-504
Medvedev, Zores, 190, 212-213,
    277-278, 281, 305, 395-396
Mercalob, M., 105
Mehnert, Klaus, *Soviet Men*, 78-
    79
Men-Years-Life (Ehrenburg), 72
Mikhailov, Artiomi, 109, 316-317,
Mikhailov, Mikhailo, "Moscow
    Summer, 1964," 64-65
Ministry of Internal Affairs, 84, 98
Mordvinia, camp at, 158
"Moravia" (Tvardovski), 287
"Moscow Summer, 1964" (Mik-
    hailov), 64-65
Moscow, University of, 67, 94
MVD. *See* Ministry of Internal
    Affairs
My Testimony (Marchenko), 244-
    245, 389

Narica, Mikhail (pseud. Narymov,
    M.),
    The Unsung Song, 115, 116

Narodniki, 144 n.3, 224 n.5
Narymov, M. *see* Narica, Mikhail
Naumova (public prosecutor),
    265
Neck. See Seja
Neizvestny, Ernst, 71
Nekrasov, Viktor, 72
Nekrich, Aleksandr, 260
    *History of the Communist Party
        of the Soviet Union*, 148-149
    1941-22. Ijunja, 174-175
Neo-Marxism, 94
Neo-Stalinism, 47-48
New Class (Djilas), 149, 208
New World. See Novy Mir.
"New Year on the Danube" (Levi-
    tanski), 285
Nilsky, V., 106
1941-22. Ijunja (Nekrich,) 174-
    175
NM. See Novy Mir.
Nobel Prize, for Literature, 146
    to Pasternak, 50
    to Sholokhov, 279
    to Solzhenitsyn, 278-279
Noon (Garbanevskaya), 252, 258
Nor, N., 101, 105, 314-315
"Normans and the Russians of
    Kiev, The," 229
Not by Bread Alone (Dudintsev),
    43-44
*Notebook of Social Democracy.
    See Tetradi*
Novodvorskaya, Valerija, 248-249
Novol Russkol Slovo, 25
Novotny (Czech political leader),
    99
Novy Mir, 36, 43, 46-47, 62, 66-67,
    76, 86, 125, 267, 274, 284-288
NRS. See Novol Russkol Slovo

NTS, (Russian émigré organization), 153 n.3, 154-156

NZZ. *See Neue Zürcher Zeitung*

Obschestvo Russkogo Slova, 144

October Revolution, 21-22, 64, 75,
93, 103, 108, 130, 296

October. See Oktyabr.

Ogurcov, A., 169

Ogurcov, Igor, 208-209, 296

*One Day in the Life of Ivan Deni-
sovich* (Solzhenitsyn), 65-67,
72, 86

Onezskaya, A., 105

O-P. See Ost-Probleme

"Open Letter" (Jakir), 178

"Open Letter to Mikhail Sholokhov" (Chukovskaya), 177

Organization of Communist Youth.
See Komsomol

Organization of Independent
Youth, 195-196

Oktyabr, 43

Okudzhava, Bulat, 79, 101, 277

Osipov-Kusnecov Group, 210

Osipov, Vladimir, 103

Oveckin, Valentin, 37

P. See Posev

Panova, Vera, 35, 37

Pankratov, Uri, 101

Paramonov (army officer), 225-
227

"Party and the Intellectuals, The"
(Rumjancev), 83

Party of the True Communists, 197

Pasternak, Boris, 22, 34, 49-53, 69,
111, 125

Dr. Zhivago, 49-52

Paustovski, Konstantin, 44, 125,
270

Pavlinchuk, V., 242

P.E.N. Club, 291

Penal Code, 126, 135-136, 149

Penkovski, Colonel Oleg, 221-222

People Commissariat of State Security. *See* KGB

Peoples' Labor Alliance of Russian
Solidarists. *See* NTS.

Peredelkino, Writers' Colony at, 51

Petrograd, 109

Petrov-Agatov, Aleksandr, 104,
209, 239-240, 316

Phoenix. See Feniks

"Phoenix, The" (Kuschev), 319-
320

Pilniak, Boris, 23, 33

Pimenov, Revol't, 190 n.9

Pisarev, S., 242, 264-265

Platonov, Andrei, 84

Platonov, Vyacheslav, 209

Plenum of the Board of the Union
of Soviet Writers, 46

Plenum of the Writers of Moscow,
46

Pliseckaya, Maya, 174

Pliusch, Leonid, 164, 179, 468-473

Plotkin (professor), 250

Poetry, Day of, 57

Polevoi, Boris, 209

Pomerancev, Vladimir, "Concerning the Integrity of Literature,"
35-36, 227

Pomerantz, Grigory, 148

"Prague spring, the," 99, 170, 241.
See also Czechoslovakia

"Program of the Democrats, the," 298

Progress, Peaceful Co-Existence and Intellectual Freedom (Sakharov), 181-187

Posev, 25

Posev Publishing House, 26, 102, 204

Pr. See Pravda

Pravda, 62, 72, 83, 179, 279-280, 284

Program of the Democratic Movement in the Soviet Union, 211-219, 226

Pseudonyms, use of, 26, 106, 116-117, 123

"Psychiatric clinics," 265-266

Pushkin, A. S., 181, 295

Radischev, Aleksandr, 111

Radzievski, Pavel, 136

Revised Marxist Party, 197

Richter, Sviatoslav, 51

"Right to Think, The" (Tvardovski), 287-288

Rips, Ilia, 249-250

Romm, Mikhail, 174

Ronkin, Valeri, 203

Rostropovich, Mstislav, 278, 280-281

Rozov, Viktor, 289

RSFSR, 102, 135-136

Rublev, Andrei, 111

Rudenko (prosecutor general), 140, 261

Rumjancev, A. M., "The Party and the Intellectuals," 83

'Russian Road of Progress toward Socialism and Its Results," 149

Russian Soviet Federated Republic. *See* RSFSR

Russian Ward. See Russkoe Slovo

Russkaia Mysl', 25

Russkoe Slovo, 144-145, 522-525

Ryleev Club, 141, 144-145

Ryleev, Kondrati 144-145, 221

Sado, Milkhail, 208

Sakharov, Andrei, 22, 27, 76, 140, 174, 188-191, 212-213, 226, 241-242, 281, 296, 493-504

Progress, Peaceful Co-Existence and Intellectual Freedom, 181-187

Samizdat, 23, 25-27, 101-113, 164, 177, 189, 194-195, 230, 233, 237, 250, 277, 280-281, 287, 305

Saripov (writer), 271

Sceglov, M., 36

Sciences, Academy of, 305

Seasons, The (Panova), 35

Second All-Union Congress, 76

Second Congress of Writers, 36-37

Secret political police. *See* KGB

Seja, 107

"Self-publishing house." *See Samizdat*

Semichastni, V., 50

Serbski Institute, 265-266

Sergeev, Leonid, "For Aleksei Dobrovolski in Friendship and Love," 322-323

Sfinsky, 107-110, 112-113

Shashenkov, E., 243

Shklovski, Viktor, 45

Sholokhov, Mikhail, 86, 129, 133, 146-147, 170, 223-224, 271, 279, 344-356

Nobel Prize for Literature to, 146

"Silence is Golden" (Galich), 109

"Silver Age, The," 45, 102

Simonov, Konstantin, 36, 47, 271, 288-289

Siniavski, Andrei (pseud. Terz, Abram), 19, 22, 27, 34, 40, 51-52, 86-87, 93, 115, 118-121, 123-135, 146, 165-166, 283, 345-347, 356-358

"In Defense of Pyramids," 147

"Socialist Realism," 124, 147

White Book of Daniel and Siniavski trial, 127-129, 328-345

Sintaksis. See Syntax

Sirena, 107

Slavophiles, 296 n.2

Smirnov, Chief Justice Lev, 125

Smirnov, P., 525-534

Smirnov, Sergei, 171

SMOG, 110-113, 127, 139, 146, 263 n.8

April 14, 1965 demonstration of, 324-328

Sobolev, L., 82

"Socialist Realism" (Siniavski), 124, 147

Socialist revolution, 98 n.18

Society of the Russian Word, 144

"Song of the Old Party People" (Golovin), 108

Soldatov, Sergei, 226-227

Soloviev (philosopher), 208

Solzhenitsyn, Aleksandr, 18, 23, 26-27, 33-34, 48-49, 51, 53, 65-67, 115-116, 267-281, 285-286, 395-396, 454-461, 473-476, 542, 545

Cancer Ward, 66

One Day in the Life of Ivan Denisovich, 65-67

Soviet Commission for Human Rights, 189-190

Soviet Men (Mehnert), 78

Soviet Writers' Union, 23, 27, 36, 49-50

Sphinx, The. See Sfinksy

Stalin, Stalinism, 27, 31-34, 39-43, 55, 61-62, 64, 66, 72, 75, 77, 81, 83-85, 93-94, 99, 120, 134-135, 148-149, 157, 165, 170, 174-179, 183-185, 195, 204, 222, 238, 243-244, 260, 277, 287, 304, 426-428, 430-433

White Book concerning victims of, 94

Stefanov, J., 107

Stefanov, Yuri, "Descent into Hell," 317-319

Student opposition, 94-95

Sug-Sucht, A., 91, 103

Surkov, Alexei, 36-37

Suslov, Party Secretary M., 168, 204, 369-372

Svezie Golona. See Fresh Voices

Svinski, Georgi, 275

Svirski, G., 462-468

Syntax, 101-103

Talantov, Boris, 512-520

Tamm, Igor, 174, 186

Tarsis, Valeri (pseud. Valery, Ivan), 111, 115, 289
  Ward 7, 117-118
TASS, 222
Tendriakov, V., *The White Flag*, 64
Tertz, Abram. *See* Siniavski, Andrei
Tetradi, 143-144
Thaw, The (Ehrenburg), 34-35
Third Congress of Soviet Writers, 62
Tolstoi, Lev, 293-294
Tretiakov, Sergei, 33
"Trial of the Four," 20-21, 24
Turchin, Valeri, 187-189, 212-213, 275-276, 281, 493-504
Tvardovski, Aleksandr, 36, 47, 66, 76, 86, 270-274
  "From Distant Reaches," 62-63
  "Moravia," 287
  "The Right to Think," 287-288
Tverdochlebov, Andrei, 189
Twentieth Congress, of the Communist Party, 39, 42, 55, 91-92
Twenty-Second Congress, of the Communist Party, 61, 129
Twenty-Third Congress, of the Communist Party, 85-86, 174

Ubozhko, Leo, 230
Ukranian Messenger, The, 194
Ukranian Writers, 18
"Union of the Commune-ists," 480-485
Union of Democratic Republics, 213
Union of the Kommune Members, 203-204

Union of Soviet Writers, 23, 290-292
United Nations, 198-199, 212-214, 262
Unsolicited Witnesses (Litvinov), 363, *See also* The White Book of the January Trial
Unsung Song, The (Narica), 115-116

Vachtin, Boris and Yuri, 163-164
Vaculik, Ludvik, 242
Vagin, Yevgency, 208
Valery, Ivan. *See* Tarsis, Valeri
Valilov, Nikolai, 45 n.8, 76
Varga, Yevgeny, 149
Vasilev, Arkadi, 125
Vecerny Leningrad, 119
Vechernyaya Moskva, 102
Vesennij List. See Leaf of Spring, A
Vestnik Ukrainy. See Ukranian Messenger, The
Vishniakov, E., 289
Visnevskaya, Julia, 113, 128
Vladimin prison, 158-159
Vladimirov, A., 104
Vladimov, Georgi, 23, 270
Voloshin, Maximilian, 283
von Rauch, Georg, *The History of Bolshevik Russia*, 208
Voprosy Literatury, 125
Voronin, Victor, 164-165
Voskresenski, Vladimir, 144
Voznesenski, Andrei, 49, 71-72
  "It's Impossible to Write Any More," 284-285
Vremena Goda, 107

Ward 7 (Tarsis), 117-118
White Book, The
  concerning Constitution Day
    (1966) proceedings, 137
  of Daniel and Siniavski trial
    (Ginzburg), 127-129, 328-
    345
  concerning Delone and Kuschev
    (Litvinov), 142
  of the January Trial (Litvinov),
    153
  concerning victims of the Stalin-
    ist purges, 94
  concerning Yakhimovich, 370
White Flag, The (Ikramov and
  Tendriakov), 64
"Who Killed Trotsky?," 143
"Will the Soviet Union Survive the
  Year 1984?" (Amalrik), 230
Workshop. See Masterskaya
Writers' Congress, Soviet
  Fifth, 132
  Fourth, 269-271, 285-286
  Third, 62
Writers, Soviet, Union of, 23, 269-
  271, 273-278, 290-292

Yakhimovich, Ivan, 168, 250, 261,
  296, 369-372, 380-381, 414-418
Yakir, Petr, 165 n.10, 167
Yakobson, Anatoli, 161
Yashin, Aleksandr, 45
Year of Human Rights, 161, 191
Yesenin, Sergei, 33
Yesenin-Volpin, 113, 115; 120-122,
  142, 152-153, 167, 407-410,
  520-522

Free   Philosophical   Treatise,
  120-121
Leaf of Spring, A, 70
Yevtushenko, Yevgeny, 32-33, 46,
  55-57, 71, 82-83, 247, 270, 277,
  289
  "Babi Yar," 72
  "Bratsk Station," 147
  "Heirs of Stalin, The," 57-58, 72
  "Letter to Yesenin," 143
  "Zima Junction," 42-43

Zamiatin, Yevgeny, 33
Zhadanov, Andrei, 37
Zhadanovscina, 37 n.11
"Zima Junction" (Yevtushenko),
  42-43
Zionist movement, in U.S.S.R.,
  194, 302-303. *See also* Anti-
  Semitism
Zionists, Russian, 194
Znamia, 49
Zolkovskaya, Irina, 158
Zolotuchin, Boris, 156
Zoschenko, Mikhail, 34
Zorin, Leonid, *The Guests,* 35
Zorin, S., 237-238